Sir Mackenzie Bowell

Also by Barry K. Wilson:

Politics of Defeat: The Decline of the Liberal Party in Saskatchewan

Beyond the Harvest: Canadian Grain at the Crossroads

Farming the System: How Politicians and Producers Shape Canadian Agricultural Policy

Benedict Arnold: A Traitor in Our Midst

Cover art: Loose Cannon Designs
              Portrait of Mackenzie Bowell from the painting by Joanne Tod
              Copyright of House of Commons Collection, Ottawa/
              Collection de la Chambre des communes, Ottawa

Sir Mackenzie Bowell
A Canadian Prime Minister Forgotten by History

Barry K. Wilson

LIBRARY AND ARCHIVES CANADA CATALOGUING IN PUBLICATION

Title: Sir Mackenzie Bowell : a Canadian prime minister forgotten by
history / Barry K. Wilson.
Names: Wilson, Barry K., author.
Description: Includes bibliographical references.
Identifiers: Canadiana 20210186992 | ISBN 9781988657257 (softcover)
Subjects: LCSH: Bowell, Mackenzie, Sir, 1823-1917. | LCSH: Prime
ministers—Canada—Biography. |
LCSH: Politicians—Canada—Biography. | CSH: Canada—Politics and
government—1878-1896. | LCGFT:
Biographies.
Classification: LCC FC526.B69 W55 2021 | DDC 971.05/5—dc23

Published by
LOOSE CANNON PRESS

www.loosecannonpress.com

TABLE OF CONTENTS

ABBREVIATIONS

LAC — Library and Archives Canada
CABHC — Community Archives of Belleville and Hastings
County

DEDICATION

To Julianne, as always, for her support, understanding, tolerance and advice during the years in which Sir Mackenzie Bowell was an ever-present ghostly partner in our marriage. And to our grandchildren Alice, Benjamyn, Charlotte, Sam, Jeff and Jessie. May they grow up loving Canadian history and Canadian stories as their Grandpa does.

ACKNOWLEDGEMENTS

Special thanks also go to the staff of the Canadian Parliamentary Press Gallery who cheerfully offered assistance and support when needed. Through almost four decades of association with the Gallery, several generations of clerks have done yeoman service as my friendly, savvy enablers. My very un-Liberal friend Wilbray Thiffault spent many hours squinting at microfilm screens housed at the back of the Archives, scanning sometimes difficult-to-read faded stories in the very Liberal Toronto *Globe* newspaper about the politics of the 19th century Bowell years, offering a glimpse of how his critics saw him. Thanks, Wilbray.

I am indebted to Bowell great-great grandchildren Blake Holton and Kathy Holton Masson of Port Hope, Ontario who shared family stories and showed me Bowell artifacts and MaryJane HoltonSimon of Toronto who was generous with her time and information as well as patient with my many questions. She also gave me the priceless gift of her grandfather's First World War diary recording the day on the war's front line when he learned of his grandfather's death. All were gracious, welcoming hosts to a nosey researcher.

Of course, the research journey was not mine alone.

My supportive wife Julianne put up with a husband who was missing-in-action for much of four years. As well, I was helped and encouraged by Alex Binkley, friend, fellow Canadian Parliamentary Press Gallery journalist and a published science fiction writer. He generously read and critiqued each chapter as it left my computer. Alex has been the first line of defence against my errors, incomprehensible sentences or dull writing. Gratitude is extended to both fellow travellers, as is absolution from any responsibility for errors, flaws or uninspired writing that made it into the text.

Finally, Bob Barclay of Loose Cannon Press took over my typescript and, with a little technical input, turned it into a book.

Sir Mackenzie Bowell, 1823–1917

PREFACE

Why should anyone care about Mackenzie Bowell, Canada's fifth prime minister? In 21st century Canada, the truth is that few people even recognize his name or know anything about the man and his place in the Canadian story, oblivious to the fact that they are missing a rich slice of our history. What little they do know likely is negative or mocking about his role in Canada's first half century. Perhaps the answer to the question in the first sentence is contained in the second. Bowell's story is a classic tale of an immigrant kid with limited education who by any standard grew up to become a success in his new country; a businessman, a senior minister in multiple portfolios and a prime minister, one of just 23 in Canada's first 150 years.

He remains one of the longest serving parliamentarians in Canadian history.

Bowell was a trusted confidant and lieutenant for Sir John A. Macdonald and was in charge of several key foundational economic policies in the nascent Canadian nation. Yet to paraphrase the Canadian songwriter Stan Rogers and his lament about the anonymity of Lieutenant Colonel John Macdonell and his fatal heroism at the 1812 Battle of Queenston Heights: 'Not one in ten thousand knows his name.' In Bowell's case, the odds of anonymity would be much greater. It begs the question: Why has the colourful, history-making saga of the life and times of Sir Mackenzie Bowell been confined largely to neglected bins in the Canadian history vault, pried open only occasionally by historians, intent on denigrating his legacy as insignificant at best and an embarrassing catastrophe at worst? This book's attempt to present a balanced and more complete portrait of Canada's forgotten prime minister is my answer to that question.

In truth, despite my lifelong interest in prime ministerial history, I too was a latecomer to the challenge of unearthing the elusive traces of Mackenzie Bowell's authentic footprint in 19th century Canadian history. I did not seriously start to take an interest in his life until the turn of the 21st century. The catalyst was a frustrating search for a Bowell signature to add to my assortment of memorabilia and signatures connected to the 19 men and one woman who had occupied Canada's top political job during the first 135 years of Canadian history to 2002. It was years before I recognized it, but the birth of the prime ministerial collection occurred one day in 1964 when this 15-year-old farm kid from the Gatineau Valley of West Quebec received a letter from Prime Minister Lester B. Pearson's office thanking him for a flag design submission. I kept it, and the letter showed its staying power later by narrowly surviving a farm fire.

During the almost four decades following, other items were added: letters, posters, photographs, a hand-sewn political tapestry, prime ministerial sculptures and busts, copies of speeches and historic books, as well as 19 original signatures. However, to that point, Mackenzie Bowell had eluded me. The collection contained no artifacts connected to him and no signature. The lack of success in Bowell's case perplexed me. As something of a prime ministerial history geek whose academic studies included degrees in political science (with some Canadian history classes along the way), journalism and a Master's Degree in Canadian Studies, I knew a bit about Bowell's career and figured he must have signed many thousands of documents during his life.

Bowell had been a late-19th century prime minister, a longtime cabinet minister, a half a century Parliamentarian, a newspaperman and businessman for 80 years, a prominent community figure in Belleville, Ontario and Canadian leader of the then-powerful and mainstream Orange Lodge Protestant fraternity. All of these activities would have required signatures on many letters, documents and decrees. Yet not a single signed document (at least one that could be acquired) had surfaced in my long search. Finding signatures of John A. Macdonald, Wilfrid Laurier, R.B. Bennett, Arthur Meighen and the others had been relatively easy, although luck and perseverance often were my best friends. Mackenzie Bowell had been the elusive exception.

Finally, my break came in early 2004 when representatives of the Seventh Town Historical Society of Ameliasburg Township (once part of Bowell's political fiefdom) contacted retired Belleville area Liberal MP and former agriculture minister Lyle Vanclief, with news that they had several Bowell signatures they would donate to my collection. I jumped at the offer and the exchange happened on a snowy winter's afternoon at a Prince Edward County ceremony. The collection was temporarily complete; at least until more prime ministers entered the history books and more memorabilia and signatures were required.

As a happy unintended consequence, the signature search had piqued my curiosity about the man, his times, his record and the reasons behind his lack of recognition. I quickly discovered there was in fact little information or insightful analysis available on this influential player in a formative period of Canada's history. The limited analysis and commentary existing from some of Canada's most celebrated historians and authors was overwhelmingly critical and at times mocking about his place in the Canadian story. An inquiring, curious mind wondered how it was possible that this seemingly interesting, successful and influential life could so routinely be dismissed as an insignificant failure. Getting to the bottom of the story became my challenge. I decided there was a more balanced Canadian story to be told and a more accomplished, principled, flawed and complex man, politician and prime minister to be discovered.

This resolution began long project of interviews and review of mountains of paper detailing the political, parliamentary and government debates and records that defined the evolving Canadian nation and Bowell's role and decisions during that evolution. His critics' motives and responses emerged from the evidence. So, the journey began, as did my life as a library rat at Library and Archives Canada and the Library of Parliament (surely the most beautiful and inspiring library room in Canada to have as a work site). It was a fascinating voyage that took me from Ottawa through Belleville, Prince Edward County, Winnipeg, Toronto, Port Hope, Montreal and many points between. Along the way, I met proud descendants of Bowell as well as skeptics who considered him the incompetent, weak, indecisive and inconsequential political player so often portrayed.

I also met an army of skilled, helpful, friendly and professional librarians and researchers who encouraged and aided me in my detective work to find pieces of evidence depicting the real Mackenzie Bowell, flaws, strengths, prejudices and all. They accessed material and guided me through countless files at the Community Archives of Belleville and Hastings County, the Perth, Ontario library and archives, the Manitoba Archives, McGill University rare book collection and the aforementioned LAC and Library of Parliament. Through years of research and persistent requests for information and documents, employees of the Archives and Parliamentary Library were unerringly accommodating, helpful, cheerful and welcoming. They are part of the treasures contained in those two amazing national institutions.

Along the way on my journey, I sat at a table once owned and used by Sir Mackenzie Bowell in his home, read his voluminous collection of letters and found a four-leaf clover he had saved a century before to use as a bookmark. I also had the honour of sitting spellbound for hours reading a 1695 King James Bible Bowell had owned and used, one of only 12 commissioned by and delivered to William III of England (William of Orange), that was given to Bowell in 1873 to honour his Orange Lodge work. It now resides in near-perfect condition in a temperature-controlled Library and Archives Canada facility in Gatineau, Quebec.

Canadian historian Christopher Moore has wisely written: 'History is not the past. It is an argument about the past.' This book is my argument that Sir Mackenzie Bowell merits acknowledgement of his role in Canadian history, a higher profile and a more nuanced and balanced portrayal of his successes and failures, strengths and flaws, when Canada's story is being told.

Chapter One
NOW AND THEN

M onday, January 5, 1896 dawned as one of the most dramatic days in Canadian parliamentary history. A scene unfolded of an unprecedented cabinet revolt against a sitting prime minister and the effective end of Sir Mackenzie Bowell's abbreviated and controversial term in the prime minister's office. With Parliament Hill in the grip of a cold Ottawa winter as the political temperature inside Parliament soared, Finance Minister George Foster rose in a hushed House of Commons to announce that he and six other ministers had lost confidence in the prime minister and had resigned. From his seat in the Senate, Bowell initially had little comment about the 'bolter' crisis because he had not been given the courtesy of a copy of Foster's speech before it was delivered down the Parliamentary hallway. However, he had an inkling of what was coming.

The announcement followed a weekend of Conservative Party intrigue, conspiracy and backroom machinations in a capital city accustomed to a more sedate brand of colonial politics. It also ushered in weeks of political uncertainty, Opposition Liberal anticipation and ultimately, a cruel and bewildering Conservative Party compromise. As Canada's fifth prime minister, Bowell was to remain for almost four months as a lame duck leader on a short leash with little authority or credibility while effective control shifted to his eventual replacement, Sir Charles Tupper. Remarkably, Bowell's parliamentary and political career continued for another two decades while the triumphant conspirators soon were tossed out of government. Equally noteworthy was the fact that Bowell's ascent to the highest political office in the land was not the crowning moment of his long political career but the nadir of an exemplary, influential and accomplished political and parliamentary record.

In many modern-day historian assessments of that tumultuous and pivotal late 19th century era in the young nation's story, Bowell's prime ministerial moment cemented his reputation as one of Canadian history's losers even though by any reasonable standard, his Canadian saga was an immigrant-makes-good success story. After arriving as a nine-year-old British immigrant in an Upper Canada (Ontario) backwater community in 1833, Bowell earned a place in the history books more than six decades later as the nation's prime minister. Along the way, he developed a love of journalism and after beginning as a pre-teen at the lowest rung in the Belleville *Intelligencer* newsroom, he ended up as the owner and publisher of the newspaper that was pivotal in his life for seven decades. He became a successful businessman and respected community leader in the Bay of Quinte area, elected by his fellow citizens as an MP in the country's first post-Confederation election. Bowell also became a prominent national and international player in the politics of the mainstream Protestant Loyal Orange Lodge of British North America in an era when its 50,000 members carried significant political clout. However, as a politician, he also exhibited a strength of character by defying his Orange Lodge brethren on a question of principle when he invested significant energy and political capital in defending the right of minority Manitoba Francophone Roman Catholics to have public funding support for a separate school system.

He spent half a century in Parliament, becoming the fourth longest-serving parliamentarian in Canadian history. He was an associate (either as ally or foe) of most of the prominent 19th century players who were creating the story of the young nation. As Customs Minister, Bowell implemented the protectionist National Policy, the signature economic development policy of successive John A. Macdonald governments. He was Canada's first trade and commerce minister, led the inaugural Canadian foreign trade mission (to Australia) and organized an influential intercolonial conference to discuss relations between British colonies and Great Britain. Queen Victoria knighted Bowell for his service to Canada and the British Empire. Along his life's journey, he achieved one political milestone unique in Canadian history as the only politician who served continuously in Parliament throughout the entire first half-century of Canadian nationhood after July 1, 1867.

During his tumultuous and ultimately unsuccessful 16-months as prime minister, Bowell also lived through a constitutional crisis when he became the first sitting prime minister and party leader in British parliamentary history to be forced from office by his own caucus despite the fact that he led a majority government. Another century would pass before Canadians again witnessed the spectacle of a prime minister and party leader who commanded a majority in Parliament (Jean Chrétien) being pushed into resignation by dissidents fighting an in-party civil war for power.

Yet despite his prominent role in the political life of Canada's first half century, Bowell has not fared well when the stories of those early formative years of Canadian nationhood are told. Historians writing about Canada's political leaders who played a role in seeing the country survive and develop in its early decades have not been kind. During the half century following his 1917 death, Bowell was all but forgotten when the history of the country was being told. At best, he rated an asterisk noting that he was the prime minister between Sir John Thompson and Sir Charles Tupper. More typically, he was recognized only as one of the four brief Conservative prime ministers who inadequately followed Canadian founder Sir John A. Macdonald after his death in 1891, before Sir Wilfrid Laurier ushered in the Liberal Century five years later.

Then, the build-up to Canada's 100th birthday milestone in 1967 helped end Bowell's historical anonymity and not in a good way. Historians and writers, inspired by or cashing in on the buzz around the Centennial celebration, discovered Bowell and things went from neglect to worse: criticism, ridicule and scorn. Since then, contemporary interpreters of Canada's political history have built on the 1960s portrayal of Bowell as a political failure and piled on. One author, Regina writer Maggie Siggins, used her acclaimed 1994 biography of 19th century Métis leader Louis Riel to write an influential condemnation of Bowell for his parliamentary role in having the rebel leader expelled from the House of Commons in 1874. Riel had been an instigator and mastermind of the 1869 Red River rebellion against Canadian and Crown forces. She depicted Bowell as a small-minded Protestant whose religious prejudices coloured his legacy a deep shade of orange. 'In this Parliament [the third Parliament 1874–78], the forces of Orange Ontario were large and powerful,' Siggins wrote. '…Mackenzie Bowell [was] a grand master of the North Hastings Orange Lodge, a future prime minister of Canada and a man about as bigoted as they came.'[1] Although she got his credentials wrong, her point was made.

Another acclaimed historian who penned a 1971 account of 19th century Canada used a reference to Bowell's 1895 elevation to knighthood by Queen Victoria as a vehicle to mock him as a vain braggart. Respected Dalhousie University historian Peter W. Waite wrote:

> Few of the knights named to serve the Queen on New Year's Day, 1895, could have been more pleased than the pompous, ponderous, decent old newspaperman from Belleville, Ont. who now rejoiced in the rotund appellation of Sir Mackenzie Bowell. He was seventy-two, ripe with whiskers, politics and vanity… Bowell was not a bad man but his talent for leadership was non-existent… [He believed] he could follow the precepts of Macdonald but stupidity usually imitates the worst… He was, in short, a little man in a big place, fatuous, petty and on important matters, untrustworthy.[2]

In 1964, Bruce Hutchison—a leading Canadian political journalist of his time and author of classic books celebrating Canada and its potential—took his turn as a Bowell basher by referencing his background as a Protestant-promoting Orangeman, depicting him as a man unfit to be prime minister and finishing with a bit of vindictive about Bowell's physical appearance. Bowell's leadership in Protestant Orange politics was his ticket to influence and political usefulness, Hutchison argued in a centennial-inspired book about the prime ministers of Canada's first century:

> Though he was a tiny, stupid man, his influence over the extreme lunatic fringe of the Tory vote represented a political asset of sorts. He also had some minor talents as a small-town political fixer and a certain cunning… When he entered the Prime Minister's office, the

3

crumpled face behind the whitening beard gave him the look of a bitter Santa Claus with crafty eyes. In anything like normal times, such a man would have merited no more than a footnote in the history books but these were not normal times. The forces flowing had placed in this pitiable personage the future of the Conservative government, the Liberal Opposition and the nation's fragile unity.[3]

Then the scholarly judges of historical performance got involved. In 1999, academics J. L. Granatstein and Norman Hillmer collaborated on a book that ranked the 20 prime ministers who had occupied the political centre stage to that point in Canadian history. Bowell ranked 19th, ahead only of Kim Campbell, Canada's sole female prime minister who served just 133 days in the office in 1993 before leading the Progressive Conservatives from majority government status to a two-seat parliamentary rump. They ranked Bowell behind such short-term and unaccomplished (at least in the top job) first ministers as John Turner (80 days in the summer of 1984), John Abbott (528 days in 1891–92) and Sir Charles Tupper, whose 1896 time in office lasted a record-brief 69 days. In assessing Bowell as prime minister, they wrote:

> He was not a skilled leader and he proved completely inept at making decisions or managing his cabinet or Parliament. His cabinet—'a nest of traitors' he called them—treated him with contempt and in January 1896, half the cabinet resigned in protest at his leadership…[4]

Then in 2016, a year after Justin Trudeau became Canada's 23rd prime minister, *Maclean's Magazine* published a prime ministerial ranking that divided the leaders into categories of 'long-serving' and 'short-term.' Among the 10 designated short-term prime ministers, Bowell placed eighth ahead of only Turner and Campbell.[5]

However, the apex of the modern trend to diminish and ridicule Bowell's place in Canadian history came in 2004 when the Canadian Parliamentary Affairs Channel (CPAC) aired an hour-long program on Bowell as part of a 14-part series on Canadian prime ministers. The background narrative for the Bowell episode liberally cited anonymous historians and journalists with negative views of Bowell. At one point, the narrator intoned that a journalist had written: 'His good looks and silver beard disguised his weakness.' The script also claimed that Bowell's long-time position as Macdonald's Customs Minister charged with the pivotal assignment of implementing the protectionist National Policy after 1878 meant Bowell was 'among the least prominent in the federal cabinet. He was minister of customs—a tax collector!'

The program featured as commentators a collection of Bowell detractors, some of them with dubious credentials as sources of prime ministerial historical knowledge. Parliamentary Poet Laureate George Bowering, for example, said he had researched the former prime minister before being interviewed for the project and concluded that Bowell had neither the credentials nor intellectual capacity for the job.[6] 'My impression, given the amount of time I spent reading about Mackenzie Bowell, is that he was a dolt.' Bowering, 66 when appointed as an award-winning poet, then offered this assessment of what Sir John A. Macdonald thought of his long-time customs minister:

> He was the kind of guy that no prime minister could like… the prime minister doesn't like him but he can't get by without him, right? He can't dump him. If he dumps him, he probably doesn't last very long because of the guy's following among the 'racist, bigoted Protestant right wing'.

In fact, Bowell was one of Macdonald's most trusted ministers, regularly hand-picked to fill in for other ministers when they were absent from Ottawa; finance, post office, railways and fisheries, among others. In the CPAC Bowell profile, Belleville florist Blake Holton, Bowell's great-great grandson, was the only sympathetic voice but he acknowledged the negative view of his ancestor held by many. Holton recalled a time in his student days when his ancestor was dismissed by a history teacher who had been working his way through prime ministers, giving students brief lectures on their time and legacy in office:

> I knew that the day he mentioned Sir Mackenzie Bowell's name, I would put up my hand and say 'Sir, that man was my great-great grandfather." The prof walked in one day and he put his books on the floor and he opened up his notes and said 'Sir Mackenzie Bowell—we are not going to spend much time on that clown'.

In 2017 Holton recalled that the professor began by telling the class he was going to talk about 'probably the worst prime minister in Canadian history' and the great-great grandson figured 'he had skipped a number of generations and that he was going to talk about Joe Clark. When he said the clown's name was Mackenzie Bowell, I felt I had been slapped in the face.'[7]

So ingrained is the negative view of Mackenzie Bowell as a hapless, incompetent, unaccomplished and vain leader in Canadian prime ministerial history texts that it even has made it into histories about other aspects of the politics of Canada's first century. A 2017 coffee table book on prime ministerial residences in Ottawa before 24 Sussex Drive became the official residence in 1952 includes this brief description of Bowell: 'Small in stature, he was thought by his peers as stupid and weak. Sometimes described as a bitter Santa Claus, he was apparently grumpy and quick-tempered.'[8] Similarly, in his acclaimed 1997 history of the political and personal machinations that produced the Canadian Confederation bargain, historian Christopher Moore detailed the growing power of political party leaders in the federal system that evolved in Canada in the decades after 1867. However, the power of the leaders had its limits as the 19th century drew to a close, Moore argued. Party leadership could still be removed at a moment's notice. In 1896, the Conservative cabinet forced the resignation of prime minister Mackenzie Bowell; 'a weak, vain, decent old mediocrity,' in historian Peter Waite's phrase, which seems to be the kindest thing anyone has said about him.[9]

Really? Was being labeled 'a weak, vain, decent old mediocrity' the high-water mark of praise for Mackenzie Bowell's legacy? Perhaps it appears that way if the pool of judgments being assessed is confined to those written in hindsight, in times far removed from the era in which Bowell was a key political player. However, his contemporaries who watched him in action, who knew him and judged his impact from personal experience, were far more admiring and generous.

In late December 1894 after his appointment as prime minister, the Bowell family's Belleville *Intelligencer* printed a smattering of the newspaper coverage and reaction from across the country. All of it was positive and while the prime minister's ties to the newspaper no doubt influenced the choice of coverage reprinted, even Liberal-aligned newspapers were complimentary. A December 20 story from the Conservative Ottawa *Journal* described him as 'a man of broad democratic ideas, progressive and liberal…' He was the senior member of the late cabinet and his long connection with government had made his name one of the most widely known in Canada. He was not a man of dazzling brilliancy, of profound learning or polished address or extraordinary oratorical gifts but on the contrary is a plain matter-of-fact statesman of long experience, sound judgment and steadfastness of purpose. The capital city newspaper saw him as a strong, practical leader:

> He is a man of unblemished character, of businesslike address, forcible and vigourous in debate, clear headed, familiar with all the great political questions of the day and one in whom Canadians can place the utmost confidence, assured of the fact that his administration will be honest, economical and progressive.[10]

The newspaper commentary assured readers: 'The almost unanimous opinion of the leaders of the Conservative Party is that the new premier is the right man for the place.' The Liberal Ottawa *Citizen* also endorsed the decision:

> Mr. Bowell is a thoroughly capable, strong politician. His judgment originally sound has been ripened by long experience and an intimate acquaintance with public affairs… Unsurpassed as an administrator and an able debater, he has other qualities equally important. His disposition is genial and his manners attractive. No one is more

popular wherever he is known. His honesty is beyond question.

In Saint John, New Brunswick, the *Sun* gave him credit for 'long experience, ripe judgment and high standing in the country. He has never yet turned his back on the enemy or feared to face a situation.'[11] The Montreal Conservative newspaper *La Minerve* praised Bowell for his parliamentary work as 'the imperial defender of the rights of the different classes and creeds which form the Canadian nation.'

The enthusiastic assessments continued as Bowell grew older, even after the lofty journalistic predictions of a successful prime ministerial tenure turned out to be far too optimistic. On July 21, 1905 after Bowell announced he was stepping down as Opposition leader in the Senate and would sit as a simple Senator without a designated leadership role, the Conservative Toronto *Mail and Empire* opined that his record of service and achievements were unprecedented. 'There is not in our history a better illustration of the truth that work—constant work—united with rectitude brings its reward than that we have in the life of Sir Mackenzie.'[12] After his December 10, 1917 death, tributes by his contemporaries (both foes and friends during his long life) were effusive and generous. The Toronto *Globe* newspaper, founded by early Reform (Liberal) Party leader George Brown and a fierce critic and opponent of Conservative Bowell throughout his career in politics and government, marked his death with many columns of praise and tribute. 'Sir Mackenzie Bowell was one of the very last of a long line of distinguished Canadians whose activities preceded Confederation and who rank among the great builders of the Dominion,' it said in a front-page story December 11, 1917. It later asserted that had he not been defeated in his first attempt at parliamentary office in 1863, he would have been a Father of Confederation:

> Sir Mackenzie enjoyed the respect of both political parties and the warm affection of his own. He had the bluff manner which is supposed to be characteristic of the typical Englishman but behind the outward mask there beat a warm heart for personal friends irrespective of political affiliations.'[13]

The Montreal *Gazette*, a Conservative Party supporter, saw him as a nation builder. 'It is given to few men to tread continuously the stage of public life for so long a period,' it told readers December 12:

> For fifty years a member of the Parliament of Canada, he not only saw the Confederation grow to greatness but he was in no small degree instrumental in contributing to the provisions which made that greatness possible. Mackenzie Bowell was one of the active builders of a foundation upon which today a splendid structure stands.[14]

While the *Gazette* noted he had reached the highest office, it made no claim that it was the pinnacle of his career:

He was for a brief period Prime Minister of Canada but perhaps his strongest claim to a place in Canadian history is based upon the work which he did as a departmental administrator, in his organization of the Department of Trade and Commerce and in the large share which was his organizing the system of colonial conferences. Through all the long period of his public service, he enjoyed a reputation without blemish. He was at all times and to all men kind, considerate and courteous and he will be remembered as typifying Canadian citizenship at its best.

In a memoir written after Bowell's death, his long-time personal secretary and professional intimate E.L. Sanders described his former boss as the epitome of public duty, civic mindedness, good judgment and tolerance. 'It was my privilege to study his character from a point of vantage for a number of years and I know that I shall have the concurring judgment of all those who know him best when I say he owes very much to his prodigious energy, his masterly grasp of detail, his urbanity of manner and his spotless integrity of life.' Sanders concluded with a summation of what he thought Bowell represented:

In short, he has been a capable man who has commanded popular trust. He stands for what the world recognizes as 'an all-round man', gifted with acute sagacity in many things and bringing a robust common sense to bear on all things.[15]

When the Senate where Bowell spent the last 25 years of his political life next gathered several months after his death, the men from both parties set aside their political divisions March 21, 1918 to remember and honour their former colleague. They had worked with him and watched his performance as a senior minister and Senate leader both in government and in opposition. Many of those who spoke tackled head-on the allegations that had dogged Bowell throughout his political life, that because of his Orange Lodge affiliation, at heart he was an anti-Roman Catholic bigot. His political friends and adversaries instead remembered a man who regularly faced down members of his own political party and Orange fraternity to defend and advocate for the constitutional right of religious and linguistic minorities to have publicly supported schools for their children.

Montreal Liberal H. J. Cloran remembered him as a Grand Master of the Orange Lodge who was 'the bosom friend of bishops, canons, parish priests and clergy of every denomination… He was a man who believed in equal rights, equal justice to all classes, all creeds and all races in this Dominion of ours.'[16] Conservative government Senate leader Sir James Lougheed recalled Bowell as a politician motivated by a drive to make the world better:

No man in Canada was ever actuated by a higher sense of public duty than our late colleague. He was a bulwark of strength to this Chamber. We were proud on both sides of the House to call him our friend and in his death, we can only say a great Canadian has departed from amongst us.[17]

These were the positive assessments, the heart-felt praise of politicians, newspapermen and Bowell intimates who knew him, followed his career, lived in the political society in which he played a role for half a century and considered him an honourable and accomplished political player of his time. Why, then, did that view change and the assessments of Mackenzie Bowell's life, career, performance and impact become largely negative and dismissive by historians and writers almost a half century after his death? The answer, it seems, lies to a large extent in the 1960 Canadian book publishing season that came more than six decades after Bowell left the prime minister's office and more than four decades after his contemporaries praised his memory and his reputation as a significant, important and successful post-Confederation national politician.

NOTES

[1] Siggins, Maggie, *Riel: A Life of Revolution* (Toronto: HarperCollins Publishers Ltd. 1994), 231.

[2] Waite, Peter B., *Canada 1874–1896: Arduous Destiny* (Toronto: McClelland and Stewart Ltd. 1971), 252.

[3] Hutchison, Bruce, *Mr. Prime Minister 1867–1964* (Toronto: Longman's Canada Ltd. 1964), 104-105.

[4] Granatstein, J. L. and Hillmer, Norman, *Prime Ministers Ranking Canada's Leaders* (Toronto: HarperCollins 1999).

[5] The quotes cited were taken from a transcript of the 2004 Mackenzie Bowell profile provided by CPAC.

[6] The Parliamentary Poet Laureate position was created in 2001 to improve the profile of poetry and to 'encourage and promote the importance of literature, culture and language in Canadian society,' according to its parliamentary website. Appointments by Commons and Senate Speakers are for two-year terms.

[7] All quotes from CPAC transcript and 2017 interview with the author.

[8] Hadaya, Hagit, *At Home with the Prime Minister: Ottawa Residences of the Prime Ministers Prior to 1952* (Ottawa: Self-published, 2017), 35.

[9] Moore, Christopher, *1867, How the Fathers Made a Deal* (Toronto: McClelland & Stewart, 1977), 220.

[10] *Belleville Intelligencer* collection in the Community Archives of Belleville and Hastings County (CABHC).

[11] ibid.

[12] ibid.

[13] *The Globe* (Vol. LXXIV, No. 21,187) Toronto: December 11, 1917.
[14] *The Gazette*, Vol. CXLVI, No. 297, Montreal: December 12, 1917.
[15] E. L. Sanders memoir (Trent University Archives, Mrs. E. Kayser fonds), undated
[16] Debates of the Senate (1st Session, 13th Parliament, Vol. 1), 40.
[17] ibid, 38.

Chapter Two
THE REPUTATION ASSASSINS

As Canada entered the 1960s with Centennial year celebrations planning well underway, its literary community was blossoming and Canadian readers were embracing what was seen as the beginning of a golden age of letters. They were seeing their country—its stories, history and myths—reflected in published works in unprecedented numbers. Some of the most prominent Canadian fiction and non-fiction writers were prominent on book best-seller lists. The Governor General's 1960 literary awards list included Brian Moore's seminal novel *The Luck of Ginger Coffey* for fiction, Frank Underhill's influential political analysis *In Search of Canadian Liberalism* for non-fiction, and celebrated journalist and author Pierre Berton's *Just Add Water and Stir* for humour (and the Stephen Leacock Award).

The book-publishing season in the first year of the 1960s also featured the appearance of two unexpected and influential historical documents—one a diary and the other a memoir—that cast significant new light on the political turmoil inside the late 19th century Conservative Party. It was an episode that roiled the party and the nation during Mackenzie Bowell's time in the prime minister's office and ultimately brought him down. Neither book was kind to Bowell, providing plenty of judgments about his culpability for the chaos and inability to control events and outcomes. An unacknowledged undercurrent to those harsh judgments was that both authors were 19th century political insiders with grievances that predisposed them to criticism of Sir Mackenzie Bowell—party leader, prime minister and the old Orangeman from Hastings County.

The texts—personal perspectives of two well-placed witnesses to that tumultuous period in Canadian politics, written decades before their publication—proved pivotal in changing Canada's history narrative in the 1960s. Contemporary writers welcomed the new information as a base to revise, reinvent and add colour to a little-understood period in the 19th century Canadian story.

The timing of the publications was perfect for maximum impact.

They arrived in bookstores and libraries on the cusp of a renewed interest in Canada's political history as the Centennial celebration loomed. They were manna to historians and writers looking for new angles to freshen up stale tales about the first Canadian half-century that many found to be rather dull fare. There also was an appetite for historical revisionism at the time and the newly published first person, subjective accounts offered raw material galore. They shed new light on the political volcano that erupted in the mid-1890s, triggering a seismic shift that heralded the end of three decades of Tory rule, largely under the skilled manipulations and political management of Sir John A. Macdonald. The new information also offered new insight into the beginning of the 20th century Liberal successes started by Sir Wilfrid Laurier and continued by his heirs for the next century and beyond.

In the aftermath of that pivotal publishing season, Bowell's memory and place in the Canadian story, while resurrected from neglect and obscurity, suddenly became a cautionary tale about political mediocrity, indecision and ineptitude. Later generations of Canadian history writers and commentators have found the portrayal of Bowell and the snappy putdowns irresistible. A career and life judged successful and exemplary by his contemporaries and peers quickly was transformed into a cartoon, a Canadian history gag line.

The first of the pivotal 1960 publications off the presses was *The Canadian Journal of Lady Aberdeen, 1893–1898*, the fascinating private diary of Ishbel Maria Marjoribanks who arrived in Ottawa in September 1893 with her husband, new Canadian Governor General John Hamilton Gordon, a Scotsman and 7th Earl of Aberdeen. [1] She quickly began to play an active behind the scenes role for her husband, providing him with vivid detailed accounts of what really was going on beneath the political surface in his new fiefdom. Lady Aberdeen quickly made friends in Ottawa's political and social circles and they kept her abreast of developments and gossip. They acquainted her with the intrigues playing out in what still was in many ways a small, rough and tumble lumber town chosen by Queen Victoria to be the capital of the new Dominion of Canada.

She also was a regular and astute diarist with a sharp understanding of politics and the egos of the men who pursued the political game, and she had a catbird's seat from which to view the action. In a decision not possible within today's Parliamentary rules and traditions, she was given a seat on the floor of the House of Commons beside the Speaker's Throne where she could watch and listen to debates, talk to MPs and overhear the stories and gossip MPs traded as political coinage. She and her Governor General husband regularly discussed political developments and affairs of state and with her inside knowledge, Ishbel was not afraid to offer opinions meant to influence the discussion.

John Saywell, a 30-year-old University of Toronto assistant professor of history, who later became one of Canada's most renowned historians and political scientists, edited the diary and considered it an instant Canadian history classic about the tumult of the heretofore little understood era. 'As printed, it at once becomes the most important published document for the [late 19th century] period,' he wrote. 'Not only was Lady Aberdeen an acute observer but more important, her political and religious convictions, her personality and experience alike demanded that she become a participator.'[2]

However, Lady Aberdeen was not entirely an unbiased observer of the political drama unfolding in Ottawa. Ishbel Majoribanks also was an unabashed British Whig (Liberal) and such an admirer and friend of British Liberal Prime Minister William Ewart Gladstone that she displayed his picture or initials in every room of Government House in Ottawa. [3] Conservatives were not her favourite people, nor were Orangemen. She had decidedly mixed private views about Bowell and developed a strong dislike and disapproval of Sir Charles Tupper. Not surprisingly, she also quickly developed an affinity for Laurier, the dashing leader of the Canadian Liberal Party and Opposition Leader in Parliament. As the Bowell government became ripe with subversion and intrigue against the leader and prime minister, Lady Aberdeen was being kept abreast of developments and through it all, she maintained an unseemly line of communications to the Liberal leader that gave him a clear and unwarranted understanding of the political chaos that existed across the aisle of Parliament.

While a persistent private denigrator of Bowell's performance in office, Lady Aberdeen's diary also records an ambivalent view of Bowell the man. It was on display in her first substantive mention of him on December 13, 1894. In her journal that day, she mused about possible successors to the late Prime Minister Sir John Thompson, who had died in England unexpectedly the previous day, forcing the Governor General to choose a replacement. There was no obvious successor although as the senior minister in cabinet, Bowell had been acting prime minister in Thompson's absence and therefore a logical choice. 'Mr Mackenzie Bowell himself is 75, rather fussy and decidedly commonplace, also an Orangeman, at one time the Grand Master of the Orangemen of N America and also presided at one of the tip-top grand Orange affairs at Belfast—but he is a good and straight man and he has great ideas about the drawing together of the colonies and the Empire…' she wrote, referring to a Colonial Conference Bowell organized and chaired the previous year in Ottawa. [4] In fact, she exaggerated Bowell's age by four years. He was two weeks shy of his 72nd birthday. References to his Orange Lodge background reflected her religious, progressive and British distaste for the Orange brand of Protestant political agitation.

After some indecision, her husband chose Bowell for the job and during his time in the prime minister's office, she became critical of what the Governor General saw as his secretiveness and refusal to share with Government House all of the details of his work on issues and with other cabinet ministers. This led her, as the Aberdeens prepared to embark on a long trip to western Canada in the summer of 1895, to break all protocol by forming an alliance with Sir Charles Hibbert Tupper behind the prime minister's back. Tupper was a minister in Bowell's cabinet and the leader of the anti-Bowell fifth column within the government.

Despite the clear protocol that the prime minister was to be the government contact for the Queen's representative in Government House, Lady Aberdeen recruited Tupper to secretly keep her informed while they were away from Ottawa about the inner workings of the government. 'I asked him to write me as a friend so that there might be no impropriety about seeming to pass by the Premier...' she wrote in her July 18, 1895 diary entry. 'Sir Charles entirely entered into the position and its delicacy and readily assented to my proposition and then proceeded to speak to me very frankly about the difficulties which the Government were experiencing with Sir Mackenzie as Premier.'[5]

Bowell obviously had good reason to be circumspect about how much he should share with the Aberdeens and how much he could trust them. He also likely was suspicious of their clear Liberal leanings and in the small circle of Official Ottawa, may well have heard rumours of the improper relationship with Tupper. Still, despite her Machiavellian behind-the-scenes machinations, Lady Aberdeen maintained some of the early ambivalence about Bowell as well as some sympathy. Later, as his close political associates were undermining the prime minister, she confided to her diary that upon reflection, she had decided that he was not being treated fairly.[6] Sympathetic and nuanced or not, her judgments of Bowell as indecisive, secretive, untrustworthy, weak and out of his depth as party leader and when they were published more than six decades after they were written, gave ammunition to the late 20th century Mackenzie Bowell reputation assassins.

The second 1960 publication that served as a foundation for Bowell's negative modern-day reputation was a memoir written by Sir Joseph Pope, one of the most influential federal public servants of the late 19th and early 20th centuries. He was in government during Bowell's brief tenure and was not impressed. Unlike Lady Aberdeen, whose diary judgment of Bowell was a mix of criticism and sympathy, Pope was unequivocal, uncompromising and direct in his condemnation of both the fifth prime minister and the Governor General who appointed him.

By late 1894, when Sir John Thompson died in office, 'all the [Conservative] chiefs had disappeared with the exception of Sir Charles Tupper who on Thompson's death should have been summoned without delay,' Pope wrote, 'but who for some inexplicable reason was passed over by Lord Aberdeen in favour of Mr Mackenzie Bowell, a worthy loyal man but one as little qualified to be prime minister of Canada as Lord Aberdeen was to be Governor General.'[7] To make certain the point was clear, Pope added: 'Then followed days which I never recall without a blush, days of weak and incompetent administration by a cabinet presided over by a man whose sudden and unlooked-for elevation had visibly turned his head—a ministry without unity or cohesion of any kind, a prey to internal dissensions until they became a spectacle to the world, to angels and to men.'[8]

In the on-line *Dictionary of Canadian Biography* (Volume XV) published in 2003, Dalhousie University historian Peter B. Waite wrote the Pope biographical entry and described his view of the Bowell appointment in low-key prose: 'After Thompson's death in 1894, Governor General Lord Aberdeen called on Mackenzie Bowell to form a government. Pope had a low estimate of Bowell's talents and thought Aberdeen's judgment deplorable.'[9] However, in his own writing about Bowell, Waite was not as restrained and amply demonstrated that he shared the cabinet secretary's disdain.

Pope's scathing view of Bowell's performance and competence presumably flowed from a genuine belief that he did not have the skill to manage the complexities of political leadership, to control cabinet egos, to display vision, cunning and decisiveness the way Pope's political hero Macdonald managed to do for decades. However, it also is true that Pope was influenced by the fact that he was nursing a personal grudge he held against Mackenzie Bowell. In his memoir, Pope recounted bitterly that Bowell refused during the last days of the Conservative government in 1896 to fulfill a Macdonald promise that he would be appointed Under-Secretary of State for Canada, the senior bureaucratic position in the federal government.

Bowell justified inaction on the grounds that appointing Pope would be an affront to French-speaking officials. He could not replace the former French-Canadian Under-Secretary of State with the English-speaking Pope because it would upset the delicate balance of Canadian religious and linguistic politics. 'Though the appointment of a deputy minister was always held to be in the gift of the Prime Minister, Sir Mackenzie Bowell would do nothing and I bade fair to be sacrificed to this ignoble racial prejudice,' Pope complained.

Ultimately, he appealed to the incoming Prime Minister Sir Charles Tupper Sr who found a way to make the appointment effective April 25, 1896—Tupper's first day in office as Prime Minister and Secretary of State. Although the appointment was recorded as happening during Bowell's last day of leadership, 'I feel and have always felt that I owed to Sir Charles Tupper,' wrote Pope.[10] His unflattering portrayal of Bowell's performance carries weight in Canadian history because Pope was one of the most powerful federal public servants in Ottawa, serving prime ministers from Macdonald to William Lyon Mackenzie King.

Pope had been Macdonald's private secretary in the final years of his time in office, was an ardent admirer of The Old Chieftain, an author and editor of Macdonald's 1894 memoirs, and one of the executors of his will.

Eventually, Pope was appointed assistant clerk of the Privy Council before becoming the first and long-serving chief bureaucrat in the Department of External Affairs created by the Laurier government in 1909.

Oddly, given his view of Bowell, Pope also was one of the 22 signatories of a flattering letter from senior public servants presented to the retiring prime minister after he stepped down in April 1896, praising him for the 'affability and courtesy' with which he treated senior public service officials and affirming their 'great personal regard' for him. An irony of history is that Bowell played a role in Pope's first encounter with Macdonald, who became his hero while Bowell was the anti-hero. In autumn, 1881, customs minister Bowell was acting minister of marine and fisheries, replacing Pope's uncle for whom the nephew worked. One day, Bowell asked his young aide to go to his Privy Council office to retrieve a file and while Pope was going through Bowell's desk looking for it, Macdonald came into the room, spotted a stranger not authorized to be there and angrily had him removed. Bowell later explained the circumstances to Macdonald and changed the leader's view of the unauthorized intruder. The rest, as they say, became history.

Pope retired in 1925 and died the following year with his memoir half finished. His son Maurice completed the job and it finally was published 34 years after his death. 'Pope was the quintessential civil servant—capable, careful, perceptive,' wrote Waite, one of the modern historians who have ensured this model civil servant's 19th century scathing judgment of Bowell continues to influence the telling of history.[11]

While cause and effect is impossible to pin down, it is reasonable to at least wonder whether Mackenzie Bowell's negative and scant portrayal in Canadian history writing has influenced the fact that he is the least publicly recognized deceased prime minister in the country. Macdonald, Mackenzie, Laurier, Tupper, Abbott, Thompson, Pearson, Diefenbaker, Meighen and the rest have multiple public memorials that mark their once-prominent position in the nation: buildings, schools, streets, highways, parks or other public spaces named for them as well as statues, plaques and various public markers of recognition. Sir Mackenzie Bowell's legacy has almost no such memorial recognition, even in Ottawa where he fashioned an exemplary political career for half a century or in Belleville where he lived as a leading citizen for more than 80 years. In fact, the Belleville graveyard is one of the few places where Bowell's life and death are noted and even that site has problems.

In the aftermath of Sir Mackenzie Bowell's 1917 death, one of his Senate colleagues and admirers proposed that his gravestone carry a simple chiselled tribute attesting to his honourable life. It did not happen, but even if it had, modern-day visitors to his gravesite likely would be none the wiser. Federal inspection reports obtained in 2017 by *The National Post* newspaper indicate that over the years, federal governments of all stripes have failed to maintain most of the grave sites and monuments for the 15 deceased prime ministers buried in Canada.

At the Bowell grave, the Ottawa *Citizen* reported, the base of the monument has eroded, inscriptions have largely become illegible and his portrait had 'significantly faded.' [12] However, at least there is a graveyard memorial. Almost no other public recognitions exist for Bowell across the country.

Belleville exemplifies the lack of recognition. It is where he lived for more than 80 years, where he served for a decade as chair of the Belleville Board of Education, where he owned the local newspaper, was a leading businessman and for 50 years was Belleville's representative in Ottawa. Yet precious little public recognition of Bowell's prominence in hometown history greets a visitor. Once there was a school, but the Sir Mackenzie Bowell Public School closed in June 2014. The Sir Mackenzie Bowell 'Educator of the Year' Award established in 1967 was abolished in 2014. It honoured the fact that for many years, Bowell had served as the chair of the local school board and was an ardent advocate of education and the opportunities it brings.

No buildings or streets bear his name and, other than his gravesite and a graveyard federal plaque, the only recognition that Belleville is one of just a handful of Canadian communities to be represented by a prime minister comes in the form of an Ontario government plaque in front of his downtown William Street house, a plaque at the Belleville Armoury for his role creating a militia unit in the 1860s and a Sir Mackenzie Bowell meeting room tucked away inside City Hall.

The experience of long-time Prince Edward-Hastings Liberal MP Lyle Vanclief illustrates the lack of local recognition. Vanclief was a successor to Bowell, representing the city in Parliament for 16 years (1988–2004) and as agriculture minister was the only Belleville representative since Bowell to be a Queen's Privy Councillor. Yet he recalls that throughout his entire schooling in city schools, he learned almost nothing about the former hometown prime minister. 'You can't say I was raised in his shadow or was influenced to get into politics because of his example because really, I was never taught about him that I can recall,' Vanclief says. 'His story, if it was told at all, didn't stand out in my schooling.'[13]

Other than those small Belleville offerings, it would take a trip of thousands of kilometres west to find what may be the only other remaining public reminders of Bowell's time in the political limelight. The first stop is southeast Alberta. Beside a lonely, windy stretch of the Trans-Canada Highway cutting through Cypress County between Medicine Hat and Brooks stands a solitary 'Bowell' roadside sign, the remnants of a Canadian Pacific Railway train station and a small village long since disappeared.

In late 2015, the *Medicine Hat News* reported that the County might remove the Bowell sign and the story led Jonathan Koch—affiliated with the 'Forgotten Alberta' website project preserving provincial history—to take to the web. He lamented the news while conceding that the name and sign had been, 'the butt of countless drive-by [puns]' and bodily function jokes from locals over the years because of the name's spelling proximity to a certain vital body part. Originally, the train station and the town that grew around it was given the Bowell name by CPR builder William Van Horne to recognize the-then Customs Minister who often was involved in federal government negotiations with the builders of the railway over progress, or lack of it.

In the province further west stands the largest physical memorial to Bowell: a mountain. Mount Sir Mackenzie Bowell, at 10,301 feet the 97th highest mountain in the province, is part of the Premier Range of the Cariboo Mountains in the east-central interior. It acquired the name in 1927, one of the first of the Premier Range to receive its prime ministerial appellation.

In northern Ontario, railway officials in the late 19th century chose the name Bowell Township to designate an area outside Sudbury when the CPR track was being installed. In the 1970s, Bowell Township became part of the Greater Sudbury town of Valley East and the name all but disappeared. In a way, the Mackenzie Bowell story is a classic example of the often-fleeting nature of fame, particularly political fame. In *Smoked Glass*, a 1977 book of poems written by New Brunswick novelist, playwright and poet Alden Nowlan—1967 winner of the Governor General's Award for English Poetry—Bowell's story is used ironically as the symbol of that reality. The torchlight victory parade the New Brunswick poet imagines could well have been a description of one of the Belleville parades staged for Bowell, transporting him from the train station to his home. The parades typically were organized late in the night after another personal election victory had been declared through seven consecutive successful House of Commons campaigns (1867–1891). A similar parade was organized in winter 1895 when newly appointed Prime Minister Bowell returned triumphant for a home-town celebration.

ELECTION SONG
Down the street they came with torches,
Like a roaring human sea,
Chanting 'Up with Sir Mackenzie Bowell!
Statesman! Man of Destiny!
Mackenzie Bowell. Mackenzie Bowell
May thoughts of your vanquished fame
Help us keep things in perspective
As we vote for what's-his-name.'[14]

Of course, before Canadian history could forget about Mackenzie Bowell, and then the few historians who remembered casually set out to malign his memory, there had to be a story to forget or malign. It began in the fourth decade of the 19th century on the cold icy shores of Lake Ontario when a young boy landed with his family after a life-changing journey from the Old World to the New. On that chilly first day in his new country, young Mackenzie likely was a kid full of dreams but it is difficult to imagine that even if he had a fertile imagination, his dreams were expansive enough to think that one day he would join the select few who would rise to become the leader of a prosperous country that spanned the North American continent. To arrive at that day in the unimagined future, it would require a lifetime-long history-in-the-making journey. Along the way, it would be filled with hard work, ability, character strengths (and flaws), perseverance, good luck (and bad), determination, circumstances and the good fortune of living through and influencing some of Canada's most interesting and nation-forming times.

It would be Mackenzie Bowell's story.

NOTES

[1] *The Canadian Journal of Lady Aberdeen, 1893–1898*, edited and with an introduction by John Saywell (Toronto: The Champlain Society, 1960). Just 600 copies of the book were printed. 50 for 'editorial purposes' and the remaining 550 for Champlain Society members and libraries.

[2] ibid, xxiv.

[3] ibid, xxvii.

[4] ibid, 161. The ground-breaking 1894 inter-colonial conference in Ottawa referred to by Lady Aberdeen was instigated by and chaired by Bowell to discuss trade and communications relations between Great Britain and her colonies. It will be examined more thoroughly in Chapter XII.

[5] ibid, 246.

[6] ibid, 301.

[7] Pope, Maurice (ed.), *Public Servant: The Memoirs of Sir Joseph Pope* (Toronto: Oxford University Press, 1960), 104.

[8] ibid.

[9] Waite, P. B., 'POPE, Sir JOSEPH,' in *Dictionary of Canadian Biography*, vol. XV (1921–30), University of Toronto/Université Laval, 2003, accessed September 25, 2017, http://www.biographi.ca/en/bio/pope_joseph_15E.html.

[10] op cit, *Public Servant*, 107.

[11] op cit, *Sir Joseph Pope*.

[12] Ottawa *Citizen* (March 13, 2017) FP1.

[13] Interview with Hon. Lyle Vanclief in Belleville, June 13, 2016.

[14] Nowlan, Alden, *Smoked Glass* (Toronto: Clark, Irwin & Company, 1977), 51.

Chapter 3
KID FULL OF DREAMS

Through most of his life, Mackenzie Bowell was a man of words. He penned and published hundreds of thousands of them during an 80-year affiliation with journalism and contributed millions more to the printed records of Parliament through daily Hansards that recorded hour upon hour of marathon speeches throughout his 50-year parliamentary career. Yet he wrote precious few personal records of his life; no diary that has surfaced, no memoir, little personal information in the letters that have been preserved and very few reminiscences about personal incidents in his long and rich life. It therefore is impossible to pinpoint exactly when the future Prime Minister first caught a glimpse of the wilderness community of Belleville, Upper Canada (Ontario) that he would call home for 84 years. Nor is it possible to describe definitively the boy's first impressions of his new country, although it is easy enough to speculate about excitement, wonderment and perhaps apprehension for it was nothing like what he came from in England, the only place he had ever lived. Like all immigrants young and old, the young Mackenzie undoubtedly looked around his new home and quietly yearned for stability, family, comfort, fitting in and belonging in his new life: adventures, opportunities and new friends. It also is a safe bet that upon arrival that day on the shores of Lake Ontario, nine-year-old Mackenzie Bowell was a kid full of dreams.

This much is certain: it was approaching winter, 1833 when he arrived with his family. By his own late-in-life account, it also was at the end of a long and dangerous journey that took him from his home in Walsham-le-Willows, Suffolk in eastern England to Yarmouth, the nearest east coast English port and from there across the Atlantic Ocean to England's North American colonies. He had made the journey with his parents John and Elizabeth and his younger sister Mahamah. According to Bowell biographer Betsy D. Boyce, Suffolk County records indicate that Mackenzie was born out of wedlock almost three months before John Bowell and Elizabeth Marshall married March 19, 1824. His March 13 baptism certificate records that his mother was 'Elizabeth Marshall, spinster.'[1] In January 1914, just weeks after his 90th birthday, Bowell offered his fullest published account of the trip all those years before when interviewed for a profile in the magazine *Canada*. 'He describes the passage from England in detail,' wrote journalist W. A. Craik, 'a trip which lasted over eight weeks. From Quebec, the family travelled to Montreal by steamer. From Montreal, they were conveyed as far as Prescott in Durham boats hauled by French ponies and from Prescott to

Belleville, they went in the Sir James Kemp, one of the earliest steamers on Lake Ontario.'² Boyce speculated that the family arrived in early December with ice already forming along the shores of Lake Ontario. It would have been one of the last runs of the season for the Sir James Kemp before it was grounded for the winter. Its arrival at the shores of the Bay of Quinte, part of the Lake Ontario system, likely happened on a chilly late afternoon in the growing dusk of shortened late autumn days.

Even if Bowell did not leave an account of conditions during the voyage across the Atlantic written in his own hand, a contemporary immigrant to Hastings County did and it was not pretty. The previous year, John and Susanna Moodie made a similar trip from the Scottish port of Leith to Belleville and then to a farm east of the small community. She was to become one of Canada's earliest celebrated female writers. The Bowell and Moodie families, although near neighbours in their new home, shared little in common other than the fact that they were part of the same mass migration wave that flowed from the British Isles to the North American colonies in the 1830s. It was a decade of record emigration from Britain to Canada that saw more than 600,000 risking the trip. The mass migration also meant that space on seaworthy (and sometimes not-so-sea-worthy) ships was at a premium. Those willing to gamble that a long, risky voyage was worth it for the chance of more opportunity in the New World or to escape hunger and poverty had little bargaining power with busy captains. It was a sellers' market and the ship operators simply were looking to rent out their limited space for the best price they could get. There was no shortage of customers. The Moodies had embarked July 1, 1832 on the passenger ship Anne and spent two months on the ocean (like the Bowells) before reaching Quebec City. There, they cobbled together transportation links westward on the St. Lawrence River to the Upper Canadian wilderness. However, while the logistics of the trip would have been similar for the two families, conditions during the journey almost certainly were not. According to Susanna Moodie biographer Charlotte Gray, the family was affluent enough to afford the relative luxury of a deck cabin for the voyage. It came with the benefits of fresh air, leg-room, walking space and better food because they often dined with the captain.³ It is unlikely John Bowell, an English town carpenter with a wife and two young children, would have had the means to afford a deck cabin. The alternative would have been the less expensive, crowded and less hygienic steerage accommodation below deck

Based on records kept by Moodie, Gray wrote a description of conditions in below-deck steerage quarters on the 1832 voyage: 'Steerage class passengers had a miserable time,' she wrote. 'The Anne was a relatively small boat and its 72 cheap-fare passengers were crammed into a space only sixty feet long by 10 feet wide and 5½ feet high.' Rough plank berths filled the space, hastily nailed together to convert a storage hold that had been filled with timber from North America on the last trip across the ocean into accommodations for passengers. 'Baggage, utensils and food supplies jammed the aisle and there was little ventilation. Children played in the fetid darkness. Dirty bilgewater slopped across the floor. Rats swarmed up from the hold. On long storm-plagued voyages, the smell of unwashed bodies, rotting food and vomit was suffocating.' While ship captains were supposed to feed all passengers as part of the fare, few loaded sufficient supplies of biscuits, flour, salt pork and fresh water to last the whole voyage. 'When the daily provisions were distributed, they were almost always too meagre and often spoiled.'[4] With those conditions not uncommon, ships transporting the tidal wave of British, Irish, Scottish and Welsh emigrants desperate for a new start in a new country sometimes were referred to as 'coffin ships.' They regularly arrived off the shores of North America with steerage class human cargo suffering from typhoid, cholera or other infectious diseases. On the St Lawrence River island of Grosse Ile east of Quebec City, a government quarantine station was established where passengers were examined before they landed on mainland Lower Canada (Quebec). The sick were detained until they recovered or died. Grosse Ile was the final resting place for thousands of 19th Century would-be immigrants. The island houses the largest Irish graveyard outside Ireland. Today, a towering Celtic cross commemorates the National Historic Site graveyard and quarantine station, part of the Parks Canada system.

The closest Bowell came to pinpointing the timing of the emigration journey for his family (except in several interviews in the latter years of his life that produced journalistic paraphrasing) was in a January 29, 1894 letter to James Bowell of Port Arthur, Ontario. James had written to enquire if the two were related. He provided the then-Trade and Commerce Minister with his English grandfather's name, hoping to find a common ancestor. Perhaps suspecting an impending follow-up request for a government job or favour from his newfound 'relative', Mackenzie replied with the unlikely assertion that he could not confirm a connection because he did not remember his grandfather's name in England. He did, however, remember the trip over, including its start. 'My father John Bowell left Suffolk in the summer of 1833 to come to Canada where he remained until his death,' Bowell wrote. 'I was then a boy of nine years of age.'[5] The letter serves to correct one of several errors about Bowell's life that made their way into on-line Government of Canada biographical sketches about the life of the fifth prime minister. One claimed he arrived in 1832 at age eight, a year before he did. Another trimmed 11 years off the 50 years Bowell spent in Parliament, mistakenly claiming he left the Senate in 1906 when he stepped down as Opposition Senate leader instead of in 1917 when he died. He remained active in the Senate until months before his death.

There is no record of where the Bowell family lived after they arrived on the cusp of an Upper Canadian winter in 1833, but one later account of his life suggested John Bowell moved to Belleville because a relative already lived there, perhaps offering lodging until the new arrivals could settle. The Belleville that existed during the Bowell's first winter in the New World was a primitive small town with a population of little more than 1,000 and a rudimentary economic base that included a gristmill and sawmill catering to local forestry and farming enterprises. The area was the site of a First Nations settlement, and in the 1830s First Nations encampments on the edge of town were part of the community. The first European settlers had migrated to Canada from the Thirteen Colonies when United Empire Loyalist refugees fled north after the American Revolution. They created a community that adopted the motto: Loyalty Tradition Progress. Police board regulations reflecting rules and conditions existing in the Belleville of the1830s described 'a rustic village where pigs strayed around the town, horses and cows might wander untethered and people left their rubbish on the street—everything from junk to dead animals.'[6] Within three years of the Bowell family arrival, according to local historian Gerry Boyce, Belleville was a community with a rapidly expanding economic base. 'By 1836, there were five wharves and the port was one of the busiest in Upper Canada,' he wrote. 'According to a newspaper account in 1837, exports included 10,000 barrels of flour, 40,000 bushels of wheat, 1500 barrels of potash, 1,000,000 staves and 2,000,000 feet of timber.' Surrounding land was being developed for agriculture.[7] By the time the Moodie family moved to Belleville in 1840 from their Peterborough-area farm after John was appointed sheriff of Victoria district, the town had grown considerably. 'Belleville's economy was thriving thanks to two flour mills, two carding mills, four sawmills, three breweries, seven blacksmith's shops and two tanneries,' wrote Gray. 'At its wharves, sailboats bringing goods from northern New York State via the Bay of Quinte jostled with fishing boats and steamers carrying passengers along the lakefront. Its 26 shops and 12 grocery stores carried imported goods from the United States, the West Indies and Europe as well as locally grown produce.'[8] The community also boasted a bookstore, a library, four churches, street lamps, limestone houses for the richer citizens... and still free-range pigs and garbage on the streets.

Throughout his life, Mackenzie Bowell possessed a strong religious and church connection. Belleville was a strongly religious settlement, or at least its residents built, attended and supported numerous churches. An 1840 survey of the community's 3900 residents provided evidence that the population claimed affiliation with at least nine different denominations. In his Belleville history text, Gerry Boyce argued the churches provided town residents with spiritual instruction, good works and some religious or denominational discord for good measure: 'Although occasional external and

23

even internal religious disputes interrupted the churches' work, the fact remains that they made a very positive contribution to the life of the community in pioneer times,' he wrote. 'Certainly, they ministered to more than the spiritual needs of the citizens. They were community social meeting places, welfare and education centres that improved the lot of the individual.'[9]

Lacking active state agencies, churches provided the program infrastructure and services that governments now are expected to provide. The Bowell family was affiliated with the Wesleyan Methodists, the largest denomination in the community. The Church of England (Anglican) was a close second. It began Bowell's lifelong connection to Ontario Methodism that defined an important part of who he was, although as with most affiliations and causes in his life, the relationship was complicated and not always an easy one. In fact, he apparently never officially become a church member even though he was a regular attendee and financial supporter. Belleville Methodist pastor Dr E. N. Baker, who ministered to Bowell during his time as prime minister, told the Toronto Star in 1935: 'He was a member of my church—the Bridge Street Methodist—and we got to be close friends. I'd have prayer with him in his office… but when I wanted him to join the church, he always said there were certain rules that he couldn't accept.'[10]

Bowell clearly was not a blind follower of religion and his church. He had doubts and concerns about the actions some took in the name of their religion. Over the years, he voiced public and private scepticism about some church practices and internal political feuds. In August 1893, for example, he responded sympathetically to a letter received from Toronto preacher John Burton who had left his congregation in a dispute over divisive debates about doctrine and church governance. 'I fear I should be out of my element if I attempted to deal with questions of theology or church government,' Bowell wrote. 'I may say, however, that I am fully in accord with your views so far as denominationalism and Christian unity are concerned. My experience has been that those who fight with the greatest bitterness for some alleged denominational dogmas have possessed the least Christianity in their composition, if I understand Christianity.'[11]

Years later while speaking in the Senate, Bowell showed his church scepticism again when he bluntly accused them of exploiting elderly church supporters to raise money for the institution. He noted that churches and preachers were restricted by a law that dictated when and how they could solicit donations from dying parishioners. 'We may as well be frank,' he said. 'That provision was made for the purpose of preventing a clergyman or anyone else from working upon the religious susceptibilities and prejudices of a dying man to induce him to make bequests to churches or other religious bodies which under ordinary circumstances, when in full possession of his intellect and mind, he would leave to his wife and family rather than to a religious corporation.'[12] Bowell's sceptical views about church tactics did not

24

always make him popular at church gatherings. Nonetheless, despite his doubts, discomfort and tensions with the church and fellow Methodists, Bowell continued to attend and support the church of his youth. When in Ottawa on weekends during his parliamentary career, Bowell was a regular attendee at the downtown Dominion Methodist Church (now Dominion Chalmers United Church), a close walk from his room at the Russell House hotel. Dominion Chalmers annual reports for the years before and when he was prime minister indicate a payment of $80.00 in 1892 including $15.00 for church renovations, $50.00 in 1893-94 to reserve a pew and contributions through 1895 and 1896 to a missionary fund and a church education fund. 'The payments ceased in 1897 and thereafter, presumably because he was no longer Prime Minister and his official residence and home church was in Belleville,' Dominion-Chalmers archivist Garth M. Bray concluded. Sir John A. Macdonald also was a regular worshipper at Dominion Methodist, joining Bowell in his pew some Sundays.[13]

When in Belleville, Bowell attended Pinnacle Street Wesleyan Methodist Church and also supported Bridge Street Methodist Church several blocks from his William Street home. When the Bridge Street church was destroyed by fire in early 1886, Bowell sent $500.00 to the rebuilding fund, a significant sum at the time and a major contribution to the church's $7500.00 fund-raising campaign[14] He also did not shy away from touting his church connections if it helped his image or his political cause. While prime minister, Bowell granted an interview to an American church newspaper, *The Northwest Christian Advocate*, that proclaimed him Canada's first Methodist prime minister and referred to him as a 'Methodist layman... It will interest our readers chiefly to know that the recently-appointed prime minister is a Methodist from conviction and choice.' It reported that Bowell had married 'a godly woman' and every Sunday, he was in the pews of Dominion Methodist Church 'among its most attentive hearers.'[15] Beyond his support of the church in the here and now, Bowell clearly also had a spiritual core that presumed an afterlife. As his 67th birthday approached in late 1890, he wrote to a Montreal Senator about recently deceased Roman Catholic and Methodist clergy: 'As time rolls on, we lose many of those we hold most dear. The best we can do is to live in hopes of meeting them in a better world.'[16]

Almost six decades earlier, a young Mackenzie Bowell likely had reason to wonder whether a 'better world' awaits those who die. At age 10, Bowell lost his mother Elizabeth, who died soon after childbirth on October 4, 1834. Her newborn infant Elizabeth died October 16, according to church burial records housed in the Community Archives of Belleville and Hastings County. It left John Bowell as a single working parent with two young children and a need for a coping plan. The former English carpenter had joined with a partner in Belleville to create a woodworking shop that sold furniture to a growing town population and it took up much of his time. He decided that Mackenzie, although he had little formal education from his childhood in England, should start to work in the family business helping in the shop rather than attending the local public school. Formal 'book learning' was not a priority for the working class in early 19th century Upper Canada. Besides, his father already had taught the boy rudimentary reading and writing skills. John then arranged to have his young son apprenticed to a local businessman so he could learn a trade. A condition of the apprenticeship agreement was that it came with room and board, sparing the father some of his single-parent obligations. At an age when many young boys were just beginning to think about their futures, Mackenzie Bowell was obligated to leave home to enter into a form of servitude. It marked an important turning point in his life, one that effectively would set him on a path to the prime minister's office. For the next three years, young Mackenzie was under the direct control and care of Belleville newspaper owner George Benjamin, who became arguably the most influential person in Bowell's life, initiating and influencing the personal journey he would embark upon, the interests and skills he would develop and the paths he would choose. Bowell's affiliation with Benjamin was to last the better part of three decades.

In the beginning, as an apprentice in a printing plant and part of the *Intelligencer* newspaper operation (a 'printer's devil' in newspaper industry parlance), the pre-teen lived and slept at the shop, had his meals provided, worked long hours and made little money. He also learned the power of words, information and journalism in the rough-and-tumble political world of 19th century Canada. Years later when Bowell's long-time political private secretary E. L. Sanders told the apprenticeship story in a handwritten undated and unpublished memoir about his former boss, he noted that the arrangement was not unusual for the period. 'The new boy started off as a "printer's devil" and from confessions of mischievous pranks in those early days, it may fairly be assumed that the appellation in his case was not altogether misplaced,' wrote Sanders, based on Bowell's recollections. 'His apprenticeship took him from his home and brought him wholly under the care of his employer, as was the custom in those days.'[17] His entry-level position as a print shop apprentice 'had all the inconveniences and primitive makeshifts of a country weekly in a practically pioneer settlement.' Yet when his three-year apprenticeship obligation ended, Bowell signed on as an employee under Benjamin's watch, working his way up through the newsroom and printing plant hierarchy for the next four years.

When he was 18, Bowell realized he needed a broader education if he was going to make his way in the world. It was a plan he pursued despite Sanders' view that 'there are few schools more thorough and practical than a newspaper office.' Bowell quit his job at the *Intelligencer* to enrol in a Hastings County school in the nearby town of Sydney. Within six months, he had earned a diploma that allowed him to teach in the public system and had lined up a job as a school principal. Then fate, in the form of George Benjamin, intervened to change his life path once again. As Sanders recounted: 'On the Saturday preceding the week he was to begin work as a rural dominie [a Scottish term for school master], he met his former employer [on the street] and was induced to go back to the *Intelligencer* office as foreman at the munificent salary of $10 a month with board and washing, which probably was as much as he would have received in those days as a school teacher.' [18] The die had been cast for a different journey than Bowell envisioned. Benjamin would continue be his leading influence, teacher and mentor. However, although Bowell's choices appeared on the surface to follow Benjamin's example in areas ranging from journalism and politics to Protestant promotion, Sanders said Bowell insisted it was coincidence. 'He neither set up Mr Benjamin as his ideal nor sought in any way to follow his footsteps in life.' Whatever the truth, he could hardly have chosen a more interesting or storied mentor, example and influence than George Benjamin. He was 'one of the most intriguing characters in Nineteenth Century Canada,' author Charlotte Gray concluded, even as she detailed the toxic view of Benjamin held by early Belleville area author Susanna Moodie. It was a view of Benjamin based both on Moodie's politics and racist views. [19]

British-born Benjamin emigrated to the United States as a young man and lived in North Carolina for several years before traveling north to Toronto in April 1834, just months after the Bowell family had settled east of the capital of Upper Canada. He arrived in Canada as an accomplished linguist and educated man, hoping to make a living as a language teacher to the growing population of Toronto (York), the colonial capital. In July 1834, Benjamin advertised himself as offering language lessons in French, Italian, German, English, Hebrew and Spanish. The 35-year-old recent arrival had a young wife to support, Isabelle, a New Orleans native whom he had married two years before when she was 12. Their marriage, with its brood of 12 children, lasted throughout his life. [20] Just two months after advertising himself as a language teacher, Benjamin moved east to the growing town of Belleville to start the weekly *Intelligencer* newspaper as a forum for conservative views in a deeply divided political Upper Canada.

Despite its generally conservative and Conservative leaning population, Belleville also reflected the bitter divisions of the times, both religious and political. Opposition to executive rule by the wealthy and well-connected Toronto-based Family Compact was growing and a noisy chorus of Reformers (and their newspapers) was calling for a move toward at least rudimentary democracy and 'responsible government'. In less than three years, armed hostilities would break out during the Rebellion of 1837. It was a milestone on the path to representative government.

The drama of the time also left a strong impression on young Bowell, barely into his teens and witnessing the growing tensions from the vantage point of his work at the newspaper. Almost 60 years later, in Belleville to attend a banquet in honour of his rise to the Prime Minister's office, Bowell told a story about the day he could have been conscripted into the looming 1837 insurrection. While his employer Benjamin was hostile to the growing agitation, the *Plain Speaker* was launched in Belleville as a Reform newspaper to challenge the Establishment mouthpiece. As Bowell recounted the story, a Methodist visitor arrived at the Bowell house to speak to his father. 'Your son knows how to set type. I want him to work for me,' he said. John Bowell, in the middle of dinner, asked for details about the potential employer and found it was *The Plain Speaker*. 'My father laid down his knife and fork. "When I want to send my son to the gallows", he said, "I will let him work for you".' A fanciful tale or not, it illustrated the dangerous, careful path newspapers on both sides had to walk in pre-insurrection days.

Benjamin (and by implication his employee Bowell) clearly had staked out a position on the side of the conservative Establishment. At the time, he also lived with a potentially damaging semi-secret in a conservative town: Benjamin was Jewish by birth, born Moses Cohen in Brighton, England and only changed his name to Benjamin (his mother's maiden name) after he left home in his early twenties. The reason for the name change remains lost to history. His racial and religious background apparently was only a 'semi-secret' in Belleville because while he did not openly practice his Judaism in a community without a synagogue or a Jewish population base, many people knew of his origins including his Reform opponents, John and Susanna Moodie among them. The Moodies were friends of early Reform leader Robert Baldwin who had been elected to the Upper Canada Parliament in the Hastings County constituency. John Moodie also held politically influenced public jobs including sheriff and election returning officer charged with making sure the Hastings riding elections in 1841 and 1842 that featured Baldwin as a celebrity Reform candidate were free and fair. Tories saw Reform bias in Moodie's performance and that made him a target in *Intelligencer* coverage. The partisan dispute between her husband and Benjamin brought out Susanna's racism. She was the celebrated author of *Roughing it in the Bush*—what has been called one of Canada's earliest classics—an 1852 book describing her 'painful experience as a pioneer in the Canadian backwoods and her sense of geographical, cultural and social dislocation.' According to Gray, Moodie is an inspiration for modern female Canadian writers including Margaret Atwood.[21]

Susanna was also anti-Semitic. In 1843, Moodie published an allegedly fictional book based in Jamaica—*Richard Redpath: A Tale*—about the experiences of two English gentlemen shipwrecked in a backwater country where slaves were one of the commodities for sale. The story included a portrait of a 'villainous [newspaper] editor' who opposed abolishing the slave trade. Local readers could quickly see it as a commentary on the *Intelligencer's* opposition to political reform in Upper Canada. Benjamin Levi, the 'fictitious' editor profiled bore a striking resemblance to the Belleville Benjamin. He was 'a bull-like bespectacled man,' a 'living, laughing impersonation of a gratuitous thief, a moral hyena… His salient characteristics are all negative. He disguises his Jewishness by passing as a Christian.'[22] In fact, Susanna Moodie did not hide the fact that Benjamin was the model for the caricature. In a January 1854 letter to a publisher about her book, she warned that it might be too harsh and close to home for public approval. 'The Jew Editor is a true picture drawn from life which so closely resembles the original that it will be recognized by all who ever knew him or fell under his lash… A man detested in his day and generation.'[23]

It was far from the only public anti-Semitic incident Benjamin endured. In April 1838, while Bowell worked at his newspaper as an apprentice, he came to work one day to find an effigy of his employer hanging outside the office door at Bridge and Front Streets. Days later, the Kingston *British Whig* newspaper wrote about the incident and published a poem titled 'Elegy on the Execution of the Belleville Jew' with an accompanying commentary which speculated the hanging may not have been the cause of death but rather eating pork. 'For pork's the meat Jews must not eat. No doubt it killed the Jew.'[24]

In their biography of Benjamin, authors Sheldon and Judith Godfrey imagined the day when young Bowell uncomfortably brought the day's mail to the editor, including the Whig newspaper copy with the poem. 'Mackenzie Bowell, his apprentice who had just brought in the paper with the rest of the day's mail, shifted as he uncomfortably watched his employer [read it].'[25] There is no record that Benjamin ever responded in public to the anti-Semitic attacks. Nor is it clear that he ever 'disguised his Jewishness by passing as a Christian,' as Moodie wrote of her 'fictitious' editor. In fact, Benjamin only formally joined a Christian church—St Thomas Anglican Church—when he was baptized in 1864 before his death so he could be buried in the church cemetery. Perhaps she was alluding to the fact that Benjamin was a long-time Orangeman (possibly joining before he left England) and national leader of the Loyal Orange Lodge of British North America, an organization formed decades before in Ireland to promote and defend Protestant interests against Roman Catholicism. Shortly after moving to Belleville, he was commissioned by the LOL to form a local Lodge, No 102 in Thurlow Township. Benjamin's involvement with the Orange Order appears to be a mysterious anomaly. Did he pass as a Christian or was the entry qualification requirement not that he be Protestant but that he not be Roman Catholic? Either way, the evidence is that he preached a tolerant form of Orangeism and Conservatism that included a 'live and let live' attitude toward Catholics. As an elected member of the Canada West (the former Upper Canada) Parliament for the Hastings North constituency from 1856 to 1863, Benjamin advocated and voted for civil and political rights for Roman Catholic citizens. It led the Hastings Chronicle newspaper in its August 7, 1861 issue to report that Benjamin won office with support from Catholic voters because they believed 'that no other man willing to extend to them their rights and privileges as a religious body presented himself for their suffrages [votes].' The message was that Benjamin 'had been the only one of the candidates to sympathize with the aspirations of the Catholics to exercise civil and political rights equally with other religious groups.'[26]

It led Bowell, by then the owner and publisher of the *Intelligencer*, to write during the 1857 local campaign in support of a controversial Benjamin position to support a legislative proposal incorporating a Roman Catholic order by law: 'Let every Protestant ask this simple question. Should we not give the Roman Catholics the same rights—civil, religious and political—that we ourselves enjoy?' It would presage Bowell's own accommodation and defence of Catholic rights throughout his long political career. In their 1991 biography of Benjamin, Sheldon and Judith Godfrey enunciated his precedent-setting achievements in his adopted homeland: first Jewish notary public, first recorded Jewish candidate to be elected to a municipal council, the first Jewish country registrar of deeds and justice of the peace. 'He was to become, with one possible exception, the first Jew permitted to retain a seat as a member in a Canadian Parliament before Jews had sat in the Parliament of Great Britain or the Legislatures of most American states.' John A. Macdonald also offered Benjamin a cabinet post (he declined) 'More than 100 years before the next Jewish Member of Parliament was offered a federal cabinet position.'[27] That was Windsor, Ontario Liberal MP Herb Gray in the early 1970s. Whether Bowell credited him or not, through their years of association, Benjamin was an example to his young apprentice of the principle of religious tolerance. His example helped Bowell become an unusually tolerant 19th century Conservative. He also introduced his young apprentice to three of his lifelong passions and pursuits: journalism, the Orange Lodge and politics. Bowell's journalism journey began first and it remained arguably, his greatest passion.

NOTES

[1] Boyce, Betsy D., *The Accidental Prime Minister* (Ameliasburgh, Ontario: Seventh Town Historical Society, 2001), 12

[2] LAC, Mackenzie Bowell files, W. A. Craik, *Canada Magazine*, January 3, 1914.

[3] Gray, Charlotte, *Sisters in the Wilderness, the Lives of Susanna Moodie and Catharine Parr Traill* (Toronto: Penguin Books Canada Ltd, 1999).

[4] ibid, 52-53.

[5] LAC, Mackenzie Bowell Papers, Vol. 48 (January 29, 1894 letter to James Bowell).

[6] Boyce, Gerry, *Belleville, A Popular History* (Toronto: Dundurn Press, 2008).

[7] ibid, 13.

[8] op cit, *Sisters in the Wilderness*, 151–52.

[9] op cit, *Belleville*, 56.

[10] Lamb, J. William, *Bridging the Years: A History of Bridge Street United/Methodist Church, Belleville 1815–1990* (Winfield, British Columbia: Wood Lake Books, 1990), 243.

[11] LAC, Bowell Papers (Vol. 95), 126-27.

[12] Senate Debates 2nd Session, 12th Parliament Vol 1, (April 1, 1913), 336.

[13] Copies of Dominion Methodist Church annual reports provided by Dominion Chalmers United Church archivist Garth M. Bray.

[14] op cit, *Bridging the Years*, 166.

[15] CABHC, Bowell scrapbooks.

[16] LAC, Bowell Papers (Volume 66).

[17] Trent University Library and Archives (Mrs. E. Kayser fonds, Accession 75–1022), E.L. Sanders Memoir.

[18] ibid.

[19] op cit, *Sisters in the Wilderness*, 169-170.

[20] Godfrey, Sheldon and Judith, *Burn This Gossip, The True Story of George Benjamin of Belleville, Canada's First Jewish Member of Parliament.* (Toronto: The Duke & George Press, 1991). The book is the best source of information about Benjamin's life, accomplishments and influence in colonial Canada.

[21] Gray, Charlotte, *The Promise of Canada (150 years—People and Ideas that have Shaped Our Country* (Toronto: Simon and Schuster Canada, 2016), 174-175.

[22] op cit, *Burn this Gossip*, 25

[23] ibid, 115.

[24] ibid.

[25] ibid.

[26] ibid, 115.

[27] ibid, 5.

Chapter 4
INK-STAINED WRETCH

For Parliament Hill reporters in 1895, it was hardly surprising that one of Sir Mackenzie Bowell's first public acts as Prime Minister was to reach out to journalists who would be reporting on his government, whether for Conservative-leaning or Liberal newspapers. They had chronicled his political career for years and their published profiles of the country's new political leader almost always noted his cordial relationship with front-line reporters, whatever he thought of their bosses. 'He has always been a staunch but not a bitter Conservative,' the Vancouver *Daily World* wrote in an 1894 profile just months before the unexpected elevation of Bowell from trade and commerce minister to the top job. 'He entertains a warm attachment for members of the Fourth Estate as befits one who toiled at case and desk.'[1] Of all Canada's prime ministers, Mackenzie Bowell was the most intimately connected to journalism and newspapers. He also was the most attuned to the role newshounds and their newspapers played in the Body Politic of his time. Several other prime ministers, including Pierre Trudeau and Joe Clark, had a brief involvement in the business, but Bowell's lasted a lifetime. For more than eight decades, he experienced it in its various guises: inside the industry as apprentice, printer, writer, editor, publisher, and newspaper owner, and on the receiving end as the subject of extensive news coverage. Despite a sometimes-hostile relationship with Opposition-aligned newpapers and journalists, he was genuinely sympathetic to the practitioners of the craft. Throughout his later life, Bowell was nostalgic for the days when he was more actively one of them. Ironically, it was the Toronto *Globe*—a Liberal newspaper that was a critic and the biggest thorn in Bowell's side throughout his political career—which made the point most directly and accurately. Despite all his political and government achievements, the newspaper once wrote about his career, at heart he always was a newspaperman who loved 'the smell of printer's ink.'[2]

It was not out of character, therefore, with memories of newsroom scents and sounds still lingering in his mind, that within weeks of being appointed, Prime Minister Bowell sent a note to the parliamentary pressroom inviting reporters to meet him in his Parliament Hill office. In a scrapbook, he kept a newspaper clipping that recorded the gathering of the band of brothers. 'Canada's premier is a veteran journalist and is not ashamed of the fact,' wrote the unidentified reporter. 'He has a soft spot in his heart for newspapermen and no one was surprised, therefore, when a notice was posted at the Press Committee room, Ottawa, intimating that Sir Mackenzie

Bowell would be pleased to meet the visiting knights of the pencil in his office.' When they crowded into his room, there first were the greetings and congratulations and then the old familiar story. 'Sir Mackenzie established a bond of sympathy with his visitors by recalling some of his early experiences as a member of the Fourth Estate. He recounted the steps by which he had risen gradually from printer's devil to proprietor of the Belleville *Intelligencer*.'[3] Around the same time, Bowell showed up at a going away dinner for a Toronto *Mail and Empire* reporter returning to head office after four years of covering Parliament Hill. 'Premier Sir Mackenzie Bowell paid a high tribute to [Tim] Healy's ability and closed with expressions of sincere wish for his future prosperity,' the Toronto *Herald* reported.[4] Then, as usual, he reminisced about his time in the journalistic trenches.

Was this a genuine affinity for working journalists or an effort by a savvy veteran politician to curry favour with reporters who covered him and would define his image and legacy? Whatever the motive, his one-time private secretary J. Lambert Payne suggested that the press-friendly attitude produced some positive payback for the Conservative leader. In a memoir, Payne recounted the story of a night in Parliament when Bowell became enraged at a Liberal heckler and strained parliamentary rules by attempting to throw a glass of ice water at the heckler across the Parliamentary aisle. He missed his mark and instead doused a nearby Conservative MP snoozing in his seat. Reporters in the press gallery ignored the embarrassing incident, Payne recalled. 'Bowell was a journalist and the free masonry of the craft saw to it that not a syllable of this incident got into print.'[5] Beyond the potential payback, Mackenzie Bowell consistently displayed affection, and even fraternity, to reporters unlikely to reward him with favourable coverage... or helpful silence. On December 30, 1893, for example, he had recently returned from an extensive trip to Australia and wrote a letter of complaint to London, England newspaper the *Westminster Gazette*. He asked for a correction to a *Gazette* story about his Australian visit that contained one crucial factual error that he feared could stir up trouble with Ireland. However, he was careful not to criticize the reporter or to suggest he had used deliberate journalistic spin to make it a more explosive story. 'This I am sure was an error on the part of your correspondent whom I found to be both intelligent and courteous,' Bowell wrote.[6] Privately, he even allowed his regard for other newspapermen to trump his life-long hatred of his bitter political opponents, the Liberals. In May, 1890, journalist L. G. Jackson from Newmarket wrote to Bowell with a dilemma. Ontario Liberals were urging him to abandon journalism and run for the party in the next election for the Ontario Legislature. What should he do? Bowell set aside partisanship in his advice. 'I always like to see newspapermen come to the front and all I have to say is if the nomination is offered, go in and win,' he advised. 'When elected, you will pursue such a course as your conscience may dictate.'[7]

As Senate Opposition Conservative leader in 1901, Bowell was equally generous with a recently appointed political opponent, Liberal Senator and former Saint John, New Brunswick newspaperman J. V. Ellis. Although Bowell's partisan job was to criticize the Liberals across the aisle, he began a speech with kind words for a fellow former journalist. As a Conservative, he said, he opposed government proposals and the Liberal free trade agenda but as a member of the newspaper family, he welcomed the new Liberal Senator. 'Without wishing to appear egotistical, permit me to congratulate the House on the fact of having another addition to it from the Fourth Estate,' he said to Senate applause from both sides.[8] It was not the first time the Conservative true believer had articulated his view that loyalty among newspapermen was stronger than partisanship. It had been Bowell's belief for more than four decades.

In 1859, he was a key player in a decision by leading newspapermen from both sides of the political divide in the North American British colonies to create the Canadian Press Association. It was an attempt to bridge the partisan rancor that characterized newspaper coverage of the heated pre-Confederation politics of the day. A 1908 history of the CPA as the country's first journalism organization told the story of its founding. 'The honest zeal of men for their own opinions had gone too far, the spirit of moderate compromise necessary to support any political fabric seemed to be vanishing altogether,' wrote the authors of the account. 'At its founding meeting Sept. 28, 1858, fifty or sixty Canadian journalists had expressed their willingness to throw aside their political differences in order that they may commune together for the purpose of mutually benefiting each other in matters pertaining to the welfare of the Fourth Estate.' Forty years later in 1898, as the recently appointed Senate Opposition leader, Bowell used a speech to a CPA meeting in Ottawa to advance the same view that being part of the newspaper community was bigger than the rancor of politics. He had served as president in 1865 and Bowell had not lost faith in the bipartisan sentiment expressed all those years before despite his sometimes-bitter experience in politics over the years and what he considered unfair reporting. Nor had he lost his nostalgia for the calling of journalism. 'I can assure you that my heart is still with you, just as strongly as it was before I entered the political world,' Bowell told the crowd. 'I always remember with pleasure that I was of some assistance in forming in the earlier period of my life an association in which I have formed friendships—with many with whom I am not in political accord—which have never ceased to exist in the present day.'[9]

Given the partisanship of the Canadian newspaper industry and Bowell's criticism of his treatment in the Liberal press, it was an open display of his divided loyalties, depending on the hat (political or journalistic) he was wearing. The affection flowed in the other direction as well. Just weeks after

Queen Victoria had honoured Mackenzie Bowell with a knighthood and a title—Knight Commander of the Order of St. Michael and St. George—members of the Canadian Press Association recognized the achievement with a short, whimsical poem. Past-President T. H. Preston read it aloud at the January 31, 1895 annual meeting of the CPA:

> When I was a boy I served my term
> As a junior imp in a printing firm
> I washed the windows and scrubbed the floor
> And daubed the ink on the office door
> I did the work so well, d'ye see
> That now I'm a Premier and a KCMG.[10]

It was indeed a remarkable ascent from newspaper 'printer's devil' apprentice to Prime Minister of the country, rivaled only by the speed at which he advanced as a young man in the newspaper business. After the fateful encounter with George Benjamin in 1841 at age 17 that persuaded Bowell to return to the *Intelligencer* as a foreman rather than become a school principal, he became a full partner in the business at age 23 in 1847. Benjamin arranged the partnership and a decade later, Bowell became the sole owner and publisher of the newspaper when his mentor decided to concentrate on a developing career as a Conservative politician. Owning and running the community's largest and most influential newspaper instantly made Bowell one of the most prominent figures in Belleville and Hastings County with a platform he could use to promote the town, local business… and himself.

The pages of the *Intelligencer* became a vehicle that argued the need for railway expansion and improvement to service local businesses and to get their products to important markets. When gold was discovered north of Belleville in 1866, the newspaper proclaimed the launch of a new era of development: more immigration, more construction, more jobs. A stage-coach line was planned between Belleville and the nearby town of Madoc. The gold deposit, the *Intelligencer* gushed, was 'rich not only in the ordinary use of the term but very rich.' Bowell capitalized on the economic boom by turning the weekly newspaper he had purchased into a daily in 1867. Even though the gold glitter began to fade in 1868, promotion of business expansion and growing prosperity became the narrative of town leaders and its newspaper booster.

'Throughout the entire process, the Belleville *Intelligencer* remained a strong supporter of mining ventures in Central and North Hastings,' said a local history of Belleville's early decades. 'This could be explained by the potential advertising revenues, the fact that Mackenzie Bowell represented North Hastings in the first Parliament of the Dominion of Canada and the strong support that Bowell and the community's business leaders were giving to the development of a railway reaching into North Hastings.'[11] Beyond the advertising and circulation revenues that contributed to Bowell's bottom line as one of the community's more successful businessmen, ownership of the newspaper also gave him a vehicle that he used to help and support his family. Over the years, he employed son-in-law James Jamieson as editor, found a position for son Charlie (eventually as editor) and at one point even employed grandson Mackenzie Bowell Jamieson in the profitable printing side of the operation. However, the greatest benefit Bowell received from ownership of the *Intelligencer* operation arguably was its value as a tool to promote his own political career and the fortunes of the Conservative Party in the parliamentary seat-rich area of eastern Ontario.

The 19th century newspaper business and fraternity that Bowell embraced was a deeply political and partisan one. Virtually all newspapers were aligned with one of the two political parties and ideologies competing for the allegiance of inhabitants of an emerging Canada: the Liberal Reform side and the Conservative Tory camp. Former Carleton University Dean of Arts David Farr, director of a 1990s project to convert newspaper accounts of early House of Commons debates into official Hansard parliamentary transcripts, described the state of parliamentary coverage he found. 'The newspaper reporting of the debates was frankly partisan since a political point of view was a hallmark of the Canadian press in the mid-Victorian period,' he wrote. 'Partisanship was most usually shown by the shortening of the opposing party's contribution to a debate and a fuller reporting of your own party's position. Occasionally distortions and half-truths were resorted to in the political wars of the newspapers...' [12] Rivalries between competing newspapers revolved around political messaging and alignments as much as they did over the typical industry battles for subscribers and advertising revenue. In the last half of the 19th century, newspapers were highly influential in communities as the main source of information. The days of the town crier as the purveyor of the latest news were largely over and the age of omnipresent electronic news coverage was far in the future. As a source of information about community affairs, world and local events, consumer products available and the political issues of the day, the newspaper industry had a near-monopoly.

Paul Rutherford, University of Toronto historian and analyst of media influence, has argued that the late 19th century was something of a Golden Age for Ontario newspapers. The provincial education system had launched a highly successful literacy campaign as a building block for an emerging society. 'In the last half of the century, illiteracy rates in Ontario fell from as many as one-third to less than ten percent by 1900,' he wrote. 'And that led to an explosion of newspaper and magazine subscriptions.'[13] Political parties, their leaders and operatives naturally saw this as an opportunity to spread their message by enlisting editors and owners as allies. 'The typical politician saw newspapers as essential vehicles of publicity, indeed a surrogate for organization which could confound foes, strengthen party discipline and morale and educate electors,' Rutherford argued. He cited as evidence a 1901 letter from Liberal Prime Minister Wilfrid Laurier: 'The publication of a newspaper is a very great advantage always for the prosperity and well-doing of a political party.' Rutherford then added his view of Laurier's enthusiastic embrace of the game. 'He was quite prepared to reward friendly journalists and to punish the disloyal or hostile.'[14]

However, there also was a clear potential downside as well for political parties that became too closely identified with their newspaper supporters. Two decades earlier, politically astute Conservative leader Sir John A. Macdonald acknowledged the usefulness of 'party newspapers' and their support but cautioned that politicians should not expect reporters and supportive newspapers always to parrot the party message in a way that helped the cause. Their loyalty and support could not be taken for granted. 'This government, like other governments, are exceedingly glad to have the support of the newspaper press,' he told the House of Commons in May 1883. 'If the newspapers support the government, we thank them for it [and] if they go against us, we are sorry for it. But no government worthy of the name of a government can submit to having any organ and no newspaper worthy of the name of a newspaper can submit to being called a servile organ of any government. The moment that is understood, that moment the newspaper is valueless.'[15] Macdonald was advocating the need for some distance between the party and its media friends for a practical reason. If one of the newspapers that embraced and endorsed the Conservative Party went too far and became offensive in its partisan attacks, it ran the risk of alienating undecided voters who saw parties and their supportive press as indistinguishable. Politicians needed the wiggle room to distance themselves from excesses of media supporters that could do more harm than good.

Privately, Bowell called on his years of experience in the news business and politics to reinforce the danger of being too politically aligned with media. If published comments meant to help conservatism were too vicious or extreme, it could offend middle-of-the-road voters and hurt the party, he acknowledged. 'There is a large class in the community that does not hold extreme views on either side in politics and it is that class which the wise and judicious journalist will strive to mollify and win over but brutal conduct on the part of an opponent never accomplishes that end,' he wrote in December 1884.[16] It was a warning about limits to the usefulness of the supportive partisan press coverage of the day and Bowell had considerable experience with over-the-top personal attacks directed his way in Opposition newspapers. As a longtime Conservative MP and cabinet minister, he was subjected to some vicious name-calling; 'stupid,' 'bigoted,' 'unimportant' and 'senile' being among the least pointed allegations. He also understood that media criticism can create sympathy for a politician. Unfair or vicious attacks sometimes strengthened his standing in Hastings North where supporters rallied to the local boy under attack from 'outsiders.' They elected him in seven consecutive campaigns despite hostile Liberal newspaper coverage. A decade after Bowell voiced his warning about the dangers of political parties being associated with extreme partisan attacks, the Montreal *Star* came to the same conclusion in a defence of the then besieged prime minister. 'Some of the attacks upon Sir Mackenzie Bowell are nothing less than brutal and more worthy of Bulgaria than of Canada,' said the *Star* editorial. 'Such methods in the long run prove more dangerous to those who use them than to the object of their wrath. If a certain class of journalists cannot discuss a political question without coarse abuse of the premier and savage speculations about his death, they must find his position difficult to assail.'[17]

Still, despite the risks of media strategies backfiring, political parties continued to believe that collaboration with friendly newspaper owners, editors and journalists was effective much of the time. It was an efficient and cost-effective way to disseminate their message and policies to voters and to undermine their opponents. In an age before mass communications and targeted advertising appeals, it was a political strategy that worked over many decades despite its sometime unpredictability, uncertainty and headaches. Each side needed the other. 'Journalism and party seemed inextricably linked by tradition and necessity,' Rutherford concluded, but they did not always speak with one voice. 'The party chieftains had difficulty realizing that their reputed organs must curry the favour of a wide range of readers and this meant these dailies had to be more than just mouthpieces of a party.'[18] Of course, political parties planning to use supportive media to their advantage had more tools than simple persuasion and a shared goal to help nudge and keep newspaper allies in line. On the other side of the relationship, newspaper owners and practitioners also had benefits to reap from the alliance with political players, particularly those in government. It gave them an influential entrée into the exciting and profitable world of politics and offered the prospect of some concrete professional and commercial rewards useful to poorly paid denizens of the political journalism universe.

The government's ability to offer lucrative patronage, advertising or printing contracts and preferential access to information and power were major incentives used to encourage newspaper loyalty. With deep knowledge of the ways, needs and ethos of the newspaper trade, Mackenzie Bowell was a natural to be involved in actively arranging to dole out the goodies; money and access. He was particularly helpful to the government in dealing with Tory media players in rural Ontario and Manitoba, where Macdonald decided that Bowell had the contacts and history to be a useful intermediary, particularly in Manitoba. As Customs Minister, he was a familiar figure in the West and travelled frequently through the Prairies to visit staff and customs posts along the border and throughout the territory. He also had family in the West and actively promoted Prairie settlement and agriculture. 'Sir John, after consultation, has consented that I should pay particular attention to your section of the country,' Bowell announced to a Conservative-friendly and influential Winnipeg newspaperman in late 1882.[19] The minister eagerly got to work behind the scenes fulfilling the prime ministerial mandate. He was the government's point man in meeting the needs and massaging the egos of Tory-friendly newspapers 2,400 kilometres west of his eastern Ontario base. His success offers a glimpse into Bowell's reputation as a hard-working, partisan practitioner of the political arts of paying attention to details, looking for practical solutions and keeping the machinery of government running to his and his party's advantage. He was an expert in the political game.

A significant tool available to the government for rewarding supportive newspapers was the ability to direct advertising and printing contracts to friendly publishers. Mid-March, 1883 found Bowell busy in Ottawa lobbying other ministers to favour the Brandon *Times*. He asked a cabinet colleague to include the newspaper 'on the official list to receive government patronage. The *Times* is the recognized newspaper of the party in that section of the country.'[20] In 1880, he also went to bat in Ottawa for the Conservative-supporting Winnipeg *Times* when it became involved in an angry spat with the government over Ottawa's decision to award the printing contract for Canadian Pacific Railway construction documents to the Liberal-supporting Winnipeg *Free Press*. The *Times* complained it had a deal with Public Works Minister Sir Charles Tupper to receive the contract and the business but had been betrayed. Bowell wrote to Tupper that in order to boost a supportive newspaper in the Manitoba capital 'it is necessary that such a journal should receive all the patronage which the government has to dispose of.'[21] He won that Parliament Hill battle. On the other side of the issue, he also lobbied in cabinet to have the government remove advertising and printing contracts from an Ontario newspaper recently purchased by a Liberal.[22]

Beyond advertising dollars from Ottawa, government tools in the campaign to woo favourable newspaper coverage included the ability to dole out news 'scoops' to friendly journalists. An example unfolded behind the scenes when Bowell set out to repair relations with important Manitoba media. Likely in a bid to smooth ruffled Manitoba feathers from the earlier dispute, Bowell offered the aggrieved Winnipeg *Times* editor Amos Rowe another of the government's available carrots, the promise of news tips in advance of their newspaper rivals. In late December 1882, Bowell wrote that he and the Prime Minister had decided 'it would be well to give you an intimation in advance of what is to be done in matters affecting your province. I trust I shall in future be in a position, to use a familiar expression, to "keep you posted" in order to enable you to foreshadow what may possibly be done in reference to Manitoba.' It would, wrote Bowell, 'give your paper an official status and enable you to direct public opinion in advance into the proper channel.'[23] As well, even if unstated, throwing that bone of early exclusive access to pending announcements also helped ensure government decisions would be given a positive first airing to influence Manitoba voters' minds.

Throughout his ministerial dealings with newspaper allies, Bowell's goal clearly was to gain Conservative advantage. The premise was that it was the job of Conservative allies in newsrooms to advance the cause of the party, despite his view that newspapers should not be considered mindless mouthpieces for the party nor simple unquestioning appendages. He revealed his bottom-line attitude toward the proper and supportive political role of the press near the end of his prime ministerial days as he enumerated his Conservative Party credentials while defending himself against dissidents working for his ouster. Bowell's long history of running and owning a Conservative-friendly newspaper was one of the feathers he believed adorned his Tory cap. Bowell considered his decades of ownership and leadership at the Belleville *Intelligencer* an integral part of his long record of political work and promotion of Conservative Party interests. They appeared to be one and the same in his mind. One of the ways he served the Conservative Party during 50 years of promoting the political cause was 'in conducting a journal advocating the policy of the party with which I have been connected from its inception to the present,' he said in January 1896 speech to establish his Conservative credentials against those in the party who wanted him ousted.[24] While Bowell was prone to wax nostalgic about journalism as a noble profession and journalists as his brothers-in-arms who rose above partisanship in pursuit their shared passion, his view of the role of journalism had its limits and a cynical side. Journalism's role in society was far more than simply supporting democracy by exposing the truth. He stopped well short of considering it the lifeblood of political accountability or the instrument of an educated electorate that is the foundation of a robust democracy. Instead, Bowell clearly saw his chosen profession as being at its best when it served the higher purpose of helping make sure the Conservative Party and its vision for Canada were in charge.

That partisan view of journalism clearly extended to the local level where his political power base was rooted. Owning the dominant newspaper in the community he represented on Parliament Hill was a clear political advantage for Bowell during his long Parliament Hill career and he was not reluctant to use it. During volatile election periods, the *Intelligencer* became a Mackenzie Bowell propaganda sheet, part of his campaign. Liberal-leaning newspapers circulating in his riding offered the same service for his political opponents.

In 19th Century Ontario politics, it was how the newspaper game was played and later 20th century critics of the news business argued that not much had changed over the previous century. In a 1960 essay in *The New Yorker* magazine, American journalist A. J. Liebling wrote: 'Freedom of the press is guaranteed only to those who own one.'[25] For more than half a century since that critique was published, those 12 words and many variations of them have been a clarion call for critics of media and the powerful influence that news outlet owners wield in the public debate. Mackenzie Bowell was among the small minority of citizens and politicians of his day who 'owned one' and used it to his political advantage but he was far from the only politician of his era in the same privileged position.

In the decades after Confederation, many leading politicians also were newspaper owners. From early Reform leader George Brown (the Toronto *Globe*) and long-time New Brunswick Liberal MP and House of Commons Speaker Timothy Anglin (Saint John *Weekly Freeman*) to Ontario MP Thomas White (Hamilton *Spectator* and Montreal *Gazette*), the Canadian political class contained dozens who played dual roles as active politicians and press barons. Belleville *Intelligencer* coverage of the local campaign in the Hastings North race for the first Parliament of the new Dominion in late summer of 1867 offers a glimpse of the powerful political tool 'freedom of the press' could be for politician newspaper owners. It was a harbinger of the favourable election coverage Mackenzie Bowell would receive from the hometown newspaper throughout his 25-year run as the MP for Hastings North.

A week after aspiring candidate Bowell attended a Belleville picnic to celebrate the July 1, 1867 birth of the new Canadian nation, the *Intelligencer* reported that he would be willing to run for office in the pending first federal election to the new Canadian Parliament in Ottawa. The vote across the country would be spread out from August 7 to September 20. At a meeting to discuss possible candidates 'Mr. Bowell said he would stand if selected. He was quite willing to be held responsible for all he might say as he usually knew what he said and only said what he meant.'[26] The story added that he would support whoever was selected as the Tory candidate 'as he did not think the riding had been properly represented.' This was an unsubtle shot at the incumbent Member of the Legislative Assembly of the Province of Canada Thomas C. Wallbridge who had defeated Bowell in his first attempt at election in 1863. The incumbent almost certainly would be the Reform/Liberal candidate in 1867. The next day, Bowell's newspaper reprinted a vicious 'profile' of Reform leader George Brown first published in the Conservative Toronto *Telegram*. It called him 'a mere demagogue and like every demagogue [is] intensely selfish, loud-mouthed and foul-mouthed... God help the country that has George Brown as its saviour.'[27] The pattern of coverage had quickly been established. Bowell was chosen

41

candidate at a July 18 meeting. The *Intelligencer* reported that he expressed concern about his electability after his 1863 defeat at the hands of the same opponent but 'he had taken a tour through the riding and he must say that promises of support were sufficiently flattering to warrant his acceptance ... His remarks were well received and his friends feel sanguine of success.' There followed published stories about election meetings where Wallbridge was 'abusive' while Bowell outlined his opponent's 'treacherous' performance in the last Legislative Assembly and where the Conservative candidate won favour. 'His prospects of election by a large majority are very cheering and we trust every one of his friends will do his utmost between this and election day to swell the majority,' reported the August 1 edition.

After two weeks of such coverage, the *Intelligencer* on August 14 assessed the candidates running in the three Hastings County constituencies and surely to no one's surprise, endorsed Bowell and his fellow Conservative candidates. It referenced Bowell's military service, his business success and his 'practical' approach to problems:

> Above all, we want reliable, honest men—men who when they get into Parliament will carry out what they profess, who will not seek their own aggrandizement at the sacrifice of their constituents' interests… men in brief in whom the people can place the utmost confidence that they will honestly and faithfully perform their pledges and carry out the wishes of their constituents.

As the September 9 first day of voting approached, the newspaper that listed Bowell as 'Publisher' warned readers that 'the Wallbridge Family' was taking electors for granted. 'Will you not rather, by supporting Mr Bowell, teach them that the people of Canada will not brook insolent dictation as to how to exercise their franchise?'

On Tuesday, September 10, Bowell was declared elected with 59 percent of the vote and coverage of the election result was exuberant. THE NORTH RIDING REDEEMED screamed the capitalized boldface headline. WALLBRIDGE DEFEATED. It launched Mackenzie Bowell's quarter century run as MP for Hastings North and in each of the seven elections, he received the enthusiastic endorsement and fawning coverage of the hometown newspaper. Twenty-nine years later, Mackenzie Bowell returned to his journalism roots after allegedly distancing himself during his years of political prominence in the upper echelons of the Canadian Parliament and government. As soon as he could after losing the prime minister's job in 1896, the 72-year-old Bowell resumed his official position as a newspaper owner, publisher and columnist even as he continued his political work in the Senate. In a statement published in the December 3, 1896 issue of the *Intelligencer*, Bowell announced that he was back and proclaimed: 'It will be the endeavor of the publisher to… keep the *Intelligencer* in all respects up to the best standards of journalism.' It would never betray convictions for 'temporary applause or for personal gain.' He said the newspaper under his renewed control would live up to its masthead motto of 63 years: 'Let there be harmony in things essential, liberality in things not essential, charity in all.'[28] However, it is doubtful if Bowell ever really was 'away' from ownership in or influence over the *Intelligencer* during his time in government. The evidence is mixed, including after 1875 when he said he gave up sole ownership and converted it to a joint stock company in which he had no involvement. Immediate family members, including his son-in-law Jim Jamieson, were involved in running the newspaper and in holding a financial interest. Bowell unconvincingly insisted he was arm's length, at least in a narrow definition of the term despite evidence that he was kept abreast of issues at the newspaper, freely offered advice and influenced decisions. Still, he maintained the illusion of a keeping a distance from his relationship with the hometown newspaper that promoted and praised his career.

In an August 1882 letter to a Kingston resident who complained about a story in the newspaper, for example, the then-Customs Minister responded: 'I beg to inform you that I am not the proprietor of that journal nor am I a member of the company owning it, not holding one dollar of its stock.'[29] Two years later during a Commons debate, he rejected an allegation from Liberal MP David Mills that the *Intelligencer* was 'the organ of the Minister of Customs.' When Bowell denied it, Mills said it was common knowledge that in the years after he was elected, he remained connected to the newspaper 'either was the editor or controlled the newspaper.' Bowell again denied the allegation: 'Neither the one nor the other.' Yet in the early 1880s, he was accused under the Independence of Parliament Act of directing government advertising dollars to a company in which he claimed to have no interest; the *Intelligencer*. A Commons committee with Conservative MPs in the majority found substance to the allegation and the penalty under the law was that Bowell had to resign his seat. As was the custom, he immediately ran in a by-election and was re-elected unopposed. In his exchange with Mills, the minister referenced the incident without claiming he was falsely accused. 'I challenged you and your party to contest it [the by-election] and you did not dare do it,' he taunted his opponents.[30] Years later, a magazine profile clearly stated that Bowell never ceded control of the newspaper. There was no public disclaimer after it was published. In the January 3, 1914 edition of the magazine *Canada*, a profile to mark Bowell's recent 90th birthday included a reference to his long association with the newspaper and the connection he maintained even in government. Writer W. A. Craik reported: 'His ministerial duties removed him partially from the management of the paper but he never gave up control.'[31] Rather than denying the claim, Bowell kept a copy of the profile in his files.

Whatever the reality of his connection to the newspaper during his years in Parliament and government, he was unabashedly and enthusiastically back in charge by the end of 1896, writing editorials and columns and plotting the direction of the journalistic project he had served and nurtured for six decades. Among his journalistic admirers, it added to the legend. In a 1907 profile of the seven Prime Ministers who served during Canada's first forty years, the Ottawa *Citizen* noted that after his stint at the top political job, he returned to his first love. 'A practical printer and a journalist, he at once resumed his connection with the press as editor and proprietor of the Belleville *Intelligencer*, a position which he fills to this day—vigorous and clear-headed despite his burden of four-score and four years.'[32] The Hamilton *Herald* enthused that despite his political accomplishments and knighthood, Bowell was 'still in love with the work, went back to the business and is still cheerfully and vigorously doing his duty as a newspaperman on the same old paper in very much the same old way.' In his old age, he was 'a journalist-statesman,' said the *Herald*, an accolade and appellation Bowell no doubt cherished. In fact, despite his history of using journalism in the service of Conservative Party and personal political interests, Bowell apparently saw himself in a different light: as an honest, fearless presenter of the truth throughout his newspaper career. During a raucous 1889 House of Commons debate about customs department conduct, Bowell complained that Montreal newspapers had taken up the cause of those importers found guilty of smuggling. Liberal MPs needled him for being an 'old hand' at journalism now reduced to turning on his old colleagues with criticisms. Bowell took umbrage. 'Yes I am [an old hand in the business] and I used to write just as I thought, as plainly and honestly as I know how and I was never taken into court nor did I ever have to apologize for what I said,' he bragged.[33]

In what may be considered Bowell's definitive reflection on his self-image as a straight-shooting, fearless journalist, he wrote to a young newspaperman about what is required to be true to the profession and to himself. A journalist had to stand up to his critics, consequences be damned, Bowell advised in 1882. 'During a long experience, I have learned that to be successful in conducting a journal, politically independent or neutral, the only way is to have an opinion, express it freely and tell grumblers to go to the devil and shake themselves and then go on in my own way as usual.'[34] For a politician nearing 60 who professed continuing nostalgia for the news business, it must have been a comforting view of himself that he once was a fearless young journalist standing up for what he believed was right and true, the critics be damned. The actual record of his use of journalism as an instrument of his career is decidedly more mixed.

NOTES

[1] LAC Bowell Papers MG 26E(A) Vol. 110 Part 2 (Vancouver *Daily World*, September 12, 1894).

[2] Toronto *Globe* (Vol LXXIV No. 21 December 11, 1917), 1.

[3] LAC Bowell Papers (MG 26E Vol. 97) undated newspaper clipping.

[4] LAC Bowell Papers (MG 26E Vol. 128) Toronto *Herald* February 26, 1895.

[5] Cited in *Canadian Parliamentary Anecdotes*, Marc Bosc, editor (Peterborough: Broadview Press, 1988), 51.

[6] LAC Bowell Papers (MG 26E Vol. 95) December 30, 1894 letter.

[7] LAC Bowell Papers (MG 26E Vol. 90). May 8, 1890 letter.

[8] Debates of the Senate of Canada, 1st Session, 9th Parliament (February 11, 1901), 14.

[9] The Canadian Press Association, *A History of Canadian Journalism in Several Portions of the Dominion with a Sketch of the Canadian Press Association 1859–1908* (Toronto: 1908).

[10] CABHC Bowell collection.

[11] Boyce, Gerry, *Belleville A Popular History*, 112–114.

[12] House of Commons Debates, 1st Session, 3rd Parliament, Vol. 1 (1874): Introduction (April 2011), i.

[13] Rutherford, Paul, *A Victorian Authority: The Daily Press in Late Nineteenth Century Canada* (University of Toronto Press, 1982), 26–27.

[14] ibid, 212.

[15] House of Commons Debates, 4th Session, 4th Parliament Vol. II, (May 7 1882).

[16] LAC Bowell Papers (MG 26E Vol. 82) December 2, 1884 letter to J. B. Plumb of Niagara, Ontario.

[17] LAC Bowell Papers (MG 26E Vol. 128) Montreal *Star*, July 23, 1895.

[18] op cit, *A Victorian Authority*, 212.

[19] LAC Bowell Papers (MG 26 Vol. 80). April 18, 1883 letter to Winnipeg *Times* editor Amos Rowe.

[20] LAC Bowell Papers MG 26 Vol. 42 (March 14, 1887 letter.

[21] LAC Bowell Papers (MG 26E Vol. 18) Letter to Sir Charles Tupper (date illegible).

[22] While Bowell worked to arrange government patronage for supportive Conservative newspapers, there is little evidence he did the same for his own family-owned newspaper. During the 1895–96 fiscal year when he was prime minister, the Belleville *Intelligencer* received just $159.85 in federal government advertising payments, while the Conservative Montreal *Gazette* hauled in $1057.27. Rutherford: *A Victorian Authority*, (217). However, it did not stop occasional Opposition allegations that Bowell was in a conflict of interest for favouring his newspaper with federal contracts.

[23] LAC Bowell Papers (MG 26 Vol. 80) Letter December 20, 1882 to Amos Rowe.

[24] Senate Debates, 6th Session, 7th Parliament, (January 9, 1896).

[25] Liebling, A. J., 'The Wayward Press: Do You Belong in Journalism?' *The New Yorker*, May 14, 1960.

[26] CABHC Archive files, Belleville *Intelligencer*, July 8, 1867.

[27] ibid. All election citations are taken from the *Intelligencer* file at the Community Archives of Bellville and Hastings County.

[28] LAC file (MG 26E Vol. 130 (*The Belleville Intelligencer* December 3, 1896), 26.

[29] LAC Bowell Papers, Vol. 133.

[30] House of Commons Debates, 3rd Session, 5th Parliament Vol. III (May 11, 1885).

[31] LAC microfilm file F CC-4 no. 02527 NL. Queen's Printer 1889 pamphlet *Speech of Hon. Mackenzie Bowell, Minister of Customs.*

[32] LAC Bowell Papers, Vol. 104, Ottawa *Citizen*, August 1, 1907.

[33] LAC Bowell Papers, MG 26 E Vol. 79 (43).

[34] LAC Bowell Papers, Vol. 78. May 8, 1882 letter to H. C. Kennedy.

Chapter 5
AN ORANGE HUE

In 21st century multicultural and increasingly secular Canada, it requires imagination to conjure up a time when the young nation was riven and often defined by religious tensions between its founding communities. Yet a key feature of the 19th century Canada in which Mackenzie Bowell lived was the existence of a chasm of acrimony, hostility and distrust between Roman Catholic and Protestant populations. It was a reality that influenced and shaped his career trajectory. He was both a beneficiary and a victim of the religious divide. In the beginning, Bowell's leadership role in the Protestant Loyal Orange Lodge (LOL) fraternity helped launch and sustain his political ambitions. In the end, his promotion and defence of the political and educational rights of the Roman Catholic minority in defiance of the Orange Lodge was a core issue in the controversy that derailed his prime ministerial term. It turned one-time Protestant supporters into some of his most fierce critics and opponents. Bowell was a prominent player in the religious divide and his political career was deeply influenced and affected by the denominational tensions of the day.

Mackenzie Bowell was the country's leading and most honoured Orangeman at a time when the Protestant Loyal Orange Lodge mattered. The tens of thousands of Orange Lodge supporters and sympathizers in the Canadian population were a key part of the Conservative Party voter base as well as Bowell's constituency. His Orange ties also were a source of controversy. The LOL was a Protestant fraternity created in Ireland in 1795 to commemorate a 1690 victory by Irish Protestant forces over Roman Catholics. Irish immigrants brought their Orange allegiance to Canada in the 19th century and the Lodge quickly found space in a country in which trying to craft an accommodation between French-speaking Roman Catholics and English-speaking Protestants in the face of those who would exploit the divide was a political preoccupation. Well into the 20th century, the Orange Lodge packed a political punch by flourishing in the fertile soil filling the gap that divided the two solitudes. At the time, it was a powerful and influential political and social force throughout the British Empire, especially in Canada and particularly in vote-rich Ontario.

As Grand Master of the LOL of British North America through most of the 1870s and a leading Belleville area Orange leader before then, politician Bowell saw Orangemen as a natural base of support. Yet he pointedly preached a message that did not embrace the belligerent, militant anti-Catholic LOL faction that often was part of the package. He was an Orange leader who promoted Protestant pride and history but with a side order of tolerance, coexistence and equality for other religions including Roman Catholic neighbours. Over his 70 years of involvement in Orange Lodge politics, Mackenzie Bowell lost some battles but won more. He faced down critics who called him a bigot and those who chastised him from the other side for being too cozy with Catholics. He also won public honours for his Orange efforts and during his long association with the fraternity, no day was more memorable for him than September 6, 1873.

On a sunny Belleville Saturday morning, Bowell put on his finest clothes to prepare for an occasion like no other in his life. He was scheduled to host a visit from Captain William Hodden, leader of the Orange Order of Ireland, the country considered ground zero for Orange adherents around the world. Hodden made the long journey from Northern Ireland to rural eastern Ontario to present a precious gift, a rare Bible printed in 1695 for British King William III, the 'spiritual' father of Orangeism whose legend inspired the founding of the Orange Order in the early years of the 19th century. William's Protestant fame came from a military victory in 1690 when, as the Dutch Prince William of Orange with a largely Protestant army, he had defeated Roman Catholic forces led by former British King James II at the River Boyne near Belfast. King Billy, as he was (and is) depicted in annual July 12 Orange parades leading the way on a white horse, had assumed the British throne the year before the Bibles were printed. His victory at the Boyne five years earlier sealed Great Britain's status as a Protestant-ruled kingdom. His defence of Protestantism in the face of Roman Catholic opponents inspired the Irish creators of the Orange Order almost a century after William's 1710 death. The dedication handwritten in the Bible presented to North American Orange Grand Master Bowell explained its storied origin: 'It is one of only XII copies extant, printed by order of His Majesty King William III for presentation to his friends and in memory of his victory at the Boyne.' In part, the gift of the rare Bible honoured Bowell's position as the leading North American Orangeman from 1870 to 1878. In part, it commemorated the fact that he had presided over an international Orange conference convened in Belfast that summer. As the only Orangeman of his generation honoured with a William of Orange Bible, it also recognized Bowell as one of the most celebrated Protestant leaders of his time.

The four-inch-thick bible given to Bowell—1,475 pages printed in Old English text and bound in a 12 by 18-inch volume—now resides in a climate-controlled Library and Archives Canada (LAC) Preservation Centre in Gatineau, Quebec across the Ottawa River from Parliament Hill.[1] Stored at a constant temperature of 18°C and in a stable relative humidity of 40%, it is a rare-book treasure and a priceless national artifact more than three centuries old, with fingerprints of Bowell and William of Orange literally all over it. Yet few Canadians have seen it or know of its existence. There is no

48

record that LAC has ever publicly displayed the Bible. It is a one of several priceless surviving symbols of Bowell's role as a key player in the religious debates that were prominent in the politics of his era.

In 20th century Canada, Bowell's well-documented attachment to and involvement in the Orange Lodge became a major black mark on his reputation. As seen through the eyes of contemporary historians, the Orange movement was purely a divisive historic relic that primarily provided a refuge for bigots. Other Orangemen prime ministers—John A. Macdonald, John Abbott and (possibly) John Diefenbaker, among several—largely have escaped condemnation for their Orange tinge. For Bowell, Orange affiliation has led to a modern narrative that sees him as a narrow-minded Protestant extremist. It is a perception fuelled by the fact that he was not just a casual member of the Order but a proud defender and an energetic leader who promoted the Orange cause whenever the opportunity arose. A small but telling piece of evidence of his commitment to the Orange cause came in 1864, on the cusp of his mainstream political career, when Bowell used his newspaper's printing presses to publish an incendiary new edition of a book describing the Irish roots of Orangeism. In gory detail, *A History of the Rise, Progress, Cruelties and Suppression of the Rebellion in the County of Wexford* told the story of a bloody Irish Roman Catholic uprising in 1798, atrocities against Protestants and the subsequent formation of Protestant defensive forces. No other Canadian publisher would touch the project in the midst of growing Catholic/Protestant tensions in the early Confederation debates. The Belleville newspaperman was happy to put his name to a project that some saw as little short of a spark that could turn smoldering Canadian religious tensions into an open flame.[2] But did his Orange affiliation, leadership, support and actions actually provide evidence for the Bowell-as-bigot narrative? Like many threads in the Mackenzie Bowell story quilt, it is a complicated question within the context of the times that does not easily qualify him for the bigotry label.

In his political career, Bowell preached religious accommodation and reconciliation as central to the Confederation bargain between French and English, Protestants and Catholics. As an Orange leader, he advocated tolerance toward others as a founding principle of the Orange Order and this view sometimes put him in direct conflict with many of his members. Indeed, Orange activists often were among Bowell's harshest political critics and at one pivotal point almost derailed his political ambitions. Still, the Orange Order of 19th century Canada was far more than the modern stereotype of a home for violent Catholic haters populated by 19th century versions of Reverend Ian Paisley, the regular television dispenser of Orange vitriol during the Northern Ireland Troubles of the 1970 to 1998 period. Paisley's anti-Catholic diatribes delivered on nightly newscasts with his hate-twisted, spittle-spewing ruddy face filling the screen became the modern image of the

Orange Lodge to millions. Yet to apply fairly a contemporary judgment about Bowell's lifelong commitment to Orange causes, it should be acknowledged that the Orange Lodge of his day had a broad and often-progressive political and social agenda that ranged far beyond a single-issue, anti-Catholic focus. It wielded significant mainstream influence on political issues as broad and liberal as worker rights, immigrant integration and poverty mitigation while providing a host of social services to the needy in an often-unforgiving early Canadian capitalist economy.

By the mid-1850s, Canada was straining to integrate a torrent of immigrants, many from Ireland and often concentrated in growing urban areas and poverty ghettoes. 'Immigrants constituted between one-half and one-third of Toronto population throughout this period 1867-1892,' according to Gregory Kealey, University of New Brunswick historian emeritus and prominent analyst of working-class history in Canada:

> Ethnic voluntary societies in general and the Orange Order in particular were extremely significant in workers' lives. Historians have generally focused only on the Order's bigoted role in national politics but we see the Order in a local context which shows its varied uses within the working-class community.'[3]

Kealey documented the Orange movement's involvement in fighting for union rights and the nine-hour workday, as well as providing services to the poor. It faced off against opponents, including Liberal elder statesman and Toronto *Globe* founder George Brown. In the 1870s, Brown was using his newspaper to campaign against proposals for a shorter workday as a 'communistic system of leveling' while denouncing his own unionized employees who supported the campaign.[4] Ironically, Brown died from an infected leg wound after being shot in his office by a former pressman and union supporter he had fired. 'The Order offered much to many quite different people,' Kealey concluded. 'For some there was the obvious patriotic and Protestant-defender appeal [but] for others there was the confidence that came from belonging to a society which would help carry them through the difficulties of working-class life': aid to the unemployed, medical coverage in illness, payment of funeral expenses with additional financial aid to the widow and children. The Lodge even operated a cross-Canada system of orphanages.[5]

Orange activists also were deeply engaged in the Canadian Confederation debates of the 1860s. Prominent McGill University historian Hereward Senior, a specialist in Orange and Canadian Loyalist history, saw them as key players, particularly in swaying the debate in New Brunswick in Canada's favour. 'Orangemen were an important and indispensable element in the consensus which brought about Confederation,' he concluded in a history of the Canadian Orange Order. Senior argued they saw it as the most effective way to resist the northern creep of American republicanism.[6] Even on the contentious issue of the Orange track record on Canadian relations between Protestants and Roman Catholics, the evidence is less black-and-white than often portrayed. Queen's University historian Donald Akenson, an authority on Irish history and diaspora, argued the Orange bite was more benign than the sound of the bark. 'Locally [in 19th century Ontario], the Orangemen went through their anti-Roman rituals with all the solemnity of a politician deprecating government waste while day-by-day, they got along peacefully with the Catholics who lived on the next farm.'[7] The Lodge's progressive agenda on many issues was evident in the pages of its influential weekly magazine *The Sentinel* founded in 1875, published in Toronto and circulated throughout North America. In a 1983 Wilfrid Laurier University master's thesis analyzing the magazine's content and influence between 1877 and 1896, Andrew Thomson noted that while defending the Lodge from its critics, Sentinel writers also promoted the nascent union movement, better social services for the poor and immigrants and political moderation. It endorsed appointment of Sir John Thompson as Canada's first Roman Catholic prime minister in 1892 and supported voluntary temperance but not coercive legislation.

Even on the issue of public funding for separate schools, the Orange-controlled newspaper opposed the proposal but continued to support the Conservative government despite its attempts to mediate between Protestant and Catholic interests on the explosive issue. 'The Sentinel exercised a moderating influence on the Protestant movement in Canada,' Thomson concluded. '[It] supported the Conservatives at the federal level in Canada.'[8] That made the Orange publication an ally for Bowell in fulfilling one of his key roles in Macdonald governments. Having an influential caucus member with one foot in the powerful Orange Lodge and the other in the Conservative Party paid political dividends for Macdonald. It was a bridge that helped keep Canada's large pool of Orange voters firmly, if at times grudgingly, in the Tory camp. One historian depicted them as the 'storm troopers of the Tories' during election campaigns.[9]

On a personal level, Orange membership and leadership also proved to be an important stepping-stone for Bowell. In largely Protestant Belleville, it was a key power base for a businessman, community leader and aspiring politician. He joined the Orange Order in late 1841 or early 1842 in his late teens and remained an enthusiastic adherent for the following 75 years of his life. As late as July 1916 at age 92, Bowell made a grueling trip across the country from a Vancouver family visit to a Toronto Orange convention. The Toronto *Daily News* published a photo of the old warrior standing at the meeting clad in a jacket and vest, carrying a cane. The newspaper reported he was taking an active part in debates.[10] It was a display both of his stamina in old age and his dedication to the cause. Since there is no evidence that his father brought Orange affiliation with him from England in 1833, Bowell's teenage decision to become an Orangeman likely was a case of emulating his employer and mentor George Benjamin.

Bowell joined Orange Lodge No. 2, created almost a decade earlier by Benjamin as only the second in Upper Canada.[11] At first, the new Belleville Orange outpost had been a forum where newcomer Benjamin could meet influential local contacts helpful in advancing his business and political interests by establishing community leadership credentials. Obviously, the strategy worked. By the late 1840s, he was the leading North American Orangeman and a successful Belleville newspaper owner. A Benjamin biographer said his rise to the position of North American Orange Grand Master made him 'the leader of what was probably the largest and best organized political lobby in the province.'[12] According to author Charlotte Gray in her biography of Belleville–area writer Susanna Moodie, the regular Orange meetings were the place for both Benjamin and Bowell to meet and bond with leading players in the community. 'Belleville's numerous Irish Protestants had established one of the most active Orange Lodges in the province,' she wrote. 'All over Upper Canada, Orange Lodges were well on their way to becoming the most important club in every small town—boisterous, populist and passionately pro-British but the Belleville Orange Lodge was particularly forceful.'[13]

During the years following his introduction to the ways of the Lodge, Bowell learned the ropes of the organization and gradually increased his position and influence in eastern Ontario Orange affairs. He was filling a void left as Benjamin's attention was shifting to the larger national and international Lodge stage and to politics. However, Bowell also soon discovered the pitfalls of miscalculating how far he could go to impose an Orange agenda on outsiders. It was a lesson he would take to heart after one of the most embarrassing political missteps in his life. His actions helped deprive Royalist Belleville of a planned 1860 visit by the heir to the British throne, a blunder that could have had dire implications for an aspiring young local politician. Eighteen-year-old Albert Edward, Prince of Wales and heir-presumptive to Queen Victoria, was despatched by his mother in the summer of 1860 for his first visit to Britain's North American colonies. First up was a visit to Ottawa, his mother's controversial choice as capital city of the new united province of Canada that comprised present-day Ontario and Quebec. On September 1, he officiated at the laying of a marble cornerstone for Parliament's signature Centre Block. Then, it was on to Montreal where he dedicated the Victoria Bridge as the first to span the St Lawrence River. A century and a half later, the bridge remains a major link between downtown Montreal and the South Shore suburbs. To end the royal tour, Prince Albert was scheduled to head west to visit communities along the St. Lawrence shore including John A. Macdonald's base in Kingston, the growing community of Belleville and finally, Toronto. In royalist Belleville, 1,500 people showed up in the brightly decorated downtown to greet the Prince. At that point, the Prince's schedule went off the rails and Belleville's young Orange leader was at the centre of the debacle.[14]

Orangemen staged a series of demonstrations to show their loyalty to the Crown with marches. They prominently displayed Orange flags and regalia, first in Kingston and then in Belleville. The problem was that in Great Britain, displays of Orange symbols were banned as offensive to the Queen's Catholic subjects. The young prince's government handler, Colonial Secretary Henry Pelham-Clinton, refused to allow Prince Albert to go ashore in Kingston since it would involve mingling with the Orangemen and their symbols. The ship then sailed to Belleville, arriving late September 5 for the planned September 6 visit. No LOL symbols were obvious when they arrived but overnight, Orangemen from Kingston and Belleville decorated the procession route with Orange emblems, and again the prince was not allowed to go ashore. The entourage sailed west. On September 8 when the ship docked in Toronto, 300 Belleville politicians and influential townspeople including Grand Master Bowell were on hand to greet the prince with apologies and promises that if he returned for a visit, there would be no Orange emblems or flags on display. The Prince said he accepted the apology that had cleared up 'all painful feelings occasioned by the proceedings' but his schedule could not be changed to allow a return visit.[15] He quickly returned to England where he would have to wait more than 40 years for his short term on the Throne as King Edward VII. In the aftermath of the fiasco, Bowell had some political repair work to do, although it was a ham-handed effort. George Brown's Reform-supporting Toronto *Globe* newspaper had some fun with the sorry incident, accusing the Orange Lodge and its Conservative friends of insulting the monarchy that they claimed to support and revere. In Bowell's *Intelligencer*, however, it was all a 'misunderstanding' and a controversy precipitated by the Roman Catholic Church that protested a public display of Orange Protestant loyalty while 'dragging a Protestant Prince through Romish Colleges and Nunneries [and] the complimenting and extolling the education taught therein' during Albert's visit to Montreal.[16]

Although Bowell survived the embarrassment of the Royal visit fiasco and the citizens of Belleville clearly forgave his miscalculation by repeatedly electing him to represent them in Parliament, it gave his critics more fodder to taunt him about his Orange connections and poor judgment. An underlying theme of the taunts was that despite his regular stance that Orangemen should respect the rights of fellow citizen Roman Catholics, his actions as an Orange Order leader was not always so benign. It was Opposition ammunition in a nasty mid-summer 1891 House of Commons exchange that exposed both Bowell's defensiveness on the issue as well as his feisty, combative nature. The flare-up began during an innocuous July Monday afternoon parliamentary debate over whether binder twine should be on the duty-free import list as a farm product. Bowell chided the Liberal champion of the idea—southwest Ontario MP John Charlton (North Norfolk)—for being inconsistent as a protectionist when in government but a free trader in opposition. Charlton fired back by arguing that Bowell's career had its own inconsistencies: elevated to cabinet in 1878 only because an Orange delegation pressed Sir John A. Macdonald to include him as their representative and yet willing to abandon his Orange friends when it was in his political interests. This made him 'an unworthy ex-Grand Master of the Order he was supposed to represent here.'[17] A heated war of words erupted. Bowell rose to deny the claim of Orange pressure to get him into cabinet. Two days later, Charlton restated his claim, citing an 1883 *Globe* article about the day in 1878 when an Orange delegation travelled to Ottawa at Bowell's request to lobby Macdonald for a cabinet post 'should he succeed in carrying the approaching election. As Orangemen, they discharged their duty in that respect and the result was that Mr Bowell was taken into government.'[18] The besieged minister denounced the former Orange official quoted in the *Globe* story as unreliable and an intolerant bigot who had been expelled from the Orange Order.[19] Then the debate drifted to a Liberal claim that in 1878 before he joined cabinet, Bowell had sent Ontario Orangemen to a Montreal demonstration that almost led to violence. Bowell insisted he opposed the plan to send a delegation to Quebec and had not attended himself. 'Were you afraid to go?' a Liberal MP heckled. Bowell saw it as an attack on his backbone; fighting words. 'I do not think, as far as my courage is concerned, that the honourable member will put it to the test,' the enraged Minister of Customs shot back across the aisle that separated the political combatants, designed to be two sword lengths in width from the days when British MPs could be carrying weapons.[20]

Years later in the Senate, Bowell ruefully summed up his view of attempts over the decades to saddle him with a label of intolerance because of attachment to the excesses of Orange partisans: 'The Orange Order seems to be a ghost that haunts some people from morning until night,' he lamented.[21] After close to four decades in Parliament, he would know from experience the sometimes-burden of Orange affiliation on a reputation. In his acceptance speech after being nominated by Hastings North Conservatives to contest the 1891 election as their candidate, Bowell recounted what he considered to be his lifelong attempt to reconcile an Orange Lodge allegiance and his belief in tolerance and coexistence between Protestant and Roman Catholic Canadians. It was, he argued to the crowd that included Protestant partisans, a political position he had been taught as a core principle of Orange belief. He told the Madoc, Ontario meeting:

I surrender to no man my allegiance to Protestantism but I tell you this as your representative. As long as I occupy the position I do in the councils of the country, you must distinctly understand that there is only one principle on which I can consent to assist in governing the country and that is equal rights to all classes of the community... These were the first principles I was taught in the Lodge room— that every man could enjoy freedom to live and worship God as he pleased as long as he doesn't interfere with you and with me.[22]

It would be the 'live and let live' guiding doctrine for Bowell's long political career that saw him gain the support of Roman Catholic as well as most Protestant voters through a quarter century of election campaigns. He advocated for Orange issues but also did not back down from confronting Orange leadership when he thought their positions undermined the Canadian compromise of coexistence between religious and language communities. However, there was no denying his record included some moments that were red flags for Roman Catholic voters. When Bowell first came to wide public attention in 1874 as a backbench Opposition MP, there was a strong Orange connection to his new notoriety. He spearheaded the parliamentary campaign to have Manitoba Métis leader Louis Riel expelled from the House of Commons. Bowell, like many Ontario Conservatives, had been outraged by Riel's leadership of the 1869 to 1870 Red River Rebellion that was put down by a Canadian expeditionary force including volunteers from his rural Ontario riding. He saw the rebellion as an act of treason against Canada and the Crown. There also was a personal connection for the third-term MP. During the rebellion, Riel had authorized the execution of Thomas Scott, imprisoned by the provisional government and convicted of treason for his violent and racially tinged attitude toward his Métis captors. Riel biographer Maggie Siggins described him as 'the obnoxious Thomas Scott... the quint-essential Orangeman and he was foul-mouthed, bigoted and outrageously abusive in his never-ending heckling of the "damned depraved half-breed".'[23] Scott also was an immigrant from Ireland who settled in Ontario's Hastings County not far from Belleville before moving to Winnipeg. He was an Orangeman and militiaman known to the Hastings North MP both through the Lodge and his own leadership in the local militia. While he never defended Scott personally and there is no evidence that they were friends, Bowell condemned his 'murder' by Riel forces.

When Riel was acclaimed MP for the Manitoba riding of Provencher west of Winnipeg in the 1874 election, Bowell insisted he should not be allowed to sit in Parliament and moved a motion to expel him (although at that point Riel had not shown up to claim his seat). The acrimonious Commons debate on the issue pitted mainly English-speaking MPs who saw Scott as a victim of insurrection and murder against Francophone Quebec

Liberal MPs, who saw it as an issue underpinned by racial, religious and language prejudice. Bowell tried to distance himself from that interpretation. When he rose in the Commons April 15, 1874 to move his motion for Riel's expulsion, he insisted the critics were wrong. It was not about Riel's language or religion. In the third-person style of the Hansard during that Parliamentary period, Bowell is recorded as telling the House:

> He regretted exceedingly that the discussion upon the subject had narrowed down into these questions... He looked upon this question as one affecting a British subject. The man put to death in the Northwest was a British subject and he was foully murdered while in defence of the Crown and the country.'[24]

When a vote ended the debate, a large majority of MPs voted for Bowell's position including Prime Minister Alexander Mackenzie, Conservative Party leaders and a number of Liberals, although most Quebec Liberal MPs opposed the motion.

In his third parliamentary term, Mackenzie Bowell finally had attracted attention, both celebrity and notoriety. Riel-related proceedings of the Select Committee of the Commons that included Bowell were extensively covered in newspapers, as was the Commons debate and the vote. The Orange Lodge certainly took note. In 1875, delegates to a Sarnia, Ontario convention of the Grand Orange Lodge of British North America re-elected Bowell by acclamation on July 2 as North American Orange leader. Then, after an afternoon river cruise, delegates gathered to lavish gifts on him including an engraved silver tea set worth $1,200.00 carrying images of scenes from the 1690 Battle of the Boyne and other Catholic/Protestant Irish battles as well as the Bowell family crest. The inscription proclaimed it to be 'in grateful recognition of the eminent services rendered by him to the Orange cause and as a tribute to his worth as a man and a Member of Parliament.' Speakers praised Bowell for his opposition to 'demands made by the Popish hierarchy and for the marked ability and determination displayed by you in obtaining the expulsion of the arch-rebel and murderer Louis Riel from the Dominion House of Commons.'[25] Within years, many of those Orangemen would find themselves at odds with Bowell for being part of a government that refused to support several hardline anti-Catholic policies that Lodge members embraced. For now, though, he was an Orange hero. The tea set is housed in a Mackenzie Bowell collection at the Glanmore National Historic Site mansion in Belleville.

As a senior member of successive Conservative governments who brought with him close ties to the powerful Orange voting base, Bowell had to perform a delicate political balancing act. He was called upon to alternate between dispensing political carrots to placate Orange supporters and wielding a stick to use when dissidents threatened party cohesion and hegemony. Party leader John A. Macdonald expected it from Bowell as his contribution to the effort to keep the Conservative French/English, Catholic/Protestant, Orange-Green coalition together. On one side of the balancing act, Bowell had to keep his Orange credentials polished and the voting base convinced they were getting something in return for their support, despite occasional displeasure over government compromise policies. He had to demonstrate that Lodge goals were being given a hearing in government. He had to defend the Orange Order when it was depicted as a nefarious, bigoted anti-Catholic secret society. He had to be seen as bringing rewards for Orange loyalty to the party. Patronage was one of his most effective tools. Fellow Orangemen saw Bowell as a friend in government who should ensure that his Lodge brothers were in line for patronage jobs when they were available. Of course, he also had to be careful not to be perceived by the broader voting base as merely an Orange puppet always tilting government opportunities their way.

Bowell's personal papers are rife with evidence that he often pushed back against the Orange assumption of entitlement, insisting that merit rather than religious or political affiliation should be the primary criterion for government appointments. Still, if competing candidates for a job were deemed qualified, Bowell also made clear that religion and Orange affiliation could tilt the balance. A prime example occurred in June 1887 when a Protestant Customs officer in Kingston died. The Orange Lodge in Macdonald's hometown passed a resolution that the deceased's son should be hired to ensure the position remained in Protestant hands. Bowell responded to the demand with a lecture about his view of the ethics of government staffing. While it was true that Roman Catholics regularly lobbied to have a Catholic replaced by a Catholic, must Protestants do the same? 'You now claim that because an Orangeman held the position of landing waiter, therefore the vacancy must be filled by another of the same Order,' he complained. 'Permit me to dissent from this principle, upon which no government could be carried on. What we must consider is first, that the man's qualified and second, that he is a friend.' The principle of staffing, he wrote, is that 'equal justice should be shown to all and I have no doubt that in filling the vacancies at Kingston, this course will be followed.'[26] In the end, the son received the appointment.

Despite his protests, Bowell also understood that part of his role as government Orange liaison was to make certain LOL partisans received at least a fair share of government appointments. He therefore kept track of Orangemen appointed to government jobs. The list also proved to be a useful record to be used in self-defence when he faced inevitable complaints that in an attempt to be fair to all, he was being unfair to his Protestant 'brothers.' A prime example of its value came in 1894 when a Charlottetown Orangeman wrote to ask that a Lodge member receive a Senate appointment.

He said there were 'many complaints' that Orange applicants were under-represented in appointments. Bowell was quick to refute the insinuation of reverse discrimination, using his little black appointment record book as evidence. 'There is no cause for what is said so far as members of our Order are concerned,' he wrote before naming 13 Orange executives who had been given appointments during his time in government. He could add to the list 'scores of privates in the ranks who hold various positions under government.'[27] Besides, Clarke Wallace was Grand Master of the Orange Order of British North America and a junior cabinet minister as Controller of Customs. 'That ought to be an answer to these gentlemen,' Bowell concluded. Balance maintained!

He also polished Conservative Orange credentials by making annual appearances at July 12 Orange parades, which were the highlight of the Lodge 'marching season.' As well, flattering perks were offered to members of the movement including: private arrangements with the CPR to provide rail cars to transport Orangemen to their parades and demonstrations; an invitation to an Ottawa Orange Lodge leader to accompany Bowell in the government carriage on a cross-Canada rail trip; and making sure other government ministers were available to meet with visiting Orange Order members. Meanwhile, Liberal leader Laurier occasionally helped Bowell's partisan efforts to retain Orange allegiance by making it clear, at least to receptive Quebec Francophone audiences, that Orangemen were anti-Catholic and not welcome on the Liberal ship. 'Thank God there are no Orangemen among us, the Liberals,' Laurier said erroneously during an 1895 campaign speech in Chicoutimi, Quebec, a comment quickly spread by Conservative newspapers.[28]

The other side of the delicate political balance that Bowell was expected to maintain for the government on the Orange file was to preach moderation and tolerance. He tried to steer Orange leaders and members away from more extreme positions while keeping the tens of thousands of Orange voters in the Conservative tent even when their instincts clashed with Conservative reconciliation policies. It often involved standing up to Orange leaders, even if it potentially jeopardized his personal political survival. When French/English, Catholic/Protestant disputes arose that threatened the Conservative coalition, Macdonald often turned to Bowell to lower the temperature by convincing Orange leadership to temper their anti-Catholic rhetoric. The Jesuit Estates controversy that broke out in 1889 and threatened to tear apart the Conservative coalition before the 1891 election proved to be one of Bowell's greatest challenges in fulfilling that part of his balancing act bargain with Macdonald. Throughout the tense episode, he displayed skill, strength and courage in helping the party weather the storm.

Tuesday, May 28, 1889 was a particularly long and tense workday for Mackenzie Bowell in Goderich, Ontario. It stretched into the wee hours of

May 29. He had been dispatched to represent the government at the 60th annual meeting of the Orange Grand Lodge of Ontario where a motion to condemn Protestant Conservative MPs for their actions in the latest flare-up of the perennial Catholic/Protestant wars was being debated. In an analysis of the issue, University of Saskatchewan history professor J. R. Miller described it as a moment that represented 'a serious threat to the close alliance of Orange Association and Conservative Party.'[29] Bowell successfully doused the fire with a 5:00 a.m. speech pleading for Orange unity and understanding of the government's predicament. He asked for appreciation of the constraints on federal power under the constitutional order of the land. The inflammatory motion did not come to a vote. Bowell reported back to Prime Minister Macdonald that it had been a 'jolly fight' in which Conservative interests 'succeeded tolerably well.' The Orange delegates present were not happy but they did not vote for a rupture in the relationship with the Conservatives. They decided to cut Bowell some slack despite the fact that 'the Orange Lodges, like many Protestant ministerial groups, refused to see the question in the same light as former Grand Master Bowell.'[30]

The 'question' at issue in the tense parliamentary debate was a decision by the Macdonald government, supported by most House of Commons Liberals, to refrain from using federal power to disallow a Quebec law; the Jesuit Estates Act. It would send hundreds of thousands of dollars to Quebec Jesuits in compensation for lands seized by the British in the late 18th century after the Conquest. The legislation was an attempt by Liberal Premier Honouré Mercier to settle a long-standing divisive dispute over the land seizure and whether compensation money should be used to finance public schools or Catholic schools. The British North America Act of 1867 gave the federal government the right to disallow provincial legislation but also assigned education and property issues to provincial jurisdiction. In Ottawa, Justice Minister John Thompson (a Roman Catholic) decided provincial jurisdiction should prevail rather than the federal power to disallow provincial bills. The Macdonald government agreed and it was left to Bowell to sell the decision to outraged Orange members in Ontario. The uproar was so toxic that it threatened to break the Conservative Party asunder. Senior Conservative minister, Ontario Conservative Party chair and Macdonald favourite D'Alton McCarthy bolted the government to form the Equal Rights Association to defend Protestant rights. He vowed to challenge the Conservatives for the loyalty of Protestant voters and it was Bowell's assignment to counter McCarthy's argument and head off the threatened split in the party. To begin, Bowell made clear to the critics that his position did not flow from love of the Jesuits or support for Roman Catholic school funding. He confirmed his personal opposition to public funding for denominational schools. However, he called for recognition and respect of the Canadian constitution and its federal-provincial division of powers, as well as his strong belief in the need to keep the peace between Canada's two founding religions. He told one critic:

> I have as little sympathy with Jesuitism as you have but I do not deem it my duty to interfere with the legislation of local governments which deal with their own funds. The Federation Act gives them this right and power and I cannot see why any man of common sense should ask us as a Dominion to interfere. Jesuitism is to Orangemen what Orangeism is to the Roman Catholics.[31]

The argument presaged his position of principle a half decade later during the Manitoba School Question crisis.

On August 21, 1890, Bowell attended a national Orange Lodge meeting in Saint John, New Brunswick where Jesuit Estates again was a hot topic. He reported back to Macdonald that the Equal Rights Association 'malcontents' received little support and 'did not even get an audience.' Acceptance of his defence of the government position produced 'without exception one of the most pleasant and harmonious [meetings]… in years.'[32] Throughout this acrimonious debate, Bowell made a point of not challenging his critics' sincerity nor right to their own honestly held opinion. However, neither did he back down from his view that a Canada based on the views of the critics could not survive. 'A moment's reflection will show you that an exclusively Protestant Party could not govern a country like Canada,' he told one critic. 'The only principle on which a government can exist in this country is that of equal rights and privileges to all.'[33] In the end, Bowell triumphed despite accusations of being a 'traitor' to Protestants, a Vatican 'toady' and in at least one case, being warned of a possible attack against him at a public meeting. He responded by saying he was not afraid and didn't need a bodyguard. The Equal Rights Association fielded candidates in the 1891 election but made few gains. It disappeared from the political landscape a few years later.

Mackenzie Bowell's private library at his Belleville home included extensive newspaper clippings chronicling his public deeds over the decades and one of those stories shone a light on his success in maintaining the respect of the Orange Order despite their battles. It was a late-life eulogy written by an unnamed Past Provincial Grand Master about Bowell's Orange Lodge years. The undated story may have been published in *The Sentinel* as he approached his tenth decade. It noted 'how deeply rooted was the affection of his brethren' despite his periodic and often bitter disputes with the Orange community when its stance on Catholic/Protestant relations clashed with his view of the need for tolerance and 'equality for all' if Canada was to survive. It also noted his continued involvement in Orange affairs despite those disagreements. 'When it is possible, he may be found today, as of yore, an attendant at his own primary lodge or on days that commemorate great historic events, marching with his brethren behind an Orange flag, keeping step to music of fife and drum.'[34] Even after an often-tense relationship between the two sides over the many decades, it read like a heartfelt acknowledgement of a balancing act well executed.

NOTES

[1] The Bible was part of Mackenzie Bowell's extensive private library inherited by his great grandson Douglas Mackenzie Holton of Port Hope. 'Mack' donated it to the Library and Archives Canada, along with other Bowell papers and files September 23, 1994.

[2] Taylor, George, *A History of the Rise, Progress, Cruelties and Suppression of the Rebellion in the County of Wexford in the year 1798*. 3rd Edition. (Belleville: M. Bowell, Intelligencer Office, 1864). Carleton University Archives and Library, Barry Wilson Collection.

[3] Kealey, Gregory S., *Toronto Workers Respond to Industrial Capitalism 1867–1892*. (Toronto: University of Toronto Press, 1980), xv.

[4] ibid, 133.

[5] ibid, 113.

[6] Senior, Hereward, *Orangeism: The Canadian Phase*. (Toronto: McGraw-Hill Ryerson, 1972), 69.

[7] Donald Akenson, *The Irish in Ontario: A Study in Rural History* (Montreal: McGill-Queen's University Press, 1985), 280.

[8] Thomson, Andrew, *The Sentinel and Orange and Protestant Advocate, 1877–1896: An Orange view of Canada* (Master of Arts thesis for the Department of History, Wilfrid Laurier University, Waterloo, Ontario, 1983).

[9] Senior, Hereward, 'Orangeism in Ontario Politics 1872–1896,' *Oliver Mowat's Ontario*, Donald Swainson (ed.) (Toronto: Macmillan of Canada, 1972) 147.

[10] *Daily News*, July 28, 1916 story in CABHC files, Belleville.

[11] Godfrey, *Burn This Gossip, 37*.

[12] ibid, 59.

[13] Gray, *Sisters in the Wilderness*, 153.

[14] Boyce, Gerry, *Belleville A Popular History*, 104–106.

[15] ibid, 106.

[16] LAC Bowell Papers Vol. 115 (Belleville *Intelligencer*, September 7, 1860).

[17] House of Commons Debates, 1st Session, 7th Parliament (July 6, 1891), 1847.

[18] ibid (July 8, 1891), 1967.

[19] On July 20, 1891, Bowell also sent a private letter to a member of that delegation to Ottawa asking for confirmation that he had not asked for their help in winning a cabinet appointment. (LAC Bowell Papers, Vol. 65).

[20] House of Commons Debates (July 8, 1891), 1970.

[21] Debates of the Senate, 1st Session 10th Parliament, Vol. 1, July 18, 1905, 579.

[22] LAC Bowell Papers Vol. 111, file 4.

[23] Siggins, Maggie, *Riel: A Life of Revolution* (Toronto: HarperCollins Publishers, 1994) 159.

[24] House of Commons Debates, 1st Session, 3rd Parliament (April 15, 1874), 116-117.

[25] Belleville *Intelligencer,* June 3, 1875. CABHC Bowell collection.

[26] LAC Bowell Papers Vol. 43. (June 9, 1887 letter to Jason Marshall).

[27] LAC Bowell Papers Vol. 96. (March 17, 1894 letter to J. M. Duncan of Charlottetown), 268–270.

[28] LAC Bowell Papers, Vol. 104, File 1.

[29] Miller, J. R., *Equal Rights: The Jesuits' Estates Act Controversy.* (Montreal: McGill-Queen's University Press, 1979), 92.

[30] ibid, 78.

[31] LAC Bowell Papers Vol. 52. Letter to George Bartlett of Hybla, Ontario, May 7, 1889.

[32] LAC Bowell Papers Vol. 190 (August 22, 1890 letter to Macdonald), 79.

[33] Bowell Papers Vol. 52. (Letter to Chater, Manitoba Protestant minister Rev F. M. Finn, April 12, 1889).

[34] *The Sentinel,* 'Centennial Issue 1875–1975' (Toronto: The British America Publishing Co. Ltd., 1975), 6.

Chapter 6
POLITICAL APPRENTICESHIP 1863-78

As it is for many young men, the approach of Mackenzie Bowell's 40th birthday in 1863 was a time to reflect on what to do with the rest of his life. At age 39, he had accomplished much in the three decades since arriving as a child immigrant. He was a successful newspaper owner and publisher as well as a leading local official in the Loyal Orange Lodge with a gold watch given to him in 1857 for his leadership. He had become a prominent local businessman and civic politician actively engaged in the affairs of his Belleville community. He had a seat on the school board as a trustee, was a Chamber of Commerce player and a Belleville Cemetery board member. He wondered if it was time to embark on a new challenge. At this moment of stock taking and uncertainty, Bowell's friend and mentor George Benjamin opened up a potential new life path opportunity for his protégé as he had so often in the past. He encouraged Bowell to consider political service and elected office as the next phase of his life and he offered a way to make it possible. After seven years as a Member of the Legislative Assembly of the Province of Canada, the ailing Benjamin had decided not to contest the impending 1863 election and informed Bowell of his decision. He died the following year at age 65. Benjamin's decision to retire from politics opened up the Hastings North seat for a successor and Bowell was an obvious contender. It seemed like a good fit. As publisher of the Belleville *Intelligencer* and long-time Benjamin supporter in Conservative politics, Bowell was not a stranger to the complexities and uncertainties of the political battlefield that so often became a minefield in the partisan heat of religious and language politics of the day. He knew the issues. By late May, after some typical hedging and protestations that there might be better candidates available, Bowell was ready to commit to taking the political plunge. The decision eventually would launch one of the longest parliamentary careers in Canadian history. It also cemented a relationship with Kingston lawyer, Conservative party leader and co-Canadian premier John Alexander Macdonald that would last throughout the remainder of Macdonald's life. With a decision made, Bowell faced the challenges of securing the Conservative nomination and then winning his first election campaign. The latter would prove to be a much steeper hill to climb than the former.

From the beginning, the newspaperman with a prominent community profile was Macdonald's choice to be the Hastings North Conservative candidate in the wake of Benjamin's retirement. Immediately after learning that Bowell was considering a candidacy for the August election, the leader sent a letter offering party funds to defray campaign costs. Bowell refused the offer, telling Macdonald he did not need the money. 'Accept my thanks for your kind offer but as I do not intend spending money, I shall not require it,' he wrote in a May 29 letter. 'Should I receive the nomination and accept, I will write you.'[1] He also said he would decline the nomination if a better, more electable candidate came forward, although that likely was modesty posturing since Bowell had a high opinion of his own abilities and qualifications and a stronger candidate was unlikely. Lacking competition, he was proclaimed candidate and Bowell officially donned the cloak of politician. His first act as a candidate was to predict his own defeat, warning Macdonald he might not be able to retain the seat. 'To tell you the truth, I am fearful of the result,' he wrote. 'There is not the slightest doubt that Benjamin would have been beaten and probably the man who takes his place at the present moment may not be more successful than he would have been.'[2]

The issue he would face as a candidate in 1863 was one that would haunt Bowell throughout his long career. He had to contend with Protestant voter opposition to what they saw as Tory catering to Roman Catholic interests. Bowell's long-cultivated Orange Lodge base in Hastings County would prove to be his most difficult campaign challenge. The issue was whether taxpayers should be forced to see their tax dollars used to support separate Roman Catholic schools. Macdonald, with backing from both Benjamin and then-publisher Bowell, supported the public funding of separate religious schools because it had been promised in the 1841 deal creating the united Province of Canada. The policy was used to fund schools for both the Roman Catholic minority in Ontario (Canada West) and the Protestant English minority in Quebec (Canada East). Bowell personally opposed separate school funding but on principle, he believed that the deal which underpinned the 22-year-old political union should not be breached retroactively. In the interests of equal treatment for all religions, Benjamin (with Bowell's editorial endorsement) also had supported legislation allowing incorporation of Catholic organizations. Consequently, angry Orange leaders and organizers were urging their members to vote for George Brown's Reform Party and its anti-separate school and anti-Catholic stance. In Orange Kingston, Macdonald also was not immune to the Protestant backlash although his higher profile, prominent political position and superior organization made him better able to withstand the opposition. In his May 29 letter to the leader, Bowell pinpointed the Hastings North problem. 'There are a large number of the same kind of Orangemen in the riding as you have in Kingston,' he lamented. 'They have got [hostility to separate school funding] so completely rooted into them that you nor anyone else can knock it out of them, hence the difficulty in bringing them back to the party.' On August election day, Macdonald withstood the opposition in his own riding but with a victory margin well reduced from 1861 levels. Bowell did not fare as well. Belleville lawyer and Reform candidate Thomas Wallbridge defeated him and Bowell would have to wait four years for a rematch when conditions and issues were vastly different and more weighted in his favour. Meanwhile, he had four years to work on his credentials for the job.

In Belleville and surrounding rural Hastings County, name recognition would not be a problem for the aspiring novice politician. It was an asset Macdonald clearly valued as he courted Bowell to become a candidate. The new Conservative recruit began his search for a political career with some clear advantages and a high profile. As owner and publisher of the local newspaper, he and his employees were gatekeepers over what narrative the majority of voters received and how it was presented. It gave him a powerful position of influence over information, a key currency of political debate. Beyond Belleville, he had a profile as a founder and leading member in the Ontario Press Association. As a prominent Orangeman and local church supporter, he had a strong built-in Protestant base, despite some opposition to his stand on separate school funding. As a supporter of equal rights for all religions, he also could count on some Catholic support. In addition, as a prominent businessman, Bowell had extensive land holdings in the area, created jobs, advocated pro-business policies and promoted enhanced transportation links for the community. Beyond ownership of the *Intelligencer*, he also held corporate positions that made him a key player in the local business elite. Among his high-profile positions, Bowell was well known for being prominent on the boards of leading businesses including the Hastings Mutual Fire Insurance Company, the Farren Manufacturing Co., the Dominion Safety Glass Co. and the Belleville and North Hastings Railway. He was a founding member of the Belleville Chamber of Commerce and adding to that profile was his status as a promoter of education as a ticket to advancement for Belleville's youth, Bowell served for many years on the local school board until 1867 including 11 years as chairman of the Belleville Board of School Trustees. Eventually, a school and a local education award bore his name in recognition of his training as a teacher and lifelong support of education, although both namesakes now have disappeared.

Bowell also benefitted from high-profile military renown in the community. As a volunteer militiaman in 1864 during the American civil war, he had served on the Canada/United States border for four months guarding against threats that refugees from the Confederacy living in Canada on the shores of Lake Erie would use it as a base to attack Northern Union forces, potentially dragging Canada into the conflict. 'Fortunately, we had no necessity to fight and all we did was practice with blank cartridges,' he said later. 'The Canadian volunteers were sent there to maintain the neutrality of Canada and prevent one portion of the Yankees attacking the other.'[3] He also saw military service in 1866 during Fenian raids across the border aimed at capturing Canada to make it a bargaining chip in demanding Irish independence from Great Britain. His volunteer militia company was sent to Cobourg east of Belleville where Fenians were gathering on the U.S. side of Lake Ontario. No invasion force arrived and Bowell recounted years later that he acted as a trumpeter for one of the volunteer officers.[4] His military profile in the community was enhanced by the fact that he was an organizer and funder of the Belleville 15th Militia Battalion and retired with the rank of Lieutenant Colonel in the 49th (Hastings) Battalion of Rifles. It was a title he proudly used throughout his life. In 1867, No. 1 Company, 15th Belleville Battalion presented him with a ceremonial sword 'in recognition of the esteem in which he was held when in command of that company.' It now is displayed in the Belleville Armoury. The Hastings and Prince Edward Regiment, one of the most battle-tested and decorated regiments in Canadian military history, has its roots to Bowell's 15th Battalion.

Political success typically flows in part from good timing and a candidate's record and Bowell was blessed on both counts. Community affiliations and reputation, accomplishments, work habits, vision, and promises are assessed by voters and judged. Electors in the small community of Belleville-Hastings would judge Bowell the candidate on all of that and more. Judgments about such intangibles as personality traits, character, honesty, likeability, reliability and trustworthiness also play a role in forming political opinions and choices.

After three decades of deep involvement in the affairs of the community, most voters likely had a good idea of the attributes, talents and foibles that Bowell brought to his political pursuits. His basket of character traits, skills and tendencies often were assets in his public office quest, although in some cases, his personality quirks also were to prove a drag on his ambitions and skills as a politician. In January 1896, almost 30 years into his successful political career, the Conservative Ottawa Evening Journal decided to turn to the 'science' of physiognomy to get a read on the characters of the key political players on Parliament Hill, including Bowell. The newspaper defined the term that dates back to ancient Greece as 'the science of reading character by the face.' Bowell's strong, determined and non-threatening visage fared relatively well in the exercise. 'Here we have the face of a man whose geniality and tendencies to enjoy the sociabilities of life are his most marked characteristic,' the newspaper rhapsodized under a sketch of the Prime Minister. 'Taken all around, the face is one that if you did not know the owner, you would trust... as one worthy of your confidence, a man of integrity.[5] Had the physiognomy test been applied to Bowell 30 years earlier as he prepared to offer himself to the voters of Hastings North constituency for the first time, it might have hinted at some candidate character traits and self-image perceptions that would reveal themselves during his political career. His strong, relaxed facial features might have suggested pride in his accomplishments based on effort and merit. He saw one of his strengths as being a self-made man, rising from a humble background to local prominence through diligent hard work, industry and strong work ethic rather than a privileged background or good connections. Bowell clearly thought his personal formula for success could be a template for others. 'I went into a printing office at a very early period of life and that taught me [that] to be successful either in business or in fighting a political battle, a man must never weary of well doing,' he later would tell an audience of young Conservatives. 'If he puts shoulder to the work, he must never hesitate but keep pushing, pushing until he attains the top and it is by plodding industry... that you will be led to success.'[6]

Deep into his political career, Bowell reflected that his story was proof positive of the fact that Canada was a land of opportunity, offering success for those, like him, willing to work for it, irrespective of background. 'No matter what position I have held or in which you have placed me, I am one of yourselves,' Bowell once told his constituents as he asked one more time for their electoral support. '[It] must convince very one of you that we live in a country in which no matter how humble a man may be, if he has only industry, temperance and perseverance, he can aspire to the most eminent positions in the country.'[7] A corollary of that work-ethic philosophy was a lifelong disdain for those who argued for special treatment in life or before the law because of their connections or status. He had an egalitarian streak. In March 1883, as an example, Customs Minister Bowell penned a caustic reply to a plea for lenient treatment from a well-connected Montreal Conservative businessman caught smuggling goods into the country. 'It is quite time these frauds were put a stop to and when we arrest a Negro, fine and imprison him for smuggling on Pullman cars, I can see no reason why the frauds of those in a higher social position should go unpunished.'[8] In defining his character traits from his face, Bowell's steely stern visage could have been a hint of vanity that led him in later years to scribble on collected and preserved newspaper clippings a judgment of press coverage based on whether the illustration used to portray him was 'very poor' or 'first class.'[9] His square jaw could have offered a hint of his inner resolve to stay fit and tough. As the son of a carpenter, Bowell was raised doing manual labour and stayed in shape throughout his life. In his later years, he continued to embark upon arduous trips on the high seas to destinations abroad or on cross-Canada trips by rail, wagon and on horseback.

Well into his 80s and 90s, Bowell travelled extensively and even in his 70s, more sedentary reporters marvelled at his fitness and stamina. In 1895 when he was 71, the Toronto *Mail & Empire* reported on a trip of almost two months that took the Prime Minister from Ottawa to British Columbia and back. 'The premier has covered more territory than most of his younger colleagues,' said the newspaper. 'His visit to the West... has entailed a great deal of laborious traveling which only a man of iron constitution could at his age undertake [even with] physical comfort. That he not only crossed the continent but travelled almost to the confines of civilization in the most primitive conveyances speaks well of his endurance.'[10] Bowell often visited border customs stations across the southern Prairies on horseback, sleeping in tents along the way.

If the photograph used for the journalistic physiognomy assessment of character showed him with the hint of the smile that he sometimes displayed, it might have been interpreted as a sign of a man with a humorous side. Indeed, he had a sense of humour although it usually was a trait revealed only in private rather than being displayed in public pronouncements. Since Bowell was an avid reader, it sometimes involved word play as illustrated when he commiserated with a letter writer who complained that a land speculator named Wrong had taken property from him on the Prairies. 'Of course, it is not right for Wrong to do this but you will have to grin and bear it,' he responded. In Parliament, the Senate and Senators often were the butt of his jokes. In October 1881, he told an applicant for a Senate seat he would do what he could to help but held out little hope considering the number of pleas for the single seat vacated by a death. 'The applicants are numerous enough to fill the Senate if all were dead,' he wrote.[11]

Even after he was elevated to the Senate himself, Bowell continued to poke fun at the institution and its inmate colleagues. After listening to a Liberal Senator who once had been a Senate critic extolling the virtues of the Upper Chamber, Bowell responded: 'It only proves to me the moment an honourable gentleman enters the Senate, benign influence by which he is surrounded... so mollifies his opinion that he becomes as mild as a suckling dove—one of ourselves.'[12]

Bowell also brought into his political career a reputation for physical toughness and fearlessness that would sometimes be seen as a political asset, a sign of strength, and sometimes as a detriment and evidence that he was thin-skinned, rash and a bully. A striking example of his tough side occurred in winter 1885 as the 61-year-old Bowell was walking in Ottawa one evening. He came upon a street brawl involving a small man attacking a much bigger man with his fists and a riding crop while the intended victim tried to fend off the blows. After surveying the scene, Bowell intervened, separated the two and sent them on their separate ways. Later, he made light of it. 'I must confess it was about as amusing a sight as I ever witnessed,' he wrote to a friend. '[The small attacker] reminded me very much of a bantam cock attacking a Shanghai rooster.'[13] As part of his 'tough guy' package, he was not a man to be threatened. After being offered protection following warnings that there could be violence at a Montreal meeting he was to address, Bowell replied simply: 'I do not know that that [fear] has been a feature in my character in the past and I am not aware that it is likely to be in the future.' There was no need for a bodyguard.[14] When a party supporter from his riding warned that her husband would retaliate if he did not receive a coveted mail delivery contract, Bowell was angry and blunt. 'If anything would prevent me from interfering in the matter, it is such a threat.' To burnish his reputation for toughness, Bowell also may have occasionally made up or embellished stories. He once told a much-repeated story that he defeated then-Liberal leader Edward Blake in a House of Commons wrestling match. 'I suppose I'm the only man who ever lived that took Edward Blake down, once on the floor of the House and once in the lobby,' he told a reporter who duly reported what sounds like a fanciful tale not recorded in parliamentary records. He said Blake started ribbing him late one parliamentary night after adjournment and Bowell told him to stop or 'I'll take you down right here.' Blake said he couldn't so Bowell floored him. Several days later, Blake charged him in the Commons lobby and Bowell 'downed' him again. 'I was never a very big man but what there was of me was hard as nails,' he bragged to the reporter.[15]

While perhaps a fanciful tale, it was not an incident or a story fuelled by alcohol for when it came to liquor, Bowell was an abstainer or at least a very temperate drinker. It made him something of an anomaly in a profession in which deal making, gossip and debate often were conducted over and aided by a glass or many. Still, he generally was tolerant of those who considered alcohol a form of political fuel. In his younger years, Bowell had flirted with supporting legally enforced temperance but later concluded it could not be policed and would not be effective. Discouragement and voluntary abstention or moderation became his preferred solution.

However, he was less tolerant of those who drank excessively in his employ. As Customs minister, employee drunkenness was one of the biggest problems in his department and he disciplined offenders for undermining departmental effectiveness. Perhaps that same desire for better performance motivated his later successful campaign to have the Senate liquor bar shuttered. His distaste for excessive imbibing came through in a letter to an Orange Lodge acquaintance who had informed him that the Lodge was imposing a drinking ban for men wearing the colours. 'I note your remarks as to the prosperity of lodges owing to the doing away of their former drinking habits,' he wrote. 'Depend upon it. A policy of this kind will tend to establish your own respectability and do much good in the eyes of the community.'[16]

Throughout his political career, one of Bowell's personality traits that sometimes became a liability was his ingrained independent streak. It sometimes caused him problems with his voters in the constituency and rebuke from his party's head office gatekeepers. In Parliament as a backbench MP in the 1860s and 1870s, he often criticized his party's positions and sometimes voted with the Liberals. On the campaign trail, he bluntly told his electors over the years that he while he owed them his hard work and advocacy, he also owed it to himself to be governed by his own core beliefs. Elections were their chance to judge whether he achieved the right political balance. A classic illustration of the tightrope he walked with supporters came during a meeting in Madoc where the Conservative candidate to contest the 1874 campaign would be chosen. Bowell already had served two terms as their Conservative MP and was asking for a chance to win a third. Tory supporter John Hagerman stood to nominate him as the candidate but first he chastised Bowell for his failure to adhere to party policy. 'He, with a good many others, thought Mr Bowell had not been as true to his party as he might have been,' the *Intelligencer* newspaper reported from the meeting. 'He was too independent.'

Rather than back down, the aspiring candidate stood his ground. If elected to the new Parliament and if the Liberals under Alexander Mackenzie won government 'he would do what he had done with Macdonald. He would support the Mackenzie government when it proposed something good and oppose it when it proposed bad policy.' Bowell noted that as a Conservative backbencher under Prime Minister Macdonald 'he had voted against some Macdonald policies even when they were confidence motions.' One of targets for his opposition had been a government bill to create pensions for government employees. Despite this refusal to guarantee party loyalty, Conservatives at the meeting apparently appreciated the honesty and independence. He was chosen as candidate for the 1874 election campaign and won, withstanding a Liberal popularity surge that put Alexander Mackenzie into power in Ottawa. [17] Years later, a published analysis of Bowell's political successes noted that the independent streak also extended to his dealings with Orange Protestant voters. He risked losing their support by standing up to Orange Lodge leadership on the issue of equal rights for Roman Catholics. 'Though a thorough Orangeman trusted and honoured by the Order as no man ever has been before him in North America, Mr Bowell has always had a mind of his own,' read a Kingston newspaper analysis after his appointment as prime minister. [18] These were among the character traits known and on display as he prepared to offer himself to the voters in the new nation of Canada in 1867.

As Mackenzie Bowell braced for a decisive summer political campaign, preparing to sell himself as the best candidate to represent the Belleville-area riding, he likely nursed some anxiety about what he privately considered his greatest political handicap. He was pursuing a career in which the main currency that decided success or failure was the spoken word. Public speaking and words were the weapons of choice in the political battlefield. Yet by his own admission, Bowell was not a fluent, natural or engaging public speaker. He privately confessed to a dislike for public speaking. In fact, two decades into his political career in 1887, he declined an invitation to speak at two public rallies for a friend and fellow Conservative candidate with a frank admission: 'I think you are asking too much—a speech during the day and another at night. You know that I dislike speaking.' As a newspaperman, he had mastered the printed word but as suits the profession, he preferred to be a fly on the wall observing rather than the centre of attention on the stage. Once as Canada's first trade minister, Bowell began a major Toronto speech on potential export markets by warning assembled manufacturers not to expect a sparkling address. 'I may state before proceeding further that it is not my intention to attempt any oratory,' he said. 'Those who know me know that is not my forté.'[19]

J. L. Payne, Bowell's private secretary during many of his years in government, was one of those who knew him well and his assessment was that his boss 'was not a great debater.'[20] Even the Methodist minister who delivered the December 1917 eulogy at Bowell's Belleville funeral said he did not possess 'conspicuous abilities as an orator.'[21] His awkward way with words could be embarrassing. Once, during a tour of Berlin, Ontario. (now Kitchener), Bowell was trying to pay the community and its largely German population a compliment. The local newspaper recorded the clumsy outcome. 'Mr. Bowell, in his quaint way, said there is not much 'ruin and decay' visible in Berlin,' it reported. The local Conservative MP whom Bowell was there to support probably hoped there would be no more words of praise from his prominent visitor.[22]

Even Conservative-supporting newspapers conceded that while a popular government player, Bowell could not hold audience attention with his eloquence. At a huge 1891 election campaign rally in Toronto, for example, the veteran of countless political speeches over more than two decades was one of four featured speakers. He largely bombed. 'Mackenzie Bowell was received with a cheer,' reported the Toronto *Evening Telegram*. 'He is not a magnetic man, however, and though listened to with interest, did not rouse the enthusiasm of the house.' He also had difficulty being heard by the crowd of thousands despite a 'heroic' attempt to shout. 'His throat went back on him and he got hoarse as a crow in a few minutes,' reported the Conservative-friendly newspaper. 'It finally broke down with him altogether, like a water-works pump.'[23]

Still, over the course of his half-century in the Parliament of Canada, Bowell was renowned for his long, detailed speeches and answers, usually delivered without notes. He uttered and committed to Hansard or journalistic records millions of words over his career and occasionally, perhaps despite himself, he could use words well and movingly. In a eulogy to Sir John Carling, a former agriculture minister in both Ontario and federal governments and long-time colleague, Bowell in a few eloquent words displayed

71

how he thought it proper to measure a political man's accomplishments. It wasn't necessarily through statues or monuments. In Carling's case, Bowell said, it was through his ministerial legacy of government-run agricultural research farms   (that still exist more than a century later). 'The experimental farm in Ontario [Guelph] and the Central Experimental Farm here, organized when he was a minister of the Crown, are the best monuments that could be erected to his memory, better than anything that could be raised in marble or brass.'[24] Whether he was an eloquent, natural-born speaker or a verbal stumblebum, Bowell's risky decision in 1867 to leave his journalistic comfort zone to throw himself into the word-fuelled political arena proved to be a good career choice. He turned out to be a formidable and successful political campaigner with the skills, character and work ethic to become one of Canada's leading and most durable politicians and parliamentarians.

During the following 11 years, he would fight four election campaigns and sit as a backbench MP in three Parliaments. It served as a productive period of political apprenticeship for the Belleville newspaperman. During those years, he learned the ways of politics and Parliament and through hard work, developed a reputation that made him stand out from the crowd, admired by supporters and denigrated by foes who thought him effective enough to warrant a counter attack. During those years of apprenticeship, he established himself as a backbench MP and a rising political star in Conservative Party circles. Still, in the summer of 1867, the aspiring politician had yet to win his first campaign or to learn the survival skills needed to navigate through the political swamp. It was his first political hurdle and it all began at the birth of Canada.

July 1, 1867, dawned sunny and warm in Belleville as residents dressed in their finery to attend a picnic marking the official birth of Canada. A canon was fired at midnight to announce the creation of the new nation. For the hundreds who turned out to celebrate, there were bands, games and horse draws to watch.[25] With an election looming, the politicians also were there, glad-handing the crowd in search of votes. The first federal Canadian election would be taking place in little more than a month with voting staggered over six weeks. Enfranchised male electors in Hastings North would vote in late August. Reform candidate T. Campbell Wallbridge was there to promote his record of defending and promoting constituency issues over the past four years since defeating Bowell to win a seat in the last Legislature of the United Canadian colonies. As the nominated Conservative candidate, Bowell also was there in campaign mode, arguing that his opponent had let voters down. He joined Wallbridge detractors in blaming him for failing to vigorously support legislation that would have financed construction of a local railway serving Hastings County and connecting Belleville with Marmora and its iron mines. In the Legislature, the Reform Member had introduced a bill to support railway construction but then took no action to move the bill forward. It languished on the legislative agenda for weeks and then when the Legislature session ended. Undoubtedly, the issue was a hot topic of debate on the fairgrounds.

Although Bowell had warned supporters that victory was not a sure thing given his 1863 defeat to the same opponent, he knew that the political landscape was far different four years later. The focus in mid 1867 was the recently concluded Confederation bargain that included acceptance of separate schools as the price of union rather than as fuel for religious animosities. During the campaign, Bowell had the benefit of representing the main political architects of the Confederation bargain that created Canada and later, his long-time private secretary E. L. Sanders summed up the change in political mood since 1863 that explained the local outcome of the 1867 vote 'The electoral riding of North Hastings was composed then, as it is today, of strongly Protestant elements and on general principles, separate schools found no favour in the community but they realized that these concessions formed part of the basis for Confederation and they accepted them as being outside the pale of useful controversy.'[26] And unlike the previous election vote, Wallbridge had a record to defend against an opponent recognized inside and outside the riding as an important addition to the Conservative team. 'In the North riding, Mr Wallbridge has found a powerful rival in Mr M. Bowell of the *Intelligencer*,' wrote the Montreal *Gazette*. 'Mr. Bowell ought to have an easy victory.'[27] When the votes were counted, Bowell indeed was elected with almost 60 percent of the 1565 votes cast. After weeks of partisan coverage that favoured Bowell and disparaged Wallbridge, the Bowell-owned local newspaper crowed in a dramatic and capital letters headline: 'NORTH RIDING REDEEMED.' Nationally, the vote was much closer with the Conservatives winning a 21-seat majority and 50 percent of the vote but in ballots cast, the opposition came within one percentage point of the Conservatives. The new Canadian electorate was almost evenly divided. Still, Mackenzie Bowell was on his way to Ottawa, having avenged his 1863 defeat. With extended stays looming in Ottawa when Parliament sat, Bowell was leaving behind Harriet, his wife of 20 years and their five surviving children: Louisa, 19; Caroline, 16; John, 10; Evalyn, 8; and newborn Charles.

Almost five years later, Bowell's next electoral political test was a relatively quiet affair that featured a second rematch between the same candidates. Once again, the Montreal *Gazette* (perhaps taking its cue from the *Intelligencer's* biased pro-Bowell coverage) predicted that the riding was safe for the Conservatives. It was a chance for riding voters to judge the performance of their rookie MP and Bowell's continued business and political prominence in the constituency helped his cause. 'As usual, Bowell was elected in 1872,'

73

local biographer Betsy Boyce reported matter-of-factly.[28] Although fewer voters turned out, he held his share and won by more than 200 votes. His reputation as a hardworking, independent-minded and honest representative, coupled with extensive campaigning in small towns throughout the large rural riding, carried the day. Wallbridge's argument that for four long years the rookie MP had supported the government agenda at the expense of local issues gained little traction. Bowell's solid victory came despite disappointing national results for the Conservatives. Macdonald held his 50 percent share of the national vote but the distribution of votes this time favoured the opposition. Alexander Mackenzie's Liberals closed the margin of Tory victory to just six seats. With rumours and allegations of shady dealings by prominent Conservatives during the previous government term, signs of weakening Conservative support were evident. Little more than a year later, the weakened Macdonald government fell as the Pacific railway funding scandal unfolded. Mackenzie was invited by the Governor General to try to form a government and the new prime minister and quickly dissolved Parliament and called an election, looking for legitimacy and the advantage of a fresh mandate granted by disillusioned electors. The young country was thrown into its third election in just seven years and this time, John A. Macdonald's legendary campaigning skills were not enough. Mackenzie swept to power with a strong 60-seat majority.

The January 1874 campaign in Hastings North tested Bowell's political mettle, strength and credibility. He had a new opponent in prominent Belleville lawyer E. D. O'Flynn and spent much of the campaign on the defensive over the Pacific Scandal that had brought down the Conservative government although did not implicate him personally. He later called it the most bitter election campaign he ever fought.[29] At the core of the scandal were allegations backed by strong evidence that the Macdonald government had received election campaign funding in 1872 from American-backed businessmen lobbying to build the Canadian Pacific Railway. Despite the evidence of Macdonald telegrams begging for campaign money from Sir Hugh Allan who led the syndicate that was awarded the CPR contract, Bowell had used the pages of his newspaper during the previous year to deny the facts, attack the Liberals and defend Macdonald. Critics said Bowell contaminated himself in the messy affair by constantly insisting it was not a scandal but a Liberal smear campaign. Before the bitter 1874 campaign even began, a Liberal-aligned newspaper recommended that Bowell be sent back to private life since 'he is fast proving himself to be mentally incapable, morally delinquent and utterly devoid of patience under criticism.'[30] However, despite the disastrous national result for the Conservatives and the loss of 24 seats, the late-January election night was another triumph for the Hastings North incumbent, one of just 73 Conservatives elected to the 206-seat Parliament. Bowell held the seat by 95 votes (fewer than half of his 1872 victory margin) and in the bitter cold, supporters whooped it up by feting him in Madoc where he spent election evening, then Stirling and finally Belleville at midnight where celebrants carried him to his house after a short victory speech. Within weeks, Bowell was on the train heading back to Ottawa and Parliament Hill to begin his third term as an MP when Parliament reconvened in late March. His first three electoral victories had given him a decade of parliamentary experience, an invaluable political apprenticeship as a backbench MP during which he was a keen student of the skills required to succeed in the political theatre. His third term represented a new learning opportunity from a different perspective. It was his only House of Commons exposure to life as an Opposition MP, a chance to hone parliamentary skills and an opportunity to develop a higher profile. As an experienced veteran MP in a sharply diminished and demoralized Conservative Opposition caucus, Bowell would have a better chance to be noticed than he had during his seven years as a backbencher in a large government caucus.

The third Canadian Parliament would prove to be a crucial turning point for the ambitious Hastings North MP. It elevated him into the ranks of Conservatives to watch and one of Macdonald's chosen. His performance and rise in caucus status and public profile led to a growing relationship with Macdonald during those Opposition years. Of course, for his potential to be recognized and the lessons learned during the apprenticeship to pay off, Bowell would eventually have to triumph for a fourth consecutive time in an election that Prime Minister Mackenzie was constitutionally obligated to trigger by late 1878 before his five-year mandate expired. It would turn out to be a milestone election, not just for Bowell but for the Conservatives and the young country as well. While every national election can legitimately be cited as an event that changed the country's history in ways big or small, only a handful truly qualify as game changers. Election day September 17, 1878 unquestionably was one of them. By bringing Macdonald and his Conservatives back into power with a National Policy platform of protectionism, the young country was launched on an economic path that built a tariff-protected domestic industrial base. It was supported by a policy foundation designed to withstand the northern expansionist pressures of the booming American capitalist machine.

A century after the launch of the National Policy, the Journal of Canadian Studies analyzed its successes and failures over 10 decades. 'The national tariff policy was not to be a temporary expedient but a permanent feature of the country's economic structure, the stability of which would be a source of encouragement to industrialists and to the economic development they alone could provide,' editor Ralph Heintzman wrote. 'In this, [Macdonald] was not to be disappointed.'[31] Protectionism versus freer trade with the United States remained a recurring election theme for 110 years even as integration of the North American economies happened incrementally. The 'free trade' election of 1988 finally appeared to settle the matter on the side of less protection; at least in principle.

In political terms, the Tory move to protectionism and the National Policy that was the defining issue of the 1878 campaign happened quickly, driven by circumstances, changing economic conditions and Conservative opportunism. In less than two years after winning a large 1874 majority on promises of ethical government and prosperity, the Mackenzie Liberal administration by 1876 was presiding over a growing recession. Unemployment was rising and many Canadian businesses faced competition from dumped American products. It sparked a growing chorus of Canadian business voices calling for protection. Macdonald heard the sounds of protest and saw an opportunity, beginning to allude to the need for 'incidental protection.' Then, as Macdonald biographer Donald Creighton reconstructed the story, Liberal finance minister Sir Richard Cartwright handed the Opposition leader a gift in his February 25, 1876 budget speech. Cartwright declared that increased taxes, including higher tariffs, were 'a positive evil in itself. This is no time for experiments.' John A. Macdonald had found his cause and his opportunity to return to voter favour. 'He would overwhelm Mackenzie's government with the national policy of protection,' wrote Creighton in a seminal biography of the Old Chieftain. 'With the national policy, he would revenge the humiliation of the Pacific Scandal and reverse the verdict of the election of 1874.'[32]

As in most ridings in the build-up to the 1878 election campaign, the national question largely overwhelmed local issues in Hastings North. Businessman Bowell was a protectionist by inclination and he eagerly bought into the national campaign theme. A letter circulated to eastern Ontario farmers, for example, warned them 'not to be misled and deceived by free trade theorists. Do not allow foreign rivals to get all the profits from the Canadian buyers.' Ironically, despite a decidedly anti-American bent, Bowell claimed to have learned his protectionist theology from a prominent American political writer and journalist. 'From reading many years ago the editorials of Horace Greely in the New York *Tribune* which used to come to my office,' he reminisced, 'I formed my opinion as a boy upon the question of trade and I confess I have not changed them since but as I grow in years, I am still more firmly convinced of the correctness of that policy.'[33] Election night in Hastings North produced another solid victory for Bowell. He captured 55 percent of the vote against his businessman opponent O'Flynn, more than doubling his 1874 victory margin to 241 votes. The high election stakes had produced a 40 percent increase in voter turnout. Nationally, Macdonald and the Conservatives won 53 percent of the vote and a 68-seat majority in a 206-seat House of Commons. Bowell quickly began preparations to head back to

Ottawa, this time to sit on government benches in a rejuvenated Tory regime. Almost certainly unbeknownst to him, a surprise would await him in the capital. Macdonald had been watching Bowell during his apprenticeship years and apparently had been impressed by his performance and development as a government and Opposition backbencher learning the parliamentary ropes. The Conservative leader clearly had started to think that Mackenzie Bowell might be in line for promotion as he considered how to construct his new cabinet.

NOTES

[1] LAC Sir John A. Macdonald Papers, Vol. 189 (Letters from Hon. Mackenzie Bowell, 1863–1885), 78,688–78,691.

[2] ibid.

[3] Debates of the Senate, 1st Session, 9th Parliament, March 29, 1912, 887.

[4] ibid, 885.

[5] Ottawa *Evening Journal* (Vol. XI No. 31).

[6] LAC Bowell Papers Vol. 128 A, February 8, 1895 address to a Young Conservative Club meeting in Toronto.

[7] ibid, Vol. 111, File 4. LAC Bowell Papers Vol. 25, Speech to constituents in February 1891 after being selected the Conservative candidate for the March 5 federal election.

[8] ibid, Vol. 25, March 17, 1883 letter to Montreal Conservative George Smith who had written asking leniency for a businessman friend.

[9] ibid, Vol. 128, A typical file of clippings had scrawled judgments about how flattering the illustration was rather than the news content of the articles.

[10] ibid, *Mail & Empire* (September 15, 1896).

[11] ibid, Vol. 19, October 17, 1881 letter.

[12] Debates of the Senate (3rd Session, 8th Parliament, February 8, 1898), 11.

[13] LAC Bowell Papers, Vol. 82, Letter to J. R. Philip of Whitby, Ontario, February 23, 1885)

[14] ibid, Vol. 25, January 21, 1889 letter to a Montreal Conservative organizer.

[15] CABHC Bowell Files. Augustus Bridle, *The Canadian Courier* (December 27, 1913) 'A Remarkable Ninetieth Birthday.'

[16] ibid, Vol. 36, January 23, 1886 letter to constituent.

[17] CABHC Bowell papers. *Intelligencer* January 24, 1874.

[18] LAC Bowell Papers, Vol. 112, File # 1. The Kingston *News*, ibid, January 13, 1895.

[19] LAC Bowell Papers, Vol 105, file 1. Toronto *Globe* February 15, 1894.

[20] Payne, J. L., *Recollections of a Private Secretary* (Montreal *Star* articles 1923-24). Quoted in Hill, Mary, O., *Canada's Salesman to the World, the Department of Trade and Commerce 1892–1939* (McGill-Queen's University Press, 1977).

[21] Belleville *Intelligencer* (December 11, 1917).

[22] LAC Bowell Papers Vol. 110 Part 2, File 1, Berlin *Daily News*, September 22, 1894.

[23] CABHC Bowell Papers. The Toronto *Evening Telegram*, February 7, 1891.

[24] Debates of the Senate, 1st Session, 12th Parliament Vol. 1. November 24, 1911, 45–46.

[25] Boyce, Gerry, *Belleville, A Popular History* (Toronto: Dundurn Press, 2008), 119.

[26] E. L. Sanders memoir, Trent University Archives.

[27] Montreal *Gazette* Vol. XCIII No. 205, August 29, 1867.

[28] Boyce, Betsy D., *The Accidental Prime Minister* (Ameliasburgh, Ontario: Seventh Town Historical Society, 2001), 147.

[29] ibid, 152.

[30] CABHC, *Daily Ontario* newspaper, August 30, 1873. Cited by Boyce.

[31] Heintzman, Ralph, 'The National Policy, (1879–1979),' *Journal of Canadian Studies*, Vol. 14, No. 3, autumn 1979), 2.

[32] Creighton, Donald, *John A. Macdonald, The Old Chieftain.* (Toronto: The MacMillan Co. of Canada, 1955), 210–212.

[33] Debates of the Senate (5th Session, 12th Parliament, March, 1915), 253.

Chapter 7
MACKENZIE AND SIR JOHN A.

The sequence of experiences that led prime minister-elect John A. Macdonald to consider Mackenzie Bowell as potential cabinet material in late 1878 had started decades earlier. The first archival record of direct dealings between the two men is the May 1863 letter in which the Conservative leader offered party financial aid to the Belleville publisher if he agreed to stand as a candidate in the pending election to the Legislature of the Province of Canada. Perhaps the fact that Bowell turned down Macdonald's offer of campaign funding support was an early signal to the leader that his new recruit was not entering the political game for personal gain. However, according to Bowell's later telling, their relationship first began almost two decades earlier in the 1840s and lasted almost half a century. Macdonald got to know him over the years in his role as owner of a Conservative-friendly newspaper, a supporter and friend of Conservative politician George Benjamin and an influential Orangeman, an organization that counted the Tory leader as a prominent member. Besides, they were almost neighbours. Bowell's Belleville base lay just 50 miles west of Macdonald's' Kingston home riding. As well, the mid-19th century pool of leading Canada West Conservative activists was relatively small and club-like. Presumably, therefore, when Bowell was elected a Member of Parliament and joined the Conservative caucus in 1867, Macdonald already would have taken some measure of the man. He would have known the new MP as a successful businessman familiar with living within a budget and managing employees, tough in the face of opposition or competition and opinionated on religion but an advocate of equal legal rights for Protestants and Roman Catholics despite his Orange leadership. However, John A. undoubtedly also understood that rising to the top in a small rural community would not necessarily translate into success in the rough and tumble, high-pressure and partisan lion's den that would be the 19th century Canadian Parliament.

When the 181 recently-elected MPs met for the first time in the new Nepean Sandstone parliamentary Centre Block in downtown Ottawa November 6, 1867, Macdonald began to keep track of the 100 MPs in his caucus, gauging their performance, their strengths, their weaknesses and their potential to help the government achieve its goals. Fifteen were appointed to his first cabinet—many of them veterans of the Confederation debates—and the remaining 85 had much to learn and something to prove. Most were political rookies. Macdonald, whose assessment of caucus members would determine their political futures, was watching to determine the quality of political clay voters had sent him to mold into a sustainable government. In hindsight, Bowell concluded that this process of judging character and potential was one of the leader's greatest strengths during his long political career. 'I believe the strongest characteristics of the late Sir John A. Macdonald were his thorough knowledge of men and how to use them,' Bowell wrote shortly after Macdonald's 1891 death.[1]

Several years later as fifth Prime Minister, Bowell spoke at a ceremony unveiling a statue of the first Prime Minister in Kingston and he expanded on his praise for the skills and intuition of his political mentor. 'He understood human nature as few have known it,' Bowell told the gathered crowd. 'He knew most people better than they know themselves and not only did he know them, he possessed the rare faculty of drawing men to him and inspiring them with zeal and affection stronger than party ties.'[2] For Bowell, it clearly was a personal reflection of his experience with the man who had made possible his unlikely political journey to the top.

In the aftermath of the 1867 election when he turned his gaze on the rookie MP from Hastings North to try to gauge where he fitted in or could best be used, Macdonald must have alternated between being perplexed, annoyed, bemused, entertained and ultimately impressed. As a Prime Minister with a vision, a platform to implement and promises to keep, Macdonald could not have been pleased by Bowell's tendency to defy government policies, particularly in the early Parliaments. Although clearly ambitious, Bowell quickly indicated he would not jettison personal principles or constituency priorities simply to stay in party good graces, even if it might have been a good career-advancement strategy. For Conservative parliamentary leaders and backroom power brokers who had Macdonald's ear, the willingness of the new MP to stand against government positions when it suited him must have smacked of self-serving disloyalty and a sign of unreliability. Even in an era that featured lax party discipline and 'loose fish' MPs who regularly were persuaded to defy party positions during votes, Bowell's willingness to bite the party hand that supported him was audacious.

It surely led to an early reputation in Conservative circles that Bowell could not be trusted to stand by the party when it needed him.

From Mackenzie Bowell's perspective, it simply was a case of honouring his 1867 pledge to constituents (repeated in subsequent elections) that he would serve as their representative in Ottawa and not blindly support his party if he thought its position wrong. It was a political *modus operandi* he defended throughout his career, defining it not as disloyalty but as principle trumping partisan expediency. 'In matters to which you allude, I stand in the same position as when I entered cabinet,' he wrote in 1891 as the party and government struggled to adjust to serving a new leader after Macdonald's death. 'In whatever the leader of the government thinks best, where no principle is involved, I deem it my duty as a party man to acquiesce.'[3] With the 'principle' caveat thrown in, it hardly was a ringing declaration of toe-the-line party solidarity. From the beginning of his parliamentary career, Bowell created a record of independent thinking that strained party patience.

Bowell's first recorded intervention in the new Canadian Parliament came on April 21, 1868 when he defied Defence and Militia Minister Georges-Etienne Cartier, a Conservative icon and John A. Macdonald's main partner in the Confederation project. The issue was legislation proposed by Cartier that would authorize spending to build fortifications and to fund organization and maintenance of a defence force that included both draftees and volunteers. It offended Bowell, a veteran militia volunteer and organizer of a Belleville regiment, as a plan that would discriminate against and downgrade the status of volunteers in Canada's fledgling armed forces. He noted the bill would require volunteers to serve for three years while conscripts would be released after two. He complained that Cartier's proposal to pay volunteer officers just 50 cents per day to lead drills was insulting and he spoke from experience. 'To a man who had spent his hundreds and thousands of dollars in uniforming and keeping his corps efficient, such an offer was an insult to his manhood and his loyalty,' the parliamentary Hansard reported from Bowell's speech.[4]

Three weeks later when the legislation came up for debate, Cartier was conciliatory and paid Bowell the compliment of referring to him by his militia rank but he did not really back down, offering instead a minor concession. The government wanted volunteers to be 'first in the field of honour but to meet the views of Col Bowell, he would introduce an amendment to give credit to volunteers for the time already served as part of the three years service,' Hansard reported. Bowell thanked him but then saw all his amendments voted down by the Conservative majority.[5] Days later, the freshman MP got his revenge, voting with Opposition and other disgruntled Conservative MPs against higher pay levels for permanent military staff. When Cartier complained that Quebec MPs who voted against the government were 'betraying their nationality,' the rookie Ontario MP went on the attack, chiding his party's Quebec leader and party icon. When in trouble, he complained, Cartier 'appealed to the national cry and sought to rouse a feeling which he, of all others, should be the first to discountenance.'[6] With his first MP performance, Bowell effectively put down a marker that in Parliament, he would be his own man and not defer to party luminaries or agendas.

Two years later, Bowell joined the Liberals in opposing an education provision in the Manitoba Act setting out the terms of Manitoba's entry as Canada's fifth province. It guaranteed minority language and religious education rights in the province, reflecting the deal that had been negotiated between Canadian and Manitoba leaders, including Louis Riel, after the Red River rebellion had been quelled in 1869. In Parliament, Bowell and his new Liberal colleagues argued that education rules should be set by the province under the British North America Act and not imposed by federal legislation that would be Manitoba's de facto constitution. The renegade Conservative MP and Opposition allies on the issue lost the vote 81 to 34. In defiance of the Confederation bargain struck between Ontario's Macdonald and Quebec's Cartier in the mid-1860s, Bowell used the debate to make clear he personally opposed government support for a separate school system to serve Roman Catholic or French-speaking minorities.[7]

At the time, his position was applauded and honoured by the Orange Lodge and the Reform/Liberal party. A quarter century later, the issue came back to haunt Prime Minister Bowell. By then, he was resolutely on the other side of the separate school funding debate on the grounds that whatever his personal opinion, he had been on the losing side in the 1870 vote and it was now a constitutional promise that must be honoured.

Four years later again, as detailed in Chapter 5, Bowell again found favour in Orange Lodge circles by successfully proposing expulsion of Riel as a Member of Parliament. That time, when the divisive and acrimonious debate ended and a vote was held, the Hastings North MP found the majority of his party, including its leaders, were on his side. Still, then-Opposition leader Macdonald likely wished that his freelancing MP from Hastings North had not once again laid bare the national open wound of language and religious divide. For the future of the country, the Conservative leader desperately wanted to see the issue managed through tolerance and compromise rather than confrontation. However, as Macdonald kept his critical eye on Bowell throughout his decade of parliamentary apprenticeship as a backbench MP on both sides of the House, the leader clearly looked past the irritating independent streak. He saw develop a maturing politician gaining notice far beyond the politics of minority education, Louis Riel, military issues and independence from party discipline. He was becoming an effective House of Commons man. 'His restless energy took him quickly into the active business of the House,' former private secretary Sanders wrote in a memoir about his long-time boss. 'His natural fondness for details and fearless methods of analysis soon made him a conspicuous figure in the shaping of parliamentary measures.'[8]

Several personal strengths helped make him effective. His work ethic, financial knowledge, communication skills learned during his journalism days and his interest in the minutia of issues that many MPs preferred to gloss over in search of the 'big picture' enabled him to master the mechanics of Parliament. Bowell absorbed the detail of issues that came before Parliament, making him a must-listen-to speaker during many debates as he offered a primer on a bill's contents. He was an effective and hard-working member of parliamentary committees. He learned to craft and deliver long and detailed—if not eloquent—speeches. As he developed as a House of Commons man, Bowell also became a leading proponent of creating a system of verbatim Hansard transcript accounts of parliamentary debates that was launched in 1874 and became the invaluable record of parliamentary history.

Despite the occasional display of independence from the Conservative Party agenda and discipline, Macdonald also would have noticed approvingly that Bowell was increasingly displaying partisan flair as a Conservative attack dog against the Liberals. In one notable example, he led an 1876 parliamentary assault that resulted in the resignation of prominent Liberal MP and Commons Speaker Timothy Anglin. His parliamentary sin had been allowing the New Brunswick newspaper he owned to take a $6000.00 federal printing job in contravention of the Independence of Parliament Act prohibiting MPs from being beneficiaries of government contracts. Anglin resigned, ran in a by-election and quickly was sent back to the Commons by Saint John voters but his reputation was damaged and his parliamentary career never really recovered.[9]

Ironically, as detailed in Chapter 4, several years later Bowell was convicted by the Commons of the same sin: allowing government money to flow to the newspaper in which he had a stake (although he claimed no ownership interest). He too was quickly re-elected unopposed in a by-election but unlike the Anglin case, it had no obvious impact on his subsequent political success.

Another factor Macdonald would have considered when pondering whether to pluck Bowell off the backbenches for a seat in cabinet was the relationship of collaboration and trust between the two men that had developed during the previous decade. Although it started as the normal to-and-fro relationship between a leader and a member of caucus, including Macdonald's role in helping decide which parliamentary committees Bowell would join and on which issues he would concentrate, the breakthrough moment in the relationship likely came in a private letter of congratulations and support the MP sent his leader in late 1875.

During the two years since losing power, Macdonald had sunk into depression, heavy alcohol consumption, disinterested leadership and public silence even as flaws in Prime Minister Alexander Mackenzie's governing agenda and issues management skills were becoming obvious. The country was sliding toward an economic recession and yet the Conservative leader was conspicuously missing in action by not challenging an increasingly vulnerable political opponent. Party supporters were beginning to wonder if the leader still had the energy, interest and desire to lead. They remembered his despondent suggestion in November 1873 after losing power that the party should consider choosing 'a younger man' to replace him.[10] However, a fiery Macdonald speech in late 1875 began to change the party's gloomy mood, the political dynamic and Macdonald's reputation. At a Montreal dinner to honour a defeated Conservative candidate, he delivered a spirited attack on the performance of the Mackenzie government. Bowell was one of those who responded enthusiastically in a letter that Macdonald retained in his files. The Old Chieftain had sent a note to Bowell outlining some of his points and their reception by the partisan Montreal audience. Bowell quickly responded. 'I am in receipt of your note and I am glad to learn that you have again made the Grits feel that you are not politically dead yet and I am also glad to know that you have broken a silence which was being misunderstood,' wrote the clearly relieved Hastings North MP. 'Hoping that now you have broken the ice, we may often hear from you.'[11]

The following summer, Macdonald's resurrection continued as he headlined a series of political picnics across Ontario that drew thousands. It gave the rejuvenated leader an opportunity to hone his anti-Grit rhetoric and message. Bowell played a role in that effort as well. The last of the picnics was held in Belleville September 12, 1876 and Bowell used it to showcase his political skills and organizational abilities. Donald Creighton, pre-eminent Macdonald biographer, recorded that a crowd estimated at close to 15,000 strong gathered on the town picnic grounds for a rally that left the leader 'elated—Undoubtedly, the climax of the Conservative efforts came at Belleville.'[12] Needless to say, the *Intelligencer* gave the event extensive coverage, claiming '15,000 STRANGERS IN TOWN' in one headline and 'NOTHING TO EQUAL IT' in another. The newspaper credited Macdonald with claiming 'it was the most magnificent political demonstration I ever saw. It would be difficult to surpass it in any country.'[13]

Clearly during the Conservative Opposition years of the 1870s when Macdonald travelled the difficult path from defeat and despair to rejuvenation and optimism, Mackenzie Bowell proved himself to be a loyal and effective supporter of his leader. It no doubt was noted as Macdonald kept track of who stood by him, encouraged and enabled him in his dark hours.

There was one curious incident during those years, though, that could have raised questions about the sincerity of Bowell's support of his leader. It was never explained. In 1874 when a despondent Macdonald was talking of the need for a new, younger Conservative leader, the Saint John, New Brunswick *Globe* newspaper wrote about possible candidates to replace him. Recently re-elected third term MP Bowell was featured as one with potential. The newspaper wrote that he had distinguished himself in Parliament, was credible on financial issues and clearly had some qualifications to be a contender. The Toronto Telegram reprinted the Saint John *Globe* article and then the *Intelligencer* followed suit without comment or denial by Bowell of any such ambition.[14]

Since by any measure, the prospect of a Bowell leadership run at that stage in his career was a non-starter, perhaps it simply was a matter of ego, letting his hometown readers and voters know that he was being noticed from afar. Whatever was behind it, there is no evidence that Macdonald ever saw the article or if he did, that he raised it with Bowell. Perhaps he understood the power of ego to warp judgment.

After enjoying a boisterous late night hometown celebration of his re-election with an increased majority September 17, 1878, Bowell spent some days with his family and political supporters in Belleville before catching the train back to Ottawa. The capital was in the throes of speculation about the cabinet Macdonald would assemble to lead the government into its new life with a mandate to reform and in some ways to reinvent the Canadian economy. Depending on how it was designed and implemented, the campaign's signature policy proposal—the National Policy—would nurture a reinvigorated industrial economy behind a wall of protective tariffs. It would make Macdonald's choice as Minister of Customs one of the key economic ministers in the new government. In earlier post-Confederation Conservative regimes, Maritime Fathers of Confederation Sir Leonard Tilley and Sir Charles Tupper had presided over a customs department regarded primarily as a revenue generator through import taxes. It was not considered a major portfolio, often attached to the finance minister's responsibilities. With a new reworked and enhanced stand-alone department, its minister would be the gatekeeper for a new economic vision.

Several weeks after arriving in Ottawa to settle back into Parliament Hill routine, Macdonald contacted Bowell to discuss the possibility of a cabinet appointment. The Intelligencer reported the meeting 'on good authority,' presumably directly from the mouth of the newspaper's owner. A week later at Rideau Hall, Governor General Lord Dufferin confirmed the speculation when he swore Bowell in as Minister of Customs in one of his last official acts before leaving the job after six years in Canada.

It undoubtedly was seen within political and government circles as a gamble. Bowell, after all, was an inexperienced first-time cabinet minister with no track record of running a sprawling bureaucracy nor of managing the implementation of a complicated government policy file. Now, he would be in charge of a central piece of the government's agenda. Critics then and now credited Orange Lodge lobbying for the surprise appointment. Orange leaders certainly tried to claim the credit, bragging about having successfully lobbied the Prime Minister for the result. Macdonald undoubtedly had a broader perspective on Bowell's qualifications for the job.

The editor of the *Intelligencer* (and presumably its owner) credited Bowell's appointment to his work as an Opposition MP. In a profile after the appointment, the newspaper suggested he blossomed as a critic of the Liberal government. 'Not until his party was in opposition did he display his abilities to their full effect—winning for him a very high position amongst leading members of the Conservative Party.' [15] In office, he clearly did not disappoint. Over the ensuing dozen years that featured multiple cabinet shuffles through three successive Macdonald-led governments, Bowell kept the job and during that period, the Macdonald-Bowell relationship broadened and deepened. The two men worked well together in a close and effective political and governmental relationship based on trust, respect, shared goals and an appreciation of the other's strengths.

Their relationship was close, congenial and complex if not intimate. It was close enough that they developed a system of communicating in tele-graphic code, presumably sharing information they did not want to risk falling into Opposition or press hands. Sometimes, however, the telegraph operator 'misspelled' the code gibberish and the result was a frustrating miscommunication. On June 27, 1882, for example, Bowell telegraphed from Manitoba to Macdonald in Ottawa: 'Lisgar dominate practices—Ily supposing nipping Dominand Vinter reimbursing verify apparement.' The message was incomprehensible to the leader and so the next day came a second telegram: 'Message you received yesterday to Sir John A. Macdonald signed M Bowell should read as follows: "Lisgar dominante practically supposing nipping dominance Vinter reimbursing Verify apartment".' Whatever that meant, it apparently cleared up the confusion although the miscommunication problem was to crop up again over time as the use of coded telegrams continued between the two.[16]

They also were relaxed enough in communication to put some humor into the mix. In late 1882, the Macdonald-appointed Chief Justice of Manitoba (a former Hastings County Liberal/Reform politician) returned to his hometown of Belleville to be feted by local lawyers. Macdonald wrote to complain to Bowell about Chief Justice Lewis Wallbridge's bad teeth. He groused that a mouth full of rot did not reflect well on the legal profession. Could Bowell speak to him privately and ask him to have some dental work done? Bowell, who had won two out of three local elections against Wallbridge's brother Campbell, could not resist some word play in his response, nor some digs at the judge's Liberal past. 'The question of teeth or no teeth I find is somewhat difficult to solve,' he replied. While 'a mouthful of good teeth' would add to the dignity of the bench, when you consider the extreme egotism of the Chief Justice of Manitoba and the difficulty of approaching him upon a subject of such gnashing importance, you will see the difficulty of accomplishing the effect you have in view.'[17]

In the end, the mission was not accomplished.

For Macdonald, Mackenzie Bowell was a reliable, trustworthy and effective lieutenant; an efficient campaign organizer, a candidate recruiter and a political intelligence gatherer in Ontario ridings who kept his leader honestly briefed on party prospects and political moods. He often was dispatched to campaign for the Conservatives in other provinces. He was a link to the party's powerful Orange voter base and he was a reliable workhorse in government. When the Old Chieftain was away from the capital, particularly during his months-long holidays at his summer home by the St Lawrence River in Riviere-du-Loup, Quebec, Bowell regularly sent letters or visited to update him on government business and Ottawa dynamics.

His work ethic, mastery of detail, understanding of bureaucracy and financial affairs and management of employees made him Macdonald's go-to minister to fill in for other members of cabinet when they left Ottawa. Through successive governments in the 1880s, he acted variously as fill-in Minister of Finance, Marine and Fisheries, Postmaster General, Secretary of State and Militia in addition to the heavy workload that overseeing the sprawling Customs department imposed. Bowell clearly did not see the job of 'acting minister' as merely a caretaker assignment. He delved deeply into the departmental files to make sure his decisions could be justified.

In the summer of 1885 as acting Finance Minister preparing to table a request that the House of Commons vote more money for departments, for example, he contacted the Deputy Minister of Indian Affairs for an explanation of some of the department's spending proposals. In one case an official slated for a salary increase 'has not qualified himself for promotion,' Bowell had decided. And 'an explanation is also required of the item $4000 for purchasing cattle, establishing agricultural exhibitions, ploughing matches etc.'

Sometimes, even the workaholic Bowell found it onerous. Through the spring of 1885, the Customs Minister also was acting Finance Minister during Leonard Tilley's lengthy absence and de facto Government House Leader in the Commons as the Macdonald government struggled against Liberal obstruction to pass voter list reform legislation.

By late July, Parliament was on the verge of rising for the summer and Bowell was relieved. 'After a six-month siege with plenty to do in my own department and Sir Leonard's, I feel as fresh as a daisy but nevertheless I propose at the earliest opportunity to indulge in a couple of week's laziness when I will try to get out of the reach of postal facilities and telegraph wires,' he wrote a friend.[18] As evidenced by his growing workload, Macdonald clearly appreciated his reliability and ability to get the job done, whatever task was assigned. He could count on his minister to offer blunt assessments about situations and people. Nevertheless, it did not mean the relationship between the two men was free of tension. Bowell regularly resisted Macdonald pressure to use the fruits of power to show Custom Department favouritism or special treatment to friends of the Prime Minister or party. Bowell was a by-the-book operator when running his department and enforcing customs rules. He would stand against pressure to cut corners or play favourites, even if it would displease the boss.

Macdonald was one of the most active behind-the-scenes advocates of lenient departmental treatment for friends or party acquaintances. 'My dear Bowell,' he wrote in a June 1884 note to his minister, 'listen to our friends.' He regularly asked Bowell privately to reward supporters with patronage appointments or to be lenient when they were caught breaking Customs import rules. Just as regularly, his Customs Minister resisted the pressure. An incident from summer 1884 illustrates the point. A Conservative ship owner in New Brunswick was caught smuggling alcohol into the country. Under the law, he faced the possible consequences of cargo confiscation, a fine and/or seizure of his schooner. Macdonald privately pleaded with the minister for special consideration and that the ship not be seized. 'Let him off as easily as your conscience will allow,' he wrote. Bowell pushed back and Macdonald backed down.

Two weeks later, the Prime Minister sent a follow-up letter with a change of heart. 'I quite agree with you that the most rigorous steps should be taken to condemn the vessel and to bring all the parties possible to justice,' he wrote. 'In fact, no expenses should be spared in this matter.'[19]

The Liberal Toronto *Globe* told the story of a Conservative businessman facing punishment for breaching the law who went to Macdonald, asking him to call off his minister who was planning to apply the rules and penalties. The Prime Minister promised to help and then asked which minister he should contact. Mackenzie Bowell, he was told. 'Good heavens, man. I can't do anything with him,' Macdonald reportedly replied. 'If Bowell says so, it goes. I'm extremely sorry but I don't have a tittle with Bowell. Take my advice and settle up at once.'[20]

From Bowell's side of the relationship, he was in awe of his leader, showing respect and admiration as a student would to his most revered teacher. He was grateful for the opportunities Macdonald had given him and impressed that he had the latitude to do his job even if it meant standing up to the old man. In tributes, Bowell made clear he had been inspired by Macdonald's political skills at managing issues and people as well as his vision and understanding of the compromises needed to attain it. In pursuit of a goal, he could convince friends and adversaries alike to work with common purpose. Critics noted, and Bowell acknowledged, that these were not skills he personally held in abundance.

In a speech at the July 1, 1895 unveiling of the Macdonald statue that still casts a Parliament Hill shadow from its base beside the Centre Block, Bowell, as a Macdonald successor in the prime minister's office, summed up his side of the relationship with his former leader and mentor: 'I was struck with an admiration, which never ceased, of the genius of Macdonald,' he told the crowd of thousands packing the parliamentary lawn. 'I entered public life as his supporter. To his fortunes I adhered in good and evil times. It is now my pride to know that I shared his confidence and joined in his policy to the day of his death.'[21] But there is no definitive evidence to indicate that through the years, they were intimate friends or that they circulated in the same off-hours social circles during their long years of association and collaboration. They were very different personalities.

Bowell was a loner who by his own admission spent most Ottawa evenings working in his Parliament Hill office or in his rooms at the Russell House hotel, a stone's throw south of Parliament Hill. Macdonald, by contrast, was a social animal who often entertained in evenings, using his off-hours to make or strengthen contacts or to wheel and deal with free-flowing alcohol as a conversation lubricant. As a mark of Bowell's respect and tolerance, even on the touchy issue of Macdonald's legendary drinking habits, he was prepared to cut his leader some slack. Despite his status as a likely abstainer, Bowell generally was tolerant of others who were not and he kept liquor handy for visitors who indulged. 'When you visit Ottawa you shall have not only one glass but as many glasses of old rye as you like to tuck away under your skin without troubling yourself as to whether the excise duty has been paid or not,' he wrote to a Halifax Customs Department official in 1891.[22]

As a government employer, he was very intolerant of people who allowed alcohol consumption to interfere with performing their duties. Macdonald was an exception. 'Sir John has been down with a slight attack of his old complaint—he has only been able to attend [Privy] Council once during the past fortnight,' he wrote to a friend in 1882 with no hint of reprimand.[23] The term 'his old complaint' was one of the euphemisms used by contemporaries to refer to the leader's frequent sprees. 'By 1856 and at intervals for 20 years, Macdonald was a problem drinker, subject to intermittent binges that rendered him incapable of attending to his responsibilities,' concluded an historian who researched his romance with the bottle.[24] Bowell's comment indicates the binge problem continued well into Macdonald's time at the cabinet table but his Minister of Customs was uncharacteristically willing to turn a blind eye even when it affected his effectiveness.

In early 1890, two old friends and comrades—Bowell and Macdonald—indulged in some reminiscing about their long association. The leader had sent his Customs Minister an engraved medallion commemorating events in 1840 when the two Canadian colonies of Upper and Lower Canada united as Canada East and Canada West in a new political union. Bowell responded that he had a similar engraved medal given to him by George Benjamin in 1844. 'Nearly half a century has passed since then and here we are, fighting the battles of life—for how long we know not,' he wrote. 'Well, I suppose we must make the most and the best of it.'[25]

Little more than a year later, on Friday, May 22, 1891, fate and happenstance assigned Mackenzie Bowell the role of a bit player in the story of Sir John A. Macdonald's last day on Parliament Hill, a venue he had dominated for a quarter century. In light of Bowell's long association with Macdonald, it seemed fitting. On that final day, MPs gathered at 3:00 p.m. in Parliament and spent most of the following eight hours in 'committee of the whole' examining government spending with a short 6:00 p.m. recess for dinner. As the evening progressed, Liberal MPs pressed Macdonald—aged 76 and still exhausted from the rigors of the spring election campaign recently completed—to justify a government decision to bring Sir Charles Tupper back to Canada from his post as Canadian High Commissioner in London for several days of Tory election campaigning. One of his speeches had been in Kingston on behalf of Macdonald, who was tied up in Ottawa. Opposition MPs complained it was unethical and a conflict of interest to have 'a leading civil servant of this country' engage in partisan campaigning while being paid to be a neutral government employee. Had Macdonald in fact sent him to Kingston to give the questionable and partisan speech? demanded Liberal William Paterson.

In one of his last parliamentary interventions, Macdonald agreed that he had and rather than apologize, praised the momentum Tupper had brought to his re-election campaign. His electoral victory margin had increased to 483 in 1891 from 17 four years earlier, he joked. 'You see, I was pretty wise in my generation in asking Sir Charles to go there and make a speech for me.'[26]

Macdonald biographers have offered two versions of what happened later that night after the House of Commons adjourned at 11:00 p.m. Both involved Bowell. 'He lingered for a while on the terrace outside, chatting with his Minister of Customs Mackenzie Bowell,' Donald Creighton wrote in his 1955 biography. Finally, he decided to call it a night. 'It is late, Bowell. Goodnight.'[27]

Fifty-six years later in a 2011 biography, Richard Gwyn offered a different version of the late-night exchange between the two veteran political warriors. He suggested it happened in the Commons as the parliamentary day was winding down. 'Mackenzie Bowell, one of his ministers, teased Macdonald into agreeing that it was time for two oldsters like them to be 'at home in bed.' Macdonald responded: 'I will go. Goodnight.' These were the last words he ever spoke in the House of Commons.'[28] If so, they were not recorded in the official Commons Hansard for May 22 since the official part of the parliamentary day had ended and there was no other official record of the exchange. Bowell did not mention it in letters and neither author cited the source of their version of the exchange. At the very least, the incident as variously described has entered into the folklore of Macdonald's end days.

That weekend at home in Ottawa, Macdonald suffered what likely was a stroke from which he never recovered. In the days that followed, Bowell was one of Macdonald's few colleagues given access to the dying leader. 'Our Old

Chieftain will in all probability have gone to his long home before this reaches you,' he wrote a friend June 2. 'I was at Earnscliffe about midnight and the doctor told me there was no hope. What the result will be God only knows!'[29]

On June 6, Sir John A. Macdonald died.

As widespread mourning broke out across the country, Bowell was privately devastated. Two weeks after he lost his leader and colleague, the 67-year-old minister wrote of his grief to a constituency friend. 'We all feel like boys who have lost their father and mother,' he said; heartfelt words of anguish and loss he did not commit to print when his actual father John died.[30] In the years that followed as the Conservative Party that Macdonald had built first floundered, then descended into civil war and finally into Opposition, Bowell was one of those who regularly eulogized his late leader as the architect and overseer of a golden Conservative era. He also learned to poke fun at some of Macdonald's legacy, particularly his tendency to keep people happy by promising future rewards. Hinting at a future Senate appointment had been one of the Old Chieftain's favourite ways of keeping favour seekers at bay and five months after Macdonald's death, Bowell had to deal with a claim by a Trenton, Ontario Conservative supporter that a Senate seat had been promised by Macdonald. 'As to the Senatorship, that is a matter altogether in the future,' Sir Mackenzie replied. 'If the promises alleged and otherwise by our late Chief are carried out, I fear it will require a periodical epidemic to clean out the Senate and make room for those who have been promised seats.'[31]

Even in his grief and loss, Bowell still could have a laugh over the Old Man's political management skills.

NOTES

[1] LAC Bowell Papers, Vol. 66, November 11, 1891 letter.

[2] LAC Bowell Papers, Vol. 128, Text of a speech delivered Oct. 23, 1895.

[3] ibid, November 11, 1891 letter to A.H. Moore of Magog, Quebec who had written to ask Bowell's position on funding Roman Catholic schools.

[4] Debates of the House of Commons (1st Session, 1st Parliament, April 21, 1868).

[5] ibid (May 12, 1868), 681.

[6] ibid (May 16, 1868), 722.

[7] Debates of the House of Commons (3rd Session, 1st Parliament, May 10, 1870).

[8] Sanders Memoir (Trent University), 5.

[9] Boyce, Betsy D., The Accidental Prime Minister (Ameliasburgh, Ontario: Seventh Town Historical Society, 2001), 151.

[10] Creighton, Donald, John A. Macdonald, The Old Chieftain. (Toronto: The MacMillan Co. of Canada, 1955), 210–212.

[11] LAC Sir John A. Macdonald Papers Vol. 189 (Letters from Hon. Mackenzie Bowell, December 9, 1875), 78717–78718).

[12] op cit, *John A. Macdonald, the Old Chieftain*, 225.

[13] op cit, *The Accidental Prime Minister*, 169.

[14] CABHC, *Intelligencer*, June 6, 1874).

[15] ibid (October 21, 1878).

[16] LAC Macdonald Papers Vol. 189, 78831-78832.

[17] ibid, 78870.

[18] LAC Bowell Papers Vol. 83, (July 20, 1885 letter), 376–377.

[19] ibid, Vol. 3, file 3. Macdonald letters (July 18 and July 29, 1884).

[20] The Toronto *Globe* (December 11, 1917), 7.

[21] LAC Bowell Papers Vol. 112, file 2 (Ottawa *Citizen*, July 2, 1895), 1.

[22] ibid, Vol. 62 (Letter to John White of Halifax, March 18, 1891).

[23] ibid, Vol. 79 (Letter December 20, 1882).

[24] Martin, Ged, 'John A. Macdonald and the Bottle,' *Journal of Canadian Studies*, Vol. 40 Number 3, Autumn 2006), 163.

[25] LAC Bowell Papers, Vol. 90 (March 25, 1890 letter).

[26] Debates of the House of Commons, 1st Session, 7th Parliament. (May 22, 1891), 426.

[27] op cit, *John A. Macdonald, the Old Chieftain*, 563.

[28] Gywn, Richard, *Nation Maker. Sir John A. Macdonald: His Life, Our Times, Vol. 2.* (Toronto: Random House Canada, 2011), 575.

[29] LAC Bowell Papers Vol. 91, 408.

[30] ibid, Vol. 63 (Letter to constituent June 20, 1891).

[31] ibid, Vol. 92 (Letter to D. R. Murphy, November 10, 1891).

Chapter 8
MINISTER OF CUSTOMS

When Mackenzie Bowell emerged from his swearing-in ceremony on October 19, 1878 as Canada's fourth post-Confederation Minister of Customs, he could be forgiven for thinking that after years of paying his dues, the immigrant kid finally had made the political big time. Although a disparaging 2004 television profile[1] mocked the significance of Bowell's position in the Macdonald government as 'among the least prominent in the federal cabinet—minister of customs, a tax collector,' that is not how contemporaries viewed it. His assignment was nothing less than overseeing implementation of the central promise of the triumphant Conservative election campaign: the development of a high-tariff, protectionist National Policy. Its ambitious aim was to foster the beginning of a transformation and a rebalancing of the Canadian economy from primarily agrarian to increased industrial goods production. He would be in charge of one of the government's biggest departments with hundreds of employees in Ottawa headquarters and across the vast country in Customs offices and border outposts.

Bowell would also be responsible for collecting much of the money the government needed to pay its bills. In the era before the 1917 introduction of 'temporary' income taxes to finance the war effort, the Department of Customs and its duties on imports was the major source of government revenue. In addition, he would be responsible for orchestrating a radical change in the mentality and core mission of the Customs Department from a 'tax collector' with a loose and lax mandate to police cross-border smuggling into a key driver of the Prime Minister's vision of a more activist government role in shaping the new country.

Macdonald's decision to elevate Bowell to a key position in the new Conservative government was not a shock to political watchers at the time, despite the judgment of some modern historians that it was a surprising and uninspired choice. Laurent-Olivier David, a Quebec journalist who covered politics for Liberal newspapers, reported that as his new Customs Minister, the Prime Minister had chosen one of his caucus stalwarts. Years later as a Liberal Senator, David paid tribute to Bowell, remembering the rookie minister in 1878 as a senior Macdonald Tory 'occupying a high position in the front ranks of the Conservative Party, amongst the best fighters in that party. All of his outward appearance showed signs of firmness and energy, of a resolute mind, of a tenacious will.'[2]

Bowell's long-time private secretary E.L. Sanders described his elevation to cabinet as neither unexpected nor controversial. 'No one was surprised that Mackenzie Bowell should be given the important portfolio of Minister of Customs in the new government,' Sanders wrote in a memoir. He cited Bowell's performance in Opposition, his experience and qualifications.[3]

A century after Sanders committed his assessment to paper, a present-day analyst and student of late 19th century Canada and the National Policy concurred that it was a good choice. Bowell was 'an extremely important minister' under three prime ministers, concluded a 2008 academic research project examining the role and impact of the National Policy and the Minister of Customs.[4] 'It was Bowell's administrative personality with all its peculiarities, strengths and shortcomings that would come to shape the operation of the National Policy (NP) both in terms of his own enforcement of the tariff system and those engagements mediated through his deputy minister James Johnson,' wrote author Braden Hutchinson. 'Bowell became the firewall of the National Policy. His attitudes and administrative rigidity supplanted the old informality which had hitherto allowed a loose, casually administered tariff system which sought only revenue, not the reorientation of Canadian economic life to co-exist with smuggling all along the Canadian border.'[5]

Beyond this, it was a policy 'aimed at imbuing the population with a sense of belonging to and forming part of the Canadian social body; it invested the border with a new, more rigorous administrative reality, making it a central feature of the definition of Canadianness.'[6]

Bowell obviously could not see his role through the lens of 21st century political and social academic jargon but he clearly bought into the view of the National Policy as a nation-building instrument and more than just a more efficient money-raising tariff collector. 'A national protective policy means the encouragement of all industries in all sections of the country,' he wrote in early 1883. 'Situated as we are with our diversified interests stretching from the Atlantic to the Pacific, we must learn this important fact—that if we desire to prosper and become a great people, we must have sufficient forethought and breadth of intellect to learn to "give and take".'[7] Even Dalhousie University historian P. W. Waite, usually a critic of Bowell's competence and effectiveness, saw his 'administrative talents' as a good fit for the portfolio. 'He was conscientious, hard-working and scrupulous,' Waite wrote. 'Customs with its large bureaucracy, steadily changing schedules of rates, stream of demands from manufacturers and importers and detailed fiscal components required such talents.'[8]

Nevertheless, Bowell's full understanding of the broader implication of what the Prime Minister had asked him to do came only after several years of experience in the job. With that understanding came the more sobering realization of the political, economic and bureaucratic pressures, obstacles and special interests that would make his job one of the most challenging in government. After more than 13 years running and guiding the department, the stress and aggravation would lead him to beg the Prime Minster of the day to move him to another, less stressful and contentious cabinet assignment. On that heady late autumn day in 1878, though, when he basked in the honour of being invited into cabinet, it is doubtful he had even an inkling of the enormity or complexity of the assignment. He was a cabinet rookie facing a formidable and pivotal challenge. As to predicting how the assignment would unfold, Bowell's preferred response when asked to anticipate what would happen in any situation was: 'The answer to that lies in the womb of the future.'

At the core of the Conservative's 1878 National Policy were short-term and long-term goals, both domestic and international. Near-term, it aimed to stimulate the faltering Canadian economy before voters passed judgment in the next election four years hence. Over the longer haul, it would build a nation north of the 49th Parallel less susceptible to Yankee domination and bullying. The policy's architects imagined that Canadian companies and workers would have more opportunity to create the goods required by the unfolding Canadian Dream if they were protected from cheaper American imports. In lockstep, aggressive immigration policies would expand the consumer base and workforce while a promised coast-to-coast railway would deliver the Canadian-made products to markets where they were needed. Cities would grow and the working class would expand, integrate and prosper.

This, at least, was the original rhetorical vision that Sir John A. Macdonald and his new government were selling in the late 1870s as the core of its interventionist domestic economic plan. Then, with the next decade featuring Opposition Liberals embracing North American free trade and closer ties to the United States as their response to Conservative protectionism, the National Policy increasingly was portrayed as foreign policy as well; a bulwark against American annexationists.

This emphasis reached its zenith in 1891 when a Conservative election poster depicted the Liberals trying to hand the keys of the National Policy edifice to Uncle Sam while Macdonald guarded the door. In his academic analysis of the policy, Hutchinson argued that the election campaign depiction of the issue 'represents the militaristic message of "protecting" the community from those who would destroy it from within or in the case of Uncle Sam, who hover menacingly outside it.'[9]

While designing, tweaking and selling the National Policy would be a government-wide effort, Bowell would be the cabinet point man and political bureaucrat in charge of trying to make it happen. In several key respects, he was well suited to the task. His experience in the newspaper business and a decade in Parliament illustrated both a strong work ethic and a talent for ferreting out the details of an issue, committing them to memory and understanding both their importance and their context. He was a meticulous researcher and a careful communicator. Verbally and on paper, his messages were clear and unambiguous, largely devoid of the vague and hedged language that peppered many missives from politicians.

While his denigrators then and now often interpreted his flashes of pride and ego as signs of underlying and counterproductive vanity and arrogance, Bowell's self-portrayal was modest rather than swaggering. By his own reckoning, he was not an original thinker or expansive visionary but a practical implementer of plans and ideas concocted by other more gifted dreamers. In the House of Commons, Bowell once told a critic who challenged the philosophical underpinning of the National Policy that the question was 'too philosophical and metaphysical for me. I admit I was not brought up in that particular school of thought and I yield the palm to him.'[10]

The Customs Minister promoted the view that he was essentially a politician-bureaucrat rather than a vision man, a characterization used by later detractors to underscore his 'ordinariness'. Bowell insisted his job was not to make or bend the laws with his own ideas and interpretations but to implement them to the letter. 'You must bear in mind that the Customs department is one of an administrative character, being compelled to carry the law as it stands upon the statute book and having no power to change it,' he told one 1882 critic of import tariff rules.[11] To another, he wrote: 'The law is imperative and I am but the instrument to enforce it.'[12]

Of course, as Customs Minister, a member of Treasury Board and a seasoned and prominent MP, Bowell had a louder voice and more opportunity than most to advocate for changes in the law but his policy proposals were cloaked in cabinet confidentiality rules. His success in portraying himself as a mere enforcer of rules made by others also served Bowell well when deflecting demands from those who expected to be listened to and accommodated. In one example, Queen's University principal Rev George Munro Grant (great-grandfather of future Liberal Party leader Michael Ignatieff) wrote to ask the minister to exempt as a 'philosophical instrument' a lathe the university wanted to import without paying duty. The minister rejected the request by falling back on his limited role: 'This department being administrative, it is impossible for me to give orders for the free admission of the lathe. That is a question exclusively for Parliament to deal with.'[13]

Mackenzie Bowell also brought several other useful character traits to his seat at the cabinet table and to the Ottawa headquarters of the Customs Department: toughness, a belief in himself and a resolute determination to complete whatever job he started. The Quebec journalist David noted these traits and wrote about them when he first profiled the new minister in the early months of his appointment. Although he wrote for Opposition newspapers with an assignment to make the Conservative government look bad, David clearly admired Bowell as a key new kid on the block in Ottawa's political power landscape of the late 1870s. 'When I saw Sir Mackenzie Bowell for the first time, his middle-sized stature was strong, solid and well-proportioned,' the then-Liberal Senator recounted decades later. With black beard and hair and a dark frock coat, he appeared 'severe and imposing,' David said, quoting from a 'pen picture' he had written all those years ago. The admiring Opposition Senator finished with a flourish. Bowell had 'a warm heart and a firm mind susceptible to great resolution and feelings of independence—he seemed to be made of iron and steel, a born fighter in war or in politics.'[14]

This combination of character traits would prove to be an essential asset in the turmoil, controversies and pressures that confronted the Customs Minister in the years ahead.

Bowell spent the better part of his first year as a new minister getting to know the ways of government and his department. He travelled from Ottawa to visit customs stations and staff across the country and when in the office, dealt with a deluge of letters and special pleadings that opened a window on the political and bureaucratic lay of the land he had inherited.

It wasn't always pretty.

During this 'learning curve' phase, he discovered the 'day-to-day realities of attempting to make the commercial policy of the government work in the face of budgetary shortfalls, administrative incompetence and the limited administrative capacity of an only semi-professional civil service,' noted Hutchinson in his 21st century analysis of the period.[15] There also were early signs he could not count on as much political and business support as he expected for the customs reforms the Conservatives had been elected to implement with business backing.

Bowell's first jolt of governing reality during the winter of 1878-79 came when Macdonald and finance minister Leonard Tilley 'discovered' they had inherited a $2M deficit from the recession-hobbled Liberals. The messaging from upper echelons of government concentrated on cutting costs across all departments. Bowell vowed to do his part despite constant pressure from departmental managers and customs collectors for more money and staff.

In a typical example, he rejected an April 1879 complaint about staff cutbacks from a departmental employee in Nova Scotia and delivered a lecture on fiscal responsibility. 'With a deficit of over $2 million this year, it has become absolutely necessary to retrench in every department of the public service,' he wrote to the complainant. 'Hence every change which will have the effect of reducing expenditure without injury to the public service must be made—a policy which every friend of the country will I am sure approve.'[16] However, by then he already knew that not every 'friend of the country' would approve the austerity measures, nor would every Conservative 'friend' support him.

He soon was composing a caustic letter to London, Ontario Conservative MP John Carling who had endorsed the government-wide austerity order only to protest the closing of a customs house in his riding. Bowell said he thought it 'strange' that while London voters and Carling had just supported the government promise of deficit fighting, 'an attempt is made to cut off the useless branches and make the men in the public service work for their salaries [and] then we have a howl about persecution.'[17]

The austerity issue led to an early parliamentary attack on Bowell's handling of the Customs department and it came from his own side of the House. Toronto Conservative MP William Little, a self-described Independent who generally supported the government, complained in April 1880 that the minister had failed to act on evidence that in the Toronto Customs office, some Liberal appointees were being paid more than recent Conservative appointments. 'I have waited more than a year for action to be taken but [Bowell] is still in dreamland,' Little complained. 'I am afraid he will never wake up.' The MP urged Macdonald to instruct his errant minister 'to act more wisely, more ably and more justly in the future.'

Bowell quickly blamed his inaction on the financial squeeze facing the government. To increase Toronto salaries as the MP suggested would cost more than $20,000.00 annually. 'I do not see my way clear to recommend to my colleagues or the House, considering the financial condition of the country, a general increase in salary which would have to be done if the question were opened.'[18] It was part of his education about problems inside the department and gaps in the support system the government had promised to provide for his difficult task. It also was an early lesson, often repeated in the future, that his was not a job destined to win him many friends on any side of the debate.

Once in office, the Customs Minister quickly began to question the competence, dedication and honesty of many of his departmental staff. At the same time, he had reason to doubt the commitment of many of his political colleagues and allegedly supportive businessmen to seeing the policy succeed. At times, they appeared more part of the problem than allies in search of a solution. Customs employees quickly pushed back against Bowell's plans to reform the department to reflect its new, more robust mandate, all the while ignoring fiscal restraint realities to demand more money and staff. At the same time, MPs from both sides of the parliamentary aisle lobbied for appointments of their friends to sometimes-unnecessary positions and often sided with smugglers from their ridings when they were caught.

Businessmen lobbied for rule-bending and less strident enforcement even while praising the tariff protection they received. Barely a year into the new National Policy regime, Charlottetown merchants petitioned to complain that more stringent enforcement of customs rules was causing them inconvenience and losses. Mayor W. E. Dawson accused Bowell of being 'disrespectful' of business owners trying to make a living.[19]

The most immediate and persistent problem facing Bowell was the steady flow of applications for new appointments and workforce expansion even as the government slashed spending and staff rosters already were beyond full. As the government's largest department, many job seekers or their political friends saw the customs department as a potential patronage heaven waiting to be entered. Sometimes, the minister expressed his frustration over the heavy flow of applications and patronage requests through sarcastic humour. In response to a plea that he find a government job in Napanee, Ontario for a former Belleville resident, the minister wrote (with underline for emphasis) that he would be happy to help 'if it were in my power but the fact is we have about nine hundred and ninety nine and a half applications for every position in the gift of the government.'[20]

Still, demands from Customs office managers for new staff hires continued to pile up and Bowell concluded many were not being strictly honest or factual in justifying their requests. He suspected they saw the inexperienced minister as a rubber stamp for departmental demands. By September 1879, after less than a year on the job, Bowell decided to send a clear message that the former days of lax oversight and weak central control were over. A new, tough, no-nonsense minister was in charge and Montreal customs collector N. B. Simpson was the unfortunate employee on the receiving end of the ministerial declaration of war.

The minister already had flagged the Montreal office as a trouble spot; a big spending, under-performing office where there were allegations of staff malfeasance and collusion with importers who bent the rules.[21] Therefore, when Simpson wrote to the minister September 2 asking for more staff, his timing could not have been worse. It did not help his cause that he offered gratuitous advice on how other staff could be dismissed without 'injury to the service.' Bowell took offence, recalling that weeks after his appointment to cabinet, the Montreal collector had sent an ingratiating letter to the new minister bragging about how well the amply staffed office was performing. Now, there was a different message and the result was a scathing six-page hand-written letter to Simpson September 9. The sudden request for new staff less than nine months after the rosy report 'seems strange to me,' Bowell wrote, since the earlier letter had boasted of an additional 41 office positions since 1873, 'and this to collect some million and a half dollars less than was collected in 1873.'

The minister then took aim at his collector's advice that while more should be spent on additional staff that he 'needed', money could be saved by dismissing lower-paid staff and reducing wages for labourers.[22] Bowell's response was a no-holds-barred message to the bureaucracy that a new, firm hand was in charge. The message likely spread, as intended, through departmental bureaucracy.

Bowell employed the same no-nonsense approach when dealing with another perennial departmental employee problem he encountered throughout his years as minister: public servants unable to do their jobs because of alcohol abuse. In his decisions on issues of intoxication on the job, there was no hint it was a reflection of Bowell's personal tendency to abstinence. Rather, it offended his idea—likely ingrained in him as an employer—that honest people had a duty to perform the tasks they were paid to do efficiently and competently.

Sometimes when reports about inebriated departmental staff were received, the minister showed compassion if it involved a man supporting a family. Customs office managers occasionally were told to be lenient on first (and sometimes even second) offence but with the clear message to the employees that they were on probation and under scrutiny. Even so, during an era in which government jobs were considered plum prizes because they paid relatively well and offered security, Bowell had little patience with those who repeatedly jeopardized them by showing up for work drunk.

While it was a scenario repeated hundreds of times over the years as recorded in archival records, an 1889 refusal to offer leniency to a long-time Montreal customs collector impaired by booze illustrated Bowell's hard line on the issue. The head of the Montreal Customs office pleaded to be allowed to offer an early retirement package to the offending employee because of the man's many years of service. The minister refused, noting that the employee was younger than 60 and therefore ineligible for pension under the rules. No exception would or should be made. 'His incapacity [was] brought about by his own conduct,' Bowell wrote. 'You will readily understand when an officer renders himself unfit for his duties by his irregular habits, that to treat him as you suggest would look like rewarding his conduct.'[23]

As in hundreds of other examples like it, case closed.

By the end of his first year in the portfolio, Bowell also was voicing his frustration about another unpleasant and irritating reality of the job, a situation that would plague him throughout his 13-year tenure. The evidence was clear that cheating the customs system was aided and abetted by otherwise law-abiding and decent members of the public, departmental staff and sympathetic MPs who supported the National Policy in theory but undermined it in practice. Politicians who campaigned on promises to strengthen the system in fact were complicit in perpetuating its weaknesses.

In a letter to a sympathetic Conservative MP, Bowell vowed that during his tenure at Customs he would do what he could to change the culture of the department and the attitude of public and political tolerance for the law-breakers. 'I am aware that the decisions of the department in the past have been of a very lenient character,' he wrote. 'While I have no desire to be overzealous or harsh in the administration of the law, I am determined to put a stop to smuggling as much as possible—My short ministerial life has taught me that every dodge that human cunning can devise is resorted to cheat the revenue.'

A major problem in the past was that ministers usually acquiesced when political pressure was applied to have seized goods returned to the smuggler.[24] This minister, he assured the MP on the receiving end of the lecture, would be a different kind of department head. 'I flatter myself I have stamina of character sufficient to resist this,' he boasted. 'Hence I have been less yielding to political friends than to others whenever I believed them coming. False invoices and dodging of all kinds have become so numerous that I am losing my faith in men generally.'

If there was an issue that haunted Bowell during his years as Minister of Customs—that irritated him, that enraged him—it was the prevalence of customs fraud. He thought tolerance of the widely practiced form of tax avoidance illustrated hypocrisy among Canadians, the business community and sympathetic political enablers. While the majority of voters supported tougher customs import rules through four elections, they apparently expected the old smuggling system to continue as it had existed since well before Confederation, the product of what would later be called the world's longest undefended border.

Even in the Hasting County area when Bowell was growing up, smuggling across Lake Ontario had been a feature of the economy. For the minister, it seemed personal. The issue of general tolerance or even acceptance of smuggling as part of the game seemed to resonate with him on a level deeper than simple anger over loss of needed revenues or even that so many people took a casual, tolerant attitude to law breaking. For Bowell, it was an issue of honesty and morality. Smugglers were cheaters, pure and simple.

He took a dim view of businessmen who smuggled or benefitted by buying cheaper smuggled goods and when caught, defended themselves by touting their position of respect in the community. He took a dimmer view of those who defended the cheats. 'It is remarkable that we have never yet had a case of smuggling brought to our notice in which the smugglers were not represented to be the most "respectable" men in the vicinity in which they live,' he raged in late 1879 in a letter to a Conservative MP who had protested a charge against a constituent.[25]

To another Conservative MP, he lectured: 'In this case as in all others, the smuggler never intended to do anything wrong when caught but when not caught, in no instance do they ever think of voluntarily going to the Customs house to make entries. It is only when caught that they become honest.'[26] Smugglers often had friends in high places. 'I need scarcely tell you that one of the great difficulties in carrying out the provisions of the Customs

Act is that when a man is detected in smuggling, no matter to what party he belongs, his friends plead that he may be let off, threatening all sorts of troubles political or otherwise if their requests be not complied with,' he complained to a New Brunswick acquaintance.[27]

Once, in response to a plea from a New Brunswick MP to go easy on a constituent smuggler, Bowell answered by recounting a meeting he had with a southwest Ontario MP and some of his constituents. The MP told his supporters: 'This is the Minister of Customs to whom half my time is devoted to urging the appointment of people to prevent smuggling along the frontier and the other half in praying and begging to have the smugglers let off when caught.'[28]

Sometimes, the offenders themselves occupied high places in the community, raising Bowell's ire even more. When the Customs Minister received a letter from a magistrate in nearby Morrisburg, Ontario asking that the department drop a smuggling charge against him, Bowell reacted with indignity. Someone 'occupying your position socially' and employed to 'protect the laws of the country from infraction' should know better, rendering the 'crime of smuggling greater.' The minister noted that the judge was a repeat offender. 'I cannot believe the law was enacted alone for the illiterate and the poor,' he fumed in a long and angry letter. 'Such men are often led into crime from want and penury [but] the educated and well-to-do have no such excuse and therefore should be the more severely punished when they break the law.'[29] Then, to a Conservative MP asking leniency for the respected magistrate, Bowell curtly said he planned to do the opposite. 'I am going for every "religiously" respectable and gentlemanly smuggler that I can catch.'

Through the years that he held the Customs portfolio, the pressure to make exceptions for people with impeccable character references was constant from across the country and every strata of society: clergy wanting a customs break on supplies; Ontario Lieutenant-Governor J. B. Robinson seeking an exemption from wine import tariffs; prosperous businessmen who couldn't resist the temptation to make a few extra dollars in profit; and women who crossed the border feigning pregnancy to explain the bulk they carried from wearing layers of smuggled clothes.

The pleas for leniency were constant and sometimes involved businesses that have become Canadian icons. In 1883, St. Stephen, New Brunswick chocolate maker James Ganong (a founder of Ganong Bros Limited, billed in 2018 as 'Canada's oldest candy maker') complained that while they were guilty of smuggling and had been charged, others in the border town were getting away with it. Bowell refused to drop the charge but promised to crack down on the others.[30]

Then there was a demand from Montreal Cotton Co president and well-connected Tory A. F. Gault that the company be granted a reprieve from a smuggling fine in recognition of his party loyalty. Bowell stood his ground:

> I have never allowed party considerations to sway me in the administration of the customs law which was placed on the statute book for the protection of all classes of the community and should the time arrive when it has to be administered upon any other principle, the liberties of the people will cease to be protected.[31]

With the unrelenting flow of pleas from party supporters for special consideration and simultaneous accusations from Liberal newspapers that Bowell was guilty of favouring Tory friends, family and Orangemen when hiring, his years at Customs were high-pressure and wearing. Yet there also were rewards including the repeated judgment of voters at election time that implementation of the National Policy deserved their support. Then in 1887, there was some objective evidence that Bowell's efforts to rein in smuggling were paying off.

On January 1, 1883, he had taken the much-criticized step of creating within the department a Special Agent's Branch based in Montreal to investigate and bring to justice those alleged to be undermining implementation of the National Policy protectionism. It was a controversial step with critics complaining about another government attack on the businessmen of the country. The minister, therefore, might have allowed himself a small smile of satisfaction and accomplishment five years later when a 129-page independent assessment presented to the department reported significant progress in suppressing smuggling. It credited Bowell.

The investigation 'demonstrated fully the wisdom of the suggestion of the Honourable the Minister of Customs that a Special Agent's Branch should be created, the first and principal duty of which would be to attend to the "detection and prevention of frauds upon the revenue",' the report concluded. 'Cadres of actual smuggling for trade purposes are now becoming rarer because the risk attending it has become much greater since there has been organized a persistent effort for its suppression.'[32]

Bowell also could take some solace from the fact that, despite years of broadsides from his political, press and business critics, his own integrity and honesty in the administration of the customs system and the department generally was not under challenge. Bowell didn't like cheaters and no credible evidence was produced that he succumbed to the temptation to gain personal advantage through his years in business, politics or government.

Even his most fierce critics did not accuse him of applying a double standard, with the major exception of assertions by opposition newspapers that paternal influence was involved in helping a son of Bowell's to enjoy a successful career in the Customs Department. That issue will be explored in Chapter 9.

In his private affairs, Bowell was scrupulous about avoiding even the appearance of conflict of interest or rule breaking. In late 1889, for example, the minister returned six pairs of gloves sent to him by a Toronto business-man in appreciation of a successful business relationship with the depart-ment. 'I lay it down as a Principle never to accept presents of great or small value from those who have business transactions with the department,' Bowell wrote when returning the gift.[33]

Nor would he manipulate the tariff system to benefit friends or family. John Thompson, justice minister in cabinet with Bowell, could attest to his friend's insistence on playing by the rules. When some Roman Catholic Church officials in Halifax wanted Thompson to help them import statues without paying duties, he told them to forget it because Bowell insisted that not even the customs minister, never mind the justice minister, was exempt from the law. To support his point, Thompson recounted an anecdote about Bowell's refusal to turn a blind eye to the tariff rules, even for his wife: 'I know of his paying duty on some dresses for his wife a short time ago.'[34]

His personal reputation for probity may have injected some moral authority into his regular rebukes to defenders of smugglers that 'because he is your friend doesn't make the crime any less serious' or 'the crime of smuggling is in being caught.'[35]

As the first Minister of Customs in the National Policy era, Mackenzie Bowell created the template for how a strong and 'by the book' minister should run the department and try to protect the country against smugglers and customs fraud, even if the perpetrators were allies. It took the next generation of ethically challenged Canadian politicians to illustrate how the customs and tariff system Bowell helped create could be corrupted.

In the mid-1920s, explosive Parliament Hill hearings into allegations of corruption under Liberal Customs Minister Jacques Bureau in the first William Lyon Mackenzie King government (1921–25), produced damning conclusions. In his acclaimed 1952 biography of Mackenzie King, Bruce Hutchison summarized the findings:

> Officials were guilty of condoning and assisting a ring of smugglers from coast to coast. The government, on Bureau's advice, had modified or quashed the sentence of criminals convicted in the courts. Liberal hangers-on were fattening on contraband, mostly liquor, which flowed in swelling cataract north and south across the American border.[36]

The contrast with Bowell's record of upright honesty in office could not have been more pronounced. However, his success in dealing with patronage pressures was decidedly more mixed.

In the Canadian political system of the late 19th century, orchestrating patronage appointments was a key responsibility for senior political figures like Bowell. It was a part of his job description that inspired mixed and ambivalent feelings. A sampling of quotes from the minister, instructions from Sir John A. Macdonald on the topic, and a modern-day harsh appraisal of Bowell's performance on the patronage issue by a leading academic critic, illustrate the complexity and judgment-prone nature of the file:

- 'Experience has proved to me that patronage is not only a nuisance but the curse of any government and it would be well if we were rid of it.' Customs Minister Mackenzie Bowell, December 14, 1885.[37]
- 'It is this patronage for unimportant offices that does more to demoralize a party than greater questions.' Bowell, December 15, 1888.[38]
- 'My Dear Bowell, listen to our friends.' Scrawled on a letter forwarded by Sir John A. Macdonald from Charles Tupper, complaining that Bowell had not filled an open patronage position in Pictou, Nova Scotia.[39]
- Bowell was 'an expert on patronage' whose motto was: 'you consult your friends when anything is to be done.' Dalhousie University historian P. B. Waite.[40]

If the audacity of smugglers, their widespread acceptance by society and their support from well-placed 'friends' who pleaded for leniency was what drove the moralistic Bowell to clean up the system, the constant pressure on him to make Conservative-friendly patronage appointments wore him down. Staffing was an important and complicated responsibility for the Customs Minister. His response to it also was complex and often contradictory. Sometimes he played the partisan with party interests in mind but often, he insisted on rising above politics to ensure a competent workforce to implement the government's centerpiece legislation.

As the man in charge of the largest federal department, employing hundreds who were very visible in their often-small communities, Bowell had an obligation when vacancies arose to fill positions with people who could make the protectionist tariff system work. He also had to be mindful of party pressure to make appointments that were politically helpful when possible. It was a difficult balancing act with Bowell sometimes rising to the occasion and sometimes not.

Clearly, the minister was not immune to party interests in hiring. Early in his tenure, he wrote to a political friend about being lobbied from both sides of the political divide over who should be given a sensitive Customs position: 'It would never do to give it to a Grit or Rouge unless there is not a man of our party in the Dominion fit for the position.'[41]

Ironically, in the context of the time, the addition of the requirement that the successful candidate had to be 'fit for the position' actually was a step toward creating a professional public service. The previous Liberal government had dismissed hundreds of Conservative appointees after taking power in 1873, competent or not, replacing them with Liberals looking for work. Bowell insisted competence rather than party would the primary qualification for appointment although in the case of two equally qualified candidates, the Tory had the inside track.

There certainly were appointment incidents during his tenure in which party considerations surfaced in response to pressure from partisans. In one 1888 incident, in fact, the minister clearly crossed the line. He lobbied his son John, customs collector in Vancouver, to consider Belleville-area Conservative H. H. Boyce for a job in the Vancouver office. 'If Boyce is a good man, I should like for our friends in the Northumberland to have him appointed,' he wrote. 'You will understand that my object in placing Boyce would be political. See what you can do in the matter.' The decision, though, was John's and in the end, he chose another candidate.[42] Still, by the standards of the era and government hiring practices at federal, provincial and municipal levels, Bowell significantly shifted the emphasis from political hires to competence. He made clear in many responses to pleas for appointments that simply being Tory, Orange, Protestant or a friend was not sufficient credential.

He refused demands from some partisans to follow the Liberal example by purging Liberal appointees from the public payroll, sensibly arguing that ultimately, Conservatives would be the big losers once government changed hands again because most of the employees inherited by the next regime would be Tories vulnerable to dismissal. He complained that the patronage system created more party dissatisfaction than gratitude because for every Conservative who received an appointment, many others who thought themselves worthy but denied were angry and discontented. The 'expert on patronage', as Waite described him, strongly supported a system of removing most government staffing decisions from partisan consideration.

He was an advocate of the 1882 Civil Service Act establishing a rigorous test for government job applicants and once it was the law, quickly used it to rebuff an attempt by Macdonald to win appointment of a party friend in Stratford, Ontario. Bowell informed the leader that his favoured candidate had not passed the exam, adding an underline for emphasis: 'You will see in one of the subjects absolutely necessary for bookkeeping, Daly scored a duck's egg,' he wrote. 'What I want is a really clever, active man to go into the office.'[43]

In the midst of the constant pressure for patronage appointments, the minister occasionally may even have enjoyed a chuckle over being able to say 'no.' When Postmaster General John Carling wrote to ask for an appointment to a rural Ontario Customs office for 'a good friend of ours,' Bowell scrawled on the letter to be returned that it would not be possible: 'No Surveyor of Customs is required at Clifton, the office having been abolished some four years ago.'[44]

Still, the constant flow of demands for jobs or pressure from party insiders to provide them to party friends was a grinding, irritating and troublesome aspect of cabinet duties for Bowell. It figured prominently in his growing discontent with his position in government.

In late 1889, Mackenzie Bowell needed a break from the pressures and politics of Ottawa. His idea of an escape was to head west for a month-long journey across the southern Prairies from Winnipeg to Lethbridge, including 'a buck board drive of over 800 miles' that led to 'a severe cold that has been troubling me for days.'[45] He was 66 years old and feeling his age after more than a decade in the demanding Customs portfolio that received little public respect or praise and much demand for favours.

Although well compensated for his work as a senior cabinet minister ($7,000.00 annually plus $1,000.00 in Commons sessional payments, according to the 1889 Auditor General's report), he was tired of the workload, the pressure and the lack of public appreciation for his effort to curtail illegal import practices in the Canadian economy. A report to government on the success of the department in combatting smuggling summarized the problem: constant newspaper coverage of complaints from importers, smugglers, businessmen and supportive politicians about tough Customs rules gave the general public a negative opinion about the department. The result was 'a large number of honest and well-intentioned persons who from an insufficient knowledge of the points at issue are led to believe that not [only] is the Canadian customs law harsh and exceptional in its severity but its administration unjust and oppressive,' said the report authors.[46]

Bowell also had grown disillusioned and cynical about the demands of political life. In 1889 after receiving a request from an MP who wanted help in getting a complaining constituent off his back, the minister replied wearily: 'You may well say that "politicians are made to be bled" and I suppose that applies to ministers as well. Sir John once said: "That is what they are for".'[47]

To make matters worse for his mood, the Macdonald government decided in 1888 that all ministers would be ordered to cut spending in their departments. Bowell had been through that a decade before when he assumed leadership of the Customs department. He clearly did not relish a repeat of spending restraint and the resistance it would provoke inside government.

By 1890, Mackenzie Bowell was musing to friends about asking to be moved to a new cabinet position and department or possibly even retiring from politics. A tough election campaign loomed and reports from the Hastings

North constituency were not positive. Cabinet duties had limited his time in the riding in recent years and political divisions over religious questions had aroused and divided the voters yet again. His already sour mood likely darkened in late November, 1890 when he received a letter from his long-time friend and cabinet colleague Sir Joseph-Adolphe Chapleau asking for a meeting to discuss a complaint he had received about Bowell's 'competence.' Later that afternoon, a second letter arrived from Chapleau and Bowell could permit himself a smile: '*Question de notre competence*' means a question which comes within your jurisdiction when well-translated into English,' a sheepish Chapleau wrote. 'It makes a fool of the man who so translated it. With humble apologies.'

In the end, with the government about to embark on a tough re-election campaign and Macdonald growing frail, Bowell decided that loyalty to his leader demanded he should stand again. The issue of a transfer could be raised after the election. After both Bowell and the Macdonald government were re-elected with reduced majorities in 1891, he agreed to remain in the portfolio while still hoping for an early change of scenery. However, Macdonald's death in June of that year threw the government into uncertainty and left Bowell still occupying the Customs cabinet chair after John Abbott became prime minister. His quiet lobbying for a change of portfolio intensified. He was desperate to leave and he let Prime Minister Abbott know.

By the end of the year, Bowell had received prime ministerial signals that his lobby campaign would bear fruit. He had been appointed acting Minister of Railways and Canals by Abbott while still in charge of Customs, but privately was predicting he soon would lose both responsibilities. 'I may tell you frankly I do not think I shall remain in railways and it is possible I may not remain in Customs,' he wrote to a friend in late 1891.[48]

On January 25, 1892, Bowell got his wish when Abbott shuffled his cabinet, sending him to the Department of Militia and Defence. Lieut Col Mackenzie Bowell now was in charge of the military and he couldn't have been happier. 'I can assure you that I feel relieved,' he wrote to Sir Leonard Tilley. 'The War Department will I doubt not be much more peaceful than the Customs. True, volunteers are a little exacting in their demands but they are not to be compared to the army of smugglers, dishonest importers and other violators of the customs law. The change was at my request as I insisted on being relieved.'[49]

To a London general responsible for militia forces in the colonies he wrote: 'To be frank with you, I thought 13 years was long enough for one man to be battling with smugglers, dishonest importers and not the least troublesome, Members of Parliament who are ever trying to get such offenders off.'[50] But he was not quite free of the Customs Department yet. Because his replacement, Joseph-Adolphe Chapleau, was ill, Bowell kept the department as well as railways and canals for several more months.

In parting, he offered some gratuitous advice about what his successor would face and an epitaph for his own time in the department. To a Manitoba MP who had sent congratulations, Bowell wrote: 'I can assure you that a man who does his duty as Minister of Customs has not a bed of roses and I found by experience that there is only one thing to do and that is to know neither friend nor foe in administering the law. If the minister draws a distinction, he gets himself into hot water at once.'[51] They were words of wisdom learned in the trenches.

He soon would find the militia department came with its own brand of politics and lobbying but for the moment, he was free of the smugglers, their political friends and enablers. Yet as time passed, Bowell clearly looked back on his years implementing the National Policy as a success story despite all the aggravations it produced. He had overseen a transformation of Canadian thinking about protectionism, embedding the concept in the political landscape.

Even the free trade-promoting Liberals were not immune once they assumed power. Years later as Opposition Conservative Leader in the Senate, the former Minister of Customs was prone to needle Liberals as free traders in opposition and protectionists in government. During debate on the Liberal Throne Speech opening the 1901 parliamentary session, Bowell gently chided Liberal Senator Lyman Jones of Toronto, the former general manager of the farm machinery manufacturer Massey-Harris, who had seconded the Throne Speech motion and whose company had benefitted from tariff protection. He was 'a Liberal of the old school, of free trade opinions but of strong protectionist ideas,' the old Tory protectionist warrior said with a smile. 'I congratulate the present government on not having interfered with the protective policy of the old government so as not to materially interfere with the progress and advancement of that particular industry as well as with others.'[52]

Point made. Pride of accomplishment was on display.

NOTES

[1] https://www.cpac.ca/en/programs/prime-ministers/

[2] Debates of the Senate, 13th Parliament, 1st Session (March 2, 1918), 41.

[3] Sanders Memoir Kayser Fonds. (Peterborough, Ontario: Trent University Archives).

[4] Hutchinson, Braden, *The Greater Half of the Continent: Continentalism and the Canadian State in Ontario 1878–1896* (Carleton University, Ottawa: Department of History MA Thesis, 2008).

[5] ibid, 61.

[6] ibid, 63.

[7] LAC, Mackenzie Bowell Papers, Vol. 25 (Letter April 18, 1883).

[8] Waite, P. B., 'Bowell, Sir Mackenzie,' *Dictionary of Canadian Biography* Vol. XIV, 1911–1920. (Toronto: University of Toronto Press, 1998).

[9] op cit, *The Greater Half of the Continent.*

[10] Debates of the House of Commons, 6th Parliament 1st Session. (June 18, 1887).

[11] LAC Bowell Papers Vol. 23 (November 24, 1882 letter to S. G. Tattersall of Nairn, Ontario).

[12] ibid, Vol. 27 (July 27, 1883 letter to Quebec MP Robert Hall who was seeking a waiver of the tariff on imported granite for a riding church project).

[13] ibid, Vol. 23 (December 7, 1882 letter to Grant).

[14] Debates of the Senate, 13th Parliament, 1st Session. (March 2, 1918), 40–41.

[15] op cit, *The Greater Half of the Continent.*, 57.

[16] LAC Bowell Papers Vol. 16 (April 18, 1879 letter).

[17] ibid (May 18, 1879 letter to John Carling).

[18] House of Commons Debates, 4th Parliament 2nd Session Vol 2 (April 14, 1880).

[19] LAC Bowell Papers Vol. 1 (January 1880 letter from Charlottetown, Prince Edward Island Mayor W. E. Dawson).

[20] ibid, Vol. 23 (November 27, 1882 letter to Alex Henry of Napanee, Ontario).

[21] The Montreal office was not unique as a perceived problem. Bowell had just ordered an investigation of customs officers throughout the system to ascertain their honesty and productivity. There had been allegations of corruption and inappropriate behaviour, including 'turning a blind eye' to smuggling. 'Many must be very nervous,' he wrote a friend.

[22] LAC Bowell Papers, Vol. 16 (September 9, 1879 letter to N. B. Simpson).

[23] ibid Vol. 55 (November 26 1889 letter).

[24] LAC Bowell Papers, Vol. 16 (September 8, 1879 letter).

[25] ibid, Vol. 17 (December 12, 1879 letter).

[26] ibid, (November 29, 1879 letter).

[27] ibid, Vol. 81 (June 6, 1884 letter to Hon. T. R. Jones of Saint John, New Brunswick).

[28] ibid, Vol. 79 (February 3, 1883 letter to MP John Boyd of Saint John, New Brunswick).

[29] ibid, Vol. 18 (October 29, 1880 letter to Morrisburg Judge McDonald and October 23 letter to Cornwall, Ontario Conservative MP Darby Bergin).

[30] ibid, Vol. 25 (July 5 and July 1883 letters to James Ganong).

[31] ibid, Vol. 48 (August 4, 1888 letter to A. F. Gault).

[32] ibid, Vol. 6 (September 25, 1887 report to Customs deputy minister James Johnson).

[33] ibid, Vol. 55 (October 24, 1889 letter).

[34] Waite, P. B., *The Man from Halifax: Sir John Thompson, Prime Minister* (Toronto: University of Toronto Press, 1985), 470–471.

[35] LAC Bowell Papers, Vol. 52 (Letter to A. W. McLelan. April 29, 1889).

[36] Hutchison, Bruce, *The Incredible Canadian. A Candid Portrait of Mackenzie King* (Don Mills, Ontario: Longmans Canada Ltd., 1952), 107.

[37] LAC Bowell Papers, Vol. 84 (December 14, 1885 letter to a Newcastle, New Brunswick Conservative supporter lobbying for an appointment).

[38] ibid, Vol. 48 (December 15, 1888 letter to S. M. Conger of Picton, Ontario).

[39] ibid, Vol. 3 (June 14, 1884 letter).

[40] op cit, *The Man from Halifax*, 149, 260.

[41] LAC Bowell Papers, Vol. 17 (November 20, 1879 letter).

[42] ibid, Vol. 87 (January 18, 1888 letter to John Bowell).

[43] ibid, Vol. 189 (July 18, 1884 letter to Sir John A. Macdonald).

[44] ibid, Vol. 2 (July 13, 1882 letter from John Carling).

[45] ibid, Vol. 55 (October 12, 1889 letter to the Hudson's Bay Commissioner).

[46] ibid, Vol. 6 (September 1887 independent report to Customs deputy minister James Johnson).

[47] ibid, Vol. 54 (August 6, 1889 letter to Welland, Ontario MP John Ferguson).

[48] ibid, Vol. 66 (December 10, 1891 letter to Hon C. C. Colby of London, England).

[49] ibid, Vol. 68 (February 2, 1892 letter to Sir Leonard Tilley).

[50] ibid, Vol. 92 (March 8, 1892 letter to Gen Laurie in London).

[51] ibid, Vol. 68 (February 1, 1892 letter to Brandon MP Mayne Daly).

[52] Senate Debates 1st Session, 9th Parliament Vol. 1 (February 11, 1901), 14.

Chapter 9
FAMILY TIES

A s is true for many who live largely in the public eye, the decade of the
1880s imposed a special burden that required Mackenzie Bowell to lead
a complicated double life. On the surface, in the newspapers and on public
stages, he was Minister of Customs, one of the prominent faces of the new
and activist government. He was consumed through endless long workdays
by the formidable task of learning to run a large bureaucracy while
implementing the government's signature economic and social protectionist
tariff policy. At the same time and below the surface of that public persona,
he also was a family man forced to navigate through turbulent times; a
husband and father for whom the decade was a continuous and tumultuous saga
filled with drama, grief, joy, responsibility and change.

The drama, grief and loss reached its peak through the winter and spring
of 1883 to '84. In a May 8, 1884 letter to an old friend who recently had lost
his wife, Bowell confided his pain and sadness at recently becoming a
widower:

> It is only now that I can appreciate and enter into your feelings and
> can well understand the loneliness you feel. It is indeed hard at our
> age to be parted from one with whom we have spent the larger
> portion of our lives in which the battles and strife for existence and
> position are encountered. I feel as you do that I am alone in the
> world and were it not for the fact that I have children to look after,
> I do not know what I should do.[1]

On that Thursday spring day, Bowell was in deep mourning over the
death of Harriet, his wife of 36 years. She had died more than a month earlier
in the Los Angeles area, where she was staying on doctor's advice in an
attempt to recuperate from lung disease. Much of the ensuing month had
been a blur of dealing with the aftermath of her death including transporting
her body to Belleville for burial. In a letter to a friend who had written
condolences, the 60-year-old new widower was putting his raw emotions and
desolation on paper for one of the first times.

Over more than three decades together, Mackenzie and Harriet had
raised five children (four others died young) and she had been the family
anchor while her husband rose to prominence as a businessman, leading
Orangeman and successful politician. His feeling of loss would linger for
years. A decade later, the trauma of Harriet's death—the 'affliction'—was
still a reference point for Bowell. 'Let one who has had to undergo the same

ordeal in the loss of a dear wife after 36 years of married life extend his sincere sympathy to you in your affliction,' he wrote to a Halifax friend grieving a spousal death in 1894.[2] Harriet's decline had been a sad, traumatic and expensive two-year spiral that involved medical care with lung specialists in Montreal, extended stays with their son John in Winnipeg in hopes that the dry Prairie air would help and, finally, the last-ditch, unsuccessful stay in southern California warmth. In late 1883, as her condition worsened and in the midst of confusion as Bowell tried to decide the best solution for her treatment—a winter in the southern California climate seemed like the best bet, but that option was complicated by her insistence that he abandon his government duties to stay with her—another family loss occurred.

In the last week of October, Bowell's 84-year-old father John died at his home in Tweed north of Belleville. Bowell rushed to his father's house to make funeral arrangements and to bury the man who had brought him to Canada. Unlike the emotions he would display after losing Harriet, Bowell was sanguine about his father's death and life. 'We may expect a similar fate should we live to the age of 84 or 85, which let me trust will be your case,' he wrote to a friend.[3] To another, he reported: 'Fortunately he did not suffer much pain. The sands of life having run down, he quietly passed away.'

In fact, little is known about the relationship between father and son. Although he didn't mention him often in speeches or private correspondence, late in life Bowell praised his father John for his gutsy decision to leave England in search of a better life for his family. In Belleville, the carpenter had built a furniture-making business. Bowell also recalled that as a 13-year-old, he watched his father support the authorities against the 1837 rebellion in Upper Canada led by Reformer William Lyon Mackenzie. It is not clear if John Bowell took up arms to support the Family Compact that governed the colony or 'rendered service' in other ways.

After his father's funeral, Bowell raced back to Belleville to complete arrangements for Harriet to travel south. In the end, he compromised on the issue of whether to accompany his wife to California. For a month, he abandoned Minister of Customs obligations to take Harriet, son Charles, daughter Eva and a granddaughter to a cottage south of Los Angeles. Christmas day 1883 was spent with the family 'walking about the lawn in summer clothing with straw hats and parasols while I was gathering oranges in the orchard,' he reported when he returned to Canada alone in early January. 'I hope the change will do Harriet some good though I frankly tell you I think her lungs are very much diseased.'[4]

On April 1, 1884, Bowell received a telegram in Ottawa from Charles reporting that Harriet was bleeding from a lung hemorrhage. He began to make plans for an emergency trip south to be with her but she died the next day at age 56 without her husband by her side. The planned rail trip to be with Harriet became a sad journey to bring her body home and it was a long and harrowing trip from Los Angeles. 'I was delayed eight or 10 days by washouts and landslides but reached home on Sunday last [April 27] with the family and the remains of my poor wife,' he reported.[5] Son John travelled from Winnipeg to meet the family in Chicago for the last leg of the trip.

The *Intelligencer* recorded that Harriet was transported in a metallic casket with a glass window to display her face. The Belleville funeral procession included 87 carriages or horse-drawn 'rigs' viewed by hundreds of mourners and the curious. She was buried in the Belleville cemetery where her husband would join her 33 years later.[6]

Mackenzie Bowell was back at his Minister of Customs desk in Ottawa within days of the funeral but his new status as 'single father' for his children and grandchildren required some lifestyle changes even though his 'kids' were adults. Only the youngest, Charles, was still a teenager. In Ottawa, he moved out of his longtime suite of rooms at the Russell House Hotel a block from Parliament Hill to rent a house where his daughter Eva and a granddaughter could stay with him. Within months, Bowell was complaining that his landlady was imposing new restrictions including taking away the piano he had arranged for his family guests.

In late November, he moved back to his rooms at the Russell House with family in tow. In preparation for Christmas in Belleville, he rented a one-horse open sleigh for the family use over the holiday. In the years following Harriet's death, Bowell organized family travel holidays to help fill the void of her loss. In August 1884, there was a boat trip holiday through the Gulf of St. Lawrence and up the Saguenay River with daughter Eva, son Charley and several grandchildren as part of the group. The next year, he used a Grand Trunk Railway pass to take family to Prince Edward Island, although he eventually left the others on their own in to spend several working weeks, touring East Coast lighthouses and Customs Department offices.[7]

The most extensive family adventure was organized in 1887 when he and two daughters spent more than three months with two other friends traveling through the British Isles, France, Switzerland, Germany and Belgium. On his return, Bowell joked to his old friend Sir Leonard Tilley that he had learned his lesson spending that much time traveling with four females. 'You will know that I had quite enough on my hands and I have made a solemn vow not to be caught in such a trap again!' he wrote. 'Still, I am all the better for the outing.'[8]

Along with the big expenses and major trips for children and grandchildren, Bowell's 'single dad' activities also included small gestures: paying a granddaughter's tuition to Ontario Ladies' College in Whitby, sending $7.00 to a Toronto merchant 'to cover the price of feathers sent to the Misses Bowell' and sending copies of the book *Wee Willie Winkie* to granddaughters 'Miss Hattie Bowell' in Vancouver and 'Miss Lucy Holton' of Belleville in February 1894. He also lobbied a senior Canadian Pacific Railway official in Toronto to hire a grandson.

For several years in the 1880s after Harriet died, Bowell's youngest daughter Evalyn (Eva) acted as his Ottawa hostess. She had lived in the Belleville family home until her mother died and then spent some time in Ottawa with her father before marrying and moving away. By the early 1900s, she was back in Belleville as a single mom with a daughter. Dad still looked out for her. On August 4, 1905, Bowell signed his William Street Belleville family home property over to Evalyn 'in consideration of natural love and affection' and one dollar.[9] He signed the document '*Mackenzie Bowell*' in the flowing handwriting he reserved for special private family letters. His usual signature was a cramped, small 'M. Bowell'.

In a bizarre postscript to the story of Mackenzie Bowell's life and extended period of mourning for Harriet, two eastern Ontario Liberal newspapers reported that in the late summer of 1888—just four years after her death—he had proposed marriage to Napanee widow Mercy Stevenson. Bowell was 64 and she was close to a quarter-century younger. A late August Church of England wedding date was set and then a week before the event, Bowell sent a letter to call the whole thing off, according to the stories. Napanee and Trenton newspapers reported that his children had opposed the marriage and a son-in-law was sent to Napanee to gather presumably negative information about the prospective bride. The only public information source about the aborted wedding plan came in the opposition press at the time of the alleged whirlwind romance and there is not a single reference to the affair in Bowell's archived private papers. The Belleville *Intelligencer* carried not a word.

There is not even evidence that Bowell's political opponents raised the issue, although they rarely missed an opportunity to try to get under his skin in partisan debates and speeches.[10]

By 1891, after almost a decade of closer involvement in the lives of his children and grandchildren, Bowell was back to spending most of his time in Ottawa by himself, immersed in his demanding cabinet jobs and preparations for the pending March 5 federal election. He clearly was nostalgic, though, about his years as an active 'single dad.' In early January, he wistful wrote to an old Hastings County friend that he wished there was time to travel back for a visit 'and [to] have a chat about old times. As we grow older, our families become scattered... In this respect, I am worse off than yourself, not having one of my children around me. Four of them are married—two in Belleville, one in Vancouver and one in Cleveland, Ohio. Youngest boy is in Tacoma, Washington Territory.'[11] Still, the resumption of a more work-focused, solitary routine in Ottawa may have afforded him some solace as a return to the familiar.

He was back in surroundings he had occupied on and off for years, back to a predictable routine and occupying Room 61 at the Russell House that was the capital's most elegant and important political entertainment venue and hotel. The building filled most of a block in downtown Ottawa, a short walk from his ministerial office in Parliament Hill's West Block. The Russell filled the space between modern-day Sparks Street and Queen Street, extending east into what is now Confederation Square in downtown Ottawa that is the site of the National War Memorial. Bowell had a suite of rooms to call home, ate there most days, held meetings and used it as his off-Parliament Hill office.

The Russell House was Ottawa's most prestigious and politically important private space and institution during the half century after Confederation. It was home away from home for MPs, cabinet ministers, Supreme Court judges, leading parliamentary reporters, visiting officials, lobbyists and entertainers. Guests included the famous and controversial such as Irish poet and playwright Oscar Wilde in 1882 and most of the political luminaries of the day.[12]

Canadian labour movement icon, political activist and Senator Eugene Forsey recalled that his Ottawa insider grandparents who raised him in the early years of the 20th century were Russell House regulars when he was a child. In a memoire, he offered a glimpse of the venue: 'The family loved the theatre and seldom missed seeing at the Russell the great British actors and actresses whom the Governor General brought to Ottawa.'[13] A 1967 McGill University Master's thesis on the Russell House called it the 'social annex' of Parliament and noted that in 1877, renowned travel writer Peter O'Leary described it as 'one of the largest and best hotels in North America… and one which compares favourably with those in the United Kingdom.'[14] It was located close to Ottawa's central railway station and the confluence of the Ottawa River and Rideau Canal that carried passenger boats ferrying visitors to the capital. 'For many years from Confederation to its demise in the 1920s, the Russell House was the social centre of Ottawa.'[15]

An advertisement for the Russell published in the 1898 to '99 edition of the Parliamentary Guide touted it as the place to stay in Ottawa for anyone craving the centre of the action. 'This famous hotel is situated in the heart of the city and is the best headquarters from which to visit the many attractions of Canada's capital. Newly refitted and furnished with the handsomest and most modern style. Patronized by the most eminent people, within three minute's walk of the Parliament Buildings.' It was where high-profile social gatherings and holiday balls were held, where the Parliamentary Press Gallery held meetings and the political class staged celebrations for departing members of the exclusive club.

The Russell also staged non-political events that made history. On March 18, 1892 at a lavish dinner in the banquet room, Governor General Lord

Stanley of Preston unveiled the silver cup that since 1894 has been awarded to the top Canadian (now North American) hockey team: the Stanley Cup. As a Russell resident and a senior cabinet minister, if Bowell was in town, he likely attended the Governor General's banquet and unveiling ceremony.

Mainly, though, on a day-to-day basis it was the site of political imbibing, planning, plotting, gossip and intrigue. In 1875, visitors Thomas and Anne Brassy sang its praises and noted its drawbacks. 'It is a fine large hotel with very comfortable accommodations but fearfully noisy,' they reported. 'The boat leaves at 5 a.m. and the train at half past seven so everybody in the House is aroused lest there be passengers for either.'

In a 1984 book about the 'private life' of the Canadian capital in its early decades, Sandra Gwyn wrote: 'The Russell, like the legendary Willard's in Washington, was much more than a hotel. It was the capital's great meeting place and central promenade.' A Quebec journalist wrote in the 1880s that it was 'a little city within a city... all the world passes by. Would you like to meet the big and little people of politics and journalism? Go to the Russell.' Gwyn reported that the hotel housed Wilfrid Laurier during his early years as an MP before becoming Liberal leader and prime minister. Future Prime Minister Robert Borden also took a room when elected a Nova Scotia MP.

Most importantly, though, it was where political players gathered after hours. 'The Russell functioned as an extension of government. Into the famous Hotel Bar at the back of the lobby just off to the right flocked MPs, Senators, job hunters and lobbyists to be swallowed up instantly in a cloud of blue cigar smoke.'[16]

However, for the semi-permanent occupant of Room 61, that would not have been the main Russell experience or attraction. Teetotaler Bowell saw it mainly as a place to read, work and sleep, although liquor was readily available for visitors who wanted it. When friends, government officials or other politicians wanted to see him off Parliament Hill, the Russell was where he directed them. 'It is difficult for me to name an hour at which you could see me,' he wrote in a note to a Department of Agriculture official seeking a meeting. 'When I am in Ottawa, I generally spend the evenings in my room at the Russell.'[17]

It would be the hub of meetings with supporters several years later when his prime minister's tenure was under siege. The anti-Bowell plotters also used it as a convenient meeting place close to Parliament Hill. Even so, Bowell's life at the Russell wasn't entirely consumed by work and meetings. In an 1894 newspaper profile of the then-trade and commerce minister, an Ottawa reporter wrote that the minister occasionally 'indulged in a quiet game of backgammon in his parlor at the Russell in the evening but not until he has looked over his correspondence and he believes his day's work to be over. He flatters himself that he plays a pretty good game and thoroughly enjoys to win. If he is beaten, well he wants another game to recover lost ground.'[18]

For some time, Bowell also had a roommate and companion living with him at the Russell. As a sign of his status as a regular hotel resident and part of the Russell 'family,' he was allowed to cohabit with a very noisy pet. In late October 1890, a Canadian government agent in Liverpool, England sent him a talkative parrot. On November 3, Bowell wrote to the sender that the parrot had arrived safely. 'The bird arrived in good condition and was as talkative as could be required. He woke me this morning whistling and barking and when I asked what he wanted, replied: "wake up". Since then, he has done an indefinite amount of jabbering.'[19]

He did not mention how his Russell House neighbours reacted to the sudden, and relatively constant, racket next door.

While Harriet during her life was the glue that held the Bowell family together, kept the home and fussed over the offspring—particularly her daughters—Mackenzie also was deeply involved in the family throughout his life as a guardian and promoter of the financial and career affairs of his sons and sons-in-law. In many ways, he was a financial backer, always watching to make sure that his sons John and Charles were successful and that the men his daughters married were able to support their wives and his grandchildren. While much of his protective and supportive work was meant to be a private affair, these family interactions sometimes made their way into Bowell's public life, occasionally as a liability to his political reputation.

He faced Opposition charges of nepotism for his role in supporting and influencing eldest son John's career in the Customs Department where father was the political boss. Son-in-law James Jamieson was a constant drain on Bowell's bank account and patience, at one point dragging Bowell into an unnecessary and messy political controversy over a Prairie land speculation scheme. Youngest son Charles was a source of worry—fragile, sickly and accident prone—whose father ended up making sure 'Charley' had some work stability through the family newspaper business.

Son-in-law Charles Holton was a successful businessman and generally not an employment worry or financial drain for Bowell (although even he occasionally called upon Bowell for a financial advance or some mortgage payment help) but he was a *Liberal*, a fact his father-in-law often noted, sometimes with humour. Still, despite the political divide, Holton generally did not figure in Bowell family affairs complications. As for the rest, Bowell's family life and entanglements were complicated and sometimes frustrating.

John Bowell

When Customs Minister Bowell first 'heard' that his eldest son John had been hired on as a surveyor in the Winnipeg Customs department office in 1882 (age 26), he wrote a private note to his son's new boss: 'Am glad to learn that

John has got into the harness and hope he may prove useful to you.'[20] It was widely assumed that the minister played a role in his son's entry into the public service and Bowell biographer Betsy Boyce wrote as much, reporting that Bowell Sr 'sent John to Winnipeg as customs officer.'[21]

Yet less than a year later, when some ambitious departmental official presumably thought it would be a good career move to promote the minister's son within the bureaucracy, the father/minister said he was less than enthused about the idea and not happy John was an employee of his department. 'I do not think it would be advisable to make the appointment,' he wrote. 'He is already in the service, contrary to my wishes.'[22]

There is no evidence in the Bowell archival papers one way or the other on the issue of whether father helped son get a secure, well-paying public service job. However, it would not have been the first time Mackenzie helped John find a job. Out of school, he first started working in Belleville at the Bowell-owned *Intelligencer* newspaper. Then, when Bowell Sr was elevated to cabinet and the customs portfolio in 1878 to '79, he quickly brought John to Ottawa as the minister's secretary and unofficial tour guide of Parliament Hill for visitors to the capital from the riding. The next stop on his career path was the move to Winnipeg and a job in his father's department.

Bowell critics in the opposition press certainly advanced the assumption that family favouriteism was at work. The Liberal-supporting *Ontario* newspaper noted his $1800.00 salary and the prospect for advancement before opining in print: 'Mr. John Bowell must have been born under a lucky star. At any rate, he has been a lucky boy [since] his appointment to and promotion in the public service of the government cannot be ascribed to any special qualifications for such offices for we all know John to have been an ordinary lad.' It finished the homily with the sarcastic wish that Bowell Sr soon would have found positions for all his relatives since other ministers 'want a chance to do something for their friends. But is all this business nepotism? It looks like such a thing.'[23] A Winnipeg Liberal sympathizer wrote that on the bright side, John's promotion to customs collector did not appear to have required the firing of another employee 'to make room for him, as happened when he was first appointed.'

Whether or not nepotism was at play in securing John's foothold in the government workforce, during the following years Bowell Sr definitely acted behind the scenes to help his son, who was not just any employee. By 1887, John was facing an 'uncomfortable' situation in the Winnipeg office (his ties to the minister may have been part of the issue) and Bowell wrote a Winnipeg friend that he was looking for a way to find a different location for his son. 'As the place has been made so uncomfortable, when an opportunity presents, I think I shall move him.'[24] An opening soon appeared in Vancouver and John was transferred to spend the rest of his public service career as customs collector in the largest West Coast depart-mental office.

While there is no indication John Bowell was less than a competent senior departmental official throughout his long career, his father did help over the years. The help included teaching his son how to separate private and work-related messaging. At one point, he reminded John that when sending a dispatch to the department, address the minister formally. Save the more familiar greeting for private letters between father and son! In early 1891, Bowell saw a report filed by John on a customs seizure in Vancouver. The Minister of Customs thought it contained inappropriate information including the name of the informer who helped expose the smuggling. The father gave the son a chance to rewrite the report for the official record to avoid censure or uncomfortable questions about the custom collector's competence. 'I return the report and would suggest that you destroy it and substitute a new one in the terms I have indicated,' he wrote.[25]

As the *Ontario* newspaper insinuated, John Bowell received help along the way from an influential benefactor. His Liberal critics didn't know the half of it.

Charles Bowell

Youngest son 'Charley' apparently was not cut out for a career in the public service, whether his father ran a department or not. However, his father's newspaper was a fallback employment option throughout his life. He worked there as a young man and later served as president of the *Intelligencer* business for a number of years. He relinquished the position back to his father in 1906 when Bowell Sr decided at age 82 to assume full control again after stepping down as Conservative Leader in the Senate. He remained a Senator but by then, apparently considered it no longer a fulltime job.

Early on, the father had tried to equip his youngest son with a good education by paying his tuition to attend Bishop's College School in Lennoxville, Quebec but he dropped out in April 1885 before completing his year.[26] Within weeks, Bowell included his youngest son on an expenses-paid family trip to Prince Edward Island. Later, Charley moved to Montreal to take a job in the hardware business but in early 1887 he fell ill and had to leave work. A Montreal Conservative MP took him under his wing and Bowell Sr was grateful and uneasy about his son's strength. 'I think it would be well for Charley not to return to work until he has fully recovered for fear of relapse,' the worried father wrote in March. 'Accept my thanks for your kindness in looking after him.'[27] Eventually, he sent his sickly son on an expensive sojourn to the warmth of Bermuda to try to rebuild his strength and health.[28]

Illness and mishaps were the story of Charley's life that unfolded in his father's fretful private letters. By early 1894, Bowell the son had moved to Toronto and shortly after arrival, a street trolley struck him as he crossed the tracks, damaging his foot and ankle. The rest of the year was a blur of hospitals, operations, recuperation, worry and expense for the father. When he sent a cheque to S. W. McMichael who had been caring for the injured young man, Bowell added a note: 'I have again to thank you for your kindness and attention to that unfortunate boy of mine.'

Bowell travelled to Toronto to visit his son but seeing his condition, left despondent without making himself known to the suffering patient. 'I found the boy very weak and I question whether he will ever be able to do anything.'[29] In early March, he wrote to a Customs Department official in Toronto to arrange a delay in a planned ankle operation so Bowell could travel from Ottawa to be there. By mid-April he had heard from Dr B. E. McKenzie that the operation went well. 'I am glad to learn there is every probability of a successful result,' a relieved Bowell replied.[30] But the ordeal was not finished. At the end of May, Charley's Toronto landlord informed is father that the rent was due. Although protesting that he was not responsible for the debt, he agreed to pay.

In mid-June came another problem. Dr McKenzie reported that Charley was resisting a scheduled follow-up foot operation because he was afraid of chloroform and insisted his father approve the procedure before it was performed. It was Bowell's turn to sound frustrated over a grown man needing daddy's approval because he was afraid of an anesthetic. 'I cannot understand why Charley should want my approval of a thing I know nothing about,' he responded to McKenzie. 'You are the best judge of the effects of chloroform, of which he seems to have such horror.'[31] Bowell then told his 27-year-old adult son he had to have the operation.

The fallout was that Charley fell silent through the summer, ending communication with his father, perhaps in a sulk because Bowell Sr had decided not to bring him to Ottawa to recuperate as Charley wanted. By October 1, a desperate Bowell wrote to the doctor asking for a progress report because he had no information on his son's condition. 'Kindly let me know occasionally how the foot is getting on. The unfortunate boy is suffering a good deal and is likely to suffer for some time to come.' Charley eventually healed enough to be somewhat mobile although with the disability, his job prospects likely were diminished.

Not long after, his father decided Charley should be brought closer to home where a family job and some stability could be found. He came back to Belleville to take over the operation of the *Intelligencer*, running the family business until dad had time to take charge again. Charles died at age 54 in 1921, fewer than four years after his father.

J. C. Jamieson

If Bowell's relationship with his youngest son was one of worry, frustration and protectiveness, his experience with son-in-law Jim Jamieson was much more complicated and irritating. 'Jimmie' was married to Bowell's oldest daughter Louise and was father to four Bowell grandchildren (two of whom died young) so the father-in-law was determined to help ensure that Jamieson was financially stable enough to care for his family. The vehicle for that help was the *Intelligencer* newspaper where Jamieson held a job for a quarter century that included years of running the operation when Bowell was a cabinet minister in Ottawa.

Given Bowell's self-identification with journalism and attachment to the Belleville newspaper he had been immersed in since age 10, the *Intelligencer* connection became a bonding bridge between the two men, in addition to their shared love of Louise. Over the years, they exchanged letters about newspaper affairs and Bowell offered 'advice' on news stories and editorials. They purchased Belleville-area land together and they also shared a political allegiance to the Conservative Party.

On the business and financial side of the relationship, though, Jamieson was trouble. He was usually in debt, regularly did not keep up with debt payments, drove Bowell's beloved newspaper deeply into the red and was a regular drain on the Bowell bank account as he bailed his son-in-law out of financial jams and debts to keep him solvent, the newspaper alive and the family secure. Bowell correspondence with Jamieson is riddled with details of his decisions to pay his son-in-law debts and to meet loan repayment obligations over the years. In 1887, he paid $5,000.00 to buy some land from Jamieson to stabilize his finances and he also was vouching for advances his son-in-law was receiving from the Canada Permanent Loan and Savings Co. of Toronto as well as paying the interest on the debt.[32]

The following year, he was sending cheques for hundreds of dollars to cover *Intelligencer* rent and payments due on Jamieson loans with the Hastings Loan and Investment Co. Bowell was on the board of the loan company and several times was in the embarrassing position of writing on behalf of the company to tell Jamieson debt obligations were in arrears. During an October 1888 meeting between the two, it was evident that the newspaper was heavily in debt, almost half of it owing to Bowell. In a none-too-subtle hint, Jamieson said if the debt was paid or forgiven, the newspaper could break even. Bowell later told a Belleville friend in a candid letter that he had directly challenged the claim. 'I replied that it would be the first time he had made anything pay—that he had been a failure ever since he commenced business, which he knew to be true though he may have thought I was rubbing him hard. He added he had made money enough but spent it in other ways. This, of course, is confidential.'[33]

Nonetheless, Bowell appears to have forgiven the debt owing him. The constant need to supplement Jamieson's income clearly was a drain on the father-in-law's personal finances and in late 1888 he was forced to refuse a friend's request for help because, he explained, he was low in liquid assets. 'When I reached Belleville, I found I had to provide some $3,000.00 for business matters of which I was not aware,' he wrote in a clear allusion to Jamieson's request that he contribute to 'retiring' *Intelligencer* debt.[34] By early January 1893, Bowell met with Jamieson to demand a review of his finances. He returned to Ottawa with the paperwork and wrote his son-in-law to note that he was close to $1,500.00 behind in his rent for the newspaper building and his bookkeeping accounts were a mess. 'Since my return, I have been looking over your statement of account and let me hope that all your book accounts are not kept in the same manner.'[35]

By the end of February, Bowell had reached his tolerance limit with Jamieson's slipshod financial affairs. When Belleville businessman R. S. Bell wrote to complain that the *Intelligencer* had cancelled an account with his company, Bowell replied that it was the result of the newspaper's precarious financial situation. 'I see little chance of the debts of the establishment being paid off if it is run in the future as it has been in the past,' he confessed. While he would like to help his friend, he did not see his way clear to suggest more costs for the newspaper. 'As you are aware, I have altogether too much in that establishment now without getting even interest or dividends and therefore would not like to interfere in the way of increasing the expenditure.'[36]

By then, Jamieson had years of experience receiving regular financial assistance from his wife's father, even as he played the role of prominent businessman in Belleville. During an 1886 parliamentary debate, Bowell made what must have been a humiliating admission about family finances; for years he had been lending money to keep Jamieson's family financially afloat, 'an accommodation and assistance which he has received from me, to a greater or less extent as he might require it, for the past 10 or 12 years.'[37] For decades, Bowell was forced to act as a 19th century version of an ATM for his spendthrift, business challenged son-in-law.

In 1897 when 53-year-old Jamieson and his family left Belleville to emigrate to the United States where he launched an advertising business in St. Paul, Minnesota, Mackenzie Bowell must have had mixed feelings. Losing regular personal contact with daughter Louise and grandsons James and Mackenzie would have been a bitter pill but he likely was content to see his son-in-law finally out of the family business, opening a management position for son Charley, another family charity.

He also may have reminisced about a better time, the month-long trip he took to British Columbia several years before with Louise and her two sons along for the holiday. It was a break for her from the financial worries the family constantly experienced in her husband's handling of the newspaper enterprise he had been handed by her father.

On the political side, Jamieson had a knack for getting into situations that gave Bowell's political enemies ammunition to use against him. In particular, the Liberal Toronto *Globe* delighted in running stories or insinuations about Jamieson's use of his connection to the influential Customs Minister to extract favours from the government or the political system. A month before the February 22, 1887 federal election, for instance, the *Globe* published the names of allegedly well-connected Conservatives who had received timber rights on government-owned land. Jamieson's name was on the 'Boodle Brigade' list.[38]

A year earlier, the partisan newspaper had published some doggerel verse called 'Son-in-Law Jamieson's Song' after Jimmy had said that while Bowell did not have an interest in a controversial company associated with Jamieson, 'he had an interest in me.' The 'poem' included verses such as:

I'm the boy who's at Ottawa's back stairs
Do you want a friend in state affairs?
For a timber limit or a company
Son-in-law Jamieson come and see
I'll take blind shares or a salary
For a minister takes an interest in me![39]

The verse contained allusions to what was arguably the most embarrassing and potentially damaging political controversy visited upon Mackenzie Bowell by his association with J. C. Jamieson: the Prince Albert Colonization Company affair that came to a parliamentary head in Spring of 1886. Its genesis dated back to an 1874 decision by the recently elected Alexander Mackenzie Liberal government to amend the 1872 Land Act, allowing creation of 'colonization' land companies that would promote Prairie agricultural development. They were authorized to acquire Crown-owned Prairie land and then sell it to prospective settlers attracted by promises of fertile land, transportation links to markets and profits from food production on the flat and largely treeless prairie soil.

'The system of granting large tracts of land in the West to the government's favoured groups promised to create overnight fortunes to the new owners, the colonization companies,' according to an analysis of the land colonization program published in 1987 by the Métis–owned, Saskatoon-based Gabriel Dumont Institute of Native Studies and Applied Research. 'Land received for a dollar an acre could be sold at a profit to immigrants who, it was hoped, would flock to the West by the thousands.'[40] The scheme had several obvious problems. In many areas of the Prairies, the 'unoccupied' land being sold to the companies actually had been settled, occupied and farmed by Métis and indigenous families for years. In addition, many of the government land transfers were made to well-connected friends of the government who cashed in on the land colonization scheme. It became an efficient way to enrich Tory supporters. Enter the Prince Albert Colonization

Co. (PACC), created in 1882 and run by a board of directors that included a who's-who of well-connected Tories: MP John White from Hastings East, the riding beside Bowell, Quebec MP Thomas McGreevy with ties to Public Works minister Hector Langevin, friends and relatives of MPs and J. C. Jamieson, the Customs Minister's son-in-law. On June 1, 1882, the Department of the Interior entered an agreement to sell to the PACC 51,200 acres of land, much of it north of the growing community of Prince Albert that was in the running to become the territorial capital. Some of the ceded land stretched around the Métis community of Batoche.[41]

The directors were able to buy company shares and as a PACC trustee, Jamieson gave sworn statements and signed affidavits about the company to present to government officials. Although fulltime *Intelligencer* publisher at the time, he received a PACC salary and shares in a blind trust as well. The Dumont Institute analysis author Don McLean wrote:

> These [the PACC directors] were the people who were in a position to influence Sir John A. Macdonald and others in the Department of Interior. Indeed, through this influence the Métis people living on this tract of land were later denied title to the lands they occupied... The activities of the Prince Albert Colonization Co did much to create tension between the Métis and the federal government... It was this denial [of land ownership] more than any other single factor that put the Métis at the forefront of armed resistance to the National Policy of the federal government in the West.'[42]

The Liberals and their newspapers quickly picked up on that point in the aftermath of the bloody Batoche-centred Northwest Rebellion of 1885 that led to scores of deaths and the execution of Louis Riel. When it became known that Jamieson, after selling his shares, had transferred some money to his father-in-law, Bowell quickly was drawn into the allegation of complicity in causing the bloody rebellion as an alleged beneficiary of the scheme. On April 5, 1886, Ontario Liberal MP James Edgar tabled a motion calling for a parliamentary investigation and implicated Bowell in the affair. Bowell rose to dramatically endorse the motion for an inquiry as a way to clear his name. He denied any involvement in the land company, professed no knowledge of its workings and insisted there was no collusion with Jamieson nor compensation connected to the PACC. Edgar countered that 'the affair was conducted with the knowledge of the Hon. Mackenzie Bowell, then and now the member for North Hastings and minister of Customs, the father-in-law and associate in business of the said [Jamieson] and Mr. Bowell was consulted during its progress.' He said when Jamieson sold his blind shares, Bowell received a $500.00 cut, which led Bowell to counter that Jamieson simply was repaying money he perpetually owed his father-in-law.[43]

The issue was referred to the Commons Committee on Privileges and

Elections, which met in private, heard from the involved players and produced a report on May 18, 1886 which never was printed, produced no record of proceedings and never was discussed again in Parliament or in public. Even the *Globe* fell mute on the issue. A mutually agreed-upon cone of political silence descended over the affair. Clearly, the committee exonerated Bowell of any involvement or a guilty verdict would have led to his forced resignation or at least continued political criticism. Bowell did not brag about his exoneration and is never recorded as having mentioned the issue again, including during the 1887 election campaign where his constituents spoke by giving him the biggest electoral majority of his career.

There is no archived mention of the sorry affair in subsequent Bowell letters to Jamieson, who ended up suing the company for not honouring all its payment obligations to him. But the criticism and insinuations about Bowell complicity and profiteering must have wounded, embarrassed and offended him. After all, he was a politician who prided himself on being arrow straight in his conduct of public and private affairs.

Luther H. Holton

There was one other extended family entanglement that Mackenzie Bowell likely would happily have avoided if possible. When daughter Caroline married her Belleville sweetheart Charles Holton in 1872, she inherited as part of her new family her husband's Quebec uncle Luther Holton, one of Bowell's fierce political tormentors as a Quebec Liberal MP.

In the Parliamentary forum, rookie Conservative MP Bowell first crossed swords with Liberal MP Holton in mid-April 1871 during the first Parliament of the new Dominion of Canada. As often would be the case in subsequent years as the two men clashed repeatedly, the issue was contentious religious divisions and Louis Riel. On that Wednesday morning after Easter, backbench MP Bowell raged at prominent Ontario Liberal MP Edward Blake for what he considered political hypocrisy over waffling on the fallout from the Red River Rebellion of 1869. Holton rose to demand that the Speaker call the Tory MP to order for his language and what he considered the irrelevance of Bowell's diatribe.

An adversarial political relationship was born.

Three years later when the Commons debated a Bowell motion to expel newly-elected Manitoba MP Riel for his role in approving the execution of Hastings County Orangeman Thomas Scott during the rebellion, Holton rose to propose that the issue be set aside until the root causes of the Manitoba rebellion were established. He was not buying Bowell's Orange outrage or grievance. Later, when a strong parliamentary majority sided with Bowell and approved the Riel expulsion motion, Holton stood against it and during the next half decade, the two locked horns many times over many issues debated on the floor of the House. The two MPs could hardly have been different. Bowell was the son of an English immigrant, believed in the British Empire, protectionism, the Canadian Confederation bargain and Canada. He was a staunch Conservative and Orangeman. He carried the conservative small-town values of his Belleville upbringing and was a skeptic about American designs on the northern half of the continent. Holton was born in rural Upper Canada but raised by a prosperous merchant uncle in metropolitan Montreal. He was a cosmopolitan, a wealthy businessman and a son of American immigrants who as a young politician flirted with supporting union with the United States. He was an early skeptic of the terms of Confederation (although an advocate of association between English Upper Canada and French Lower Canada) and a supporter of free trade with the Americans. He was a Liberal, an anti-cleric, a Louis Riel defender and an advocate for amnesty for the Métis leader despite his leadership of an armed uprising against Canadian forces.

Luther Holton was a constant and acerbic critic of Bowell's protectionist stance and, in the early days of the National Policy, his management of the Customs department. Given their radically different perspectives, a political clash between the two in the small hothouse of Canadian Parliamentary politics seemed inevitable and natural. However, in the 13 years Bowell and Holton were hostile parliamentary adversaries, there is no evidence in writing or in the recorded parliamentary exchanges that the familial connection ever was noted. Luther sometimes visited family in the Belleville area over the years but there is no record of contact with his nephew's father-in-law. In fact, the Bowell-Holton political feud actually survived into the next generation. After Luther died in Ottawa in 1880 at age 62, his lawyer son Edward claimed his father's Chateauguay riding near Montreal and continued the campaign against Bowell's management of the protective tariff system.

In April 1886, Edward Holton triggered a parliamentary debate by moving a motion that the Customs Act be changed to 'relieve the honest importer from the danger of oppression.' He alleged that under the minister, customs officers were raking in thousands of dollars in fees charged to importers while treating importer businessmen badly.[44] After a daylong debate, Bowell spoke well into the night to refute almost all of Holton's charges, throwing in a bit of personal invective to boot. 'I do not say it offensively or intend it that way but his whole speech would come very well from one who was employed to defend all the smugglers and violators of the law in the country,' he said of his daughter's cousin by marriage.[45]

For Mackenzie Bowell the family man, recognizing the extended family connection to his Liberal Holton tormentors clearly would be taking the idea of 'family' too far.

NOTES

[1] LAC Bowell Papers Vol. 81. (May 8, 1884 letter to Thomas Allen), 451.

[2] ibid, Vol. 96 (May 9, 1894 letter to Charles Creed).

[3] ibid, Vol. 81 (November 5, 1883 letter to Ed Willis of Saint John, New Brunswick).

[4] ibid (January 5, 1884 letter).

[5] ibid (May 2, 1884 letter to Van Norman).

[6] Community Archives of Belleville and Hastings County (Scrapbook No. 5, 35).

[7] LAC Bowell Papers Vol. 83 (August 20, 1885 letter to Manitoba Lieutenant Governor J. C. Aikins).

[8] ibid, Vol. 87 (October 20, 1887 letter to Tilley).

[9] The deed and property transfer agreement are housed in the Barry Wilson Collection of prime ministerial memorabilia, signatures and documents that is part of the Carleton University Library and Archives Collection in Ottawa. https://arc.library.carleton.ca

[10] The story is recounted briefly in Boyce, *The Accidental Prime Minister*, 216–217.

[11] LAC Bowell Papers Vol. 61 (January 14, 1891 letter to W. D. Ketcheson of Wallbridge).

[12] Gwyn, Sandra, *The Private Capital* (Toronto: McClelland and Stewart Ltd., 1984), 257.

[13] Forsey, Eugene, *A Life on the Fringe* (Toronto: Oxford University Press, 1991), 9.

[14] Steiner, George P., *The Russell House: Social Annex of the House of Commons* (1967). Unpublished Master's Thesis for the McGill University School of Architecture (Montreal: McGill University Rare Books Collection) 2.

[15] ibid, 1.

[16] op cit, *The Private Capital*, 398.

[17] LAC Bowell Papers Vol. 67 (February 1, 1892 note to Alice Robertson).

[18] ibid, Vol. 103 (August 27, 1894 St. John, New Brunswick *Record*).

[19] ibid, Vol. 60 (November 30, 1890 letter to John Dyke, Liverpool, England).

[20] ibid, Vol. 79 (September 20, 1882 letter to Winnipeg customs collector).

[21] Boyce, Betsy D., *The Accidental Prime Minister* (Ameliasburgh, Ontario: Seventh Town Historical Society, 2001), 180.

[22] LAC Bowell Papers, Vol. 80 (April 21, 1883 letter).

[23] ibid, Vol. 124 (August 29, 1883 article in *The Ontario*).

[24] ibid, Vol. 80 (March 19, 1887 letter to Stewart Mulvey).

[25] ibid, Vol. 61 (January 31, 1891 letter from Mackenzie Bowell to son John).

[26] ibid, Vol. 83.

[27] ibid, Vol. 86 (March 8, 1887 letter), 185.

[28] ibid, Vol. 89 (February 5, 1889 letter from Mackenzie Bowell to the Hastings Loan and Investment Co. regarding his dwindling savings in company stock), 105.

[29] ibid, Vol. 95 (January 17, 1894 letter to S. W. McMichael of Toronto who had been looking after Charlie).

[30] ibid (April 10, 1894 letter to Dr B. E. McKenzie) 348.

[31] ibid, Vol. 97 (June 19, 1894 letter to Dr McKenzie).

[32] ibid, Vol. 87 (November 19, 1887 letter to J. C. Jamieson), 21.

[33] ibid, Vol. 88 (October 6, 1888 letter to Thomas Wills).

[34] ibid, (Oct. 24, 1888 letter to H. J. Jarman of L'Amable, Ontario)

[35] ibid, Vol. 93 (January 23, 1893 letter to Jamieson).

[36] ibid, 429–430.

[37] House of Commons Debates, 4th Session, 5 Parliament (April 5, 1886), 488.

[38] LAC Bowell Papers Vol. 124 (January 15, 1887 *Globe* newspaper clipping).

[39] *The Globe*, Vol. XLII, No. 278 (November 20, 1885).

[40] McLean, Don, *Fifty Historical Vignettes: Views of the Common People* (Saskatoon: Gabriel Dumont Institute, 1987), 121.

[41] LAC (June 7, 1882 Department of the Interior document T-12538, Vol. 272, file 42507), 8034.

[42] op cit, *Fifty Historical Vignettes*, 122–123.

[43] House of Commons debates, 4th Session, 5th Parliament Vol. 1 (Monday, April 5, 1886), 486–489.

[44] ibid (April 16, 1886).

[45] LAC microfilm collection of Customs Administration documents (F CC-4 No. 02527 NL) *Speech of the Hon. Mackenzie Bowell, Minister of Customs* (Ottawa: Queen's Printer, 1889).

Chapter 10
'MINISTER OF WAR'

Although Mackenzie Bowell's official January 25, 1892 assignment from Prime Minister John Abbott was to become Minister of Militia and Defence, the former proud volunteer soldier preferred a more dramatic title. 'You will no doubt have heard that I have left the guerilla warfare against smugglers and for a time, will be rusticating in the more peaceful position of Minister of War,' he wrote to a friend at the beginning of February.[1] In fact, Bowell did not officially take over the position until Undersecretary of State L. A. Catellier signed the Great Seal proclamation about the cabinet appointment on February 9. The new minister did not receive it in the mail until February 17 but already, the word was out and letters of congratulations were pouring in as well as invitations to visit drill halls and militia units across the country.

Volunteer troops on the ground clearly were thrilled to have as their new political leader a man who had shown interest and attachment to militia matters through all his adult life. He had volunteered a quarter century before when the Fenian raids were a border threat, had organized militia units in Belleville and used his first House of Commons speech after being elected in 1867 to take on then-militia minister George-E. Cartier during a middle-of-the-night speech in defence of militia volunteers.

For his part, Bowell clearly felt at home and comfortable in his new position. Finally, proudly using his militia rank title of Lieutenant Colonel seemed appropriate and not just pretentious. He was among his people, joking with one old soldier who wrote to say he would be willing to fight again under the new minister: 'My soldiering did not begin so early as yours but I can only hope that when I reach your age, I may be as able and willing as you are now to shoulder a musket in case of need.'[2] Bowell had recently turned 67 and muskets had long ceased being the firearm of choice.

In truth, the Militia and Defence ministry was not a major assignment in the Canadian government. It dealt with policies affecting thousands of volunteer militiamen across the country but in case of a military threat, Great Britain and its professional soldiers—light on the ground as they were in Canada—would be the first line of defence. Even so, the Canadian government took seriously its obligation to contribute to the nation's defence through a trained and properly funded militia force. Inevitably, the new minister inherited unresolved issues that required his attention and many of them would have an echo from his days in Customs.

There were pressures from friends or political colleagues for appointments or promotions within the military that Bowell resisted as he worked to reduce the costs of an over-abundance of officers. An April 1892 request from a Cobourg, Ontario officer for a promotion to Brigadier General triggered a familiar Bowell hardline response:

> You are aware that in the Customs department, I laid it down as a principle not to appoint men to positions whose services were not required and I propose to act on the same principle in the Militia Department. 'I think a moment's reflection will convince you that the throwing away of money on an unnecessarily large staff is not in the interests of the force... I prefer to expend what can be spared on the force generally.[3]

To Sir Leonard Tilley, who lobbied his old cabinet confidante to make good on a promise from the previous minister to promote the son of a friend in New Brunswick, Bowell wrote: 'I find that in this department as in others, the promises which have been made are sufficiently numerous to fill all the vacancies for a few years.'[4] Even the vexing issue of the influence religious affiliation can have on government appointments followed the minister from Customs to the Militia ministry. After Ontario Provincial Secretary J. M. Gibson urged Bowell to consider a promotion for a Major who allegedly was passed over earlier because he was Roman Catholic, he replied: 'I suppose it is fair to argue that if Sir Adolphe Caron [the predecessor minister] gave an undue favour to an Orangeman, it would only be balancing the beam if I gave an R.C. the same consideration.'[5]

Then, Bowell quickly made clear he found odious the mixing of staffing and religious questions. 'The question of religion should not be considered in promotions in the militia—every British subject standing on an equality in that respect and that as all, irrespective of creed or nationality, are expected to defend their country in time of need, all should be treated alike.'

The minister was more ambiguous and less sanctimonious about the role political allegiance could play in assessing the merits of candidates for military jobs. An attitude carried with him from his days in Customs was that while hiring and promotion should be based on ability to do the job, being a Conservative could be an asset when choosing between two qualified candidates. 'While I recognize the fact that political considerations should not prevail in military appointments, I am inclined to believe that our friends, other things being equal, should have the preference.'[6] Still, he showed little tolerance for attempts by politicians to interfere in military decisions. When an officer was ordered transferred from London, Ontario to Fredericton, New Brunswick as part of routine forces reshuffling, the affected soldier organized a political lobby to try to have the transfer cancelled and recruited London Conservative MP Joseph Marshall to the cause. The MP urged Bowell to over-ride the order and the minister was not impressed. 'As a soldier, you know your first duty is to obey orders and it does not look well for a Captain of a permanent corps to be finding fault when ordered to march,' he replied. 'His conduct in this particular is directly contrary to the Queen's regulations... The discipline and management of the Forces is exclusively in the hands of the General [and] hence it would be injudicious and improper for me to interfere.'[7]

Bowell also had no time for militiamen who supported Canadian annexation by the United States. He said they should be removed from the service. 'The sooner we snuff this kind of thing out, the better.'[8] On a less vexing issue—the role of bicycles in the armed forces—Bowell showed himself to be open to new ideas even if senior military officers were opposed. When a Toronto Captain proposed the formation of a bicycle militia unit in late 1892, the minister did not dismiss the idea despite a grumpy rebuff from a Major General. 'This is a matter which may receive consideration in the future,' the minister replied.[9]

Of course, not all the files that landed on the new Militia Minister's desk were as off-the-wall as soldiers bicycling to defend the country. The portfolio brought with it some serious unresolved issues to confront.

Bowell quickly discovered morale problems among the soldiers and issues with the performance of the existing military leadership. In many militia units, he wrote to a disgruntled member of the 30th Battalion in mid-1892, 'the work is being done by the second or third in command and the Colonel [is] taking the credit. I have spoken to the General on the subject and you may rest assured that action will be taken at an early day.'[10] He also championed the recruitment of younger men to the militia. During an April 1892 House of Commons speech defending the government against Liberal accusations that the Conservatives did not show the forces sufficient support, he said his goal was to promote a youth movement. 'There are some to my own knowledge [who] have been in the force continuously since the rebellion of 1837 but these are an exception to the rule,' he said. 'While I do not care to see smaller boys in the force, I like to see younger men enter it and remain in it for some years until they become sufficiently acquainted with the service to be useful in case their services should be required.'[11]

During the summer of 1892, Bowell also managed to resolve a military policy irritant that had been festering between Canada and Great Britain for more than three years over repairs to the dockyard at Esquimalt, British Columbia, the only British Royal Navy facility on the West Coast between the Arctic and the Antarctic. Britain was unhappy with the facility and in 1889, offered a plan to upgrade it. Britain would station a garrison of marines there and install more powerful and modern armaments for the fort if Canada would pay for the troops and the upgrade. The Macdonald government had let the issue slide, insisting that earlier Canadian investment in an 1878 battery and the stationing of a company of gunners in 1887 was sufficient. The British were not amused and increased the pressure for Canadian action.

Once installed as minister in charge, Bowell went to work to find a resolution. He travelled to Esquimalt during the summer and worked out a deal that would see Canada and Great Britain split the costs of the upgrade. Bowell's time as Militia minister ended before the deal could be consummated but his successor was ordered to finish the project based on Bowell's deal and by August 1893, British marines had arrived and diplomatic peace between the colony and the Mother Country was restored. Bowell was lauded for the 'vigour' and decisive leadership he showed on the issue.[12]

During his watch as the political boss of the Canadian militia, Bowell also became aware of a more serious and systemic problem in the military that he was not able to tackle during his tenure. By 1892, the senior British military officer in the country had concluded that a major reorganization of the forces was needed to improve their ability to protect the country. In an end-of-year report to Canadian and British government officials, Major General Ivor Herbert, General Officer Commanding the Militia, was preparing to recommend the government embrace a major shake-up to make the force more efficient and staff officers more aware of their duties and role 'which have been hitherto ignored.'

Herbert was scathing about the state of the Canadian defence forces. He complained that 'defective staff organization' had scuttled attempts to reorganize the forces during the year. 'I conclude by urging the adoption of this most necessary measure,' he wrote in the report not printed until early 1893 after Bowell had been promoted in cabinet and J. C. Patterson had replaced him as Militia minster. 'Without it, there will continue to exist in Canada a condition of military impotence for the defence of her territory, side by side with the semblance of a military body devoid of the organization which constitutes the living spirit and motive power of such a body.'[13]

Since Herbert had spent several weeks traveling with Bowell during his summer trip to British Columbia to deal with the Esquimalt base issue, he presumably would have briefed the minister on his conclusions and growing concerns about the need for reform. Herbert also apparently took his lobbying campaign higher than the responsible minister. Governor General Stanley got involved in the issue with a long March 1892 memo to Bowell suggesting improvements in equipment, troop training and militia practice. Nevertheless, the vagaries and uncertainties of political assignment ensured that Bowell would not be the minister to tackle the problem. It would be left to those in charge of the future.

During his brief tenure as Militia Minister, Bowell did not have an opportunity to become involved in any decision to send Canadian troops into a potential battlefield, a decision that could have justified his 'minister of war' self-title. That would not happen for three years and it was in reaction to a comic-opera domestic dispute. As Prime Minister at that time, Bowell signed a November 18, 1895 cabinet Order-in-Council authorizing payment of the cost to transport a detachment of the Ottawa-based 43rd Rifles to quell a potentially violent taxpayer revolt in Lowe Township in the Gatineau Valley, 40 miles north of the capital. More than 60 troops and three buglers traveled by rail north along the Gatineau River to set up camp between the towns of Lowe and Brennan's Hill. That show of force was enough to end the nascent rebellion. The appearance of guns quickly persuaded the reluctant Irish immigrant taxpayers to sue for peace and to pay back taxes without a shot being fired and little violence. 'The arrival of the militia has chilled the ardor and bravado of the mob,' reported the Ottawa *Evening Journal* the day after the troops arrived.[14]

Half a year into his tenure as Minister of Militia, and despite the array of issues on his plate, Bowell still was remarking on the slower pace at his new department after the frantic baker's-dozen years spent at Customs. 'You are correct in supposing that my time will not be so fully occupied in the new department as in the old,' he told a Quebec correspondent.[15] Luckily for the workaholic minister, Prime Minister Abbott found other jobs to fill most of Bowell's spare time. Since Abbott led the government from a seat in the Senate after being appointed Prime Minister in June 1891 with Macdonald's death, he appointed Bowell to be Government Leader in the House of Commons, shepherding bills through the legislative process and trying to lead a demoralized Conservative caucus still uncertain about a future without Macdonald's leadership.

Customs issues also followed him to his new job. For several months in 1892, he was acting Minister of Customs while his replacement recovered from illness, and the assignment threw him almost immediately into high-level negotiations with United States representatives in Washington over trade and tariff issues between the two countries. Several times, he joined Finance Minister George Foster and Justice Minister John Thompson on treks to the American capital where futile talks ensued.

In late March, Bowell reported back that the American demands for more favourable trade terms with Canada were unacceptable to the high-level Canadian delegation. In one meeting, he said, U.S. secretary of State James Blaine laid out American terms: 'We were quietly asked to "take down the bars", as he termed it, between Canada and the United States and erect a still higher tariff wall against the English and the rest of the world. When we met the next day, the question of reciprocity on those terms was dropped like a hot potato.'[16]

His 'acting' Customs Department responsibility also gave him license to continue pursuing one of the issues that had vexed and obsessed him when he was full-time minister: hard-drinking departmental employees. At the end of February, Bowell wrote to a rural Manitoba customs collector and friend of his son John to warn him that he was courting trouble. 'It is well I should inform you that complaints have reached me that you have been indulging too freely in the curse of Ireland—whiskey,' wrote the minister. 'Now let me give you a little fatherly advice. Be cautious in the future or you will be reported to headquarters and as I am leaving the department, you may not find the next minister as easy to deal with as I am.'[17]

He also was appointed acting minister of Railways and Canals in the Abbott government and that led to a steady stream of reports and lobbying on the need for more railway investments in rural areas, pleas from shippers for tariff refunds on exports and complaints about service by the Canadian Pacific Railroad (CPR).

There was even a legacy issue for Bowell to manage. It was an echo from his role in the last years of the Macdonald government as Sir John A's 'go-to' minister when something needed to be done or an absent minister temporarily replaced. During his time as Minister of Customs in the 1880s, Bowell sometimes served as acting Finance Minister when Sir Leonard Tilley was on leave because of declining health, and during one of those periods in 1887 Bowell inherited the role of leading the government's response to growing trade union activism in Canada and tension between workers and employers. Without a minister of labour in cabinet, he was tagged with continuing responsibility for the issue over several years into the 1890s, long after he had shed responsibility for the Finance Department.

The focus of Bowell's role on the labour-management file was to oversee the activities of a Royal Commission on the Relations of Labour and Capital, set up in 1887 as the first Royal Commission on the issue in Canadian history. He supervised its creation, set the terms for its work schedule and budget and led follow-up consultations flowing from its 1889 report. Macdonald announced plans to launch the Royal Commission in an 1886 speech, not coincidently just months before the planned 1887 federal election. It was a time when union organizing was increasing as details of gruesome workplace conditions, long shift hours and worker abuse in factories were emerging. Meanwhile, tension between unions and employers was rising as industrialization within the Canadian economy continued apace.

As the party of the National Policy aimed at protecting Canadian industry from import competition, Conservative Party officials were uneasy that working class voters might be drifting away from the party, seeing it increasingly as the friend of the bosses. In his announcement of the investigation of labour-management issues, the Prime Minister had promised: 'The working classes shall be fully represented as commissioners, for the purpose of enquiring into and reporting on all questions arising out of the conflict of labour and capital.'[18] Labour leaders at the time and labour historians since have depicted the Royal Commission exercise as a pre-election political ploy by the wily old politician looking to burnish his reputation as 'the working man's friend' without actually committing to doing anything for workers. He had earned labour support when he introduced the first Trade Union Act legalizing unions in Canada in 1872 but 15 years later, that support appeared to be eroding.

'The appointment of the Labour Commission was clearly an attempt to salvage the working class vote for the Conservative Party and must be seen as an attempt to deal with the vigor and the nascent political strength of the Knights of Labour in Canada,' Dalhousie University labour historian Gregory Kealey argued in an analysis of the initiative. Commission membership was a mix of capitalists, tradesmen and some workers picked by the government, a mix designed to ensure that 'a loyal and cooperative commission' led the process, Kealey concluded. 'All appointments went to politically trustworthy men [and] most had the distinct odour of patronage.'[19]

The editor of a Hamilton, Ontario labour newspaper reached the same conclusion when the announcement was made and commissioners were appointed. 'It confirms our previous estimate of the commission as a device to bolster up the National Policy and to fool the working class by the empty promise of legislation that never will be undertaken,' said the *Palladium of Labour*, a Knights of Labour publication.[20] In the end, despite the government's best efforts to ensure a Conservative-friendly and non-threatening process, the Commission became deeply divided. It split between members supportive of employer perspectives and commissioners sympathetic to labour complaints about worksite conditions, exploitation, punishing hours and low pay. Instead of a hoped-for unanimous milquetoast report recommending little government action, the two Commission factions tabled separate, conflicting reports.

One aspect of the Commission's work did leave a powerful legacy. It collected evidence of workplace and working-class realities at the time and left the information as a gift to future historians, perhaps the greatest unintended enduring accomplishment of the exercise. Commission reports from hearings in Ontario, Quebec and Atlantic Canada included transcripts of interviews with workers that preserved for posterity a vivid record of the conditions that workers of the day endured. 'Aging craftsmen, 10-year-old sawmill hands, girls from their spindles and looms describe their workplaces, wages, hours and aspects of their lives away from the job,' Kealey wrote. 'They tell us of their past and present and some of their hopes and aspirations for the future. The Labour Commission reports and testimony are essential for the study of the Canadian working class as it was being transformed by the new techniques of industrial production.'

In the end, though, the critics were vindicated in their skepticism about whether the Royal Commission would result in actual improvements in working-class protections and conditions. Almost no reforms resulted. 'In 1894, [Justice Minister] John Thompson introduced a bill to make Labour Day a holiday, the only recommendation of the Royal Commission that was ever implemented.'[21]

As minister responsible throughout the process, Bowell made sure the Commission stayed within budget. He vetoed a proposal for hearings in British Columbia because of cost and time required and made sure Commissioners met their reporting deadline and did not exceed their mandate. He did not want the process to drag on with no formal closure date imposed.

He dealt with controversy over attempts by the Commission secretary to suppress or manipulate the official report by withholding some of the evidence and tried to mediate between competing Commissioner factions. When completed, Bowell organized the printing of 2000 report copies for distribution and then led consultations over the next several years with labour and owner representatives about appropriate government follow-up. A typical consultation event was a July 1890 meeting in Toronto with the Ontario Manufacturers' Association 'to discuss trade union issues.' Agriculture Minister John Carling was invited along by Bowell, presumably to argue that higher wages for workers in the food industry put pressure on prices farmers received for their raw produce.

Behind the scenes, Bowell was more than simply the strict wagon master making sure the Commission did not meander off the straight and narrow trail that led to the predictable and timely end the government wanted. He also was deeply biased in favour of one side in the conflict; the capitalists and employers. As a small-town businessman and employer and a 19th century conservative, Mackenzie Bowell was deeply suspicious of the impact of growing labour organizations and their militancy. He often blamed the influence of radical American union organizers as a factor in making the traditionally compliant Canadian workers of Bowell's experience less willing to accept their assigned place on the lower rungs of the Canadian economy. For Bowell, the antipathy toward worker militancy was personal.

He showed his irritation after having a personal brush with the effects of growing labour assertiveness. In 1876, passenger Bowell was delayed when striking locomotive engineers facing lay-off by the Grand Trunk Railway briefly disrupted train service between Toronto and Montreal. Later in the House of Commons when the Liberal government introduced labour legislation, he used the debate to revisit the incident and to denounce both unions and the government. He was 'especially hard on pro-labour MPs and attacked the government for the mismanagement of the Grand Trunk strike.'[22] In fact, complaints about uppity employees and their demanding unions was a recurring theme during Bowell's parliamentary career. He complained that labour leaders were responsible for protecting the jobs of unnecessary workers to the detriment of employers and those who paid the bills.

In 1888, Bowell told a job applicant that as acting Finance Minister, he found the department overstaffed because of 'too kind-hearted ministers' in the past. 'When I had charge of the Finance Department, I gave instructions to have unnecessary limbs lopped off,' he bragged, using a tree pruning metaphor he often employed to describe what he considered a problem of excess employees.[23] In debate on Liberal legislation in 1903 to create a system of arbitration or mediation to resolve impasses between employers and employees during contract disputes or strikes, Bowell insisted it would not work. Only tough laws to limit the ability of unions to close down businesses unless they got their way in negotiations would be effective.

Then, there was a rant:

> It is becoming an idea and it is growing, I am sorry to say, that to possess capital is a crime unless you are prepared to divide up what you have got and give your earnings to those who do nothing but come and go as they please and dictate the terms on which they shall do your work.[24]

As an 87-year-old Senator in 1911, Bowell raged about Liberal legislation to limit the workday for men employed on government jobs to eight hours. He referred back to his experience as a newspaper owner when he expected employees 'to work almost any hours in order to get out the edition of the newspaper. The best principle to my mind is to allow people who employ labour to make their own bargains.'

Bowell recounted how he had started work as a newspaper printer's devil at age nine, 'and I have been working ever since, often 14 or 15 hours a day and I am under the impression it has not hurt me.' Legislative imposition of workday restrictions is the beginning of the end of freedom, he complained. 'I am denounced very often as an old Tory but I must confess that the radicalism of the present day as embodied in bills of this kind is more arbitrary and tyrannical than any legislation of the past to which mankind has had to submit.'[25]

The next year, he was on his feet raging again after the recently elected Conservative government of Sir Robert Borden (in whose caucus he sat) introduced legislation that would force railways to pay their employees twice a month rather than once. 'It seems to me when you step into the office of a company or a private house and dictate to the employer how he shall employ his servant and what he shall pay him, that is a direct interference with civil rights.'[26] Betsy Boyce, Belleville chronicler of Bowell's life, argued he 'believed the man who ran the business should set the terms of employment without interference from the workers. He did not like unions.'[27]

With Bowell effectively in charge, it is little wonder that the Royal

Commission on Labour did not result in any government action to improve conditions for the working class, other than adding one additional day of holiday.

In the summer of 1892 while Mackenzie Bowell was awash in details about his new government military responsibilities and basking in the slower pace of official life after Customs, he took time to issue an appeal that Conservatives rally around new party leader and Prime Minister John Abbott for the good of the party, uninspiring as he might be. A constituent had written to question the performance and appropriateness of the 71-year-old Montreal lawyer for the job of trying to follow and replace Sir John A. Macdonald. 'You can readily understand that there was some little difficulty in selecting a new leader but there was determination to hold firmly together no matter who might be selected,' Bowell replied. 'That adhesion and unity of action has surprised the Grits.' They had hoped the Tory caucus would unravel and 'bring them into power.'[28]

Although far from a ringing endorsement, Bowell did defend Abbott in a letter to an Ontario pastor enquiring about the new Prime Minister's religion. Protestant, a former Orangeman and accepting of all religions, Bowell responded. 'He is a man of great ability and a favourite with everyone, without prejudice or bigotry against any class of Her Majesty's subjects.'[29] Of course, the Minister of Militia also owed the leader some gratitude for rescuing him from Customs. Still, there is no evidence that the two men were close. His early letters to the leader began with the formal 'Dear Mr Abbott' although they became the less formal 'My Dear Sir John' after Abbott was knighted later in the summer.

But Abbott's six years in cabinet with Bowell clearly had taught the new Prime Minister that the newspaperman and Orangeman from Belleville was a competent workhorse who could be trusted to perform. He showed no reluctance in assigning Bowell significant responsibilities including a place at the table negotiating trade terms with the Americans and the key position of government point man in the Commons.

Nonetheless, it was a difficult transition for Bowell and his parliamentary colleagues to move from the exuberant Macdonald for whom politics was life-sustaining oxygen to the quiet, uninterested leader who did not want the job. 'I hate politics,' Abbott had written to a friend in the summer of 1891 while Macdonald lay dying and there was speculation that Governor-General Stanley considered the former CPR lawyer in the running as a replacement. 'I hate notoriety, public meetings, public speeches, caucuses, everything to do with politics except doing public work to the best of my ability.'[30]

Abbott was not Stanley's first choice as leader. The Prime Minister's job was first offered to Justice Minister John Thompson but he declined, in large part because he was a Roman Catholic in a country governed by Protestants since Confederation. He doubted he would be acceptable to the party or the people at a time when religion was still a sharp dividing line in Canada and the Conservative Party. It would not be many months before Lord Stanley came calling on Thompson again. Abbott resigned in November 1892 because of failing health and died the following year. Bowell, then a Senator, delivered the March 19, 1894 eulogy on the floor of the Parliamentary chamber from which Abbott had briefly led the country. 'By all of us, he was esteemed for his sterling character and admired for his great ability,' Senator Bowell said. 'In manner, he was singularly unostentatious and yet there were few men in the country of richer talents.' Abbott was a leading lawyer 'and as a statesman, he exhibited that sagacity and unshakable patriotism which made him of great service to his country... I desire to record my own deep sense of loss by the death of an old and long-time political and personal friend.'[31] It was a final tribute notable for its correct but detached and unemotional tone.

If Bowell's relationship with Abbott was correct but cool, it was a different story with Thompson. The two men got along well, admired each other and despite age and religious differences, became friends during their years together in cabinet as ministers under Macdonald and then Abbott. Thompson was a Halifax lawyer, 22 years Bowell's junior, who served as Nova Scotia Attorney-General and then as a provincial Supreme Court Justice in the 1880s before being appointed Macdonald's Justice Minister in 1885. Talented, accomplished and young, he was considered a future leader. Raised a Methodist like Bowell, Thompson had converted to Roman Catholicism after marrying Annie Affleck, the woman he loved. Religious differences clearly did not affect the growing friendship between the two cabinet colleagues. The veteran Bowell took the Parliament Hill rookie under his wing.

Shortly after arriving in Ottawa in late October, 1885 after winning a by-election in Antigonish, Nova Scotia, Thompson mentioned that he wanted to find a Windsor uniform—including a fancy-dress jacket with gold braids that was favoured at England's Windsor Castle—to wear to special state occasions. Bowell went to work to find one, contacting a friend in the Interior Department whose father had owned a Windsor. She confirmed it was for sale and a deal was struck. At Thompson's request, Bowell then contacted a tailor in Toronto to arrange for the uniform to be altered to accommodate the Justice Minister's substantial girth. Mission accomplished and several Thompson photographs from his time in national government show him resplendent in his fancy outfit.[32]

A more valuable service that Bowell provided for his new colleague was to quietly rebuke party critics uneasy or hostile about Thompson's conversion to Catholicism. Bowell argued that political judgments should be based on competence and accomplishment rather than faith. One of the prime naysayers was Sam Hughes, a Lindsay, Ontario newspaper owner and Conservative supporter who regularly contacted Bowell because of their shared Orange Lodge affiliation and Hughes' ambition to become a Tory MP. He would be elected in 1892 and become Robert Borden's controversial Minister of Militia during the early years of the First World War before being dismissed in 1916.[33]

During the 1880s before political success, Hughes' main obsession appeared to be keeping Roman Catholic influence to a minimum in the Conservative Party and the country. In one notorious incident, he used his newspaper pages to allege that a deadly smallpox epidemic in Montreal was the result of a plot by the Roman Catholic Church. To balance the bombast, Hughes then allowed that he felt sorry for the dying Frenchmen who were 'very little better than brutes. The poor creatures have for ages been kept in darkness, ignorance and superstitions til now, they are so dulled and blinded as to be insensible to the ordinary feelings of humanity.'[34]

While Bowell's open-minded Orange ideology included the right to equal Canadian citizenship and opportunity for Catholics, Hughes saw them as a curse and he quickly homed in on rising Tory star Thompson. He was inappropriately 'insolent and arrogant,' Hughes complained in an anti-Catholic, coded July 1889 letter to Bowell, who replied hopefully that Hughes would change his mind 'once he got to know Thompson better.' Privately, he thought Hughes a bit unhinged. Bowell promptly forwarded the letter to Sir John Macdonald with a cryptic and prophetic note, considering that Hughes later would be considered 'unstable' and 'mad' by his wartime critics: 'I enclose you a letter from Sam Hughes which will give you an idea of the man's saneness.'[35]

Throughout the dramatic speculation and debate about the appropriateness of a Catholic Prime Minister in weeks before Thompson's appointment in late 1892, Bowell continued his behind-the-scenes lobby to protect him from religious prejudice. 'A man's religious views should not be an obstacle to him in public life,' he wrote to a Hamilton *Spectator* contact.[36] He would continue the defence of his friend in the face of anti-Catholic critics after Thompson became Canada's fourth Prime Minister. When a rural Ontario MP warned months after his appointment that feelings in the countryside about the new leader were negative, Bowell fired back: 'I very much regret the feeling which you say exists respecting Sir John Thompson yet I know that it exists and it will only be by personal intercourse and a knowledge of the man that such a feeling can be eradicated—particularly from the minds of men who are moved to a very large extent by prejudice.'[37]

As the parliamentary session was winding down in early July, 1892, Government House Leader Bowell rose in the House of Commons to explain and defend legislation he had sponsored to end or curtail use of forged certificates being produced by Chinese travellers to enter Canada through the Port of Vancouver. The certificates were issued to Canadian residents who had left Canada to visit their families in China, certifying that they were resident in Canada and had paid the required head tax imposed at the time when they landed. The government was concerned that the certificates were being passed on to friends or family in China to allow them unauthorized entry without paying the head tax. Employing the casual racial stereotyping that was common at the time, Bowell said it was difficult for immigration officers to detect the fraud without stronger search powers. 'In some cases, there is scarcely any difference between Chinamen [so] the matter is not investigated,' he said. The Americans used fingerprinting to verify identity. 'In many cases, this is the only way of discovering whether the Chinaman is the individual he claims to be.'[38]

After twenty-five years and hundreds of thousands of words recorded in the House of Commons debate transcripts, these were the final words that Bowell officially would utter in the chamber he had called his political home since 1867.

Barely a year into his prime ministerial duties, John Abbott was a very sick man, seeking medical advice in Canada and abroad. In autumn 1892, he travelled to England to try to regain his health but was warned by his doctor that continuing in his high-pressure job could kill him. Abbott decided to quit and rest in England for a time After decades of leadership stability under Macdonald, the governing Conservative Party was facing the possibility of more leadership uncertainty.

On November 10, Prime Minister Abbott wrote to Governor General Stanley to warn him he planned to submit his resignation and recommended that Thompson replace him. It was a logical choice, largely speculated upon by the chattering classes of the day. In an influential 1956 analysis of the revolving door prime ministerial merry-go-round in the five years after Macdonald's death, 27-year-old University of Toronto political scientist John Tupper Saywell argued that in many ways under Abbott, Thompson already had been the *de facto* government leader since mid-1891. 'He was [a] leader in the House of Commons and deliberately assumed Macdonald's old seat as striking proof of his paramountcy,' Saywell wrote. 'He was the generally accepted successor whenever Abbott chose to resign.'[39] The young and ascending academic apparently did not really believe Thompson's professed reluctance to take the job, fearing it could exacerbate the Protestant/Roman Catholic divide. However, there is evidence to suggest Thompson genuinely was reticent and not simply hoping to be persuaded. In June 1891 as Macdonald lay dying and the speculation about a successor was heating up— with Thompson prominently in the running—he assured Annie privately that 'if I should have the offer, I should refuse it peremptorily.'[40]

By October 1892 with Abbott abroad and widely expected to resign,

Thompson floated the name of another contender he would support: Mackenzie Bowell. In a letter to Senator W. D. Perley, he insisted there was no rivalry for the Prime Minister's position and Bowell would be a good choice. He had the respect of everyone and 'any of us would willingly follow him while we could agree with his policy.'[41] Thompson biographer P. B. Waite, who cited the letter to Perley, quickly let it be known, 93 years later, that he could not agree with the Thompson's assessment of Bowell's qualifications even if it was based on almost a decade of close collaboration and friendship between the two. 'Mackenzie Bowell was decent and hardworking but lacked force, intelligence and the modesty that ought to have been the concomitant of their absence.'[42]

In the end, none of the speculation and jockeying mattered. On November 23, Stanley received Abbott's letter of resignation and recommendation for a successor. Two days later, Thompson agreed but an excruciating 12 days of confusion and anticipation followed until the new government was unveiled and sworn in December 7. On December 5, he had appointed Bowell to the Senate. For Bowell, who told Thompson he would be willing to resign from cabinet in favour of new blood, the uncertainty over cabinet membership was worth the wait. When announcement day arrived, Thompson made appointments that launched Bowell on a new political career path he would follow for the next quarter century, a path that ascended to great heights and descended into great depths.

Bowell was named Government Leader in the Senate and given something of a dream assignment. He would become the first Minister of Trade and Commerce with added responsibility to supervise two controllers who led departments but did not sit in cabinet: Inland Revenue and Customs. Ironically, given the topic of his last House of Commons speech, Bowell also inherited administration of the Chinese Immigration Act.

Bowell's key assignment was to organize and run the new Department of Trade and Commerce. Even Waite allowed that 'his long experience—fourteen years as Minister of Customs—and his considerable capacity for detail gave him solid qualification' for the trade job. Then, lest readers draw too flattering an opinion of the new trade minister, Waite quickly diluted his praise with a putdown: Bowell was 'a useful if uninspiring colleague [with] no brilliance or debating power in him.'[43]

The new Prime Minister, who inspired Conservative Party dreams of resurrection, apparently disagreed.

When news of Bowell's Senate appointment appeared in the Belleville *Intelligencer* on December 6, one of his Liberal political rivals in nearby Madoc likely reacted with a wry smile. Several years before, the 59-year-old E. D. O'Flynn had written his MP to lobby for a secure government job to take him into old age, perhaps a seat in the Senate. It likely was a lark since

O'Flynn ran against Bowell as a Liberal in the 1878 election and lost. Bowell owed him no favours and the chances of a reward from the Conservatives were slim. Bowell's reply verged on the sarcastic, wishing O'Flynn an old age of comfortable retirement and ease but no promise of a cozy Senate sinecure. As he sometimes did, Bowell underlined words for emphasis: 'I regret that you are not <u>alone</u> in desiring to secure a position with <u>large</u> pay and <u>little</u> or <u>nothing</u> to do. This seems to be a mania that is contagious.' He suggested O'Flynn try to join him as a cabinet minister 'when you would learn and be enabled to appreciate what real worry and troubles are. We will think about the Senatorship.'[44]

Now, here was Bowell, unashamedly accepting a lifelong Senate sinecure, although with responsibility for multiple departments and government business in the Senate, so he wouldn't be easing into old age with 'little or nothing to do.' Still, he had some words to live down. Bowell was repeatedly on the record as a critic of Senators, their work ethic, their job security and their lack of accountability. So why would he open himself to charges of hypocrisy by opting for Senatorial political job security while abandoning Hastings North voters? For 25 years through seven consecutive elections, they were loyal and chose him as their MP. Most of the answer lay in the nail-biting evening of March 5, 1891. Bowell won re-election that evening as part of a Conservative majority government but it was close; a margin of little more than 200 votes and 53 percent of the vote after sweeping the riding with more than a 1,000-vote margin in 1887.

He called it his toughest election fight ever—'the beggars spent money right and left and fought like tigers'—and while the perennial Protestant/Catholic tension was a key issue with Protestant voters, Bowell also sensed growing discontent among his electors over his performance. In his early post-election analysis, he blamed others: voters for being misinformed about the issues and the stakes in the election, business for interfering by bankrolling Liberals and his Liberal opponents for dirty tricks. Within a few days, however, he was looking more into the mirror for the answers. 'There is no doubt the election of 1887 created a feeling of over-confidence, in addition to which my own negligence in not visiting the constituency tended to create an apathy which did not formerly exist,' he wrote to a supporter days after election night.[45]

A week later, he went further in the *mea culpa* phase, agreeing with a correspondent who laid much of the blame on him for appearing to take the riding for granted: 'It is a pleasure to have someone who will frankly write you what people say,' replied the chastened MP. When living in Belleville, Bowell confessed, he paid more attention to local issues and travelled through the riding every year to listen to the people and their opinions. 'Since I have been in Ottawa, my time has been so fully occupied that I have been unable to do as I used to do and have become more or less careless.'[46]

At age 67 and after a quarter century in the political trenches, Bowell also was showing a declining enthusiasm for the fight. In 1890 as he faced strong voter pushback on an issue touching on the religious divide, he wrote with an unusual air of defeatism and weariness: 'After having represented a constituency for upwards of 20 years, to have one's motives continually misinterpreted and ones actions assailed tends to make a man indifferent to the future.'[47] He projected the air of a political warrior losing his zest for the battle, a retail politician beginning to wonder if the voters were losing interest in the product; a hardworking MP whose efforts on behalf of his constituents were not properly appreciated.

Bowell had mused before the 1891 election that he might retire but had saddled up one more time for the old leader who needed him. Would he be as willing to do it again three years down the road? Prime Minister Thompson offered him a way to stay in the political game as a key government player without ever needing to worry about electoral politics and campaigning again. Bowell grasped the gift with enthusiasm. 'Under all the circumstances, I do not know that a better arrangement could have been made by Sir John,' he enthused in a letter to British Columbia Lieutenant Governor Edgar Dewdney weeks after his appointment.[48]

The possibilities of the new assignment were beginning to sink in. Awaiting was his adventure as Canada's primary face to the world.

NOTES

[1] LAC Bowell Papers, Vol. 92 (February 1, 1892 letter), 103.
[2] ibid, Vol. 68 (February 1, 1892 letter to J. R. Gowan of Barrie, Ont.), 5.
[3] ibid (April 8, 1892 letter to Capt. John McCaughey of Cobourg, Ontario), 186-87.
[4] ibid (April 28, 1892 letter to Sir Leonard Tilley), 261.
[5] ibid (February 22, 1892 letter to Hon. J.M. Gibson).
[6] ibid, Vol. 95 (August 9, 1893 letter to J.C. Patterson, his successor as Minister of Militia), 112.
[7] ibid, Vol. 69 (August 16, 1892 letter to MP Joseph Marshall), 183.
[8] ibid (October 17, 1892 letter to a St. Catharines, Ontario informant), 342.
[9] ibid, Vol. 69 (October 20, 1892 letter to Capt. Greville Harston), 379.
[10] ibid (July 23, 1892 letter to a militia force member whose name is stroked out).
[11] House of Commons Debates, 7th Parliament 2nd Session, Vol. 1 (April 8, 1892), 1206.
[12] Waite, P. B., The Man from Halifax: Sir John Thompson, Prime Minister (Toronto: University of Toronto Press, 1985), 359-360.
[13] LAC file COP.CA./D.1, (Department of Militia and Defence of the Dominion of Canada: Report for the Half Year Ended June 30th, 1892), 5.
[14] LAC Privy Council Minutes 18 November–2 December 1895 (RG 2, Series 1, Vol. 663) and Ottawa Evening Journal, Vol. X No. 267–268 (November 16–18, 1895), 1.

[15] LAC Bowell Papers, Vol. 69 (Letter July 2, 1892).

[16] ibid, Vol. 92 (March 29, 1892 letter to E.W. Rathburn of Deseronto, Ontario), 157.

[17] ibid, Vol. 67 (February 29, 1892 letter to George Johnstone of the Emerson Customs Department office).

[18] Kealey, Gregory, Introduction in *Royal Commission on the Relations of Labour and Capital, 1889* (Toronto: University of Toronto Press, 1973), x.

[19] ibid, xi.

[20] ibid, xiii.

[21] ibid, xx.

[22] Gregory Kealey, *Toronto Workers Respond to Industrial Capitalism 1867–1892* (Toronto: University of Toronto Press, 1980), 151.

[23] LAC Bowell Papers Vol. 48 (August 8, 1888 letter).

[24] Senate Debates 3rd Session, 9th Parliament. (June 5, 1903), 256.

[25] Senate Debates 3rd Session, 11th Parliament. (April 26, 1911).

[26] Senate Debates 1st Session, 12th Parliament. (January 30, 1912), 113.

[27] Boyce, *The Accidental Prime Minister*, 178.

[28] LAC Bowell Papers Vol. 63 (June 27, 1892 letter to Tweed constituent).

[29] ibid (June 20, 1891 letter to Rev T. A. Wright of Gorrie, Ontario).

[30] Abbott, Elizabeth, *Notes on the Life of Sir John Abbott, Canada's Third Prime Minister: The Reluctant PM* (Montreal: self-published, 1997), 153.

[31] Senate Debates 4th Session 7th Parliament Vol. 1 (March 19, 1894), 4.

[32] LAC Bowell Papers Vol. 35 (December 7, 1885 letter to Lucy Pope).

[33] The controversial career of Sir Sam Hughes is thoroughly examined by Canadian War Museum Great War historian Tim Cook in his book *The Madman & the Butcher* (Toronto: Allen Lane Canada, the Penguin Group, 2010).

[34] ibid, 17.

[35] LAC Sir John A. Macdonald Papers, Vol. 190 (August 1, 1889 letter from Bowell), 79292-3.

[36] LAC Bowell Papers Vol. 92 (September 27, 1892 letter to A. F. Freed).

[37] LAC Bowell Papers, Vol. 94 (June 17, 1893 letter to Wiarton, Ontario MP Alex McNeill), 333.

[38] House of Commons Debate, 2nd Session, 7th Parliament, Vol. XXXV.

[39] John T. Saywell, 'The Crown and the Politicians: The Canadian Succession Question 1891–1896,' *The Canadian Historical Review*, Vol XXXVII No. 4, 1956).

[40] Cited in ibid, 311.

[41] op cit, *The Man from Halifax*, 346.

[42] ibid, 347.

[43] ibid, 349.

[44] LAC Bowell Papers Vol. 57 (March 28, 1890 letter to E. D. O'Flynn).

[45] ibid, Vol. 62 (March 21, 1891 letter to Jason English of Madoc).

[46] ibid (April 2, 1892 letter to Edwin Read of Frankford, Ontario)

[47] ibid, Vol. 90 (July 10, 1890 letter), 286.

[48] ibid, Vol. 93 (January 4, 1893 letter to British Columbia Lieut Gov Edgar Dewdney), 182-83.

Chapter 11
CANADA'S SALESMAN TO THE WORLD

For the second time in his unfolding political career, Mackenzie Bowell had been chosen by his Prime Minister to break new policy ground. In 1878, the assignment from John A. Macdonald was to oversee the realignment of the Canadian economic model from British-inspired *laissez faire* rules to high tariff protectionism aimed at strengthening Canada's goods-producing farm and manufacturing base. After being introduced in 1892 as Canada's first trade minister, his assignment from John Thompson was to lead the colony's early tentative steps to assert itself in the world through trade and within the Empire to demand more colonial status and responsibility.

Several rich ironies were at play when Bowell accepted Thompson's offer, including Conservative leadership in the Senate. First, despite his longstanding frustration with the complicating and often destructive role that religion and language politics played in 19th century Canadian public affairs, it now had worked in Bowell's favour. His Protestant affiliation was a key factor in Thompson's decision to make him Senate leader. Then there was the fact that after 13 years as the Customs Minister—the personification of Canada's trade-restricting National Policy—Bowell now was supposed to morph into the role of a department leader and minister that one historian called 'Canada's Salesman to the World.' The protectionist-in-chief was becoming the trader-in-chief.

The role of his religious affiliation in influencing the Senate leadership offer was easier to explain. As Canada's first Roman Catholic Prime Minister, Thompson thought it imperative to have a counter-balancing Protestant in charge of government affairs in Parliament's Upper House, tempting as it was to appoint a Quebec francophone Senate leader to balance yet another English Canadian national leader. He decided Bowell had the credentials—and the appropriate religion—for the job. Squaring the circle between his history as the leading government protectionist and his new role as chief promoter of Canadian exports was more difficult, at least at first glance.

Naturally, Bowell's critics were happy to point out what they saw as a contradiction. He insisted there was no conflict between the two policy goals, arguing that protectionism and promotion of enhanced trade both have their place in the continuum of national trade policy. It was an argument he articulated most clearly almost a year into the job as he tried to convince Australian colonial officials to open up their markets to more Canadian goods. When he was informed that Australia planned to follow the Canadian example by erecting tariffs to shield domestic industries from competition, Bowell encouraged them to do so. 'Go on precisely as we did,' he later remembered as his response. Based on the Canadian experience, he assured his Australian listeners, protectionist tariffs would allow Australian industries to grow and improve, making them able to ultimately be competitive in world trade. 'But until you have attained that efficiency in the manufacture of agricultural implements and other things that we can supply you with now, we want you to take them from us instead of the United States.'[1]

He encouraged Australians to use Canada's National Policy experience as a template for their own nascent industrial policy because he saw it as a successful experiment. Before introduction of the National Policy in 1879 'Canada was made the dumping ground for all the surplus stock that they had in the United States or nearly the whole of it,' he told them. Then, through a combination of protective tariffs and encouragement of investment in protected sectors, Canadian manufacturers transformed themselves into competitive world-class companies, 'giving evidence that they produce as good or a better article than any other country.' 'Protectionism leads to stronger industries which leads to increased trade' was an argument he would espouse throughout his tenure as trade minister. While not convincing the sceptics, Bowell gave as good as he got in in debate, defending government policy as trade-friendly.

As to be expected in the partisan atmosphere of the times, Bowell's promotion to Senate leader and trade minister drew mixed reviews. Critics like Southwest Ontario Liberal MP James McMullen were not impressed. He complained that the Senate appointment represented an unjust burden for Canadian taxpayers 'for the sake of providing a resting place for the balance of his days for an old man who has drawn a salary year after year far in excess of the value of the service he ever rendered to the country.' The Liberal Toronto *Globe* groused that he was unqualified for the new position of economic leadership. While he was good at finding 'small economies' and brought 'methodical and industrious' work habits to the job as trade and commerce minister, his skill set was not what was required. 'He has been placed in a position where these qualities will be less important than the breadth of view, a firm grasp of the financial situation of the country, genius to devise a remedy for its ills and boldness in carrying it out,' argued the Opposition newspaper. 'The job does not use the talents he has and asks for talents that he has not.'[2]

In contrast, sympathetic supporters were thrilled, considering the promotion deserved and good value for money. The Conservative Toronto *Empire* called him 'one of the hardest working members of the government' who was more than equipped for the dual role of running the Senate and creating a new department. 'The magnitude of the work might well appal a younger man [but] one of his friends remarked that the veteran minister's hair has not turned any whiter nor does his face betray any anxiety as to the formidable task which awaits him.'

The author of a history on the early years of the Department of Trade and Commerce leaned to the *Empire* argument in her assessment of Bowell's suitability for the job. O. Mary Hill concluded that Bowell's Protestant credentials were not his defining qualification for Senate leadership or trade responsibilities. 'There were sound reasons for Bowell's appointment as the first minister of trade and commerce beyond the fact that he was a staunch Orangeman from Ontario,' she wrote. 'His long experience in the Customs portfolio qualified him to discuss tariff and customs problems and Customs was to continue [to be] one of his responsibilities. Moreover, he held strong views on the necessity for diversifying Canada's foreign trade.'

Hill said Bowell saw development of a broader roster of trade partners in the world as a form of 'self-preservation' for Canada in its fight against American annexation instincts. She also noted his long involvement in Belleville business ventures as diverse as newspaper and printing company operations, insurance companies, land development and railway operation. She saw it as preparation for pursuing the 'commerce' part of his new assignment.[3]

Although the list of trade issues awaiting him was long and complex, one of Bowell's first orders of business was to introduce himself to the Senate as its new political boss. The opportunity came in early 1893 when a nervous rookie Senator Bowell debuted in the Red Chamber, nursing some anxiety. He said on January 31:

> I confess, notwithstanding the fact that I am somewhat of an old parliamentarian, having occupied a seat in the other House for over 25 years, that I feel a delicacy in rising to address the Senate on this occasion, [but] I have learned during my political career that whatever position in life I may be called to, I should attempt to do my duty to my country first and to myself afterwards.[4]

He then launched into a two-hour, partisan speech defending the National Policy and its tariffs against what he saw as an unhealthy, unpatriotic Liberal affinity to support closer ties to the United States. Ironically, behind the scenes Bowell already was contemplating a weakening of tariff restrictions to meet industry criticisms:

> I hope I may live long enough to see the time—though I am now pretty well advanced in years—when we will be under no obligations to the United States in trade relations or anything else. It is my desire to have, if possible, the most friendly relations with the United States and all the rest of the world. But I do not wish to be placed, nor do

I believe that any patriotic Canadian wishes to be placed, in the position… of playing second fiddle to or being dependent on any foreign power in order to get to market with the products of our country.[5]

By many accounts, Bowell's heated rhetorical and partisan performance blew some of the cobwebs out of the sedate Senate chamber. It was a view he embraced. While Conservative newspapers predictably fawned over his inaugural Senate speech, praise actually was bipartisan. The Liberal Ottawa *Citizen* lauded it as 'one of the ablest speeches ever delivered in this chamber.'[6] The Toronto *Mail* called Bowell's style of heated partisan rebuttals of Liberal positions 'decidedly new to the decorous dullness of the Upper Chamber.'

In a later letter to a friend, Bowell offered much the same view while admitting that his switch from the rowdy House of Commons atmosphere to the more sedate Senate did not come seamlessly. 'I confess I feel somewhat out of place among the "aged patriarchs" although I am not so young myself,' he wrote to James Aikins, who Bowell would appoint three years later to join him in the Upper House. 'Still, for the last week I think we put some life into the dry bones by breathing rather forcefully upon them.'[7] With this allusion, Bowell was illustrating his biblical and church grounding by referencing the Old Testament Book of Ezekiel and its story prophesying the resurrection of dead armies (and Israel) from the Valley of Dry Bones.

Over time, Bowell mastered the arcane ways of the Other Place, as MPs call the Senate. He proved to be an effective government leader and for a decade, Opposition Senate leader after the Liberals formed government in 1896. He also quickly learned to appreciate the less partisan nature of Senate debate. On April 1, 1893, in the final hours of his first session as Government Senate leader, Bowell said that as a 'stranger' he had been welcomed and received help 'not only from gentlemen who are in accord with the government but also from those who differ from us on the great questions which divide parties in this country… I can only say that we part not only good friends but with the hope that our intercourse will continue to be of the same agreeable character in the future.'[8]

Of course, during the early months of 1893 the major challenges and opportunities facing the newly-minted Minister of Trade and Commerce lay not in the Senate, resurrected or not, but in creating a new government department, leading a new Canadian outreach to the world and working to improve the powers of Canada and the other colonies in the still very London-centric British Empire. After the grinding, stressful and sometimes frustrating years heading the Department of Customs and then the whirlwind months as Minister of Militia and Defence, the prospect of taking on an assignment offering new challenges, exotic issues and an international focus was appealing. 'Bowell's appointment as minister of Trade and Commerce opened two years that were probably the most enjoyable of his career,' wrote one chronicler of his life.[9]

In the cold Ottawa winter months of 1893, he quickly discovered that his new duties included the mundane as well as the grandiose and interesting. Weeks into the new portfolio, the minister had to deal with complaints from Quebec dairy industry players about adulterated cheese arriving in the province from the United States and undermining the important provincial industry. Cottonseed oil or lard oil was being injected into exported American milk to replace butterfat, creating a 'filled cheese' product 'which so closely resembles the genuine article that for a time it deceives the inexpert,' said a February, 1893 industry complaint that landed on Bowell's desk. 'You can readily see that all these processes tend to hurt the farmer and hurts the good name of our country for producing a first-class cheese.'[10]

It was a dairy industry demand for government protection that would be all-too-familiar to successor Canadian trade and agriculture ministers well into the 21st century.

At the same time, a tougher early test would soon confront the new trade minister. Bowell became party to an ugly standoff between the Thompson government and Sir Charles Tupper, its High Commissioner to Great Britain. Tupper was a storied Conservative icon with an elevated view of his own importance and mandate. He was a Father of Confederation and former Nova Scotia premier, had been minister in several cabinet portfolios under John A. Macdonald and then was rewarded for his service with the High Commissioner appointment. There, the avowed British imperialist revelled in his proximity to the politics and players at the centre of the British Empire.

He also occasionally overstepped his boundaries in the job.

Tupper had been part of the British team that negotiated a trade treaty with France that bound Canada to its obligations and increased access to Canadian markets for some French goods. It also afforded the same access to the Canadian market for any other country signing a trade treaty with France, a provision odious and unacceptable to the Thompson administration.

While Great Britain was the lead Empire player in treaty making, Canada at least theoretically was afforded the right to approve the terms of any deal that affected it. As trade minister, Bowell read the fine print of the proposed treaty sent by Tupper and decided that while it would be good deal for France, it would not be for Canada. He sent detailed questions to Tupper asking for explanations on a variety of issues: details around live fish imports, dairy product definitions and treatment of other items that he found less than clear in the text.

The greater problem for Bowell and the Canadian government was that Tupper unilaterally had endorsed the draft treaty on Canada's behalf before officials in Ottawa or Parliament had even seen the details. He then assumed the Canadian government would simply accept his handiwork (and British rules) and assured the French and British they could ratify the deal because the Canadian government and Parliament were in accord. In fact, the Canadian Parliament had not voted on it and the Thompson cabinet was less than pleased with the fine print.

In Parliament, Finance Minister George Foster made a fiery speech critical of some of the key treaty provisions. The criticism from Ottawa threw the proud Tupper into a funk and led cabinet minister and son Charles H. Tupper to act as a surrogate in defence of his father. The Tupper pushback included a threat of resignation by Charles Hibbert, minister of Marine and Fisheries in Thompson's cabinet, and a confrontation with the Prime Minister when he arrived in Paris in late March.

Thompson had travelled to France as one of the British judges appointed to adjudicate a dispute between Canada and the United States over the rules surrounding seal hunting in the Behring Strait off the Pacific Coast, northwest of British Columbia and Alaska. It would turn out to be a three-month assignment. Tupper Jr, a Canadian government delegate to the Behring conference, was incensed over Foster and Bowell's questioning of the treaty's benefits for Canada and by implication, his father's performance. He waited in ambush at the train station to make his anger clear to a surprised Thompson as he stepped off the coach onto the station platform in Paris. That evening, in a 17-page hand-written letter to Bowell, who was acting Prime Minister in Thompson's absence, the Prime Minister recounted the confrontation that unfolded on the station platform. 'Mr. Tupper's objections to Mr Foster's statement were made in strong language but eventually, I succeeded in leaving the railway station and getting to the hotel.'[11]

In the end, High Commissioner Tupper got the last laugh when the British Parliament approved the French treaty in October 1894 over Canada's objections. The vote effectively brought the treaty into force. No doubt Tupper egged British MPs on from his nearby perch in London.

After the British parliamentary vote, Bowell wrote to Thompson—by then in London to be sworn in as a member of the Imperial Privy Council—that he should bypass Tupper Sr and speak directly to the British Colonial Secretary about the damage the treaty would do to Canada. 'We shall be obligated to concede to other countries the advantages we have agreed to give France without receiving any corresponding benefits in return,' the angry Trade Minister wrote. And if the British would not agree to relieve Canada of that obligation, 'we shall be obliged to ask for the abrogation of the French treaty.'[12]

In the trans-Atlantic spat, the inexperienced Prime Minister was wedged between two warring senior and proud Tories. He made little apparent effort to smooth relations between the two. In the end, Canada received no concessions. Memories of Bowell's role in questioning the deal, Tupper's judgment and his performance throughout the trade treaty fiasco may have lingered with an injured Tupper clan. Less than three years later, the Tuppers, father and son, would be pivotal figures in Parliament Hill intrigue to depose Bowell as Prime Minister and party leader.

In Ottawa, meanwhile, with Thompson out of town and other ministers traveling, Bowell found himself in the familiar position of being swamped with work... including other people's work. He was busy overseeing implementation of a new faster mail shipping service between Great Britain and Canada while resisting demands for higher government subsidies made by the steamship line owner contracted to provide the service. He travelled with the agriculture minister to an April world's fair in Chicago to promote Canadian products and then, once back in Ottawa, Bowell was in charge of railway and finance departments since Railway and Canals Minister John Haggart and Finance Minister Foster were touring the country consulting on tariff policies. 'I have had my hands full for the last month or six weeks as you could readily understand,' he wrote June 17 to Thompson, still in Paris at Behring Strait hearings. 'With the details of three departments to look after, I have not had many idle moments.'[13]

When idle moments from his departmental workload did materialize, Bowell used some of them to survey the state of politics and the voter mood at the midway point between elections. He sensed a change in political winds and it made him uneasy. New Liberal leader Wilfrid Laurier clearly was gaining some traction as a fresh and energetic alternative to the aging Conservative regime. Meanwhile, vexing and deep-seated religious tensions between Protestant and Roman Catholic communities once again were roiling the body politic, while government consultations on the National Policy tariff regime showed a growing demand for change and an increased interest in Liberal proposals for closer trade ties with the United States.

To add to Bowell's unease, an influential British newspaper assured its readers during the summer that 'the days of protection in its extreme form are numbered in both Canada and the United States... In Canada, the party in favour of free trade pure and simple is growing in numbers and influence and the present Conservative government will need all its energies to hold its own in the struggle which is even now going on.'[14]

Meanwhile, Bowell also was having some private doubts about Thompson's political leadership abilities despite their continuing friendship. Thompson, he determined, was no Macdonald. He wrote to a veteran Tory judge and former politician, appointed to the Senate a decade before by Macdonald, that election planning was beginning and the outlook was uncertain without the Old Chieftain at the helm. 'If we do not meet the requirements of the country, it will be our fault and we must suffer the consequences,' he said. 'No one knows better than you do how difficult it is for a party that has been in power for some 15 years to keep in constant touch with the wants and wishes of a growing country. Our former leader used to manage this delicate task and we must try and follow in his footsteps.'[15]

Earlier, he had fretted privately about whether Thompson would rise to the challenge. 'It is quite true as you remark that we have an able man in Sir John Thompson and it is equally true that he has not the gravitas of the "old man" nor the dash necessary to carry a forlorn hope to victory. There is, however, no telling what he may develop when necessity calls for action.'[16]

In late summer, the trade file became yet more complicated when the United States imposed a tariff on all freight being shipped to Canada through the Great Lakes port of Sault Ste. Marie. It justified the action as a response to an earlier Canadian tariff on freight traffic heading south through the Welland Canal with Canadian-owned vessels receiving a refund of tolls paid. It was a clumsy Canadian government attempt to tilt the table in favour of using Canadian rather than American ships to carry goods south. The affair turned out to be a short-lived minor tariff war that ended after negotiations and a backdown by both sides. However, exporters and importers were rattled and critics of the Conservative government saw it as a protectionist misstep that provoked the American response.

The Tory press had a different view, seeing it as a policy victory. The Toronto *World*, for example, saw a glass more than half full. 'We accept the penalty [and] while we have to pay it, we will,' the newspaper editorialized. 'We accept this hostile legislation as the warmest tribute our neighbour rivals can pay us. It is their testimony that Canada is a nation on this North American continent. It is the beginning of our history as a great people.'[17]

General public reaction to the Canada/U.S. tension reflected the increasingly favourable press assessments that Bowell's performance as Canada's first trade minister was beginning to receive. After years of newspaper carping about Department of Customs issues, the minister clearly was enjoying his better reputation. It appealed to his vanity. Even some Liberal writers were impressed. The newspaper clippings he stored in his personal Belleville library included a complimentary story by the Liberal-supporting Montreal *Herald* on the first annual report of the new Department of Trade and Commerce tabled in Parliament by Bowell in late May 1893. The newspaper allowed that even though it was from a Tory government, the report was a 'useful document' for Canadians to read. On the clipping was a note about why it was added to his preserved file of newspaper coverage. 'This so seldom. A good word comes from a Grit paper,' Bowell scrawled across the bottom. 'This is worth preserving.'

As the summer months slipped by, Bowell remained occupied by his busy schedule and the obstacles and issues that inevitably arose to demand his attention as one of the go-to ministers on Parliament Hill. He also had a project that increasingly filled the moments when he wasn't consumed by official business. He was learning about, and probably daydreaming about, the mysteries and opportunities that could await him Down Under. Although not yet officially announced, Bowell and Prime Minister Thompson had been discussing the possibility of an autumn trip to Australia for the trade minister. As a collection of Southern Hemisphere British colonies thousands of miles away, they shared with Canada both ties to Great Britain and frustrations with how they were being treated by the Mother Country.

The two men saw opportunities to develop new markets for Canadian products, to form political alliances that would strengthen the colonies when dealing with London, and to promote establishment of a communications cable between the two vast but thinly populated territories. The trip could also be used to promote another scheme forming in Bowell's mind. He was beginning to muse about organizing a first-ever conference of senior colonial officials to discuss common opportunities, common grievances and a desire by some colonial leaders to attain more status and freedom of action and decision-making within the Empire. Great Britain might even be invited to hear colonial leaders articulate dreams of a different future and relationship with the Mother Country.

First things had to be dealt with first. If the Australian gambit was to happen and to be judged successful, Bowell needed to learn about Australian conditions and market opportunities, to create contacts and a travel agenda and to assess whether Canadian businesses had any interest in developing closer trading ties with such a distant and largely undeveloped continent. The questions and possibilities created some summer distractions for the 69-year-old who was well travelled but had never ventured south of the equator. For a colony with no foreign affairs department or bureaucracy, and a dependence on Great Britain to represent Canadian interests to the world, such a trip to promote Canadian interests and to air Empire dis-contents would be unprecedented.

Promoting Canadian commercial interests in Australia was not a new idea, having already been considered for several years without a decision. One impetus for the discussions was completion of Canada's cross-country railway network in the mid-1880s. Once the last spike was driven and the Pacific Coast linked by steel to the rest of the country, the potential for Canada to become a shortcut for trading and communications connection between Great Britain and its Pacific colonies immediately became apparent. As well, after Parliament agreed in 1889 to subsidize a Canada/Australia steamship service to carry passengers, mail and goods between the two British colonies, it was launched in May 1893 with Vancouver as its Canadian terminal. The British Columbia government saw the new marine connection as a vehicle for increased trade that sceptical West Coast voters might finally see as a concrete benefit flowing from their July 1871 decision to join Canada.

In late June 1893, Reuters News Agency reported that British Columbia was stepping up the pressure for action on the north-south trade file. 'The inauguration of the new direct steamer service between Sydney and Vancouver has led to an agitation in British Columbia for free trade between Canada and the Australian colonies and [British Columbia Premier Theodore] Davie expressed the opinion that the Dominion government ought to open the negotiations,' the news agency reported. [18] It reported Bowell was positive to the idea and promised the issue would be discussed in cabinet when the Prime Minister returned from business in Paris.

Sir John Macdonald, in fact, had first seen the potential of greater contacts with Australia several years earlier. In 1888, he discussed plans to send newly appointed Montreal Senator John Abbott to Australia on a mission to scout-out trade possibilities. However, the trip dropped off Macdonald's radar as the frailties of advancing age and a tough looming election campaign crowded other items off his agenda.

Five years later when successor Prime Minister Thompson returned to Ottawa from his European business, he was ready to discuss resurrecting the idea of a trade mission and by now, the government had a trade minister as the logical person designated to set sail.

Discussions and planning in Ottawa through the summer concentrated on trade goals, empire links, the status of the colonies, and diplomacy issues that were at the core of the proposed trip agenda. However, the shadow of another key issue and a prominent Canadian with strong views on the subject frequently was present at the table. Creation of a communications cable link between Canada and Australia was a core objective for the Canadian government, but as trip planning progressed it also became a distraction and an irritant. It would develop into a sideshow that featured earnest Canadian argument, British behind-the-back obstruction, strained Anglo-Canadian relations and some comic-opera moments supplied by a famous Canadian. While the trip would record successes on trade and diplomacy issues, in the end there was little immediate progress on the communications cable file.

The shadow at the planning table that summer belonged to Sir Sandford Fleming, a 66-year-old British immigrant like Bowell with a storied record of accomplishments as a Canadian. He had been a key player in surveying and then acting as chief engineer during construction of the Canadian Pacific Railway across Canada. He was an internationally respected scientist who had been instrumental in advocating a global system of 24 Standard Time zones around the world to end the chaos of different time systems in different locations, sometimes within the same country. In 1884, Fleming helped organize a Washington conference that accepted the Standard Time system, with the Greenwich Meridian in England as ground zero, and agreed to implement it.

156

Fleming had first come to Canadian notice in 1851 when at age 24, he designed Canada's first official postage stamp.[19] He was also a proponent, bordering on being an obsessive, of laying almost 8,000 miles of communications cable between Australia and Canada's West Coast. Since the late 1870s, Fleming had been sending lengthy handwritten epistles to politicians in Great Britain and Canada advocating the idea, calling for government investment and sometimes proposing a government-supported Fleming company to oversee the project. His wordiness, persistence and single-minded lobbying irritated many of his political targets, including Thompson, even though the Prime Minister (and Bowell) agreed with the value of the proposal.

Fleming had lobbied for an official position on the proposed 1888 Canadian mission to Australia and thought he had been approved until the plan came to naught. When he caught wind of news that Thompson and Bowell were resurrecting the trade mission idea in 1893, he quickly invited himself along. 'Not wanting to miss this unique opportunity to promote the Pacific cable plan, Fleming offered to accompany Bowell,' wrote a biographer.[20]

Initially, Thomson wanted nothing to do with him and Bowell had to send the bad news to Fleming on September 1: 'Council [cabinet] decided this afternoon that only one should be sent and that one a minister,' the trade minister wrote. However, the promoter would not take 'no' for an answer.[21] Four days later, Fleming sent a long letter to Thompson arguing that it would be a mistake to send Bowell alone, considering that there was competition for the scheme and urgency in getting a deal. His arguments were brash and self-promoting. The French were proposing a rival cable that would end in San Francisco and he (Fleming) was the expert on the topic and could tip the balance in Canada's favour, he immodestly argued. The Canadian delegation needed someone who could 'apply great tact and skill based on a thorough knowledge of all the circumstances... I am so afraid that the opportunity will be lost forever that I am prepared to make great personal sacrifices to assist in averting the evil.'

In other words, Bowell could not be trusted to represent Canada effectively.

Nevertheless, this low opinion did not stop Fleming from continuing to lobby Bowell on the issue as well. He told the trade minister, who had supported his presence on the trip, that he was determined to go and would pay his own way and make his own arrangements. That proposal turned the tide. Thompson relented as long as it was not on the government dime. When Bowell's Australian odyssey finally happened, Fleming took his daughter Minnie along and for the most part was an effective advocate for the scheme although at times his bull-in-a-china-shop approach led to political and diplomatic strains that Bowell, and sometimes Tupper in London, had to

157

manage. At one point, Fleming almost created an international incident by planning to plant a Union Jack on an uninhabited island near Hawaii and proclaiming it a British possession so it could be used as part of the route for the proposed Pacific-Canada cable. An incident was averted only by the fact that Hawaiian officials were warned of the pending action and planted their own flag first to claim jurisdiction.

In the end, despite Canadian advocacy and Australian support, the Pacific communications cable was delayed for years and a contract to proceed was not awarded until late 1900 when the Liberals were in power. It did not start to operate for two more years after that.[22]

Financing issues and Great Britain's objection to any infrastructure that would allow colonies to establish direct communications or trade ties by-passing London's supervision, proved to be major factors in the delay. In fact, even during Bowell's trip to Australia that featured promotion of the cable as a key Canadian objective, London surprised him by sending documents to the Australians disparaging the benefits of a communications link.

A furious Bowell said the British arguments were 'inaccurate and mis-leading' as well as a deliberate undermining of the Canadian campaign to strengthen ties with the Pacific colonies. 'The mission on which I was engaged justified the expectation that it would obtain the support and sympathy of the Imperial government,' he wrote to High Commissioner Tupper, calling on him to reprimand the British government.[23]

Bowell was not the only one accusing the British government of trying to sabotage the Canadian initiative. In 1899, London financial newspaper *The Bullionist* blamed the delay in establishing the cable service on British government foot-dragging, subterfuge and apathy. The Canadian advocate of the scheme, on the other hand, was lauded by the newspaper as the hero of the move to unite the British Empire into a federation with more equality for member countries through better communication links. 'The man whose name will be imperishably associated with the carrying out of this magnificent patriotic scheme is a distinguished Canadian, Sir Mackenzie Bowell.'[24]

Bowell, when he occupied the prime minister's office, had one last chance to play a role in developing the communications link. On April 25, 1896, Prime Minister Bowell signed an Order-in-Council appointing three Canadians to a British-Canadian-Australian committee being created to discuss the Pacific cable issue. It would be a major step toward the 1900 contract award and was one of his final prime ministerial acts. Bowell and new High Commissioner to Great Britain Donald Smith would be Canada's official members with Fleming appointed an 'expert advisor'.[25] Fleming's brash, aggressive lobbying had paid off.

On September 1, 1893, cabinet voted to confirm Bowell's extended mission to Australia. The CPR quickly stepped up to offer him a luxury sleeper car for the trip across Canada. He would be away for more than three months and appeared to leave with low expectations of what might be accomplished. 'I confess I do not anticipate any great immediate results from our visit to Australia,' he wrote two days before boarding the train. 'The parties from whom we have been estranged so long can scarcely be brought into a close relationship at a moment's notice.' He also dreaded the prospect of weeks on the ocean. 'Unfortunately, I have never been a good sailor and consequently do not anticipate much pleasure while at sea but I will try and do the best I can.'[26]

The adventure started Thursday September 7 when the train pulled out of Ottawa station on the way to Vancouver and a passage on the new government-subsidized steamer service to Australia that Bowell had invested significant political capital to create. He was accompanied by private secretary J. L. Payne and for the Ottawa to Vancouver leg of the trip, Ottawa Orangeman John Carleton, Worshipful Master of Bowell Loyal Orange Lodge No. 25, Bowell's home lodge in the capital which met just blocks from his hotel room.

In Winnipeg, the entourage picked up local businessman W. F. Buchanan who Bowell had invited along to talk to Australian businessmen, take purchase orders and promote Canadian goods. The Winnipeg *Free Press* reported on the pass-through visitors who were traveling with an 'important duty to perform. The government is acting in conformity with resolutions passed by various boards of trade, which urged the necessity of extending trade between the different colonies to its fullest extent.'[27]

Even as he crossed the Prairies to spend a few days in Vancouver before boarding the ship for Australia, Bowell could not avoid fretting about political problems at home. That weekend, the Young Men's Conservative Convention was meeting in Toronto to debate resolutions calling for radical tariff reform. Bowell feared they would go too far and embarrass the government. Since he could not be there for the fight, he instructed successor Belleville MP Henry Corby to oppose the resolutions. Leave it to the government to propose some changes before the next election, 'and at the same time continue the policy inaugurated by our late chief,' he counselled.[28]

Once in Vancouver, Bowell spoke to the Chamber of Commerce to promote the prospect of greater trade with Australia, held meetings with local businessmen and visited with his son John and grandchildren before embarking on the three-week journey to the great unknown. It would be a ground-breaking, modest 19th century version of the Team Canada trade trips that became popular with Canadian politicians a century later. The minister carried with him catalogues from businesses describing products they hoped would find a market Down Under. On arrival in Sydney, colonial leaders including New South Wales premier J. B. Patterson were on hand to greet the rare Canadian visitor. Then, for the better part of six weeks, Bowell

159

travelled through Australia, speaking in Sydney and Melbourne among other stops, meeting politicians and homesick displaced Canadians and promoting closer ties between Canada and the Pacific colonies.

He was treated alternately as a visiting dignitary or an exotic specimen from a different world. He later reminisced about being 'kept on the move with interviews and the desire to see a "live man from the frozen region of the North".'[29] His message in part was the need to present a common front to Great Britain when demanding better treatment from the 'Mother Country' and in part to urge improved communications and cooperation between the British colonies and with Great Britain. His pitch on trade was double-headed: promoting increased commerce and cooperation between Canada and the Australian colonies while threatening trade retaliation against Australian wool unless they opened up their market more to Canadian products. He recounted later:

> In my intercourse with the Australians I candidly informed them that we were treating them very liberally, that their great staple of export was on our free list and we wanted some concessions. It might be necessary at no distant day to place a duty upon their wools should our North West Territories produce an article to take the place of that imported from Australia. (29)

Everywhere Bowell went, there were receptions, official welcomes and honours. He was given a free rail pass in Queensland to visit Brisbane and to see the colony, including a special train that took him to a rural area 'where sheering [sic] was in progress.' There were invitations from many Orange Lodge officials to attend meetings although his Australian hosts warned that fraternizing with a divisive movement could cause political problems. Bowell was greeted and entertained by the governors of several states and boards of trade in many of the major cities.

Everywhere he went, newspaper coverage was extensive and generally favourable, thanks in part to Bowell's ability to connect with local journalists. His history in the newspaper business and understanding of how it worked was put to good use as he gave local reporters clamouring for interviews three of the things journalists most crave: access, good quotes and respect. A classic incident came when he arrived in Melbourne on October 28 where a waiting reporter asked for an interview. Bowell was strapped for time but invited him to his waiting hotel room for a chat. He promptly told the reporter that he needed to wash and change his shirt before his first engagement 'but you can ask me what you like while I am getting these luxuries.' There followed a glowing account by a clearly flattered reporter about the visiting minister answering questions 'with his white head covered up by his linen and his arms struggling to extricate themselves from his sleeves. It is not often that one has a chance of interviewing a statesman under such circumstances but when the Press is waiting and the time is short, anything is excusable.'[30]

As he prepared to depart Australia for Canada in late November, a reporter from the Sydney-based *Westminster Gazette* profiled him as he waited in his Hotel Australia room:

> Truly a remarkable man in many respects, 70 years of age yet as able as a youth, a self-made man of the best type, a unique figure in British politics for he has held office as a minister for 13 years in succession... Now here on a mission, the object of which is to strengthen that 'crimson thread of kinship' which runs through the empire into close relations with Australia.[31]

During his Australian visit, Bowell also was asked by political leaders to expound upon Canada's experience with federalism. Australian leaders at the time were involved in politically charged debates about a proposal to unite the Australian colonies into a federation. He was a willing evangelist for federalism, speaking in several colonies to extol the virtues of the 1867 Canadian Confederation bargain uniting French and English, Protestants and Roman Catholics in a union that gave them strength to resist American annexation tendencies and to compete with other world nations.

On November 20 as Bowell prepared to leave Sydney for the voyage home, New South Wales Premier Patterson and six of his ministers were there with a band and a crowd of hundreds to see him off. The Premier asked the Canadian veteran of Confederation politics to address the topic of colonial union. Bowell enthusiastically accepted the challenge, adamant that Australians should set aside their suspicions of other colonies to pursue customs and political union.

He told them that on his travels through Australia, he had heard support for the scheme but seen little progress. 'Perhaps this arises because each of you is afraid of one man taking the lead and obtaining more kudos than the others,' he said. 'We were in exactly the same position in Canada twenty-five years ago. To you I can only say "go on in the matter of federation as you have begun." I do not pretend to anything like oratory [for] I am a plain practical man but I have seen enough to convince me that you have great possibilities before you, better than even you can anticipate today.'[32]

Later that day, Bowell disembarked to attend a farewell picnic organized for him in Pearl Bay up the coast from Sydney and again beat the federation drum in a speech and a final interview. 'If you can only get under one government and become one people without having barriers across every border line, it will tend in great measure to increase your importance, particularly in the English market,' he told the gathered crowd.[33]

In a 2011 book on the politics of the Australia federation debates in the early 1890s, author Thomas Keneally did not directly reference Mackenzie Bowell's interventions, but when he compared the Australian and Canadian federation debates, he made an argument that likely was influenced by Bowell's speeches.

Unlike the Canadian experience, Australians were not faced with an external threat as an impetus for union, Keneally wrote. 'In Canada, it had been stimulated by the Irish Fenian invasions of Ontario in 1866 and 1867, after which confederation and a federal defence system seemed wise. Despite hysteria to the contrary, it was unlikely that the Yankee Fenians would oblige by invading Australia.'[34]

Canadian historians of Confederation debates and politics generally have not seen the Fenian raids as a pivotal factor. Christopher Moore in his 1997 book *1867: How the Fathers Made a Deal* called the bumbling, disorganized and ineffective Fenian raids 'comic-opera' even though 'Confederation's propagandists had exploited the raids to the hilt.'[35] Bowell, on the other hand, gave the Fenian raids a higher profile in his recounting of the Confederation story. He prided his role in organizing militia and guarding the border against the threat of Fenian attack in 1866. He gave the Fenian threat more Confederation credit than many, as he undoubtedly did during his Australian speeches. Keneally likely read Bowell's interventions in his research, perhaps leading to the curious Fenian reference in his history of Australian federation debates.

As Mackenzie Bowell departed Australia for his long voyage home, more than three weeks stretched ahead of him. He would use the time to assess the accomplishments, the failures and the near misses. Failure to move the communications cable file forward (with some effective sabotage by Britain) undoubtedly was his greatest frustration and regret. On the accomplishment side of the ledger, he had received at least tentative approval from four Australian state premiers to travel to Canada the following year for an Empire conference on trade issues and relations between Great Britain and the Colonies. If he could pull it off, it would be an unprecedented event and, in his mind at least, a major step toward more status for colonies within the Empire.

Britain, not surprisingly, was lukewarm to the idea so Bowell had some promoting and organizing to do. As to the primary trip objective of creating better trade ties with Australia, Bowell's results were mixed. Officials and crowds he had addressed seemed supportive and willing to consider the idea but there were few new contracts. Ahead lay the task of stirring Canadian businessmen to try to exploit what he saw as a prime economic and political opportunity in the South Pacific. His one misstep on that file during the Australian visit had been stumbling when trying to square the circle of Canadian protectionism and the call for freer trade. In one of the last Australian press stories published about the Bowell visit, a major Sydney newspaper called him out on the issue. While praising his last speech for promoting federation among the colonies, it said he received a failing grade on the trade file. 'He was in the position of a protectionist endeavouring to explain why freedom of trade should be extended... a dilemma sufficient to tax the ablest sophist,' opined the Sydney *Daily Telegraph*. 'Mr. Bowell came out of it very badly.'

After all the good coverage, that last story must have stung, reflecting as it did the jibes he had received, and would continue to receive, from the Canadian opposition press.

On the trip back home, Mackenzie Bowell added one new country to his list of foreign stops. He stayed overnight in Honolulu, Hawaii and the former Hawaiian Queen Liliuokalani, who had been overthrown in an American-backed business coup months earlier but clung to claims of legitimacy, hosted him at a reception. Bowell was impressed... sort of: 'Although ugly as a hedge fence, she was quite refined and she performed her part in the reception with all the grace and ease of a well-educated lady,' he recorded later.[36]

When the trip had ended and he was back in Canada, Bowell in his usual understated way, reported to a friend: 'I hope that my mission, if not entirely successful, may result in some benefit to the country.'[37]

It would prove to have done so.

NOTES

[1] Debates of the Senate, 4th Session, 7th Parliament Vol. 1 (March 20, 1894).

[2] Hill, O. Mary, *Canada's Salesman to the World: The Department of Trade and Commerce 1892–1939* (Montreal: McGill-Queen's University Press, 1977), 15–16.

[3] ibid, 17.

[4] Debates of the Senate, 3rd Session, 7th Parliament (January 31, 1893), 23.

[5] ibid, 37.

[6] Belleville *Intelligencer* reprint (February 16, 1892).

[7] LAC Bowell Papers. (February 14, 1893 letter to J. C. Aikens).

[8] Debates of the Senate (April 1, 1893), 511.

[9] Boyce, Betsy D., *The Accidental Prime Minister* (Ameliasburgh, Ontario: Seventh Town Historical Society, 2001), 235.

[10] LAC Bowell Papers Vol. 11. (February 7, 1893 letter from A. A. Ayler.)

[11] ibid (March 25, 1893 letter from Sir John Thompson).

[12] LAC Bowell Papers Vol. 75. (November 1, 1894 letter to Sir John Thompson).

[13] LAC Bowell Papers Vol. 94. (June 17 letter to Thompson)

[14] ibid, Vol. 106. (August 5, 1893, *Financial Times* newspaper, London, England).

[15] ibid (June 1, 1893 letter to Senator. Sir James Gowan of Barrie, Ontario).

[16] ibid (May 9, 1893 letter to Senator Gowan).

[17] LAC Bowell Papers Vol. 126 (Toronto *World*, August 26, 1893).

[18] ibid, Vol. 105. (June 28, 1893 *Financial News* newspaper).

[19] Green, Lorne, *Chief Engineer: Life of a National Builder–Sandford Fleming* (Toronto: Dundurn Press, 1993).

[20] ibid, 154.

[21] LAC Bowell Papers Vol. 113.

[22] LAC Bowell Papers Vol. 96. (163-164).

[23] LAC Bowell Papers Vol. 74. (February 20, 1894 letter to Charles Tupper in London).

[24] LAC Bowell Papers Vol. 113, Part 1 (London, March 24, 1899 edition of *The Bullionist*).

[25] LAC Privy Council Minutes, 21 April–29 April, 1896 (RG 2, Series 1, Vol. 685), Microfilm reel 3644.

[26] LAC Bowell Papers Vol. 95 (September 5, 1893 letter to J. C. Aikens), 216-217.

[27] ibid (September 9, 1893 Winnipeg *Free Press* article).

[28] ibid (September 6, 1893 letter to Henry Corby, Belleville MP).

[29] ibid, Vol. 96 (February 1, 1894 letter to Sir Leonard Tilley, Saint John, New Brunswick).

[30] LAC Bowell Papers Vol. 110 Part 2. (October 30, 1893 Melbourne *Herald* story).

[31] ibid (November 30, 1894 article in the *Westminster Gazette*).

[32] ibid, Vol. 108, File 1.

[33] ibid (article in the *British Australian*, December 28, 1893).

[34] Keneally, Thomas, *Australians: From Eureka to the Diggers* (Sydney: Allen & Unwin, 2011), 169.

[35] Moore, Christopher, *1867: How the Fathers Made a Deal* (Toronto: McClelland & Stewart, 1997), 241.

[36] LAC Bowell Papers Vol. 95 (December 30, 1893 letter to J. C. Aikins of Toronto).

[37] ibid (December 27, 1893 letter to Walter Ross of Picton), 246.

Chapter 12
TRADE MINISTER TO PRIME MINISTER

Trade minister Mackenzie Bowell arrived back in Canada in mid-December, 1893 in good spirits after what even the self-described seasickness-prone sailor thought had been a good trip on a tranquil Pacific Ocean. 'The voyages to Australia and return were exceedingly pleasant,' he reported. 'I did not miss a single meal and was not affected by the nausea which has always attacked me on the Atlantic.'[1] His good mood at being back on Canadian soil was abetted by his conclusion that despite some set-backs and unresolved issues, he had done well on his first major excursion as Canada's face to the world. 'Under all the circumstances, so much was accomplished as could have been anticipated and I flatter myself that I did as well as anyone could have done,' he wrote a fellow Conservative MP.[2]

After several days visiting with family in Vancouver, Bowell boarded a luxury CPR car heading east, provided by the railway for the trip to Belleville for Christmas with daughters and grandchildren before returning to the Ottawa grind. The long days of travel through the British Columbia mountains, across the flat Prairies and through northern Ontario forests gave him time to reflect and write nostalgically about his exotic trip and to look ahead to what would be a busy, big-issue year ahead.

The political to-do list awaiting him on arrival back on Parliament Hill was substantial. Australian trip follow-up would include organizing the pro-posed Empire trade conference in Ottawa (his first priority) and convincing Canadian businessmen to show more skill and enthusiasm in efforts to exploit a potential Australian market. In addition, he had decided to air a few other complaints with Canadian business leaders about their performance and attitudes.

Conference preparation would include cajoling Australian leaders to confirm their attendance, pressuring Great Britain to overcome its resistance to the conference as an uppity colonial venture, finding appropriate space, setting an achievable agenda and fixing a date. There probably also would be some skeptics within his own government who needed convincing that it was worth the time, energy and resources to host the conference even if it alienated Britain.

As Government Leader in the Senate, Bowell knew he faced a tough fight guiding a new Insolvency Act through the Upper House. He was chair of the government committee responsible for the issue that he knew would pit business leaders against farmers who were a key Conservative con-stituency. In addition, the minister had to brace for a year of heated political maneuvering and debates inside government and throughout the country over how to accommodate increasing pressure for tariff reform while maintaining key National Policy protections. Bowell quickly discovered that Prime Minister Thompson had already signaled some concessions on the issue while his trade and commerce minister was out of the country.

The Prime Minister had used the occasion of a Pictou, Nova Scotia meeting, organized as a celebration of his recent knighthood, to announce that his government would match any American moves to reduce trade barriers between the two countries. While Liberal-style reciprocity was not in the cards, 'for every step taken by Congress reducing or abolishing duties on Canadian products, the Canadian government would take corresponding steps and would do everything possible to make trade between the two countries freer,' according to a news report on Thompson's speech.[3] This came as news to the trade minister who was largely responsible for the file.

After months of consultations and growing evidence that voters were warming up to Liberal promises of trade liberalization across the 49th Parallel, a strategic retreat in the pre-election year seemed to be in the offing. Bowell saw his main role in looming cabinet tariff reform debates as defending National Policy protectionist principles in the face of growing free trade enthusiasm from finance minister George Foster. On his cross-Canada railway journey back home, the minister didn't make it off the Prairies before receiving a sharp lesson in how politically contentious and tricky the looming tariff policy debate would be. It also was a clear signal that the several months of favourable press coverage he had enjoyed in Australia were over. At the Winnipeg station where his train stopped to pick up passengers, a *Free Press* reporter interviewed Bowell about his Australian adventure and then slipped in a question about tariff reform and whether the government planned to continue protectionism. 'Certainly. Why not?' responded the minister, unaware of Thompson's promise. 'Well, up here in the Northwest, it does not appear to meet with public approval,' replied the reporter. 'Winnipeg has declared for tariff reform.'

Mackenzie Bowell had found a cow patty in which to step. 'Oh, we can't help that,' he said. 'Just now, you people are a bit off.' Then the train pulled out of the station, cutting off a chance for further questions. The next day, the newspaper—whose motto proclaimed its belief in 'freedom in trade' and whose owner was Liberal luminary Clifford Sifton—published a story under a predictable headline: WE ARE A BIT OFF. It attributed the sentiment to 'Columbus Mac Bowell,' back from exploring a new world where he promoted trade while responsible for a domestic policy 'designed to limit [trade] to its smallest dimensions.'[4]

Eventually, the Toronto *Globe* would publish a pile-on follow-up story on the issue. Bowell was hypocrite-in-chief on trade matters during his tour of Australia and can be expected to play the same role in Canada, blared the

Liberal newspaper. Australians accustomed to paradoxical natural wonders such as a tree that produces its bark inside the trunk and the duck-billed platypus that is a combination of 'bird, beast and fish,' still had never witnessed a wonder of the world such as 'the spectacle of one of the high priests of protection in Canada journeying through their cities commending to their notice the advantages of free trade.'[5]

He arrived back at his trade minister's desk in the Parliament Hill West Block on December 26 and immediately began to catch up on the work backlog, including plans for the months ahead. First up was preparation for a blunt heart-to-heart talk with business leaders. During the winter of 1894, after years of privately carping about the timidity, ethos and honesty of many Canadian businessmen willing to live comfortably if unimaginatively behind National Policy protective walls, Bowell decided to confront the problem directly. He would arrange a series of meetings with business leaders to explain his point of view in blunt, plain language. He would use as a soapbox his position as Canada first trade minister, underpinned by his personal credibility as a successful businessman and a defender of business interests in cabinet. His well-known discomfort with the rising tide of union militancy undoubtedly added to his *bona fides* before business crowds.

They soon would discover the plain-talking minister had some bones to pick. He was not one of their biggest fans.

As his first and most important venue, Bowell chose a February meeting of the Canadian Manufacturers' Association in Toronto and on February 5, asked if he could attend to speak about the potential for trade with Australia. His offer was quickly accepted but while the minister had suggested the meeting be private so the discussion could be frank 'without reporters being present,' the organizers informed him his speech would be during a Toronto Board of Trade luncheon that would be public. Bowell began his February 14 speech by recounting the mix-up over whether it would be public or secret and acknowledging he would have preferred that it be private. He began:

> But like all politicians, I have to bow under the circumstances to the inevitable. I am therefore placed in the position of saying to you in as plain a language as I can command what I think is your duty as manufacturers, and more particularly as Canadians, to extend the trade of this country to other portions of the world.

As usual, Bowell predicted he would not dazzle them with his rhetorical skills. 'It is not my intention to attempt any oratory [and] those who know me know that is not my *forté*.' Then he moved to the point he presumably wanted to make more forcefully in private: there was growing evidence and public outrage over reports that behind National Policy protections, businessmen were colluding to fix prices and to gouge consumers. Bowell told them bluntly:

I don't object to men making money, provided they can make it legitimately and honestly and not by what they are accused of having done—combining to fleece the community. There are combinations which are for the benefit of the community and there are combinations which we say injure the community. I take for granted that the manufacturers of this country have sufficient intellect and good sense to know that if the latter kind of combination exists among them, it will soon recoil against them.

A better strategy, the minister advised with more than a hint of 'or else' behind his words, 'is to combine only for the purpose of acting in consort with the object of increasing trade and cheapening products in the interests of those who have to consume them.' Bowell made clear he was not opposed to business profits. A businessman who operates ethically, builds strong companies 'and has made a little money is a good citizen of any country for he is likely to do much to enhance its progress and to build up its nationality.' But he warned that his department would be keeping an eye on those tempted to abuse their position.[6]

Bowell finished by turning to the topic he ostensibly was there to discuss— trade opportunities in Australia—although it was clear his real purpose was to warn businessmen to clean up their act. In the end, the fact that the speech was delivered in public worked to his advantage. It received wide newspaper coverage and enhanced his reputation as a straight-talking, honest and tough politician while boosting the business-oriented government's reputation as also a friend of consumers. Privately, Bowell also had formed the opinion— and had bluntly expressed it—that many Canadian businessmen had become lazy and complacent as they prospered behind the tariff walls.

In April, Winnipeg entrepreneur W. F. Buchanan—who Bowell had taken to Australia to deal with business contacts and to compile a list of trade opportunities—complained that few manufacturers showed an interest in cashing in on possibilities opened by the Australian trip. 'They would like everything done for them without any cost to themselves,' the trade and commerce minister replied. 'In fact, some have modestly asked that we should send out agents to put their goods on exhibition in large centers. I told them plainly that the government was willing to do all that was possible to open up trade but they themselves must do the business.'[7]

As the government's chief commercial and trade promoter, Bowell clearly had a dim view of many of the businessmen he was working to help. Nonetheless, by August he had decided to create a government trade office in Sydney, New South Wales to aid businessmen interested in the new market. He appointed John Larke of Oshawa, Ontario as the first Canadian trade commissioner with instructions to tour Canada for several months talking to businessmen about Australian opportunities they imagined. The plan was to have Larke take up Australian residency in December with instructions to report at least monthly to the Bowell on trade prospects. The minister asked Public Works Minister J. A. Ouimet to supply the new trade commissioner with photos of Ottawa's grandest public buildings to hang in his Sydney office 'in order that strangers may see we are not still in an uncivilized state.'[8]

Within a month of his potentially incendiary speech to the Toronto business crowd, Bowell faced the task of shepherding through the Senate a tariff change package that also had the potential to displease parts of the business community. That winter Prime Minister Thomson's government had introduced legislation aimed at implementing some tariff reductions, mainly on products imported from Great Britain. It was evidence that Finance Minister Foster's freer trade arguments had won the day in cabinet debate although most of the high-tariff National Policy remained in place.

Thompson's promise to implement tariff reductions to match American tariff cuts on Canadian goods heading south was largely unnecessary since U.S. government proposals became bogged down in the swamp of Congressional wrangling in Washington. Bowell, the good-soldier Senate leader, marshaled his forces to get the amendments through before Parliament rose in June for the summer, even if he did not entirely agree with them. Reaction in Great Britain, which had embraced free trade, was enthusiastic if a bit condescending: 'It is a matter for congratulation that the Prime Minister of the Dominion, Sir John Thompson and his leading colleagues, should have come to recognize the necessity of retreating from the attitude of high-and-dry protectionism,' wrote the *Financial Times of London*. The *Newcastle Daily Chronicle* credited the government and in particular 'several long-headed Conservatives... who, discerning the signs of the times and rightly interpreting them, strove to save their party from the disaster which an obstinate resistance to the popular desire would inevitably have entailed.'[9] It smirked that 'by degrees, the scales dropped from their eyes.'

Meanwhile, the tariff reductions implemented by the Thompson government came with fiscal consequences. They reduced revenues and undermined the national budget, driving the government from surplus to deficit in the 1894 fiscal year. 'The most noteworthy feature of the receipts is the decline in Customs duties from $21 million to $19.2 million, a decline partially anticipated as a result of the tariff reductions made during the last session of the Dominion Parliament,' the federal auditor noted in a report tabled in Parliament February 4, 1895.[10]

At the same time as he dealt with changes to the tariff regime, Bowell in his role as Government Leader in the Senate was trying to manoeuver through the Senate a contentious bill to update the country's bankruptcy and insolvency legislation. The proposals would enhance the power of creditors to seize assets in the case of a debtor's insolvency. It was an opportunity to earn some political capital with a business community still smarting from Bowell's February criticisms of its operating practices. The manufacturers' lobby supported the proposal, but the politically powerful farm community did not. The minister was receiving complaints from farm representatives about its potential to unjustly shift power from producers to suppliers. The Patrons of Industry representing Manitoba farmers complained that it would 'cripple' their members. An Ontario agricultural accountant wrote to complain that the bill would empower implement suppliers at the expense of farmers. 'The law would be able to be abused, used as a sort of coercion act.'[11]

The 'Act Respecting Insolvency' proved to be time-consuming for Bowell and in the end, an impossible political sell. Like predecessor bills over the previous 14 years since the previous law was repealed in 1880, this version died unapproved in the Seventh Parliament. 'In all, Parliament debated twenty bills proposing some form of national bankruptcy regime between 1880 and 1903... and every bill failed to garner sufficient votes in Parliament,' Western University professor Thomas G. W. Telfer reported in a 2014 study of the issue.[12]

When the bill died for lack of parliamentary support, Mackenzie Bowell likely was relieved. It freed up more of his time to work on his priority project in early 1894; organizing the unprecedented Empire conference on inter-colonial trade rules and relations between the colonies and the British government. He had no template to follow, since it would be a first.

In April 1894, a disappointed Robert Reid—Minister of Defence for Australia's Victoria Colony—was preparing to head home from Canada. He had traveled thousands of miles for a colonial conference but its start date had been delayed and Reid could not change his travel arrangements. He clearly thought he would be missing a milestone event. As reported by the Montreal *Gazette*, Reid said it promised to be 'one of the most important conferences of British statesmen ever convened' and he credited Mackenzie Bowell for making it happen. The Canadian trade minister had conceived the event, won buy-in from other colonial leaders and then did the organizational heavy lifting. Reid said his government and other Australian colonial leaders had decided to take time out of a divisive domestic political battle over Australian federation proposals to attend a conference in faraway Canada because of Bowell. 'When that gentleman appeared amongst [Australians] and with cheery English words held out the right hand of fellowship, the people of Australia felt the least they could do was to stretch their hands across the sea in order to meet their brethren of the same faith and the same blood in the colder regions of the north,' Reid said in a Montreal speech before departing.[13]

Indeed, organizing the colonial conference had been Bowell's priority since returning to Ottawa in late December and it involved dealing with myriad details. He wrote letters to Australian political leaders urging them to fulfill their promises to attend or to send representatives. He urged High Commissioner Tupper in London to lobby the British government to send a high-level representative although it would be the first empire conference not initiated and led by British officials. He convinced the Thompson cabinet in mid-February to issue an invitation to delegates from other countries and colonies to travel to Ottawa 'for the purpose of fully discussing all matters affecting trade and cable communications between Canada and Australasia'. He secured approval to have the foreign delegates designated as 'guests of Canada' with free access to transportation and other facilities. He reserved a block of rooms for delegates at the Russell House Hotel, organized some side trips and entertainment for the visitors and secured approval to use the Senate chamber as the venue for some conference proceedings.

As a final detail, Bowell arranged for his son John to take time from his Vancouver customs collector job to meet the delegates arriving at the port and to arrange their travel in Canada.

As winter snow transformed into spring showers in Canada's capital, the pieces were falling into place. Great Britain had agreed to send as a delegate Victor Villiers, the Earl of Jersey, former Governor of the Australian colony of New South Wales and grandson of legendary British Prime Minister Sir Robert Peel. Recently arrived Canadian Governor General John Hamilton, the Earl of Aberdeen, had agreed to address the conference and Prime Minister Thompson planned to attend some conference-related functions.

Then Canadian weather threw a wrench into the schedule, as sometimes happens in 'the colder regions of the north.' When delegates began to arrive in Vancouver in mid-June for a cross-Canada trip to Ottawa and the June 21 conference opening, snow melt and rain had flooded the Fraser and Columbia rivers, washing out miles of CPR track that had to be replaced. Delegates had an unscheduled week to languish on Canada's West Coast, seeing the sights of Vancouver and environs. By June 21, the track was repaired and Bowell was able to write to a friend in Australia: 'They are at the moment of writing on their way eastward from Banff in the charge of my "faithful John" whom I sent out to meet them and look after their comfort en-route.'[14]

On the afternoon of June 28 in the ornate Senate Chamber, the Colonial Conference began with Lord Jersey in his seat to represent Great Britain while Bowell, Postmaster General Sir Adolphe Caron and Finance Minister George Foster represented Canada. There were delegates from New South Wales, Tasmania, South Australia, Victoria State, Queensland, Cape of Good Hope and New Zealand. After welcoming addresses from Governor General Aberdeen and Prime Minister Thompson, the meeting adjourned to be resumed the next morning in Bowell's Trade and Commerce department offices. Aberdeen called the gathering:

In no small degree unique and much of its success is due to the fact that the highly esteemed Canadian statesman Hon. Mackenzie Bowell has travelled through a large part of Australia and was thus able to personally come in contact with leading men of the Australian colonies and others to shape views and ideas about the advisability of holding a conference.

Thompson said the Canadian hope was that 'the ocean which divides the colonies shall become a highway for their people and their products.'[15] The next morning, Bowell was unanimously elected president of the conference and promptly informed the assembly he would be absent for several days to deal with a family tragedy. His granddaughter Hattie Jamieson had died in Belleville and he hurried home to comfort daughter Louise. The delegates approved a statement of condolence and 'profound sympathy.' He returned to his leadership duties July 3.

The conference was a forum for discussions about establishing subsidized fast mail service and a Pacific communications cable to connect Australia to Canada and the rest of the Empire, although there was no resolution to either file by conference end. However, the more important and overriding issue for colonial delegates was improving the ability of colonial governments to negotiate favourable trade agreements between themselves and with other countries without facing conditions imposed by Great Britain. In effect, they were demanding more autonomy and less paternalistic oversight and restrictions from the Mother Country.

In retrospect, the Ottawa conference would be seen as a significant waystation on the journey from the 19th century British Empire model of a dominant London and an all-powerful British Parliament at the centre setting rules for a global galaxy of subservient colonies, to a federation of independent, equal nations that culminated with the Statute of Westminster passed by the British Parliament in 1931. In 1894, the issue voiced by delegates was the desire not for political independence but more colonial leeway to develop trade arrangements between themselves or with other countries that worked to their economic benefit. At the time under British law, the colonies were subservient jurisdictions, prohibited from making preferential trade arrangements between themselves unless the import concessions were extended to other countries holding trade agreements with Britain, even though they had not negotiated reciprocal trade access concessions for the colonies. For Canada, another irritant was that it was forced to give preferred access to products from Germany and Belgium under the terms of an earlier treaty between Great Britain and those two countries. In addition, Canadian anger lingered over the British trade treaty negotiated with France (with

Tupper's approval) that would extend 'favoured nation' access to Canada for French products without reciprocal access.

A special complaint for the Australian colonies was that the Constitution Acts the British Parliament had imposed on them blocked negotiation of trade treaties giving tariff preference to foreign countries, including other British colonies like Canada.[16]

A published history of the first half-century of the Department of Trade and Commerce cited the 1894 conference as a key event in colonial evolution. 'At the Colonial Conference, important discussions arose over colonial autonomy in fiscal policy and more particularly over the constitutional obstacles to the making of trade agreements by the various colonies represented,' wrote historian O. Mary Hill, citing Bowell as the leader of the colonial forces. 'In one of his speeches to delegates, [Bowell] pressed for that freedom of action in commercial affairs and in tariff legislation that he felt the self-governing colonies should possess. He foresaw a sort of customs union and waxed eloquent about it.'[17]

In his speech, Bowell was blunt. He told delegates:

My desire as a British subject is to see the colonies trade among themselves and with the Mother Country if she will let us and if she will not allow us to give her any advantages over the other countries, all I can say is, as an Englishman I pity her. But if she is determined not to do that… all we have to say is 'let her release us from her bondage under which we labour and let us trade among ourselves. We are large enough, we are old enough, we are rich enough and we are industrious enough to provide each other with that which we require not only for sustenance but for living in every way.'[18]

Lord Jersey, with an order from London head office not to cede Britain's traditional dominant position in the Empire, opposed, obfuscated and demanded more information. On July 6, Canadian Finance Minister Foster, in consultation with Jersey, moved a motion that watered down Bowell's point and that stirred some colonial opposition but was approved in a five to three vote. It affirmed conference support for 'the advisability of a customs arrangement between Great Britain and her colonies by which trade within the empire may be placed on a more favourable footing than that which is carried on with foreign countries.' The flaw in the compromise resolution was that there was no obligation that Britain enter into a customs arrangement with the colonies but still, it was a symbolic step forward.[19]

In his strong advocacy for a developing empire in which the colonies had more status, respect and autonomy of action, Mackenzie Bowell was establishing himself as squarely in the tradition of Canadian Conservative leaders who were proud British imperialists and yet Canadian patriots anxious to see their country grow in power, self-government and prestige.

In the aftermath of the Ottawa conference, the Regina *Leader* newspaper argued that Bowell's push for more colonial power within the empire conjured up memories of an impassioned statement by Sir John A. Macdonald several decades earlier. It recounted an evening of discussion between Macdonald and *Leader* founder and Conservative MP Nicholas Flood Davin when the Prime Minister was asked about his vision for Canada. 'Sir John rose from his seat, got quite enthusiastic and sketched a time when the colonies would come together, would trade more with each other, would associate for mutual protection and when, as he said, the British Empire would be a "grand confederation of nations". Then he shook his head in his characteristic way and said: "That's the time I'd like to be coming up".'[20]

In 1887 as Macdonald's Minister of Justice, John Thompson, added to the push for more Canadian legal autonomy within the British Empire by writing an analysis critical of British legislation that declared 'void and inoperative' any colonial legislation that was deemed 'repugnant' to a law on the British statute books. Thompson argued that the British power of disallowance reflected a bygone era of British supremacy within the Empire:

> The minister is of the opinion that these provisions do not aptly express the true relations between the legislation of the United Kingdom in respect of a Colony and the legislation of the Parliament or Legislature of the Colony. In the case of Canada, full authority is by the British North America Act, 1867, granted to the Parliament of Canada and the Legislatures of the provinces to legislate for the peace, order and good government of the Dominion, in the exercise of which power it may become as necessary to amend or to repeal expressly or by implication some statute of the United Kingdom extending to Canada or some Province of Canada as it is to amend or repeal some rule of the common law.[21]

Seven years later, Bowell added his voice to that continuum of Canadian agitation for more independence and respect. In a post-conference speech at a Toronto banquet for delegates, the conference chair proclaimed that while born in England, he considered himself Canadian. 'If England is not prepared to allow us as colonists or British subjects to have privileges other than those which are given to foreign countries, that is her fault and not ours,' he said. 'If we make this offer and she refuses it, then we would say to the great Mother Land to allow us and our children to deal with ourselves preferentially as against the outside world.'

Delegates greeted the declaration with applause.[22]

A quarter century later, Sir Robert Borden—a Bowell successor as Conservative leader and Prime Minister—furthered the journey toward nationhood by claiming Canada's right as a wartime ally to have a seat at the Paris peace table as a separate nation and not a part of the British delegation.

In 1931, it was Conservative R. B. Bennett who presided when Canada and the other colonies were granted *de facto* independent nation status under the Statute of Westminster, the end of a journey started by the founding Tory Prime Minister all those decades before and enhanced in their own ways by his successors.

As the Colonial Conference wound down on July 9 after 12 days, Bowell took one last opportunity to urge the Australian colonies to join in a federation to increase their clout within the Empire. The Australian representatives, divided at home over the federation issue, had often found themselves at rhetorical loggerheads during conference debates. It weakened their influence, he argued. There were few concrete conference decisions to brag about immediately. Britain made no concrete concessions about colonial power. The requirement that Canada adhere to the British-negotiated access concessions to Belgium and Germany would not be dropped for four years and the Canada/Australia communication cable would not be launched for eight years.

However, the wrap-up speeches reflected a general sense that something important had transpired, that history had been altered, that relations and the power balance within the British Empire would never be the same. In his closing remarks, Lord Jersey reflected that sense of historic change when he spoke on behalf of the British government, thanking chairman Bowell for his 'genial courtesy'.

> This Ottawa conference will undoubtedly stand forth, not only in the history of Canada and the history of Australia but will stand forth in the history of the Empire as the first great step drawing together in a friendly feeling every portion of that empire, and Mackenzie Bowell, it will be your pride to think that you have presided over such a conference... If our work results as we hope it will, you may feel you have not worked for the public in vain but that you have worked for Canada and for the Empire and there is no prouder boast for any public man than to say he has been instrumental... in carrying an object which so many millions have at heart.[23]

Within months, the British Parliament passed legislation allowing the Australian colonies to make preferential trade deals with other British colonies including Canada. In April 1895, the change of British heart was noted and praised in the Throne Speech opening the new session of Canada's Parliament. The decision 'affords gratifying proof that the suggestions of the Colonial Conference are being favourably entertained by Her Majesties' [sic] government,' said the speech written by Bowell and his new government.[24]

As the conference ended and international delegates prepared to head off on tourism excursions or meetings Bowell had organized, he was able to bask in domestic and international media accolades and praise.

Several British newspapers, while cool to the idea that the colonies should have more power and preferential trade terms, praised Canada's emerging role as a leading Empire voice. The *London Echo* suggested Bowell would 'live in history as the organizer and president of the first gathering of the statesmen of Greater Britain that has assembled in a Colonial metropolis.'[25] The *Sydney Herald* (Australia) enthused: 'The stride that has been taken from the old Downing Street relations is one that is never to be recalled and henceforth, instead of waiting on the bidding of England or being dragged willy-nilly into troubles that may be none of the colonies' seeking, we have in this conference the guarantee that the voice of the colonies will be heard and listened to and valued.'[26] The Regina *Leader* said that because of his conference organizing and leadership, Bowell 'if he cares for such things, is certainly entitled to a knighthood.'

Within months, hundreds of printed copies the official report on the conference proceedings had sold out. When the Montreal Board of Trade requested a copy of the report in early autumn, Bowell had to reply: 'It would afford me great pleasure to meet this request but the demand for copies has been so great that it is absolutely impossible to do so.'[27]

With the conference over, the foreign guests departed, an intensely busy seven months behind him and Parliament adjourned for the summer, Bowell finally was able to look forward to some down time and relaxation. However, one irritant from the conference continued to trail him for much of the rest of the summer. After his post-conference speech to delegates gathered in Toronto, the minister had booked space at a downtown hotel to host a luncheon. Instead of simply a lunch, the hotel billed the government for housing 10 delegates plus three children and two maids. Bowell put government lawyers on the case, telling them 'they were only there for dinner.' In July, the lawyers accused the hotel of gouging and threatened to send the case to Justice Department lawyers to pursue if the hotel didn't back down. Since that was the last entry in the case file preserved by Library and Archives Canada, presumably Canadian taxpayers were off the hook.[28]

On the last day of August, after returning to Ottawa from a short vacation, Bowell reported to a friend that he had been able to spend some informal, private relaxation time with the Prime Minister. 'I have just returned from Muskoka Lakes where I have been spending a few days with Sir John Thompson.'[29] The respite in the luxury of a well-appointed summer home owned by Hamilton, Ontario millionaire Conservative Senator W. E, Sandford was a summer highlight for the hard-working trade minister. Prime Minister Thompson and his family had been renting an island home from

Sandford on Lake Rousseau near Port Carling since early August. He was exhausted from a hard year of politics, travel and months of stressful work as one of the arbitrators at the drawn-out Paris hearings into the Behring Strait dispute with the United States. There were intimations that the Prime Minister, overworked and overweight, was not feeling well.

Thompson returned to Ottawa from his Muskoka retreat for an August 21 cabinet meeting called to discuss what compensation Canada would accept from the US for damages caused by American seizure of Canadian sealing boats in the Behring dispute. Bowell also attended cabinet and then the two men headed north to cottage country for a week. Sandford had invited the trade minister to stay at his main Muskoka residence on Sans Souci Island. The brief getaway provided a welcome break for both of them. Thompson reported that the air was 'balmy and the water warm as milk.'[30] A Thompson biographer described their time together as 'the halcyon summer days of August 1894.'[31] A rare photograph of Bowell and the others, laughing as they gathered for an outdoor photo-op with a newfangled Kodak camera that used rolled film rather than old-fashioned and slow plates, conveyed the impression that the two politicians were comfortable and relaxed in each other's company.

The holiday also provided the public with one of the most intimate and rare accounts of Bowell at leisure as a storyteller, an animated jokester and a raconteur when in private among friends. The source of the character sketch was a story by Toronto *Empire* reporter Faith Fenton, a friend of Thompson's who showed up at the island retreat unexpectedly and wrote about it. She described Bowell as a life of the party figure, 'a jolly summer holiday companion. He can tell bigger fish stories, troll more rollicking ditties and learn a new game of cards better than anyone else in the party—excepting always the [host] Senator.' Fenton commented on 'the vigour, bodily and mental, of our minister of Trade and Customs. He is over 70, he tells us proudly, yet he has the energy and fire of twenty-five.'[32] She wrote that a young female rower 'wonders confidentially "what he must have been when he was young".'

Evenings were spent on the verandah discussing politics, his visit to Australia and the Ottawa conference. Fenton told the story of a day when Bowell was rowing other guests back to the house for dinner after he had spent the afternoon fishing. Despite his fitness, strength and effort, the boat was barely moving and finally stopped altogether as he worked up a sweat. 'Suddenly, he turned, leaned over the bow, drew in a length of dripping rope and a mud-dragged iron anchor. "Senator," he said, "I'm a fool, shall it not be found in Ottawa when the Wise Men shall again assemble".' Fenton wrote that 'echoes of laughter rang over Sans Souci harbour at Bowell's good-natured expense.' With the holiday over, the trade and commerce minister was back in Ottawa at the beginning of September, preparing for a trip through southwest Ontario to urge businessmen, farmers and the food

177

industry to take advantage of trade opportunities with Australia. At the time, he was settling the final arrangements for appointing, preparing and equipping Canada's first trade commissioner to those colonies.

In October, Thompson received word that he was being summoned to London in November to be sworn into the Imperial Privy Council for his work at the Behring Strait arbitration process. Bowell braced for another busy autumn as acting prime minister, putting out fires across the government in Thompson's absence. The Prime Minister departed Ottawa on October 29 to travel to New York and then across the Atlantic where a month of meetings were scheduled with British officials on topics ranging from negotiations with Newfoundland over joining Canada to a push by Ottawa to win approval for Canadian copyright protection, in the lead-up to the central event.

The swearing in ceremony was to take place December 12 at Windsor Castle where Thompson would become only the second Canadian to have his name on the Queen's Privy Council roll. (Macdonald was the first.) On the evening of December 11, Thompson sent his visiting daughter Helena on her way to Paris to return to school and then attended a meeting of the Colonial Institute with Sir Charles Tupper to hear a presentation on 'the National Significance of the Ottawa Conference.'

Thompson spoke in defence of the conference's significance although one London newspaper report on the meeting said he 'seemed to be extremely nervous, trembling visibly and acting differently from his usual self.'[33] Others, including his daughter, had remarked that his health seemed improved after some summer vacation and time in London. Thompson himself allowed that he felt well. The next morning, a special train left at noon for the trip to Windsor and the 1:15 p.m. ceremony.

When acting Prime Minister Bowell received a telegram late morning Ottawa time on December 12, he did not believe it. It relayed news that Sir John Thompson, 49, had died at Windsor Castle moments after becoming a Queen's Privy Councilor. Bowell thought it a 'mere newspaper rumour' and demanded confirmation. It came half an hour later from C. R. Hosmer of the CPR in Montreal, who had received the initial telegram from London.

Then, after a telegram from Sir Charles Tupper, the shocking story was pieced together with its sequence of events that had ended tragically. The Windsor Castle ceremony over, guests had adjourned to an adjacent room for lunch. Thompson fainted at the table, was revived, returned to the table, complained of chest pain and collapsed. The Queen's doctor sitting beside him pronounced him dead at 1:45 p.m. London time.[34]

Once the import of the news sank in for shocked government leaders in Ottawa, a meeting of the Canadian Privy Council with available cabinet ministers was quickly convened. Bowell wept openly and then, joined by

Finance Minister Foster and Thompson's longtime private secretary Douglas Stewart, went to officially inform Thompson's widow Annie of the news.

While arrangements for transporting Thompson's body back from London and organizing a state funeral had to be made, the first political and constitutional priority was to name a new prime minister, the fourth in little more than three years and the third consecutive one without an electoral mandate. Without an obvious successor in sight, the delicate and essential task rested on the inexperienced shoulders of Governor General Aberdeen, John Campbell Gordon, a British Liberal barely a year into his mandate.

Aberdeen and his wife Ishbel Maria were in Montreal when news of Thompson's death reached them. The Governor-General immediately telegraphed Colonial Secretary Lord Ripon in London for advice on whether as acting Prime Minister, Mackenzie Bowell should be asked to form a government. Ripon declined to offer official advice but 'as a friend' suggested Bowell should be offered the position first.[35] The Governor General's entourage promptly boarded a train to return to the capital. The Aberdeens and Thompsons had become close friends over the previous year and Lady Aberdeen wanted to be there to comfort Annie. Her husband wanted to be on hand to try to manage the leadership crisis. During the two-hour trip, the Aberdeens discussed options he faced and Lady Aberdeen later recorded the conversation in her personal diary, a text that has become the most influential account of that politically tumultuous time since its publication in 1956.[36] By her account, the Governor General considered four possible successors: Bowell, High Commissioner Tupper, Finance Minister George Foster from New Brunswick, and Railways and Canals Minister John Haggart from Perth, Ontario, south of Ottawa. Through the vice-regal eyes, each possibility carried baggage.

In Tupper's case, he had a strong following in the Conservative Party based on his decades of political performance and accomplishments. Nevertheless, it was unclear if he was interested in leaving his prestigious sinecure in London for the rough and tumble of Canadian politics, despite the active lobbying by his son Charles Hibbert Tupper for his father's appointment. Tupper Senior also had his detractors including Annie Thompson who told Lady Aberdeen that appointment of Tupper would be 'an insult to my husband's memory.' Thompson had privately referred to Tupper Senior as 'the old tramp.' He was also mocked for his egotistical tendency to portray himself as the central figure in much of post-Confederation Canadian history. The Toronto *Globe* gleefully reported during the 1896 election campaign that then-Conservative leader Tupper used the first-person pronoun so many times in speeches that Liberal rowdies began to disrupt rallies by chanting 'I, I, I' loudly enough throughout his speeches that the audience could not hear him or laughed.

Tupper also had a reputation as a lascivious 'ladies' man' during his years as a rural country doctor in Nova Scotia, earning him the unofficial title of 'The Ram of Cumberland County.' The story was so widespread that during the 1896 campaign, Tory-turned-opponent D'Alton McCarthy drew public laughs with his response when told that Tupper had lamented McCarthy's political defection because he had treated him as a 'political father' would. In a Brockville, Ontario speech, McCarthy responded that he would be 'ashamed to be numbered among the numerous progeny who claimed Sir Charles as father.'[37]

Foster, although a competent finance minister who would go on to set a Canadian political record for serving in the cabinets of seven Prime Ministers, was not seen by the Governor General as a leader who could control cabinet. Then there were puritanical 19th century prejudices against him because critics alleged that he had played a role in the breakup of his wife's first marriage, only to quickly marry her in the United States.

Haggart, Lady Aberdeen recorded, was 'the strongest man' and favoured by Annie Thompson but he also was a 'Bohemian' which made his suitability suspect.[38] In a history of Perth, Ontario, writer Larry Turner pointed out several other accusations of abuse of office that held local MP Haggart back from promotion. He used public money to build a canal in Perth that benefited a mill the MP owned (the canal was locally dubbed 'Haggart's ditch') and the fact that he and his wife lived separately in the small, conservative town created gossip. 'While he was known for bagging party and government funds, he was alleged to have "an eye for plump and accessible lady typists",' Turner wrote.[39]

That left acting Prime Minister Bowell, whom Lady Aberdeen described as 'rather fussy and decidedly commonplace' but also 'a good and straight man and has great ideas about the drawing together of the colonies and the Empire,' referring to his organization of the Colonial Conference.[40]

On December 13, Aberdeen summoned Bowell for a 'lengthy conversation' but the Governor General still had concerns about whether his Protestant and Orange past would exacerbate racial and linguistic tensions in Canada. He consulted Sir Frank Smith, a Roman Catholic Senator from Toronto who had served in every Conservative administration since 1882. Lady Aberdeen recorded that Smith was 'emphatic in favour of Mr. Bowell and he said that the latter had been so careful that he never offended a Roman Catholic.' With that endorsement in mind, her husband 'gradually came to the opinion that Mr. Bowell would under the circumstances suit best, more especially since Mr. Haggart's private life is not supposed to be able to bear inspection.'[41]

After dinner on December. 13, 1894, Aberdeen 'returned to the office in the Parliament Hill East Block and sent for Mr Mackenzie Bowell in his room at the Russell House a block south. By 11:00 p.m. as the meeting ended, he commissioned him to form a Government.'

Little more than 60 years after landing in Canada, the immigrant kid was about to become Canada's fifth prime minister… as long as he could cobble together a cabinet of political rivals willing to serve. No doubt, Bowell's moment of triumph was darkened by the knowledge that his opportunity came because of the death of his friend John Thompson. He also may have remembered with regret a late summer note he sent to the late Prime Minister who had complained that too many outsiders were crowding into the Senate space set aside for MPs on special occasions such as Throne Speech day. Bowell promised that as Government Senate Leader, he would fix it. 'I will try and have this trouble prevented, if we live to meet Parliament again.'[42]

One of them didn't.

NOTES

[1] LAC Bowell Papers, Vol. 73 (December 23, 1893 letter to London shipping company owner James Huddart.), 242.

[2] ibid, Vol. 95 (January 2, 1894 letter), 290.

[3] ibid, Vol. 106 (November 30, 1893 Reuters News Agency).

[4] ibid, Vol. 108 (December 19, 1893 Winnipeg *Free Press,* page 1).

[5] ibid, Vol. 114 Part 1 (July 2, 1894, the Toronto *Globe*).

[6] ibid, Vol. 108 (February 15, 1894 edition of the Toronto *Globe*). Its extensive coverage was widely reprinted by newspapers across Canada.

[7] ibid, Vol. 96 (April 8, 1894 letter to W.F. Buchanan).

[8] ibid, Vol. 75 (November 20, 1894 letter to J.A. Ouimet).

[9] ibid, Vol. 106 (March 29, 1894 *Newcastle* (England) *Daily Chronicle* commentary).

[10] ibid, Vol. 106 (February 4, 1895 report of the Dominion Auditor).

[11] ibid, Vol. 13 (April 30, 1894 letter from Toronto accountant C. T. Gallagher).

[12] Telfer, Thomas G. W., 'Ruin and Redemption: The Struggle for a Canadian Banruptcy Law, 1867–1919,' *The Osgoode Society for Canadian Legal History*, University of Toronto Press, 2014, 106.

[13] LAC Bowell Papers, Vol. 108 (Montreal *Gazette,* May 4, 1894).

[14] ibid, Vol. 96 (June 21, 1894 letter to F. W. Ward in Brisbane).

[15] *Report by the Rt. Hon. the Earl of Jersey on the Colonial Conference at Ottawa.* Presented to both Houses of Parliament, London, August 1894 (Queen's Printer, 1894), 37–38.

[16] Hill, O. Mary, *Canada's Salesman to the World,* 72-73.

[17] ibid, 72.

[18] ibid, 73.

[19] *Jersey Report on the Colonial Conference at Ottawa.*

[20] LAC Bowell Papers, Vol. 108, File 3 (August 9, 1894 Regina Leader).

[21] LAC Bowell Papers, Vol. 98 (July 11, 1887 report written by John Thompson in reaction to a proposed British bill titled 'An Act to Remove Doubts as to the Validity of Colonial Laws.'

[22] LAC Bowell Papers, Vol. 108 (Toronto *Mail,* July 12, 1894).

[23] *Jersey Report on the Colonial Conference at Ottawa,* 273.

[24] Bowell Papers Vol. 110, Part 1 (October 5, 1894 *London Echo*).

[25] ibid, Vol. 108 File 3 (Reprinted July 25, 1894 by the *Montreal Gazette*).

[26] ibid, Vol. 75 (October 1, 1894 letter to the Montreal Board of Trade), 314.

[27] Bowell Papers, Vol. 75 (August 2, 1894 letter from lawyers).

[28] ibid (August 31, 1894 letter), 259.

[29] Waite, P. B., *The Man from Halifax: Sir John Thompson, Prime Minister,* (Toronto: University of Toronto Press), 413.

[30] ibid, 414.

[31] Fenton, Faith, *The Toronto Empire,* September 1, 1894.

[32] LAC Bowell Papers, Vol. 112, File 3.

[33] op cit, *The Man from Halifax,* 424.

[34] ibid, 425–26.

[35] Saywell, John, 'The Crown and the Politicians: The Canadian Succession Question 189–1896,' *The Canadian Historical Review,* Vol. XXXVII, December 4, 1956, 317.

[36] Saywell, John (ed.), *The Canadian Journal of Lady Aberdeen, 1893–1898* (Toronto: The Champlain Society, 1960).

[37] Charlesworth, Hector, *Candid Chronicles: Leaves from the Notebook of a Canadian Journalist* (Toronto: The MacMillan Co. of Canada, 1925), cited in Durant, Vincent, *War Horse of Cumberland: The Life and Times of Sir Charles Tupper* (Hantsport, Nova Scotia: Lancelot Press, 1985), 96.

[38] op cit, cited in *The Canadian Historical Review,* 317.

[39] Turner, Larry with Stewart, John, *Perth: Tradition and Style in Eastern Ontario* (Self-published in 1998), 67.

[40] op cit, *The Canadian Journal of Lady Aberdeen,* 317.

[41] ibid, 319.

[42] LAC Bowell Papers, Vol. 75 (July 27, 1894 letter to Sir John Thompson), 185.

Chapter 13
INHERITING A POISONED CHALICE

On Friday, December 21, 1894, Mackenzie Bowell and members of his cabinet-in-waiting boarded a train at the Ottawa station for a trip to Montreal and a swearing-in ceremony with Governor General Aberdeen. By the end of the day, Bowell officially would be Canada's fifth prime minister. The trip to Montreal for the ceremony, rather than a short jaunt down Sussex Drive to the Governor-General's Rideau Hall residence in Ottawa as would be customary, was required because of the eight days between Bowell's selection as prime minister and the swearing in ceremony. By then, Aberdeen had shifted his temporary office and residence to 919 Sherbrooke Street in Montreal where he would spend Christmas.

The long delay was the result of Bowell's discussions with prospective ministers about their willingness to serve in his government, although there was no public suggestion that candidates needed persuasion. Still, since several ministers later claimed they had doubts about joining Bowell's cabinet, the need for persuasion may have been a factor and possibly an early hint of later problems. At least part of the delay also could be attributed to the fact that Charles H. Tupper, Bowell's pick to be Minister of Justice (and one of the doubters), was in British Columbia when Sir John Thompson died and had to make arrangements for the long cross-country journey back to Ottawa.

For anyone with even a passing knowledge of the prominent players in political Ottawa during the previous years of Conservative governments, the Bowell entourage on the train chugging its way east that morning would have looked familiar. Most were carryovers from the Thompson, Abbott and last Macdonald governments of the past 42 months. Of the 17-member cabinet, 15 had been ministers under Thompson. The 'new' cabinet included familiar names such as Tupper of Nova Scotia, Thomas Daly of Manitoba, George Foster and John Costigan of New Brunswick and John Haggart of Perth, Ontario.

It would have been accurate, even on that first day, to describe some of the Bowell team on the train as the Prime Minister's fellow passengers accepting a job offer rather than fellow travellers who embraced his leadership. Already, some were voicing private doubts about the new boss from whom they had just accepted senior government positions, questioning whether he was the appropriate leader and up for the job. The Halifax *Herald* had reported before the cabinet was even announced that Haggart could cause 'real trouble' because he thought the leader's job should have been his.

'His friends openly claim he ought to have been selected.'[1]

The official day ended with Aberdeen signing Prime Minister Bowell's first orders-in-council appointing members of his cabinet. Then, it was off to Belleville and a family Christmas before getting down to work as Ottawa's new political boss. He spent part of the holiday bedridden with a 'severe cold and cough' and that is where he was on Christmas Day when a private letter arrived from Aberdeen forwarding a note from Colonial Secretary Ripon in London. Buckingham Palace officials wanted to know if Bowell would be willing to accept a knighthood from Queen Victoria. Bowell responded affirmatively with 'gratitude and pleasure' after the Governor General had congratulated him 'upon the offer of this mark of the Queen's favour and of recognition of your public services.'

Two days later on his 71st birthday, Bowell sent a follow-up message to Aberdeen from his sick bed, trying to deflect any possible criticism that accepting the title was a self-serving decision by a vain old man:

> If this 'mark of the Queen's favour' were merely the consequence of having been honoured with the responsibility of forming a new government under circumstances which we all deplore, I should have hesitated before accepting, but as your Excellency has kindly expressed the opinion that it is a recognition of my public services, I felt I should not have been justified in declining an honour so graciously tendered by my Sovereign.[2]

On December 31, Aberdeen forwarded another letter from Ripon that began with three powerful words for a British expatriate: 'Sir Mackenzie Bowell.' It informed him that Queen Victoria had appointed him Knight Commander of the Order of St Michael and St George 'in recognition of your valuable services to the Crown and the Dominion of Canada.' News of the Royal recognition and the official swearing in of the new government launched a sweet if brief honeymoon period for the rookie Prime Minister.

Private letters of congratulations and public praise poured in, including a nod from Queen's University principal Rev G. M. Grant, a noted Liberal. He said he held a high opinion of the new Premier: 'Especially during the past year or two, he has shown not only his usual capacity for work but a willingness to entertain new ideas that promise well.' Belleville City Council approved a resolution congratulating their 'honoured and esteemed citizen... As we believe "that honour is purchased by the deeds we do", so we believe that the position has come to our new Premier. As "great honours are great burdens", we hope that he may long be spared to Canada and to our Queen.'

Newspaper commentary generally was kind. The Hamilton *Spectator* noted he was an able debater, a 'capital' department manager, knowledgeable about trade and 'he stands high in the estimation of his French/Canadian colleagues.' Perhaps most importantly, he would run an honest government.

'He is a clean, honest, upright man against whom the slightest allegation of dishonesty was never made,' said the newspaper before ending with a bad pun: 'The Conservative Party has put on a Bowelled front.'³ The Montreal *Gazette* said of the new Prime Minister: 'He is himself a public man of large experience, sagacious, well informed of public opinion and acquainted with the wants of the situation.' The Toronto *Mail* chimed in on the knighthood debate by arguing 'if any man in Canada by reason of his services is entitled to be recognized by Her Majesty, that man is certainly Sir Mackenzie Bowell.' The *Northwest Review*, backstopped by the Roman Catholic Church, assured readers that Catholics had a friend in charge of the federal government. 'We have known Mr Bowell for twenty five years and can bear testimony to his high character and fairness in dealing with men of all shades of opinions,' it reported. 'Although a man of pronounced convictions and a leader among Orangemen, we have never heard of him saying anything that could give offence to any Catholic, either on Orange or political platform or at any other time.' The newspaper concluded its tribute with a prediction of political fidelity from Roman Catholic voters if he continued to be the political man he always had been.⁴

However, in the midst of the praise some press commentaries cautioned that Bowell should not expect to remain on the political mountaintop for too long. Several quickly began speculating about who would be in the running to replace him, even before he had a chance to settle into his new leadership chair. The root of the speculation was his age and the presence in his cabinet of younger jealous rivals rather than doubts about his performance. Typical was the Toronto *Globe*'s take on the elevation of its longtime rival to the Prime Minister's office: 'It is probable that in the Conservative Party itself, it is not expected that Mr Bowell's leadership will be of long duration,' said the Liberal mouthpiece. 'His relations with the party may be compared with those of an assignee with an insolvent estate. He is to wind it up with as little disaster as possible but not to engage in new enterprise.'⁵

The Montreal *Herald* took it a step further. 'He is not objectionable to any of the factions into which the Conservative party is at present divided,' it wrote. 'His age makes acceptance of the office, in a sense, a temporary one for he is 71 years of age and in the natural course of events must shortly retire. His accession at this time therefore does not interfere seriously with the ambitions of younger men like Haggart and Sir Charles Hibbert Tupper whose designs on the premiership are but thinly disguised.'⁶

This cheeky speculation about a short-term prime minister seemed to gain some credibility several weeks later when Bowell and several other ministers took a train to Halifax Harbour to receive Thompson's body, carried across the Atlantic in a British warship dispatched by Queen Victoria. A state funeral had been arranged at a nearby downtown church. Although Bowell made it to the city, his end-of-year malady had not cleared up entirely and a throat infection kept him out of the damp Halifax air on doctor's orders. Initial news reports suggested it was something much worse. 'He is dying,' several January 3, 1895 newspapers reported in cable alerts. 'Premier Bowell is now in very serious condition. Belief that he cannot live past 6 o'clock this evening. Ventured out too soon to attend Sir John's funeral.'

Several weeks later, Bowell was able to joke about the premature announcement of his imminent death as he was feted at lavish celebrations in Tweed and Belleville where large crowds gathered to honour the hometown, healthy and fit Prime Minister. 'The city was in Holiday Dress and the people of the City and District assembled in their Thousands to Honour their Old Friend,' enthused the *Intelligencer*. A banner welcomed him with a succinct summation of his journey: FROM PRINTER'S DEVIL TO PRIME MINISTER.' With his tendency to what critics deemed to be false modesty, Bowell said 'the demonstration which has been tendered to me is one of which I feel entirely unworthy but I accept it as the highest tribute which you can possibly show to one who has been associated with you for more than half a century of time.'[7] He attributed his success to honest, hard work and saw it as a message that anyone in Canada could succeed if they persevered.

For Bowell, whether the modesty and humble words were real or a political affectation, the first months of 1895 were a rare time of celebration, accolades and optimism. Despite the leadership chaos of the past three years and clear signs of Liberal resurgence across the country with Laurier drawing increasing crowds and candidates lining up, the Conservatives were exhibiting some healthy vital signs. They had won a slew of recent by-elections that increased the government majority in the House of Commons from the slim 28-seat advantage earned in the 1891 election to a much more comfortable 60-seat majority. Unexpectedly, he was prime minister. Even more unexpectedly, he had been appointed a knight of the Queen's realm.

Life surely seemed good.

In late April when Bowell addressed the Senate for the first time as Prime Minister, more tributes and praise flowed although Liberal speakers were clear they hoped success would be short-lived and he soon would be replaced by one of their own. In response, the Prime Minister was somber rather than triumphant:

> When I consider for a moment the illustrious gentlemen who have
> been Prime Ministers of this country since Confederation, I must say
> I feel my utter inability to occupy the position and perform the duties
> attaching thereto in the manner in which they have been discharged
> by my predecessors.[8]

His words were more prescient than he would have wished. Already, evidence was emerging that the promise of a period of political accomplishment, peace and progress was a mirage. Bowell in fact had inherited a poisoned chalice that all but doomed him to failure. The Liberal-Conservative Party he led, in power for more than two decades of the Dominion's first 27 years, had been allowed under its aging founding leader to hollow out, become lethargic, uninspiring, creaky, defensive and smug. In addition, Macdonald had failed the crucial leadership test of making sure he attracted and groomed younger, talented men to become the natural next generation of leaders.

Meanwhile, the chalice of power Bowell was handed contained a volatile cocktail of party discontent and disloyalty mixed with intractable political and federal-provincial issues to be resolved; poison pill legacy issues left unresolved by Macdonald and his successors. There was a flare-up of the perennial malady of English/French, Catholic/Protestant antagonism and developing crises that would test the skills of the strongest of leaders. In an analysis of pivotal elections in Canadian history, including the campaign of 1896, author and Liberal activist John Duffy saw the political scene Bowell inherited in Ottawa as one littered with 'ambition, bigotry and dissent.' The national mood was no more promising. 'Canada in the 1890s was a combustible cloud of political, religious, regional, ideological and jurisdictional vapors,' he wrote. And while not a Bowell fan ('weak and indecisive'), Duffy had some sympathy for his position. 'He presided over a cabinet by now so badly riven that keeping it in one piece would have taxed a better man to the limit.'[9]

It would become clear sooner rather than later that for all his strengths, resolve, good intentions and accomplishments, Bowell's limited endowment of leadership skills and strengths would fall short of what was required in the circumstances he inherited. As the mantle of responsibility settled on his shoulders in the early months of 1895, the new Prime Minister immediately had to deal with two inherited and festering federal-provincial issues in two far-flung geographic regions:

- In the east, contentious negotiations with Newfoundland over whether Britain's oldest self-governing colony would join Canada had dragged on for years and pressure for a settlement was building once again. Newfoundland needed political stability and financial help that Canada could offer. Britain wanted out of the financial responsibility its ne'er-do-well colony required.
- In the west, Ottawa and the Manitoba government were in a tense stand-off over the explosive issue of public funding for Manitoba's French-language, Roman Catholic separate school system. It was a spark destined to keep the French/English, Catholic/Protestant Prairie fires raging.

Failure to achieve closure on both issues would play a pivotal role in determining history's assessment of Sir Mackenzie Bowell's time as Prime Minister.

Newfoundland Negotiations

In early 1895, Mackenzie Bowell had it within his grasp to be a latter-day Father of Confederation, the Prime Minister who completed the founding fathers' 1867 dream of someday including Newfoundland in the Dominion. The island colony off Canada's east coast had declined an invitation to become the fifth province in 1869 but as its financial situation worsened in the late 1880s, interest in Confederation was renewed and informal discussions started. In 1892, Bowell and John Thompson were part of a Canadian delegation that met island representatives in Halifax to discuss union prospects, but no deal was reached. By the end of 1894, Newfoundland finances and debt problems led Island leaders to signal they were ready for serious Confederation talks. The colony was deeply in debt, close to bankrupt and there were citizen riots on the streets of St John's to protest poverty and hunger.

Bowell was enthusiastic at the prospect of bringing Newfoundland into Canada but wary of the financial demands being made by colonial leader William Whiteway. The Canadian Prime Minister invited a delegation of Newfoundland political leaders to Ottawa for negotiations in early 1895 and personally greeted them at the railway station when they arrived April 3.

The prospect of union was anticipated in the first Throne Speech presented to Parliament on April 18 by the Bowell government. 'It will be a subject of federal congratulation if the negotiations now pending result in incorporation of Her Majesty's oldest colonial possession into the Canadian Confederation,' Governor General Aberdeen read from the government blueprint for action presented in the Senate Chamber.[10] In debate later that day, the Prime Minister told Senators a deal would 'add greatly to our country and prove beneficial to the people of Newfoundland themselves.'

It was not to be. Within two weeks, talks had broken off, the goodwill had dissipated and Newfoundland officials indicated no further talks would be held. It would take another 54 years before two wily Liberals—Newfoundland Premier Joseph Smallwood and senior federal official (and later Newfoundland MP) Jack Pickersgill—brokered a deal that made the island Canada's tenth province.

What had happened to the 1895 promise? And was the Conservative leader responsible for the failure to implement it?

Bowell critics at the time and since have looked no further than the leader of the federal government to explain the failed negotiations. They accused him of forfeiting the opportunity to complete Canada by being too miserly in his offer to the impoverished colony. In a typical Opposition attack, the Liberal Toronto *News* said Bowell 'bears the blame for possibly the greatest national mistake made by Canada since Confederation... The representatives of Canada seemed to think that the plight of the prospective province was so desperate that she would be obliged to accept any terms. They haggled over money matters.'[11] In 1903, Prime Minister Wilfrid Laurier justified his own inaction on the file by blaming Bowell as well. 'Let me say that the government of Sir Mackenzie Bowell lost a fine opportunity of settling that question. There were negotiations far advanced and I believe if there had been generous disposition shown by Canada to Newfoundland, the question would have been settled there and then.'[12]

As he was prone to do, Sir Charles Tupper Sr suggested that if he, rather than Bowell, had been in charge of negotiations, Newfoundland would have become Canadian in the 1890s. His brag was based on an 1888 unofficial visit he made to St. John's to float a trial balloon of potential financial terms. At the time, it was a non-starter. Newfoundland objected that it wasn't enough, Ottawa did not make an official offer, no enriched follow-up was promised and the matter dropped.

Yet, with a quarter-century of hindsight, Tupper claimed that New-foundland's leader Sir Robert Bond had told him 'if they would give us the terms proposed by you, we would join the union but to this they would not agree.'[13] Tupper's contention that the Bowell government botched the negotiation gained some support in later academic analysis. In a 1968 PhD thesis on Conservative Prime Ministers in the 1890s, future University of Manitoba historian and professor Crosby Clark Lovell described the Bowell government's handling of the Newfoundland negotiations as 'one of the most serious blunders of its undistinguished career. It was only by an almost incredible degree of niggardly bargaining that Bowell and his colleagues managed to thwart what at first appeared to be the inevitable consummation of Confederation.'[14]

Retired Memorial University history professor James K. Hiller con-cluded in a 2011 analysis of Confederation negotiations that despite a lack of Canadian negotiating enthusiasm, Bowell wished to succeed, but only for personal aggrandizement. 'A man of some vanity, Bowell no doubt hoped to glory in completing the confederation of British North America.'[15]

Wherever the root of failure lay, Bowell expressed disappointment for the rest of his life over the outcome. In the face of critics anxious to blame him personally, he was adamant in defending his government's negotiating position and performance. He insisted that Newfoundland's demands on Canada for per capita subsidies, completion of an Island railway and assumption of responsibility for Newfoundland's substantial debt, added up to more financial obligation than Canada could assume. He insisted that Newfoundland was offered better terms than any other province joining Confederation after 1867 and noted London's refusal to pick up a share of the costs of the proposed deal despite pleas from Canada and New-foundland.

Bowell also regularly made the point that even if Ottawa had agreed to demands emanating from St. John's, it was unclear if the agreement would have been approved in Newfoundland where political opposition to joining Canada was extensive, powerful and loud. In fact, Bowell's self defence arguments have considerable support in the literature on Canada/Newfoundland Confederation negotiations. Even the critical Lovell noted that at the time, federal finances were suffering from reduced tariff revenue and the federal deficit was more than $4.00 million 'in a day when deficit financing was far from being acceptable practice.'[16] The governing reality was that the bleak federal financial position Bowell inherited as Prime Minister severely restricted his options on Newfoundland negotiations and many other government files.

He had experienced the reality firsthand. Several months before while still Minister of Trade and Commerce, Bowell had warned departmental managers to cut costs. 'The revenue is falling by hundreds of thousands per month until the deficit runs up now to nearly two million since the 1st of July and the finance minister insists that no additional expenditure be incurred that can possibly be avoided,' he wrote to the Controller of Customs in late 1894. The emerging fiscal reality made finance minister Foster a powerful and influential opponent of Newfoundland's demands.[17]

In another strike for Bowell's version of the story, Newfoundland historian Patrick O'Flaherty argued in 2005 that the colonial government was understating the size of the financial obligation it was demanding that Ottawa assume. The Whiteway government insisted the real public debt burden was lower than the posted $16.00 million because the capital value of a partially completed provincial railway (which Ottawa was supposed to help complete and finance in future) was an asset to be deducted from the amount owing. 'Having dealt with balance sheets in his long stretch as Minister of Customs, Bowell was not inclined to accept this inventive accounting,' O'Flaherty concluded.[18]

Hiller added another disclaimer to Newfoundland's financial arguments. The Newfoundland colonial government covered social and infrastructure costs that Premier Whiteway insisted Canada should pick up in any deal. However, that was not how Confederation was structured. Under Canadian law, they were the responsibility of provinces and municipalities rather than the national government, so Bowell was correct to argue that operational welfare costs Canada would assume if Newfoundland proposals were accepted would be much larger than St. John's was claiming. 'Certainly a chance was missed but the difficulty of the task should not be underestimated,' Hiller concluded. 'Bowell was quite right to point out that it was very difficult to fit Newfoundland into the framework established by the British North America Act.'[19]

Bowell's financial reservations even had support from some prominent Liberals at the time who argued the Prime Minister was correct and prudent to reject demands that Canada enrich its offer to get a deal, notwithstanding Liberal Party attempts later to blame him for the failure. In the Senate shortly after talks collapsed, Halifax Liberal Lawrence Power—later appointed Senate Speaker by Laurier—argued that failure was the best result given the likely financial obligation that would accompany a deal:

> My own honest opinion is that the government of Canada offered reasonable and liberal terms to the Newfoundland delegates and the delegates refused to accept those terms and consequently, I feel that it is, to a certain extent, asking us to put ourselves in an undignified position to try and induce those people who do not wish to come in on reasonable terms to join us by offering them terms which are not reasonable. While the addition of Newfoundland to Canada might be a desirable thing, there is such a thing as paying too much for it and the government offered quite enough.[20]

As it turned out, the Bowell government faced little immediate political consequence for the failure of the Newfoundland negotiations with almost no public or parliamentary backlash. Historical analysis has been more damning of Bowell's role than were his contemporaries. 'Canadians were perhaps too parochial to have been stirred by such an achievement or indeed to view it in terms much beyond financial expediency,' Lovell concluded.[21]

Besides, the Newfoundland question was not the most politically urgent topic of the day. Issues facing the Bowell government in early 1895, including deficit financing and Newfoundland, 'were as nothing when compared with the trouble which was brewing for it as a result of the Manitoba School Question.'[22] The Bowell government could be excused for not seeming to be totally focused during the Newfoundland negotiations.

The Manitoba School Question

The Manitoba school funding issue—the dominant Canadian political controversy of the 1890s that haunted six national governments and was instrumental in triggering the end of Mackenzie Bowell's brief term as Prime Minister—at its core was a dry constitutional question that provoked a national, bitter and nasty political firestorm. Did Manitoba Premier Thomas Greenway, under the British North America Act designation of education as provincial jurisdiction, have the power to enact the 1890 legislation that abolished provincial public funding for the French language Roman Catholic school system? The complication was that the legislation abolished promises embedded in the 1870 Manitoba Act, a *de facto* part of the Canadian Constitution admitting the province to Canadian Confederation. Or was the 1870 Manitoba Act guarantee of a separate French Catholic school system for the Manitoba Métis minority a constitutional right the federal government was obligated to uphold and defend? The clause had been added to the bill after tense negotiations between senior federal players including Prime Minister Macdonald and a Manitoba delegation directed from Winnipeg by the Provisional Government led by Louis Riel.

The issue had been before courts for almost five years when Bowell assumed power and a final judgment from the highest British Empire court at the time—the Imperial Privy Council in London—was expected any day. News of the decision landed in Ottawa at the end of January 1895 and in a nuanced judgment, the Privy Council answered 'yes' to both questions. The Manitoba government was within its BNA education policy jurisdiction to enact the legislation and the federal government, under the terms of the Manitoba Act, had the right to demand that the Manitoba bill be overturned.

In a face-off between the two rights, Ottawa held the winning hand if it chose to play it. At that point, it became a political issue and ironically, it was a political quagmire inherited by Bowell from his political mentor. In 1870, Prime Minister Macdonald had helped write and had embraced the guarantee of a publicly funded Francophone Roman Catholic school system to operate in parallel with a Protestant system in the new province. It was the continuation of his 'Confederation bargain' of French/English accommodation.

The Manitoba Act text also gave Ottawa the power and authority to overturn any provincial attempt to subvert the guarantee. Yet in 1890 when Premier Greenway used his legislative majority to pass the 'Act Respecting Public Schools' abolishing French Catholic system funding, Prime Minister Macdonald ducked his responsibility and refused calls that his government live up to its constitutional obligation to quash the provincial law. Macdonald had two options for overturning the provincial law and restoring Manitoba minority rights. Firstly, Ottawa, as the senior national government, had the constitutional power under the BNA Act to 'disallow' provincial bills and the provision had been used dozens of times. Secondly, the Manitoba Act specifically gave the federal government the power (critics argued 'the obligation') to strike down any provincial legislation that undermined minority education and language rights.

Instead, Macdonald executed one of his classic strategic procrastinations. He put the tough decision off into the future when hopefully the issue would have resolved itself or someone else would have to make the tough call. The strategic dither tactic earned Macdonald the not entirely complimentary nickname 'Old Tomorrow.' In this case, he decided Ottawa did not have to play a lead role in resolving the issue… at least not yet. The bill could be challenged in the courts by aggrieved minorities, knowing it would take years to get a final judgment while constitutionally guaranteed rights were denied.

The Manitoba Act was clear that the Macdonald government had the power to act if it was prepared to face off against a determined, tough Liberal premier with a supportive Protestant electorate behind him. Section 22.3 of the legislation specified that if the promise to provide publicly funded schooling for Francophone Catholic students was breached by the province 'the Parliament of Canada may make Remedial Laws for the due execution of the provisions of this section.'

In an analysis of the Manitoba School crisis, University of Manitoba (St. Boniface College) professor Raymond Hébert argued the original intent of the Confederation deal with Manitoba was unambiguous. 'For most mainstream historians, these sections of the Manitoba Act made Manitoba a bilingual province where confessional rights were guaranteed,' he wrote. When the Greenway government abolished those rights as well as making English the only official language of the Legislature and the printed version of legislation, they were provincial actions 'that were to sweep away virtually all the guarantees enshrined in the Manitoba Act in 1870.'[23] Macdonald certainly would have understood the implications of postponing a response but concluded a delayed reaction was the prudent political path that would deny Greenway an issue to take to the voters in search of another strong Liberal majority government mandate.

In a March 27, 1890 telegram, the Prime Minister instructed Manitoba Lieutenant Governor John Schultz to give Royal Assent to the bills 'leaving them to be dealt with here afterwards.'[24] Even sympathetic Macdonald biographer Donald Creighton saw it as a classic case of procrastination that spared the prime minister the need for risky decisive action. It was his 'Old Tomorrow' persona at work. Putting it off to another day or year 'of course was the best that could be hoped for… it would be a long time before the test cases could end their protracted perambulations through the courts… The danger was still there but—thank heavens—it was still distant.'[25]

It would turn out to be almost five years and three new Prime Ministers before the mess landed in Mackenzie Bowell's lap. In a final irony, one of the early orders-in-council signed by Prime Minister Bowell was issued January 30, 1895 when cabinet agreed to pick up costs of $3,535.70 for one of the private citizen challenges to Greenway's law that Macdonald encouraged and that the plaintiff lost in Winnipeg court.[26]

Once invested with the responsibility to deal with the politically lethal minefield that Macdonald had bequeathed him, Bowell's position on the core issue was firm, clear and principled. It also violated his personal beliefs on the wisdom of the policy at the centre of the controversy: taxpayer support for separate religious schools. As an Orangeman and a lifelong education promoter who believed schools should be places where knowledge and skills were taught rather than religious dogma (Roman Catholic or Protestant), Mackenzie Bowell was a lifelong opponent of separate, religion-based schools. In fact, he made the point every time he spoke on the issue throughout his life, particularly when he was insisting on Manitoba's obligation to retain such a system.

His personal hostility to separate schools led him as a backbench MP in 1870 to join a small number of MPs who defied his government to vote against the Manitoba Act in Parliament. A quarter century later in the midst of a political life-or-death struggle to preserve the right of Manitoba Francophone Roman Catholics to have separate schools supported by the state, Prime Minister Bowell recalled that defiant 1870 vote. 'Believing that the Act clearly gave the right of Separate Schools to Manitoba, I voted at the time for the striking out of that particular clause,' he wrote to a friend.[27] But by 1895, Bowell was willing to stake his political leadership position on defending what he had jeopardized his political future in 1870 to oppose.

What had changed and why did he flip-flop?

Simply put, he was a constitutionalist. The Manitoba Act he opposed had been approved, became law and was one of the constitutional guarantees Manitoba had been promised as its Confederation bargain. More than personal opinions or political positions, Bowell believed in upholding the constitution as a blueprint for the rule of law and the future of a united bi-national Canada.

A promise was a promise. A constitutional promise was an obligation.

In a 1991 memoir, left-of-centre Canadian political icon Eugene Forsey— a stalwart of the Canadian Labour Congress, founding member of the Canadian Co-operative Federation and New Democratic Party and later a Senator—wrote in admiration of Bowell's defence of minority rights and the sanctity of constitutional promises. Forsey recalled how as a union organizer on the Queen's University campus in the 1950s, he defended Bowell for his principles and strength on the issue. The target was a Francophone 'dogmatic ignoramus' who argued that the federal Conservatives had done nothing in the 1890s to protect the Manitoba minority. 'I had literally to shout him down at two o'clock in the morning with a recital of the facts,' Forsey wrote. 'He [Bowell] detested Separate Schools but he thought the Manitoba Roman Catholics were constitutionally entitled to them and that settled it.'[28]

The rookie Prime Minister also brought to the dispute with the Greenway government a deeply held belief that Canada worked better as a co-operative federation than as a nation defined by federal-provincial squabbles, tensions and power struggles. The concept of Canada was bigger than inter-governmental jurisdictional disputes. He thought that compromise was possible in the interests of unity and harmony. If it meant delay in a resolution of the dispute, that was better than federal-provincial animosity and election campaigns based on religious and language disagreements that divide Canadians rather than unites them. It was not a position he embraced only when responsibility for the issue was thrust upon him. For years, he had been searching for a compromise pathway out of the Catholic/Protestant education policy quagmire that so bedeviled Canada. In 1892, as trade minister with no responsibility for the file, for example, he asked a New

Brunswick Senator for an explanation on how that province had navigated the Catholic/Protestant school issue earlier with a negotiated settlement rather than legal warfare.[29] But as the crisis developed over the following year, Bowell's attempts to avoid punitive action against Manitoba or a divisive election on the issue came to be seen by his critics inside government and by later historians as weakness and indecisiveness.

For the Prime Minister, it was a belief (naive, it turned out) that Canadian reasonableness and sense of fairness would win out in the end if given a chance.

A final complication for Bowell on the schools' file was a predisposition to be irritated by Manitoba attitudes, a personal feeling of ill will and frustration toward the province. He held a view of Manitoba as a cantankerous, ungrateful jurisdiction always looking for an advantage or more favours from Ottawa. In one 1883 incident, he exploded in a private letter to a Winnipeg friend after receiving reports that Manitobans were embracing free trade because the high tariff National Policy was denying them access to cheaper goods from the United States:

> The people of Manitoba appear to me very much like spoilt children. They have been pampered and petted, drawing from the resources of the parents to the extent they have become spendthrifts. Hence, when asked to bear any small portion of the burden or when they cannot have everything they demand, they turn up their noses and begin to threaten.[30]

Two years later, after a complaint that the federal government was not doling out enough appointments to Manitobans, Bowell fired off a 12-page rebuttal suggesting Manitobans thought it their right to be rich. It ended with a flourish: 'When you come to look at what the Dominion government has done and the amount of money expended in a short time in developing that country, no sensible man will have cause to complain.'[31] It did not improve his attitude toward the province that he also had inherited a long-running dispute between Ottawa and Winnipeg over what he considered a bogus provincial claim that the federal government was shortchanging Manitoba by hundreds of thousands of dollars in annual transfers. Bowell read the fine print detail of the 1885 fiscal deal that was at the centre of the dispute and concluded there was no case. Greenway, however, was being belligerent in pressing his point.

Yet despite his private antagonisms, Bowell also was quick to promote the province for its potential. In summer 1885, after moving a motion to send federal money to Winnipeg to settle some expense claims based on the aforementioned deal, he told the House of Commons: 'If nothing interferes to prevent the rapid progress which is going on in every section of that country, we may look forward in a short time to find it settled by a people which I hope will be wealthy and contented.'[32] When his Hastings County constituents sent him letters asking for advice on whether to move west to farm, Bowell always recommended Manitoba as the place to go. For his promotion of Manitoba development, he was made an honorary member of the Winnipeg Liberal-Conservative Association (as the Conservative Party was then named). In 1887, there were even false rumors that he would be appointed Manitoba Lieutenant-Governor.

Once the text of the Privy Council decision on the Manitoba School question was received from London and parsed by senior government members and advisors, possible responses became the topic of seemingly endless February and early March cabinet meetings. Cabinet divisions quickly surfaced, although not on the core issue. The Bowell cabinet was united in supporting the Manitoba Act guarantees, despite suspicions that Marine and Fisheries Minister Costigan and Railways and Canals Minister Haggart were lukewarm. Cabinet division was over tactics and with Macdonald-style procrastination no longer possible, the options were limited and clear. A remedial order demanding restoration of the separate school system could be issued and then an election called to gauge public opinion. Alternatively, enforcement of the remedial order could be delayed to give MPs a chance to debate it and the Greenway government time to come to its senses.

Growing doubts among some ministers about Bowell's suitability to lead Ottawa's response also played a role in the tense tone of cabinet debates then and over the following months. In his 1956 analysis of the political chaos of the early 1890s, political scientist John Saywell noted that since the dissenters largely represented English-speaking and Protestant ridings:

> It was assumed then, and has been since, that their object was to prevent Bowell from fulfilling his pledge to introduce remedial legislation if no settlement was reached with the Government of Manitoba. In this assumption, there was no truth. The movement was simply an expression of non-confidence in Bowell.[33]

In mid-March, cabinet settled on its response to the Privy Council decision. The government would publish the remedial order written by Justice Minister Tupper that ordered Greenway to back down. It would dissolve Parliament and go to the voters in a spring general election, even though some English-speaking ministers had voiced concerns that a campaign and its heated rhetoric would deepen the national crisis rather than settle it. It was the second time Bowell had been part of a cabinet vote to call an election once the government was ready with its response to Manitoba. The decision had first been taken in mid-February and Governor General Aberdeen had agreed. The March cabinet decision was a re-affirmation.

Meanwhile, the Conservative Party through the winter and early spring had been preparing, nominating candidates and holding campaign-style rallies in anticipation of a campaign. The Liberals were in high alert, expecting an imminent call to the polls. Privately, however, Bowell spent weeks after the initial February 16 decision having second thoughts. While decisive and strong willed on issues he considered matters of principle, Bowell proved indecisive on issues of political strategy and tactics and in this case, election timing. It would extend later to dithering over when to get tough with the Manitoba government as it ignored Ottawa's remedial order. This pro-crastination pattern led to legitimate complaints from his cabinet and party critics that the Prime Minister made the situation worse by erratic behavior, inconsistency and weak leadership.

At the core of his indecisive behavior on election timing was unease about fanning religious flames of discord. Bowell's worry was that calling a vote seeking a mandate to defend Manitoba Catholic minority rights against Protestant bullying simply would exacerbate the dangerous Catholic/ Protestant, French/English tensions already raging across the country. He spoke from painful personal experience about the potential fallout from the language and religious political conflict underway. During the previous six years, the former Orange leader now turned into a senior Conservative government minister had been living in the vortex of what some referred to as a Catholic/Protestant 'civil war' over federal handling of Quebec's 1888 approval of the Jesuit Estates Act.

Although a Quebec-centered controversy at its core, the broader issues of language and religion drew the federal Conservatives into the complicated thick of the political battle. Bowell was particularly enmeshed in the uproar, both as a former Protestant leader and the government's designated point person for dealing with Orange Lodge discontent. The disruptive impact the dispute had on Bowell's relationship with his Orange support base was discussed earlier in Chapter Five.

The Jesuits' Estates Act, approved unanimously by the Quebec Legislature (Catholic and Protestant MNAs uniting), was meant to correct an historic wrong, compensating the Roman Catholic Jesuit order for property seized by the British after the Conquest. Over protests from the official Roman Catholic Church (now in a dispute with Jesuits over funding a new university) and loud objections from Protestants outside Québec, the Quebec National Assembly passed a bill to return $400,000.00 to the Jesuits in compensation.

Protestant opponents outside Quebec, led by the Orange Lodge, demanded the federal government use its constitutional power of disallowance to veto the Quebec law, condemning the handover of public assets to a Vatican-sanctioned religious organization. The Macdonald cabinet, including Bowell, refused to intervene after deciding Quebec was within its

197

constitutional rights to do with its property and money as it wished.[34] All political hell broke loose. The Conservative Party split, with a small splinter group bolting to campaign against the Conservatives and Catholic 'special' rights. The Equal Rights Association was founded and led by former Bowell colleague and Macdonald favourite D'Alton McCarthy who made Bowell a particular target of his disdain. Meanwhile, Orange Lodges denounced the federal decision not to intervene and Methodist ministers did the same from the pulpit. Critics often directed their blame and anger at Bowell personally, accusing him of selling out his Orange brethren and abandoning his Protestant roots. He received torrents of angry letters denouncing him for 'approving' the transfer of public assets in Quebec to a Roman Catholic sect when in fact there was no word of approval but a decision to respect the constitutional federal-provincial division of powers.

In June 1889, Bowell responded in frustration and exasperation to one Orange Lodge resolution criticizing him. He urged them to read the bill. 'I regret that your lodge and many others have been misinformed as to the action taken by the Dominion government,' he wrote. 'The Dominion government did not confer upon the Jesuits any favour. It simply did not interfere with the legislation of the province of Quebec.'[35]

And in a premonition of the apprehension he would feel in 1895 about the price to be paid for inflaming and dividing voters with a flashpoint religious controversy, Bowell wrote after attending a Masonic Lodge meeting near Belleville in June 1889: 'I heard hardly anything discussed there but the Jesuit question. It is a consolation that there is no election coming soon and I can only hope that the feeling may abate before we appeal to the electors.'[36]

In the end, the federal government stuck to its resolve not to override Quebec's legislation despite the Protestant uproar outside the province. Nevertheless, the inflammatory incident left a scar on Canada's body politic. Bowell calculated correctly that the profound damage the Jesuit Estates affair caused was its role in exacerbating the Orange/Green divide in Canadian politics. It helped create the toxic atmosphere in which the Manitoba School issue was to play out. It prompted Prime Minister Bowell to be nervous and wary about doing anything that would trigger another damaging and bitter public debate over religious matters that would strain political civility and the fragile Catholic/Protestant entente central to the Confederation Bargain.

On Tuesday, March 19, 1895, cabinet approved the text of the Remedial Order and let out word that Ottawa expected the Manitoba government to comply. Many in cabinet logically assumed the next step to be announced within days would be an election call to seek a voter mandate to pursue the tough line. It is what they had decided... twice.

However, the Prime Minister had decided otherwise.

Having spent the past month privately agonizing and discussing the national unity implications of a religion-dominated campaign with cabinet allies, he had decided an election campaign would be too divisive and dangerous. Amazingly, he had not yet briefed his full cabinet on his doubts or decision. On March 21 he finally broke the news to stunned ministers: the details of the Remedial Order would be transmitted to Premier Greenway to show him Ottawa meant business, Parliament would be reconvened rather than prorogued and the proposed terms would be debated and then be subject to a parliamentary vote.

Meanwhile, representatives of the opposing sides in the Manitoba divide would be invited to Ottawa to meet cabinet and to discuss whether there were grounds for compromise before the federal order took effect. Within hours of the announcement to cabinet, Bowell was confronted with his first cabinet crisis. Tupper, a passionate advocate of an early vote and no fan of the Prime Minister, was outraged and humiliated. He complained that he had been excluded from discussions and blindsided while the leader secretly cooked up a delaying deal behind his back. Of course, Tupper never passed up a chance to denigrate Bowell while arguing behind the scenes that his father Charles Sr should have been named leader when Thompson died. Now he had a legitimate grievance that confirmed his view of Bowell as untrustworthy and inadequate.

Tupper resigned from cabinet and sent the Prime Minister a long, bitter letter justifying his decision. He accused Bowell of acting because he feared electoral defeat '[and] I cannot be party to a course dictated by dread of the people.' He signed his blistering attack 'I am Yours Faithfully,' a formality whose irony Bowell likely noted. Two days later, the Prime Minister fired back, denying deal-making behind Tupper's back but acknowledging that six English speaking ministers thought Manitoba should be given a chance to respond and comply before plunging the country into a bitter political brawl. Bowell wrote that rather than being afraid of the voters, he thought they were owed a chance to hear reasoned parliamentary debate on the issues before making a decision. They would not have been 'enlightened' on the issue 'while the greater portion of the electors were in a state of uncontrollable and unreasonable agitation.' The country needed a chance to give a 'calm and deliberate judgment' based on facts. To call an election 'while the political heather was ablaze throughout the whole country would be a piece of political folly, inexcusable in any public man,' the Prime Minister wrote. Bowell also coldly reminded Tupper that it was the Prime Minister's prerogative to decide election timing.

Within eight days, Tupper had capitulated and asked if he could rejoin cabinet in his former position. His March 29 letter of contrition was a masterful example of Tupper bravado and liberal use of fig leaves to cover the weaknesses in his position. His friends had said his departure would have 'disastrous consequences,' Tupper wrote. An election could be called once

Parliament approved the remedial bill. Meanwhile, he noted, Premier Greenway had not rejected it but adjourned the Legislature to 'reflect' on the federal action. 'The whole situation is changed and much of my difficulty has been happily removed,' Tupper wrote while withdrawing his resignation.[37] He did not mention that no other minster had followed him out of Cabinet in protest. He was leading a parade of one.

At the same time, during the tense week dealing with the Tupper tantrum, Bowell also got a small taste of the personal abuse he would face from former allies during the Manitoba Schools debate. On March 20, his church turned on him when the national Methodist Ministerial Association passed a resolution at a Winnipeg conference denouncing Bowell's inter-ference with provincial affairs, a concept they had advocated during the Jesuit Estates showdown. It had been nastier the day before when former senior Conservative Dalton McCarthy, now leading the Equal Rights Association, first heard the news that cabinet had agreed to demand that Manitoba back down from its plan to abolish separate schools. Speaking in Orangeville, Ontario (named for town founder Orange Lawrence and not the Loyal Orange Lodge), he said Bowell—'the ex-Grand Master of the Orangemen'—was under the influence of 'a handful of half-breeds backed by Quebec.'

Then McCarthy took off the gloves. He said the 'Protestant champion' was being forced to 'bow the knee' by priests:

> I pity the descendants of that distinguished gentleman because his administration will be known in history for all time to come as a government that sought to impose separate schools upon the people of Manitoba and I don't know of any more disgraceful slight that could be done to any public man than to have his name coupled with this infamous measure.[38]

More than a century later, Bowell descendants were clear that they did not appreciate or need McCarthy's pity. They are proud of their accomplished ancestor. Bowell great-great grandson Blake Mackenzie Holton of Port Hope, Ontario laughed when told about McCarthy's professed sympathy for Bowell descendants. He said every generation since Bowell's time had Mackenzie as a first or middle name in his honour. 'We're proud of him. He did the best he could. How many people can say their ancestor was a prime minister?' Great-great granddaughter Maryjane HoltonSimon of Toronto added: 'From a family perspective, Bowell was always revered.'[39]

The new parliamentary session began April 18 with a Speech from the Throne that first put the increasingly controversial Manitoba school issue before Parliament, albeit in the dry language of officialdom:

> In conformity with a recent judgment of the Lords of the Judicial Council of the Privy Council to the effect that the dissentient

minority of the people of Manitoba have a constitutional right of appeal to the Governor General in Council against certain Acts passed by the Legislature of the Province of Manitoba in relation to the subject of education, I have heard in Council the appeal and my decision thereon has been communicated to the Legislature of the said province.[40]

The parliamentary papers were tabled four days later and then, as a topic of conversation on the floor of Parliament, the issue largely disappeared. Through spring and summer, Parliament dealt with the mundane issues of government: Dominion Elections Act amendments, a motion about immigration rules that allowed transport of 'Jew peddlers' from Chicago to Calgary where some of them ended up in jail; cattle movement; wheat inspection; and Post Office openings and closing.

On the Manitoba school controversy, all the action was behind the scenes in communications between Winnipeg and Ottawa and within the Conservative caucus. In his 1968 analysis of the Bowell government, Crosby Lovell succinctly summed up the tone from Manitoba: 'Greenway dug in with no sign of moderating.'[41]

Still, Bowell and his cabinet allies kept finding signs (more imagined than real) of Greenway flexibility, delaying decisive action in an attempt to avoid a heavy-handed federal response. The search for compromise and optimism that the Manitoba premier would be 'reasonable' was reflected in an undated memorandum on the Remedial Order that Bowell kept in his files. It concluded that while Ottawa had the obligation and authority to take action based on the Privy Council decision:

> In the opinion of this government it does not necessarily follow that remedial legislation from either the Dominion government or the local Parliament should go to the full extent or follow the exact lines set out in the order. The object and aim of this was and is to apply to the substantial complaints of the minority that remedy which will cause the least interference with the general law.[42]

In March, Bowell had sent that message indirectly to Greenway, asking Manitoba Lieutenant Governor John Schultz to tell the Premier he should cooperate by showing Ottawa enough flexibility to give it options, avoiding 'the bad effect that is likely to result from any interference in Manitoba school matters by the Dominion government.' The 'bad effect' included the likelihood of imposed permanent federal rules much harsher than a compromise would achieve.[43]

On Dominion Day, July 1, the federal government received a message from the Manitoba government that Bowell generously interpreted as an 'intimation' the province was open to new offers from Ottawa in the interests of a resolution. He grasped at the delusion of progress and announced on

July 8 in the Senate that cabinet had decided to delay action on a remedial law until having further discussions with Premier Greenway. The result was that the issue would not be dealt with in Parliament until a new session started in the first week of January 1896. By then, the provincial position would be clear and Ottawa would act if it was deemed unsatisfactory. In a Senate statement, Bowell tried to justify the decision to delay:

> Though there may be a difference of opinion as to the exact meaning of the [Greenway] reply in question, the government believes that it may be interpreted as holding out some hope of an amicable settlement of the Manitoba school question on the basis of possible action by the Manitoba government... and the Dominion government is most unwilling to take any action which can be interpreted as forestalling or precluding such a desirable consum-mation.[44]

Over the next two days, relieved Liberal Opposition MPs had a chance to divert attention from their own party's opaque and unclear policy on the issue by mocking the government for its indecisiveness. On July 11, the situation became even better for the Opposition and profoundly worse for Bowell. He would pay a heavy price for his latest equivocation.

The Prime Minister rose in the Senate that day to confirm rumours and newspaper stories reporting new cabinet defections. His three Francophone ministers from Quebec—Agriculture Minister Sen Auguste Réal Angers, Postmaster General Joseph Philippe Caron, and Public Works Minister Joseph Ouimet—had resigned. 'They considered that in the interests of the Dominion and in the interests of those they represented and in the interests of the minority of the Province of Manitoba, it was the bounden duty of the Government of Canada to proceed at once during the present session with remedial legislation,' Bowell solemnly explained.[45] His calm, low-key and measured statement masked the fact that behind the scenes, the past three days had been a frenzy of political confusion and impending crisis.

Bowell had sent a July 8 message to the absent Aberdeen about the impending resignations and the Governor-General immediately returned to Ottawa from Quebec City and took a room at the Russell House Hotel to be close to his Prime Minister during the unfolding drama. At one point, Bowell told him other resignations could follow and the government might fall. He dodged administration collapse at the last moment when he persuaded Caron and Ouimet to return on the promise of action in January if Manitoba had not backed down. The bad news was that the respected Angers, who had been Bowell's Senate seatmate for the past three years, refused to reconsider. The Prime Minister's explanation was generous to Angers. He said his defecting friend had presented his case 'forcefully and eloquently' but the majority of cabinet had decided a continued search for compromise 'in the interest of peace and the welfare of the Dominion' as well as the affected Manitoba minority was the better course. He looked with 'much fear and great anxiety' at the prospect of imposing a federal solution on an unwilling, resentful province. 'The difficulties which present themselves in attempting to force upon an unwilling people any kind of legislation will render whatever relief we may grant useless to those whom it is the intention of Parliament to aid.'

Angers, who had listened to Bowell's speech from his adjacent Senate desk, responded that Bowell had good intentions but had been intimidated by the opponents of 'justice to the minority.' He said he did not mean to impose 'harsh' judgment upon his friend Bowell. 'The Honourable leader has in his hand the present. No man perhaps in Canada could more effectively have given remedial legislation to the minority but himself but having the present in his hand, he has not the future.'[46] Bowell retorted that he took umbrage at the suggestion that he acted because of 'outside pressure' rather than belief it was the most effective thing to do.

When the parliamentary session ended in late July, Mackenzie Bowell appeared to believe he had things under control. The mini cabinet revolt was behind him (at least he thought it was), only one vacant cabinet seat remained to be filled, and he had five months to find a solution to the Manitoba conundrum before Parliament returned. How else to explain his decision to leave Ottawa and its simmering conspiracies and growing political fires in early August for more than a month to travel through western Canada? 'He was in need of a vacation and he seems to have had an enjoyable one although it had the appearance of a working holiday,' wrote a biographer.[47]

With a small entourage including his personal secretary, he travelled to Banff, Alberta to spend several days with the vacationing Aberdeens, then to Vancouver where he picked up son John and some family for a steamship trip north along the British Columbia coast to visit First Nations villages. Before traveling cross-country back to Ottawa, Bowell visited a number of 'Industrial Schools' established for First Nations children (now called Residential Schools) to meet teachers and students and to assess conditions and educational curricula.

On any level, the decision to take the trip was a prime example of Bowell's political tin ear and bad judgment. He clearly had work to do in Ottawa to shore up his position instead of going AWOL for six weeks. Patching together a cabinet of dissidents hardly meant the behind-his-back conspiring had ceased. His administration was clearly still in trouble and increasingly looked leaderless. Assuming that a sudden conversion to compromise by Manitoba was imminent surely was based on little more than wishful thinking and even as he departed Ottawa, attacks on the government position were becoming more focused on Bowell personally and more vicious. An example was a brutal *Saturday Night* magazine profile of the Prime Minister that called him an 'old man', too old to change principles, abandon old friends or find new ones. 'So little remains for him to do in this world, life has so little to offer him that he might as well be true to himself, true to the principles he has held or feigned all his days, true to the friends who have raised him up until, in his senility, he holds a statesman's post.'[48]

Orange Lodges continued to pass motions denouncing their former Grand Master and Bowell's Methodist Church continued to oppose his position on supporting separate schools. An apex of church criticism came that summer when a prominent preacher based at the Greenwood Methodist Tabernacle in Toronto unleashed a vitriolic diatribe from the pulpit against Bowell that had to wound him after more than half a century of active membership and support, in and for the church. Speaking on one of the Lodge's symbolic 'Marching Days' in August and decked out in Orange uniform, the reverend behind the pulpit accused the Prime Minister of selling out his religion and church 'simply for the sake of party and of power... [He is] laying aside his Protestantism and Orange principles and going down on his knees before the papacy and fawning to the hierarchy of Rome.' For good measure, the preacher referred to convents as 'consecrated brothels.'[49]

Unbeknownst to the Prime Minister during his trip, he was also being undermined that summer not just by his cabinet underlings but from the top as well. The Governor General had decided that his chief Canadian minister was not being sufficiently forthcoming with information about cabinet issues and turmoil. Lady Aberdeen's solution was to make a secret deal with C. H. Tupper—one of the leading conspirators—to keep her (and by implication her husband) in the loop about what was going on in government and cabinet. She kept secret the unprecedented and underhanded deal that circumvented the Prime Minister, clearly understanding it was inappropriate. Saywell concluded: 'From that time on, Tupper was really closer to the Governor General than was the Prime Minister.' Over the summer, under Tupper's influence, Lady Aberdeen's journal entries about Bowell's performance and appropriateness for the job grew more critical and darker. She also kept in close touch with the Laurier confidantes.

Amid the negatives, there were some rare words of praise. The Conservative Toronto *Mail & Empire* reported in mid-September that Bowell and his cabinet soon would return to the capital after a summer of travel or vacation for many of them: 'The premier has covered more territory than most of his younger colleagues,' the newspaper enthused. His trip involved 'a great deal of laborious traveling which only a man of iron constitution could at his years undertake with physical comfort.'

It reported the Prime Minister was 'returning to Ottawa delighted with his trip and prouder than ever of the great country in whose destinies he plays so important a part.'[50] He was quickly off to Washington with C. H. Tupper (was he sending report cards back to Lady Aberdeen?) to conclude negotiations with the U.S. on the Behring Strait treaty and then back to Ottawa. However, the newspaper-reading Prime Minister could not have missed the evidence that his position was tenuous and his government a mess. Journalists continued to find evidence of anti-Bowell plotting and cabinet discord. The Toronto *Globe* reported that Bowell's weakness as a leader was allowing growing discord between cabinet ministers. 'He is so weak that instead of proposing a course of action, he "wobbles" and allows his fellow scoundrels to fight it out.'

The Conservative *Mail and Empire* reprinted the *Globe* report and responded with a story of the Prime Minister laying down the law to three ministers unhappy with his Manitoba strategy and threatening to resign. Bowell's vanity apparently preferred this version of the story because he underlined key phrases about himself in the copy he kept in his files:

> The premier, knowing the weakness of his colleagues, at once exclaimed: 'If you do, I will call in Mr. Laurier.' Thereupon, the threatened resignations were not presented. Full well he understood that if he told them that by resigning they would lose their offices, they would immediately abandon the idea. Thus the 'weak' Premier quieted them by a display of strength. In fact, he showed himself to be abnormally strong.'[51]

It was partisan and thin-gruel flattery that the weakened Prime Minister apparently welcomed. By December as he looked forward to the end of this tumultuous year and the showdown that lay ahead, Bowell knew he would need all the strength the supportive newspaper ascribed to him.

There was no shortage of looming issues and challenges.

He knew the cabinet conniving would continue. There was a curious and acrimonious capital punishment debate dividing cabinet that had to be resolved before the opening of Parliament. Most importantly, it would be decision time about whether Manitoba had conceded enough to let the federal Conservatives save face and the Manitoba minority to be satisfied. First, though, he would be able to celebrate his second Christmas as Prime Minister. Bowell always enjoyed Christmas with family in Belleville.

NOTES

[1] LAC Bowell Papers, Vol. 103, File 3 (Halifax *Herald*, December 14, 1894).

[2] ibid, Vol. 13 File 3 (Letter to the Governor General, December 27, 1894).

[3] ibid, Vol. 103 (Hamilton *Spectator*, December 14, 1894).

[4] ibid (*The Northwest Review*, December 26, 1894).

[5] ibid (Toronto *Globe* December 15, 1894).

[6] ibid, Vol. 103, File 3.

[7] Belleville *Intelligencer*, March 12, 1895.

[8] Debates of the Senate (5th Session, 7th Parliament, Vol. 1), 16–17.

[9] Duffy, John, *The Fights of Our Lives: Elections, Leadership and the Making of Canada* (Toronto: Harper-Collins Publishers, 2002), 35, 57.

[10] Debates of the Senate 5th Session, 7th Parliament, Vol. 1, April 18, 1895.

[11] LAC Bowell Papers, Vol. 77 (Toronto *News*, November 6, 1895).

[12] Cited by Bowel in: *Debates of the Senate*, 3rd Session, 9th Parliament, March 16, 1903.

[13] Tupper, Sir Charles, *Recollections of 60 Years in Canada* (Toronto: Castle & Co. Ltd., 1914), 311.

[14] Lovell, Crosby Clark, PhD dissertation, 1968, 376.

[15] Hiller, James K., 'The 1895 Newfoundland-Canada Confederation Negotiations: A Reconsideration,' *Acadiensis: Journal of the History of the Atlantic Region* XL, No. 2, summer/autumn 2011).

[16] op cit, Lovell, 336.

[17] LAC Bowell Papers Vol. 97 (Letter to N. C. Wallace, October 17, 1894), 488.

[18] Patrick O'Flaherty, *Lost Country: The Rise and Fall of Newfoundland 1843–1933*. (St. John's: Long Beach Press, 2005), 193.

[19] op cit, 'Newfoundland-Canada Confederation,' 111.

[20] Debates of the Senate 5th Session, 7th Parliament Vol. 1 (June 20, 1895).

[21] op cit, Lovell, 386.

[22] ibid, 336.

[23] Hébert, Raymond M., *A Cautionary Tale* (Montreal: McGill-Queen's University Press, 2004), 7–11.

[24] ibid, 12.

[25] Creighton, Donald, *John A. Macdonald, the Old Chieftain* (Toronto: The MacMillan Co. of Canada, 1955), 544.

[26] LAC Privy Council Minutes, January 30–31, 1895 (RG2 Series 1, Vol. 6266).

[27] LAC Bowell Papers, Vol. 76 (April 26, 1895 letter to a Toronto preacher and separate school opponent).

[28] Forsey, Eugene, *A Life on the Fringe* (Toronto: Oxford University Press, 1991), 85.

[29] LAC Bowell Papers, Vol. 92 (November 2, 1892 letter to New Brunswick Senator John Boyd of Saint John), 360–61.

[30] ibid, Vol. 80 (April 18, 1883 letter to Winnipeg *Times* editor Amos Rowe).

[31] ibid, Vol. 34 (September 5, 1885 to Stewart Mulvey of Winnipeg).

[32] House of Commons Debates (June 23, 1885, 3rd Session, 5th Parliament).

[33] Saywell, John T., 'The Crown and the Politicians: The Canadian Succession Question 1891–1896,' *The Canadian Historical Review*, Vol. XXXVII No. 4, 1956, 324.

[34] Miller, J. R., *Equal Rights: The Jesuits' Estates Act Controversy* (Montreal: McGill-Queens University Press, 1979), 77–174.

[35] LAC Bowell Papers Vol. 89 (June 13, 1889 letter to E. W. Hawkins of Stirling, Ontario), 306.

[36] ibid (June 28, 1889 letter to Robert Birmingham of Toronto), 329.
[37] LAC Bowell Papers Vol. 14, file 2 (March 21, 23, 25, 27, 29 & 30 between Bowell and Tupper).
[38] LAC Bowell Papers Vol. 128 (Toronto *News* March 20, 1895 edition).
[39] These comments are based on interviews conducted by the author.
[40] Debates of the Senate 5th Session, 7th Parliament (April 18, 1895), 3.
[41] Lovell, Crosby Clark, *A History of the Conservative Administrations, 1891 to 1896* (Toronto: University of Toronto PhD dissertation, 1968, 354.
[42] LAC Bowell Papers, Vol. 98, File 1.
[43] ibid, Vol. 76. (March 7, 1895 letter from Bowell to Lieutenant-Governor John C. Schultz), 91–92.
[44] Debates of the Senate (July 8, 1895), 586.
[45] ibid (July 11, 1895), 657.
[46] ibid, 664.
[47] Boyce, Betsy D., *The Accidental Prime Minister* (Ameliasburgh, Ontario: Seventh Town Historical Society, 2001), 270.
[48] LAC Bowell Papers Vol. 128 (*Saturday Night Magazine*, July 13, 1895).
[49] ibid, (*The World*, August 11, 1895 edition).
[50] ibid (*Mail & Empire*, September 15, 1895 edition).
[51] ibid (*Mail & Empire*, November 6, 1895).

Chapter 14
'IN COMPANY WITH TRAITORS'

Over the course of a late December Christmas break in Belleville with family, friends and supporters, Bowell had time to visit, enjoy grandchildren, celebrate his 72nd birthday and reflect on his first hectic year in the country's top political job. Although Newfoundland negotiations and the Manitoba Schools standoff captured most of the contemporary headlines and historical analysis later, there were other recurring issues that had demanded his attention in 1895.

The diversity of files awaiting him in the job served to quickly acquaint the rookie Prime Minister with the pressure and diverse, often conflicting demands that faced the man who occupied the office where the buck stops. A key file had been Finance Minister Foster's campaign to contain an escalating deficit while pressuring Bowell to show more leadership by imposing government-wide restraint. From the other side of the issue came voter complaints about the impact government cuts were having on services, employee morale and public support.

Prairie farmers, a key Conservative voting base, offered a prime example of the potential political implications of government spending cuts. They were demanding more federal spending rather than less. Typical pushback came from southern Saskatchewan where an 1894 drought led to calls for federal aid. 'There has been a complete failure of crops in this district and unless seed grain be given, this country will be barren and we may all as well shut up shop,' said a petition issued from a January farmer rally in Balgonie, Northwest Territories. Over Foster's opposition, Bowell shepherded through cabinet an April decision to purchase and distribute grain to farmers for seeding and $50,000.00 to be distributed as needed.[1]

Bowell also found himself under fire from Prairie voters for a decision to trim Northwest Mounted Police (NWMP) budgets. Letters poured in complaining about police positions left vacant, staff dismissals and veteran officers retiring with poor pensions. The issues for the complainants were fairness, public safety and shoddy treatment of a powerful symbol of federal authority. In March, Conservative Alberta MP D. W. Davis pleaded with Bowell to rescind the cutback order after angry western voters began to organize protest rallies. 'I cannot put the importance of this too strongly before you,' he wrote. 'It is simply vital to the Conservative cause in the Territories.'[2] With an election looming within a year, it was a message that demanded attention, and some spending was restored although Foster remained largely unmoved by the consequences of his cuts.

On the international front, Bowell took the lead on many files since the colonial cabinet lacked a foreign affairs minister. He paid particular attention to relations with the United States and the Prime Minister brought some strong personal biases to managing the file. Tariff discussions with Washington were on the agenda as well as regular demands from the Americans that Canada make concessions on trade rules. Bowell had experience negotiating with U.S. officials, had watched the Americans throw their weight around about sealing rights in the Behring Strait, and had long harboured a suspicion that annexation was the real motive behind any U.S. negotiating strategy. To make matters worse, the American president was Grover Cleveland, a New York politician who during an earlier term as president in 1888 had used a campaign speech to advocate legislation banning all Canadian products from entering the American market. Bowell saw something sinister in Cleveland's second presidency and Canadian Liberal support for closer trade ties between the two countries. 'The truth is nothing would satisfy the American people except the compete surrender of Canada to the United States in all that pertains to our own affairs,' he had angrily written to a Liberal friend who supported his party's pro-American position. 'I would rather be defeated a thousand times than seek election on such a principle.'[3]

Given his views and Cleveland's return to power, the prime minister cast a critical and wary eye at the towering southern neighbour.

As Prime Minister, he also found himself involved in time-consuming cabinet personnel management and adult babysitting—mediating a nasty feud between several quarrelsome ministers and trying to get to the bottom of anonymous allegations that Postmaster General Adolphe Caron had taken a bribe. Caron was incensed that Bowell took the allegation seriously enough to investigate and alert the Governor General about the potential issue. It required some prime ministerial coddling to keep him in cabinet.

All the while, Bowell in his new position at the head of government constantly had to deal with a deluge of letters directed to him from voters seeking jobs or other favours. One of those in February 1895 may have given him a badly needed chuckle. Quebec militiaman George Odet d'Orsommens wrote to ask for a move out of the militia and into the NWMP. The applicant managed to mix up his prime ministers, addressing the letter to 'Sir Alexander Mackenzie Bowell' and later calling him 'Sir Alexander.' The real Alexander Mackenzie finished his term as Canada's first Liberal prime minister in 1878 and three times had refused an offered knighthood that would have made him 'Sir Alexander.' Bowell's files do not indicate if d'Orsommens' got the job he wished.

When he returned from Belleville in late December to the Ottawa pressure cooker and deepening internal government divisions, the first issue to be dealt with was the perplexing Valentine Shortis murder case. It was a life-or-death issue for cabinet to settle. The Irish immigrant had been convicted in October of murdering two men and wounding a third at the Montreal Cotton Co. factory in Valleyfield, Quebec. He had been fired from his job at the factory and had returned with a gun. The court sentenced Shortis to be hanged January 3 at the Beauharnois jail. The crime, committed by an Irish English speaker against French Canadian victims, enflamed Quebec popular opinion leading to lynch mobs, riots and the need for extra prisoner protection. Meanwhile, his lawyers appealed to have the execution stayed and the sentence commuted to life in prison on the grounds of mental illness. The issue landed at the cabinet table in Ottawa and supporters of clemency deluged ministers with pleas for leniency while supporters of the sentence responded with angry insistence that a hanging would represent some justice for the victims and their families.

Cabinet was divided over a recommendation from Justice Minister C. H. Tupper that Shortis be hanged. After a number of inconclusive meetings and votes that saw some switching of head counts, a final cabinet meeting on the issue started on the afternoon of December 30 and ended at 6:00 a.m. on December 31. It produced a tie vote and deadlock. With the planned execution scheduled within days, the cabinet stalemate pushed the issue up to Governor General Aberdeen to decide. Critics inside and outside government accused Bowell of abdicating leadership on the issue and of manipulating cabinet to get the stalemate result he wanted. It became another black mark on his prime ministerial reputation as an indecisive leader and another point of tension between Bowell and Tupper. 'The government was afraid to do its duty,' former Presbyterian Church moderator Rev James Smith said from a Montreal pulpit. 'It was a pitiable sight to see the [ministers] agreeing to disagree to save their positions. It looked like a secret scheme to throw the responsibility to the Governor General.'[4]

Indeed, hours after the cabinet deadlock, the anti-capital punishment Aberdeen commuted the sentence to life in prison. Riots in Quebec ensued, the flames of French/English tension were fanned and protesters burned photographs of Aberdeen in the streets while Conservative political fortunes in the province declined. Rumours that the wealthy Shortis family had offered campaign financing to the Conservatives deepened the outrage. While Bowell was condemned for weak or manipulative leadership on the issue, there is an intriguing possibility of another explanation for his reluctance in the face of demands for execution. He may have been a closet abolitionist at a time when most 19th century Canadians favoured the 'eye for an eye' approach to justice issues.

Only once before during his 15 years in cabinet had Bowell been forced to vote on a life-or-death question and the experience traumatized him. As a member of the 1885 Macdonald cabinet that debated the fate of 16 indigenous men who had fought with Louis Riel and been convicted of capital crimes, he voted with the others to hang them 'in the interests of the country'. However, his role in the executions haunted him. Shortly after, he told a friend he never wanted to repeat the experience, although his lament was framed in the prevailing racist attitudes of the time: 'The past week has been one of no little anxiety, regret and sorrow for me and I hope never to have to pass through another such ordeal,' he wrote. 'Having to consent to the hanging of some fifteen or sixteen men, even though most of them are Indians, is a very serious matter.'[5]

Still, trauma aside, at least the Shortis debate was over and one divisive issue had been taken off the growing list of cabinet disgruntlements. It was a bonus that he did not have responsibility for another execution on his conscience. On all the other critical files facing Bowell at the end of the first year of governing, the temperature only had risen. Days earlier, Manitoba premier Greenway had removed any illusion he was willing to compromise on the school question, so the Prime Minister had to brace for a pending nasty fight over remedial legislation tactics. He would face opponents from both inside and outside government.

At the same time, unhappiness with his leadership and efforts within cabinet to overthrow him were intensifying and widely reported. He was an increasingly isolated and besieged national leader as the fateful year 1896 was dawning.

As the young Canadian nation prepared to embark on its 30th year, the Manitoba school issue loomed as the dominant, divisive and most contentious issue facing the year-old Bowell government. In fact, the first act in the political insurrection that would end Bowell's prime ministerial tenure actually had unfolded weeks earlier, orchestrated by those who thought he was being too decisive and pro-Roman Catholic on the separate school file. After months of defying his own government by speaking out against plans to restore a separate school system for Manitoba's minority, Controller of Customs N. Clarke Wallace had announced on December 11 that he was resigning and abandoning the Conservative government. It would free him to campaign against remedial legislation. In a December 23 letter to his West York, Ontario constituents, Wallace argued the cabinet decision to 'coerce an unwilling province' to fund a Catholic separate school system left him few options. He could sacrifice his 'well-matured and conscientious convictions and the best interests of our common country or leave the government. I chose the latter course. I have always been opposed to separate schools.'[6]

The Wallace announcement was not a surprise. His growing defiance of cabinet policy had become a symbol of government dysfunction and the lack of a firm prime ministerial hand. For some time, C. H. Tupper had been urging Bowell to fire Wallace for insubordination but the Prime Minister resisted, recognizing that his dissident junior minister gave voice to a section of the party. He may even have seen in his rebellious MP a small reflection of his own career path, minus the bottom line of disloyalty. Wallace was Grand Master of the Orange Lodge of British North America, as Bowell had been. He also was responsible for administering the customs department that Bowell had created, although Wallace was not at the cabinet table and reported to the trade minister.

Despite the similar career paths and Orange affiliation, the two men disagreed profoundly on the issue of minority education rights, the sanctity of constitutional guarantees, and the proper Orange position of tolerance in Protestant/Catholic relations. While Bowell spoke for the cabinet consensus on the issue, Wallace's defection and open defiance was another public sign of government disarray. He became a powerful symbol for Conservative opponents.

At the same time that Wallace was becoming a free-floating Bowell critic, Manitoba Premier Greenway unveiled his most definitive gesture of defiance by calling an early provincial election on the question of school policy. Finally, even Bowell had to get the message that the province and its premier were not willing to bend. The Prime Minister's pursuit of a Manitoba concession that would negate the need for a federal-provincial showdown was exposed as a wishful fantasy that led to wasted time and a diminished chance of resolution.

With time running out before the constitutionally required dissolution of Parliament in late April, the Bowell government would have to act quickly when a new parliamentary session started in early January. The odds for success were long and getting longer with every passing day. Of course, Greenway understood the federal deadline dilemma and knew it put him in the driver's seat on the issue. In a December 27, 1895 election campaign speech to his southwest Manitoba constituents, he was blunt in identifying provincial voters as ammunition in his political war with Ottawa:

> The menacing attitude assumed by the Dominion government with reference to the educational legislation of the province has made it necessary to take the sense of the electors upon the question this forced upon them. It is clear that nothing short of separate denominational schools will be accepted as an adequate measure of relief. We have replied definitively and positively rejecting the proposal to re-establish separate schools in any form and expressing the intention to uphold the present uniform non-sectarian system.[7]

As he expected, Manitoba voters overwhelmingly supported him against meddling by Ottawa. The Greenway Liberals won 34 seats to six for the opposition. He had his mandate to stand firm. Mackenzie Bowell clearly had misjudged the determination of the Manitoba premier although they had known each other for years, stretching back to when they sat together in the House of Commons as fellow Conservative MPs in the 1870s. Even then, Ontario MP Greenway had a defiant streak that led him away from Conservative doctrine. He eventually bolted the Conservatives for the Liberals over high protectionist tariffs introduced by the Macdonald government and implemented by Bowell after 1878.

Greenway moved west in 1879 as a land speculator, promoting settlement of rural Manitoba by Ontario and European English-speaking immigrants and farmers who quickly outnumbered the original Francophone, Roman Catholic and Métis population. His growing public profile translated into a provincial political career. By 1888, he was premier and would hold the office for 12 years. Manitoba political historian Christopher Adams noted that Greenway's 1890 decision to end 'the delicate arrangements that had been made regarding language rights originally negotiated between the Red River Settlement's founding populations' fractured traditional provincial party politics.

Out of the chaos emerged a dominant faction of English-speaking Liberals and a smaller faction of Conservatives who thought the Liberals not aggressive enough on the issue. The third faction was 'a small break-away group of Francophone and English-speaking Catholic MLAs' led by a former Greenway cabinet minister who abandoned the government over the issue. 'In effect, this third group served as the opposition on this issue.' Facing little opposition, the premier judged that he had a mandate to remain inflexible until he could deal with a new, hopefully more compliant and presumably Liberal federal government after the next election.[8]

On New Year's Day 1896, cabinet met in Ottawa for final approval of the Bowell government's Speech from the Throne that would open the parliamentary session on January 2. There were no recorded dissenters. On the only issue that really mattered in the final session of Parliament, the Throne Speech told MPs and Senators what they already knew: the Manitoba government had refused all federal entreaties to offer compromise proposals on funding for separate schools and Ottawa finally would act. The Governor General read:

> I regret to say that the advisors of the Lieutenant Governor [the Manitoba cabinet] have declined to entertain favourably these suggestions, thereby rendering it necessary for my government in pursuance of its declared policy to introduce legislation in regard to this subject.[9]

Once the speech had been delivered to its Senate Chamber audience, Parliament adjourned until the following Tuesday, January 7, when the real legislative work would begin on the Manitoba issue. That night after Parliament's opening, the Aberdeens hosted a state dinner for almost 90 people at Rideau Hall and Lady Aberdeen recorded in her diary that her presence as the only woman at the banquet kept political nastiness at bay. 'Afterwards, we had a crowded State Reception which went with a good deal of go, the ministers staying late and making themselves generally agreeable.'[10]

The illusion of political peace would not survive 24 hours.

Bowell had been working frantically behind the scenes during those cold January days of parliamentary pageantry and policy promises to quench a political fire that had been smoldering in a vacant cabinet seat for months. He had promised to fill a crucial Quebec cabinet vacancy before facing Parliament January 7. Dissenters had made it one of their key demands. In July, respected Quebec Senator and federal Agriculture Minister Auguste Angers had resigned over government delays in forcing Manitoba capitulation on separate school policy. Since then, Bowell's cabinet critics had insisted that filling the third Quebec cabinet seat with a respected Francophone minister was crucial for government credibility in the face-off with Manitoba. While Bowell could be accused of showing a lack of urgency for the task in the summer weeks after Angers' resignation, he stepped up the intensity of the search as winter approached, vowing to have the seat filled when Parliament next sat. It proved to be a difficult promise to keep as potential candidates, often under pressure from Bowell critics or Quebec Catholic Church officials skeptical about government sincerity on Catholic education, found reasons to reject the offer of a cabinet post.

Finally, an unlikely player entered into the Conservative turmoil, the legendary celebrity Prairie priest Fr Albert Lacombe who volunteered to use his strong church and political contacts to find a willing cabinet candidate for his friend Mackenzie Bowell. On the surface, the involvement of a practicing priest in such a high profile, partisan political drama would be judged unusual and inappropriate but Fr Lacombe was a special kind of churchman. He had worked for decades ministering to First Nations communities in Western Canada, advocating for indigenous rights and bluntly warning the Macdonald government that its Indian policies of oppression, dispossession, paternalism and confinement to reserves was leading to hunger, disease, intolerable living conditions, resentment and tragedy.

In Canadian history, Lacombe is revered for his defence of First Nations interests at a time when they had few advocates. An Alberta community and an Agriculture Canada research station carry his name in tribute to his historical stature. During the Manitoba School Crisis, Lacombe also was a fierce defender of French and Métis minority religious and language rights. He was assigned by his bishop to do what he could to advocate for the Manitoba minority against provincial government policy. His political connections were extensive and put to use in his crusade, including close

214

friendships with and easy access to Bowell, Laurier and Governor General Aberdeen among many other key players of the time.

The Prairie priest had an additional affinity for Bowell; both were strong advocates of federally financed Indian Industrial Schools (now referred to as Residential Schools) as vehicles for improving the lives and prospects of aboriginal children. Lacombe lobbied the federal government in the 1880s to create and finance a network of schools to be run by the churches and he helped Ottawa write the rules for the system. In fact, Lacombe opened, and was director of, one of the West's first residential schools (St. Joseph's Industrial School in Calgary) in 1884. When he discovered that the unhappy students were running away to return home to their reserves and parents, he was an early advocate of rules that would forcibly remove children from their homes and make escape from the schools all but impossible. He saw it as being in students' best interests.

A biographer portrayed the two sides of Lacombe's record as expressions of the same motivation: to support and advance the interests and welfare of his indigenous 'family' as he saw them. 'With his experience of decades of hunger and hardship spent in Indian camps came a deep understanding of Prairie Indians and he became an expert on matters affecting them,' wrote James MacGregor in a 1975 history of the famous priest. But on the Industrial Schools issue, like 'all missionaries [he] came to the conclusion that the only way to assimilate the Indians would be to operate such schools where the children could be isolated from their parents and taught the skills necessary to ensure their success in the White world.'[11] It was a view widely shared in the government and the churches of the time.

For his part, as a trained teacher and a man who used oral and written words as a base to build an 80-year career, Bowell was a lifelong advocate of education as a way forward. While not involved in planning or implementing the Indian School system, he strongly supported it and took advantage of ministerial travels to visit schools across the West, meeting with students and teachers and extoling the good work he thought they were doing.

In his political campaign to help find a new Quebec cabinet minister for the Prime Minister, Lacombe ultimately was successful but not in time to allow Bowell to keep his promise. Respected Conservative Senator, journalist and businessman Alphonse Desjardins (rumored to have housed Louis Riel at his Montreal home when the Métis leader was a fugitive) agreed to Lacombe's persuasive arguments after assurance that Bowell was committed to remedial legislation. However, the appointment could not be arranged in time for the planned January 7 resumption of Parliament. The still-vacant cabinet seat became one of the key justifications for the subsequent uprising against the leader.

In truth, however, there was no rabbit Bowell could have pulled out of his prime ministerial hat at that late date to placate cabinet opponents and to avert the leadership coup that was about to happen. It had been in the planning stage for a year and conditions were ripe in those early January days to execute the scheme that would unfold over the following weekend. A key component of the 'right conditions' was the unusual presence in Ottawa that New Year's season of Bowell's long-time colleague Sir Charles Tupper Sr, a Conservative comrade-in-arms for more than a quarter century who now was a senior official and confidante of the Prime Minister as High Commissioner in London. It is clear he manipulated Bowell to arrange a visit to Ottawa so he could be available when a leadership vacuum was created.

In late November 1895, Tupper sent a cable from London to the Prime Minister's office in Ottawa suggesting to his old friend that a trip back to Canada would be in order for consultations about British action on several policy files affecting Canada. Bowell quickly cabled approval and, in the weeks ahead, would staunchly insist that Sir Charles was in Ottawa at his instruction and not as part of the anti-Bowell cabal.

Tupper arrived in Ottawa December 15 via New York and held some meetings with the Prime Minister to brief him on British policy regarding fast mail service and laying of a Pacific communications cable. At the same time, he also met regularly with the plotting dissidents and lodged with his son, one of the leaders of the nascent coup and main advocate for his father's ascension.

Oscar D. Skelton—legendary Ottawa bureaucrat, Liberal sympathizer and Sir Wilfrid Laurier biographer—clearly did not buy the argument that the trip was requested and arranged only to brief Bowell. In his 1921 Laurier biography, Skelton suggested sarcastically that the Tupper cable was simply 'an innocent suggestion' from a senior official to his political boss with a more sinister purpose than the Prime Minister realized. 'Mr. Bowell, too guileless or too proud to question, acquiesced.'[12] It was in fact a ruse, a convenient excuse for Tupper's presence in Ottawa early in the new year when he knew a cabinet coup was being planned and he was the choice as replacement for most of the dissidents. The Tupper charade was just one of a series of backroom developments over the previous year that set the stage for the dramatic and unprecedented early January overthrow of a Prime Minister leading a majority government.

Even the Governor General's wife, and possibly Aberdeen himself, knew long before Bowell did. The trail of behind-the-scenes collusion against the Prime Minister is clearly mapped.

On January 12, 1895 with Bowell just three weeks into his tenure, C. H. Tupper had written to his father begging him to come back to oust the new leader. 'Everyone outside of our weak cabinet demands you as leader and in our cabinet, the best men want you as well,' he wrote. Tupper Sr replied that he had no interest in the rough and tumble of House of Commons politics at his age but clearly the prospect of becoming prime minister intrigued and flattered him enough to prompt a qualifier with his rejection of the plea. 'Under these circumstances, I would sacrifice the rest for which I long and go into the Senate as president of the Privy Council [i.e., prime minister] until these things are obtained and you could succeed me,' he added.[13]

Tupper Sr also made clear he would not actively seek the office but left the door open for others to create the vacancy and plead that he fill it. He did not inform Bowell about the scheming he knew was occurring behind his back. Throughout the year, the son kept the father informed of Bowell's perceived failures and cabinet discontent. On November 1, Militia and Defence minister Arthur Dickey, Tupper's replacement as Cumberland, Nova Scotia MP, wrote to urge his political mentor to return to take over government, assuring him of cabinet support.[14] As usual, Tupper said he was flattered but demurred. Still, he added the tease that he was prepared to 'make any personal sacrifice that the party demands.' He wanted the ego inflating beseeching to continue.

Several days later, C. H. Tupper secretly confided to Lady Aberdeen that a coup was in the works. 'Efforts are being made to reorganize the Government,' he wrote. 'This is, of course, very confidential. The delay in all these things is heartbreaking. Our party is terribly handicapped and it looks as if we must continue the fight under a leader who does not lead!'[15] Of course, she did not let the Prime Minister in on the secret.

Tupper Jr and Dickey were not alone in working to undermine the leader. For more than a year, Railways and Canals Minister John Haggart had made no secret of his view that he would have been a better choice to replace Thompson. The other key dissident leader was Finance Minister Foster, the Bowell government's House of Commons leader. He had opposed and disparaged Bowell from the beginning of his tenure. He later claimed that he and the other conspirators had doubts about Bowell from the beginning, joining his cabinet in late 1894 'with many misgivings' and yet had served him 'unitedly and loyally' until it became obvious he was not up to the job.[16] In the days before he had formally been invited to join Bowell's cabinet in late 1894, in fact, Foster complained to a friend in Saint John about what he saw as Bowell's main flaws, vanity and insecurity. 'B is old and vain and suspicious to a degree... He sees a cabal in every two who converse together,' he wrote in a private letter. He did not explain later why he accepted Bowell's offer, given his unflattering opinion of him as a leader not worth following.[17]

As it turned out, even if Bowell was paranoid, it did not mean there were not conspirators conspiring.

The government upheaval that Lady Aberdeen described as 'the storm... over the political horizon' informally began to take shape Friday January 3. She attributed the timing in part to two Montreal by-election losses the previous week to resurgent Liberals and 'the planned presence of Sir Charles Sr in the country.'[18] It was the day after the Throne Speech—agreed to by all ministers including the dissidents—had been presented to Parliament as a united government's plan of action for the winter session. Bowell had presided over an uneventful cabinet meeting during the afternoon to discuss impending parliamentary business and strategy.

That evening, the prime minister visited the Governor General and in the course of conversation in the Rideau Hall study, reported there was some 'caballing against him.' As if to reinforce the point, while Bowell was in the room, Aberdeen received a note from Foster asking for a meeting between himself, Haggart and the Governor General. Aberdeen responded with a note inviting them to meet the following morning, January 4. Of course, with the direct communications line between C. H. Tupper and Lady Aberdeen, the Governor General already may have known about the recent plotting. As well, if Bowell had cultivated better sources of information within his own government, he would have known that the 'caballing' had been happening in recent days right under his nose.

On January 1, the Prime Minister had stopped at Finance Minister Foster's house to wish him a happy New Year and instead of seeing the minister, he was ushered into a room where Foster's wife was entertaining. Unbeknownst to him, the reason Foster was unavailable is that he was down the hall in his study, meeting with other dissident ministers planning the coup.

At the January 4 meeting arranged the previous evening, Foster and Haggart told Aberdeen 'they felt it was impossible to go on with Sir Mackenzie, that Sir Charles Tupper was the man as leader,' according to Lady Aberdeen's diary. They said seven ministers were prepared to resign but Aberdeen insisted he could receive such news only from the Prime Minister. Aberdeen ended the meeting and then was off to the first Rideau Hall skating party of the winter. The following day, Bowell met the Governor General to brief him on the insurrection and cabinet resignations, the news having been delivered to the Russell House that morning by the two ministers. He then had met with Tupper Sr—the successor designated by the dissidents—who asked Bowell if he would agree to serve in a future cabinet, become Ontario Lieutenant Governor or High Commissioner to Britain. 'To all propositions he declined, one reason being that he would never again sit in the cabinet with some of the men who had deserted,' according to Lady Aberdeen.[19]

She attended the meeting with Bowell at her husband's request and expressed some rare admiration for Sir Mackenzie, sparked by her dislike of Tupper Sr 'One can but admire the pluck of the old man for the desertion is a most extraordinary exhibition of treachery. Of course, it has all been hatched by the old Sir Charles, who is well known as a dodger.' The Prime Minister left in late afternoon and then returned after dinner that Sunday evening, staying until after midnight to discuss the reality and the options. The days that followed were arguably the most chaotic, dramatic and bizarre in Canadian political history. The office of the neophyte British-appointed Governor General was the focal point around which the unprecedented made-in-Canada political soap opera revolved.

It all unfolded during an Ottawa deep freeze that saw temperatures plummet to minus 38 degrees Fahrenheit on January 6, the day Bowell and his remaining cabinet ministers met to pass orders-in-council appointing acting ministers to replace the 'bolters' who had resigned.[20] Bowell took on finance and militia/defence portfolios. Aberdeen urged Bowell to try to reconstruct a cabinet and he agreed only to find that the rebels were staking out railway and boat terminals to 'persuade' potential recruits arriving in the capital not to join the cabinet.

Several times, Aberdeen refused Bowell's offers to resign by insisting that the government leader who had presented the Throne Speech plan of action had an obligation to remain government leader until Parliament accepted or rejected the plan. The Governor General also offered an open door to the dissidents but refused their request that they be allowed to directly announce their resignations publicly. He insisted the news had to come to Parliament and the public from the Prime Minister.

Meanwhile, Lady Aberdeen kept her secret pipeline to Tupper Jr open for updates and, through an intermediary, she was in communication with Opposition Leader Laurier who assured her that he was ready to accept a call to government.

Parliament first heard the news officially when it resumed sittings Tuesday January 7, although newspapers had been filled with stories about the revolt for several days. At 8:00 p.m., the Prime Minister rose in the Senate with a statement to read. 'Since the opening of Parliament, seven of the ministers have tendered their resignations to the Prime Minister which were submitted to the Governor General and accepted by His Excellency,' he told Senators. Bowell then read the names of defectors: George Foster, finance; John Haggart, railways and canals; Sir Charles H. Tupper, justice; W. B. Ives, trade and commerce; A. R. Dickey, militia and defence; W. H. Montague, agriculture; and John Wood, controller of customs. He asked that the Senate adjourn for a day when he promised a full statement would be made, as well as a response to a speech Foster had made earlier that day to the House of Commons.

The resigned Minister of Finance had justified the seven resignations as a demonstration of lack of faith in the leader rather than a disagreement with government policy. Bowell said he understood from hearsay that Foster's explanation 'was unfair to the head of the government' but he would have more to say once he had read the Hansard transcript. While he may not have had a text of Foster's words, Bowell certainly knew what his former finance minister had said. He was in the House of Commons during Foster's afternoon speech, in a chair beside the Speaker's Throne where he was accorded special sitting privileges in a Chamber normally off-limits to Senators.

Lady Aberdeen was also there in a seat on the floor near Bowell and later recorded in her diary that after the speech, the Prime Minister walked across the aisle to Opposition MPs, shook hands with leading Liberals and audibly said: 'It is such a comfort to shake hands with honest men after having been in company with traitors for months.' [21] In historical retelling, this was reduced to having Bowell refer to a 'nest of traitors'—the signature phrase attributed to him—but years later he insisted he could not recall ever using the term.

After Bowell's January 7 evening Senate statement ended with a promise of more to come, Liberal Opposition Senate leader Sir Richard Scott rose to sympathize. He said Foster had insinuated that 'the premier of this country is not mentally capable of leading the party. I scarcely think that the opinion of the people of Canada will confirm the statement made by the ex-minister of finance.' [22] Liberal Senators cheered and it would not be the last time Liberals came to Bowell's defence in the days ahead, although perhaps with ulterior motives. They no doubt hoped the Conservatives would remain divided with a damaged leader at the helm heading into the summer election.

The next day did not bring Bowell's promised full response. Instead, his scheduled speech was knocked off the agenda by an event even more shocking and sobering than the cabinet revolt. As if there wasn't enough parliamentary drama in the works, Conservative Senator Henry Kaulbach, 65, had died walking in a Senate corridor that afternoon. Bowell used most of his time that evening to pay tribute. 'Last night about 10 o'clock, Mr. Kaulbach met me with half a dozen gentlemen who were standing about and in his usual jocular manner, asked me if they were all applying for the vacant portfolios,' the Prime Minister told a hushed, somber Senate. 'Little did any of us think that the Senate would be called upon in less than 20 hours afterwards to lament his death.' [23] He also (despite clear emerging evidence to the contrary) came to the defence of his 'friend' Charles Tupper Sr that evening, insisting he was not part of the plot, but in Ottawa at Bowell's invitation to discuss government business. 'I make this statement in justice to the High Commissioner who is now in Canada and to whom many improper motives have been ascribed.' Then Bowell asked for another adjournment until January 9 when he would speak 'on a question of such momentous importance to the country.'

On Thursday, Bowell rose at 3:00 p.m. to give the Senate his side of the story; to defend his reputation, to reveal that he had offered to resign for the good of the country and party but had been turned down by the Governor

General and to challenge the veracity of Foster's explanation. It was a maudlin, defensive speech during which he lauded his rise from newspaper printer's devil to prime minister, his honesty and his belief that he could have been a successful prime minister but for the undermining action of disloyal cabinet ministers. Bowell argued that had he been given the same level of loyalty by his followers as previous Conservative leaders had received, 'we would have been as successful in carrying on the affairs of the government as my predecessors, though not possessed of their measure of ability or political tact.'

The embattled Prime Minister said he did not fear 'honourable' defeat in Parliament or at the polls 'but to retire now after having been attacked in the manner already referred to without this explanation would be dishonourable and leave a stain on my reputation which I do not desire to hand down to my family.' He finished by asking for an adjournment until Tuesday, January 14 while he tried to reorganize the government. If three days passed without success, he would resign.[24]

The political agitation was not confined to the halls of Parliament. Across Wellington Street from Parliament Hill, the Russell House had been the scene of countless strategy sessions by Bowell supporters and detractors, often within earshot of each other. The previous evening, debate descended into violence. Pent up antagonisms boiled over after some post-Parliament refreshments when two MPs fought over which party would win the coming election. A newly elected Montreal Liberal MP vowed that 'Laurier could lick the Conservative Party out of its boots and it didn't matter whether Tupper or Bowell was at the head,' according to a newspaper report. A Quebec Conservative MP objected and the fight was on, to the delight of 'a crowd of fully a hundred.' The two were separated before any serious damage could be done. Peace was restored.[25]

Then, the unexpected happened. A measure of uneasy peace broke out inside the Conservative Party and government after months of division and dysfunction. A weekend of negotiations, deal-making and compromise between the warring factions produced an unusual and unexpected compromise that kept Bowell in the prime minister's office for more than three additional months and provided at least a surface reconciliation with the bolters. In return, effective control was transferred to Tupper Sr but without the title.

For once, despite his deep involvement in much of the political machinations over the past several months, Aberdeen was not a player in forging the peace treaty. Like Canadians who read about it in their newspapers, the Governor General was caught off guard by the news. It came to Rideau Hall the evening of Monday, January 13 when Bowell indicated he wanted to meet with Aberdeen after dinner. His self-imposed three-day deadline was up. 'We trembled to hear what his announcement might be,' Lady Aberdeen confided to her journal that night. Then, there was relief. 'Actually, he had come to terms with Sir Charles and consented to take the whole of the deserters back again. And this after all his protestations! However, Sir Charles serves under him.'

As a small measure of victory, Bowell had refused a request from Tupper that the two jointly break the news to Aberdeen. The arrangement was that Bowell would remain Prime Minister until the end of the parliamentary session while Tupper would compete for a House of Commons seat. If elected, he would be the government leader in the Commons and although unstated, the de facto government leader overall. Once Parliament rose, Tupper would become Prime Minster at age 74—the oldest in Canadian history—and then lead the party into the summer election. Bowell would go back to being a fulltime Senator. Aberdeen accepted the immediate arrangement but offered no guarantee that he would sanction the planned Bowell-to-Tupper transfer in three months.

The surprise arrangement was forged through the leadership of some party elders including Sen Frank Smith from Toronto, who in 1894 had assured Aberdeen that a Protestant Prime Minister Bowell would be acceptable to Canada's Roman Catholic population. The arrangement clearly required some key compromises on both sides. Mackenzie Bowell had to swallow a significant amount of bruised ego and wounded pride to agree to stay on as a figurehead prime minister and to accept the insurgent deserters back into his cabinet. Although Bowell denied it, there were many public reports that he initially had insisted he would not accept the deal if Foster, Haggart or Montague were to be in his cabinet. Tupper Sr insisted and Bowell compromised.

Bowell also showed bargaining strength in the negotiations. He rejected bolter demands that he justify the new cabinet arrangement by reading a public statement written by them vindicating their decision to resign and denounce him. The explanation Bowell insisted on reading in the Senate, and that was accepted by Tupper Sr, was much more noncommittal on the justification for the original cabinet rupture. On the other side, Tupper had to put his ambition to be prime minister on hold for a few months. In the interim, the lack of prime ministerial obligations gave him free time to campaign for a Nova Scotia parliamentary seat and then set to work bolstering the spirits and organization of the dispirited Conservative Party. It was unprepared for the looming election against a confident Liberal Party.

By accepting the compromise, the dissidents had to delay fulfillment of their dream that Tupper would be Prime Minister and Bowell banished. They also had to endure Liberal and public ridicule over their decision to cling to power under Bowell after forcefully announcing they could no longer tolerate his leadership. C. H. Tupper was the only deserter to refuse a cabinet appointment. The public explanation was that with his father assuming a lead position and a fast track to the Prime Minister's office, one Tupper in cabinet was enough. The real reason was expressed in an angry February 13 letter he wrote criticizing two of the bolter allies who became Bowell ministers. A bitter C. H. Tupper was not happy with the deal. 'Had it not been for them, Bowell would gracefully have gone and Sir C. T. would have been Prime Minister and our victory would have been certain,' he wrote. 'These men, however, played Turk... and being allied with us up to the "resignation", encouraged Bowell to play the fool until their cart was nearly upset. We have a new government not much better than the last.'[26]

A factor in bolter acceptance of a temporary continuation of Bowell's leadership was their fear that Aberdeen might declare the Conservative government dysfunctional and summon Opposition leader Laurier to form a government, allowing him to campaign as Prime Minister.

On January 15, the new/old version of the Conservative government was sworn in by Aberdeen. Foster was back at finance, Haggart at railways and canals, Montague at agriculture and Tupper Sr as secretary of state although he did not yet have a seat in Parliament. The cabinet was unveiled in the House of Commons the next day. Public galleries were packed and Opposition benches fully occupied as the foiled dissidents took their seats to catcalls and a chorus of 'The Cat Came Back.' Sir Richard Cartwright, former Liberal finance minister, said Parliament was being entertained by 'the Ottawa Low Comedy Club' and denounced Tupper Sr as 'one of the most contemptible politicians the country ever knew.'[27] In the days leading to the end of the crisis, the Toronto Globe described the public fascination with the unfolding political drama. 'Crowds crushed into the Commons and filled the galleries until they overflowed into the corridors,' it reported after one day of parliamentary theatre.[28]

The prolonged political confusion and its final compromise resolution actually brought Bowell some rare sympathy and praise from contemporary politicians, newspapers and later historians. As noted earlier, in the midst of the coup, Lady Aberdeen—not a Bowell fan—came to regard him as a victim in the drama, although a flawed victim. 'The more one meditates over it, the more does one feel that the old man has been cruelly treated,' she confided to her diary.[29]

University of Toronto chief librarian W. Stewart Wallace, in a sympathetic 1933 biography of George Foster, concluded that in different conditions and with fewer problems inherited from his predecessors, Sir Mackenzie could have been a good prime minister. 'He was a man of honour and integrity and under other circumstances might have graced the premiership but he was ill-fitted either by ability or temperament to hold together the warring elements of the Conservative Party.'[30]

Skelton, in his reverential 1921 biography of Laurier, called the treatment of Bowell indecent. 'Whatever hidden provocation may have existed, the public were shocked by the indecent publicity of the attacks on the prime minister and the party shaken by the display of jealousy and bad judgment on the part of its leaders. Out of it all, only Mackenzie Bowell himself—perhaps no heaven-born leader but an honourable and straight-forward gentleman—emerged with any credit.'[31] In the midst of the cabinet revolt, the Montreal Star argued that Canadians would side with Bowell against his attackers. 'In his present trying circumstances, he will have the hearty sympathy of the great majority of Canadians, irrespective of race or creed,' it said. 'Even his most prominent political opponents have expressed appreciation for the premier's straightforwardness and courage.' He demonstrated no lack of 'intelligence or back bone.'[32]

After the prolonged tension, party infighting and chaos that characterized the first 14 months of Mackenzie Bowell's prime ministerial term, the final months after the compromise with Tupper forces were relatively calm. Bowell even found time for some fun in the midst of his prime ministerial duties. On March 14, he joined the Governor General in a spin down the Rideau Hall toboggan run during Lady Aberdeen's birthday skating party. 'I had many companion photographers and we all lay in wait together for the event of the day which was His Excellency taking down his premier on the toboggan slide for the first time in his [the premier's] life,' she wrote. 'They came down gaily.'[33]

On Parliament Hill in the dying weeks of the Seventh Parliament, the government had a short to-do list to push through. The Throne Speech was debated and quickly approved by the Conservative majority. Next on the agenda was introduction of the contentious remedial legislation to override the Manitoba school legislation, and it faced a bumpier ride. The Liberal opposition had decided to obstruct and avoid taking a stand during recorded votes by prolonging the debate day after day. They kept an eye on the parliamentary clock that would terminate the session in late April and plunge the country into an election, leaving the issue unresolved and the Liberals not saddled in the election by having taken a definitive stand.

As government House Leader in the Commons, a testy Tupper often forced MPs to debate through the night, trying to wear down the Opposition. Even a February 21 appeal from Roman Catholic bishops' (via Fr Lacombe) for Laurier to support the Conservative remedial bill failed to change Liberal tactics. [34] Behind the scenes, Governor General Aberdeen recruited prominent Montreal Conservative MP Sir Donald Smith to act as a federal representative in search of a compromise with Manitoba. Like others before him, Smith's effort failed. He was one of his era's most prominent and successful Canadians: MP, Hudson's Bay Company chief commissioner, banker and railway builder. In his persona as Lord Strathcona, he had pounded in the ceremonial last railway spike to complete the Canadian

Pacific Railway trans-continental line in November 1885. Yet success in trying to mediate the Manitoba school issue eluded even him.

After months of secret contacts and proposals to have Greenway travel to Ottawa for negotiations, an April 2 telegram from Smith in Winnipeg informed Bowell that Manitoba had rejected the last federal proposal. The provincial government countered with final last-minute proposal to allow some religious teaching at the end of a school day for minority groups. The Francophone minority would be regarded as simply another non-Anglophone language minority in the queue for school time despite their constitutional protection. The Conservative government rejected the idea as inadequate.[35] With time running out and parliamentary approval of spending plans required to keep the government operating during the summer, debate on the Manitoba legislation ended, left to be dealt with by the next government.

After waging a vigorous by-election campaign in Sydney, Nova Scotia and brushing up on his legendary campaigning skills, Sir Charles Tupper had won a House of Commons seat February 4, 1896 and returned to the House of Commons on February 11. Newspapers reported that crowds gathered along the tracks to cheer as his train moved west toward the capital.[36] For more than two months, he would be prime minister-in-waiting.

Parliament prorogued on April 23 and the election date was set for June 23 in a cabinet order signed by Prime Minister Bowell. On Monday April 27, he visited Rideau Hall for the last time as Prime Minister and during a three-hour meeting, discussed the transition of leadership. Although Aberdeen had made clear in January that he would not be bound by the transition deal worked out between Bowell and Tupper to end the parliamentary crisis, he told his retiring Prime Minister that he saw no alternative to Tupper. There had been growing support for a Donald Smith appointment as a compromise but the Montreal MP had indicated he would not accept the top political job if asked. Instead, he had accepted appointment as High Commissioner to London, replacing Tupper.

For his part, Bowell told the Governor General not to ask him for his choice of successor but tellingly, confided that he would have served in a Smith cabinet but had rejected a request from Tupper to stay in government as a senior minister. Bowell said he would not serve in a cabinet with some of the bolters.[37] The following day, Aberdeen summoned Tupper to be sworn in as the sixth Canadian prime minister although Lady Aberdeen could not miss the chance to privately express her disgust. 'To have to send for a man whose whole life has been devoted to scheming and who will spare no means of any sort which may be of use in securing the return of his party with himself as Premier was a distasteful job,' she wrote in her diary. 'Still, there are the facts. The Conservative Party evidently chose him for their leader.'[38]

As Tupper was achieving his dream job on April 28, Bowell went back to his Parliament Hill office to supervise the packing of his papers for transport to Belleville. A reporter spotted him and asked how he was. 'He was cheeriness itself and remarked: "You can say that the ex-premier of Canada is perfectly contented and as happy as a big sunflower".'[39] He was free to leave the politics behind. He planned to play no role in the election campaign and doubted the Conservatives could win. Besides, he would not even be in the country during the campaign. As a last prime ministerial act, he had appointed himself a Canadian representative at a London conference to negotiate details of laying communications cables between Canada and Australia.[40]

After two weeks of rest at home, Bowell boarded a May 14 ship to New York *en route* to London, leaving the political pressure and uncertainty behind. The previous day, senior federal public servants and deputy ministers praised Bowell at a meeting they organized in Ottawa to thank him for his years of service and the straightforward and honest manner in which he dealt with them and affairs of the country.

He also left with an extraordinary letter of praise in his pocket from a member of Tupper's cabinet who was first brought into government by Bowell. British Columbia MP and later premier Edward Prior, Controller of Inland Revenue, wrote on April 29 to thank his former leader for mentoring him and to assert that Bowell was leaving:

> With the respect and esteem of every decent man in Canada but nowhere in the Dominion does your name stand higher than in my own province. Whatever might be said about our party, your name was always held up to the light as that of a straightforward man.[41]

On his return from London several months later to resume his fulltime Senate duties and to face some new challenges, the former prime minister awaited with an air of calm (and probably relief) the next phase of his life and career.

NOTES

[1] LAC Privy Council Minutes for April 18, 1895 (R.G. 2, Series 1 Vol. 635.

[2] LAC Bowell Papers, Vol. 14 (March 1, 1895 letter from Macleod MP D. W. Davis).

[3] LAC Bowell Papers, Vol. 52 (May 7, 1889 letter to George Bartlett of Hybla, Ontario).

[4] Friedland, Martin L., *The Case of Valentine Shortis: A True Story of Crime and Politics in Canada* (Toronto: University of Toronto Press, 1986), 171–172.

[5] LAC Bowell Papers, Vol. 84 (letter of November 15, 1885, the day before the executions).

[6] LAC Bowell Papers, Vol. 103 (Ottawa *Evening Journal*, December 31, 1895 edition).

[7] Provincial Archives of Manitoba, Greenway Papers, Box G512.

[8] Adams, Christopher, *Politics in Manitoba* (Winnipeg: University of Manitoba Press, 2008), 70.

[9] Debates of the Senate, 6th Session, 7th Parliament (January 2, 1896), 3–4.

[10] *The Canadian Journal of Lady Aberdeen* (January 2, 1896 entry), 298.

[11] MacGregor, James G., *Father Lacombe* (Edmonton: Hurtig Publishers, 1975), 268–297.

[12] Skelton, Oscar Douglas, *Life and Letters of Sir Wilfrid Laurier* (Toronto: Oxford University Press, 1921), 465-466.

[13] Sanders, E. M. (ed.), *The Life and Letters of the Rt. Hon. Sir Charles Tupper*, Vol. 2 (Toronto: Cassell and Co. Ltd., 1916), 182.

[14] Cited in Saywell, 'The Crown and the Politicians: The Canadian Succession Question 1891–1896,' *The Canadian Historical Review*, No. 4, 1956, 324.

[15] ibid (November 4, 1895 letter), 325.

[16] House of Commons Debates, January 7, 1896.

[17] Morley Scott, S., 'Foster on the Thompson-Bowell Succession,' *The Canadian Historical Review*, Vol. XLVIII No. 3, September 1987, 275.

[18] *The Canadian Journal of Lady Aberdeen* (January 5, 1896), 299. Her private diary entries during the tumultuous January days of the cabinet uprising offer the most candid insider look at the unfolding events and will be used extensively when mapping the chronology of the crisis.

[19] ibid, 300.

[20] LAC Privy Council Minutes, 2 January–7 January, 1896 (RG 2, Series 1, Vol. 669).

[21] Senate Debates 6th Session, 7th Parliament Vol. 1 (January 7, 1896).

[22] *The Canadian Journal of Lady Aberdeen* (January 7, 1896) 303

[23] Senate Debates (January 8, 1896), 8.

[24] Senate Debates (January 9, 1896), 15-16.

[25] *The Ottawa Journal*, 'Near Fisticuffs at the Russell,' January 9, 1896.

[26] Cited by Saywell, 'The Canadian Succession Question, 1891–1896,' *The Canadian Historical Review*.

[27] *The Ottawa Journal* (January 16, 1896, Vol XI, No. 32) The headline on page 1 read: 'Scorched by the Liberals, Field Day in the House of Commons.'

[28] *The Toronto Globe* (January 11, 1896), Page 1.

[29] *The Canadian Journal of Lady Aberdeen* (January 6, 1896), 301.

[30] Wallace, Stewart W., *The Memoirs of the Rt. Hon. Sir George Foster* (Toronto: The MacMillan Co. of Canada Ltd., 1933), 78.

[31] Skelton, Oscar Douglas, *Life and Letters of Sir Wilfrid Laurier*, Vol. 1 (Toronto: Oxford University Press, 1921), 467.

[32] *Montreal Star*, January 8, 1896 edition. Reprinted January 9 in the *Ottawa Journal*.

[33] *The Canadian Journal of Lady Aberdeen* (March 14, 1896), 328.

[34] LAC Bowell Papers, Vol. 103, File 4 (February 21, 1896 letter from Fr Lacombe to Laurier).

[35] ibid, Vol. 104, file 3 (April 2, 1896 telegram from Smith to Bowell).

[36] Durant, Vincent, *War Horse of Cumberland: the Life and Times of Sir Charles Tupper* (Hantsport, Nova Scotia: Lancelot Press, 1985), 195.

[37] *The Canadian Journal of Lady Aberdeen*, 340–41.

[38] ibid, 341.

[39] *Montreal Star*, September 29, 1896.

[40] LAC Privy Council Minutes, April 21–29, 1896. (RG 2, Series 1, Vol. 685), Reel 3644.

[41] LAC Bowell Papers, Vol. 15 (April 29, 1896 letter from Edward Prior).

Chapter 15
LIFE AFTER THE BIG TOP

For Mackenzie Bowell, the first summer after escaping the prime ministerial pressure cooker did not unfold quite as planned. By the time he arrived in England as a Canadian representative to the scheduled conference on plans to lay a Pacific communications cable, the meeting had been postponed until late October. It meant he had enough time to return to Canada for the final weeks of the federal election campaign leading to the June vote if he wished. He did not, opting instead to pass close to two months in England, visiting friends and relatives. After the bruising ordeal he had endured during the previous 16 months of Conservative intrigue and bare-knuckle civil war politics, he had no appetite just yet for more political theatre, Canadian style.

As it turned out, he missed the chance to occupy a front row seat for one of the most entertaining and influential elections in Canadian history. In a 2002 study of what he judged to be the five most important Canadian federal elections since Confederation, author John Duffy described the 1896 campaign as 'Canada's first great election fight.'[1] After the implosion of the Conservative government and divisions within the Conservative party, the contest should not have been close. It turned out to be a popular vote cliffhanger.

As the campaign began, on one side was an ill-prepared and disorganized Conservative Party, tired after 18 years in power and drained by the extended feud over Bowell's leadership. It was led by recently installed 74-year-old Charles Tupper who had been out of the country for the better part of the past decade as High Commissioner to Great Britain. When Tupper returned, he found a disheveled and neglected party machine unlike the electoral juggernaut he remembered from the 1880s when he last campaigned. Signs of decay had been evident for years. As early as 1893, Trade Minister Bowell had been warning party insiders the Conservatives were losing touch with the voters.[2] Now, after three more years in office, the gap between governor and governed had widened and, to add to the trouble, the party was saddled with the legacy of the unresolved Manitoba school issue that promised to bleed support from both dissatisfied Roman Catholic and Protestant voters.

In addition, the country had changed and grown in the five years since the last election and not all the change boded well for the Conservatives. The latest census showed the Canadian population was nearing five million, the voter base was shifting west where traditional political alliances were not as well entrenched, and the Equal Rights Association splinter party was drawing support from the rightwing anti-Catholic portion of the Conservative base. Since 1894, the economy also had shown signs of strain. Trade had stalled and Canadian economic growth was sluggish.[3]

On the other side of the political fence facing the Conservatives were the surging Liberals, savouring a recent series of by-election victories and led by the relatively young (compared to Tupper) Wilfrid Laurier. At age 54, he was an experienced and increasingly polished campaigner, a 22-year House of Commons veteran and nine-year party leader. He also had learned valuable lessons from his 1891 election defeat at the hands of wily political veteran John A. Macdonald. Voters then had opted for what they knew—continued protectionism offered by Macdonald—rather than risking the unknown consequences of free trade with the Americans. For Laurier, the takeaway message was that the safest election strategy was to campaign on vague, positive platitudes rather than specific policy promises that would attract opposition.

The Liberals also enjoyed the advantage of having had the pre-election campaign field largely to themselves during the past two years. They exploited it by campaigning to promote their united party and their leader while the Conservatives were distracted by internal strife and a debilitating period of political patricide. Still, for all the advantages the Liberals appeared to have heading into the campaign, in many ways Sir Charles Tupper was the great equalizer. He was a skilled politician and campaigner, a veteran of the Confederation debates, provincial election battles as Nova Scotia premier, and many federal campaigns under Macdonald. He consistently outperformed his younger Liberal opponent even as Liberal hecklers shouted him down for his self-aggrandizing style of electioneering.

The campaign for the June 23 election officially began on May 1 when Tupper was sworn in with his cabinet as Canada's sixth prime minister. Unofficially, Laurier had been in campaign mode for several years, traveling across the country to shore up and expand the Liberal base while vaguely promising to settle the Manitoba school issue using 'sunny ways' with fellow Liberal and Manitoba premier Thomas Greenway. It was an effective strategy by Liberal Party operatives to introduce a nonthreatening Laurier in person to regional voters not familiar with Canada's first Francophone Roman Catholic national political leader.

A centerpiece of Liberal pre-election campaigning was a 70-day train trip through Western Canada during which organizers hoped skeptical western voters would be impressed to find out that despite his language and lineage, Laurier was an anglophile who spoke fluent English. Duffy joked that 'if Laurier's trip in the late summer of 1894 had been a modern campaign commercial, its tag line would have read: "Wilfrid Laurier: A Frenchman you can trust".'[4] Across the country, the Manitoba school question was an issue with most voters, many of whom knew of the religious divide surrounding the controversy even if the complex and intricate details escaped them. The Conservative position was clear and Laurier promised a solution, but offered no politically dangerous details about how. History records it as a no-holds-barred vicious campaign fueled by partisan media coverage common to 19th century Canada. 'A newspaper served each community and almost every newspaper was either Conservative or Liberal,' Duffy noted. 'Government patronage was intimately involved in the business of running a paper... In return, the papers functioned as party house organs at all times.'[5]

What filled the newspaper space between the ads during the months of May and June were negative stories that dealt more often with the lying ways and unsuitability of opponents than with positive proposals for how to lead the country into better times. Political journalist and historian Bruce Hutchison wrote:

> On both sides, the campaign of 1896 was ferocious, mendacious and more than usually cynical. Any intelligent voter could see that the political process was standing on its head when an English-speaking Protestant Prime Minister appeared as the rescuer of a French-speaking Catholic minority and a French-speaking Catholic strove to make himself leader of another race by quarreling with his Church.[6]

Laurier's 'quarrel' with his church came in the weeks before the election campaign began when the Liberal leader informed the House of Commons that he had been threatened with sanction from senior church bishops if he did not support the Conservatives in their fight against the Manitoba school legislation. He was defiant, vowing to continue the fight even though he was a devout Catholic. 'I am here representing not Roman Catholics alone but Protestants as well and I must give an account of my stewardship to all classes.'[7]

The juxtaposition of Protestant Tupper and Roman Catholic Laurier taking positions that were counter-intuitive was an underground current of comment and attack throughout the election.

During the eight-week campaign, Tupper maintained a blistering schedule of speeches and travel, speaking to as many as five rallies each day in different communities. Between June 9 and 22, Tupper's campaign claimed he made 42 speeches in a final blitz through Ontario.[8] In the end, however, Tupper and the Conservatives fell short, although even in defeat they acquired some bragging rights on election night. They won the national popular vote by almost 16,000 votes and two percentage points: 413,006 to 397,194. 'The national results showed a divided country,' concluded Duffy.[9]

For historians, the takeaway story was that Laurier's Liberals won a comfortable parliamentary majority: 118 Liberal seats to 88 seats for the Conservatives, largely on the basis of an overwhelming victory in Quebec where voters embraced Canada's first French-Canadian political leader. In the traditional Conservative Quebec bastion, the Liberals won 53 percent of the popular vote and 49 of 65 seats. The 1896 election began a century of Liberal dominance in Canadian politics, made possible by an almost continuous hold on Quebec political loyalty.

On June 30, Bowell wrote from London to tell Tupper he was surprised at the Quebec result and to commiserate about the effort the Conservative leader had made. 'Trusting you are none the worse for your arduous labours during the last month or six weeks.' His sympathetic outreach was not reciprocated. In a 1914 memoir, Tupper implicitly blamed Bowell for the defeat: 'The downfall of the Conservative Party in 1895–96 was occasioned by the determination of the government not to deal with the Manitoba school question in the session of 1895,' he complained.[10]

In defeat, Sir Charles Tupper also proved to be a poor, angry loser. As the dust settled from the June 23 vote count, he made it clear he did not believe the fight had ended or that he really had lost.

Lord and Lady Aberdeen, with their barely concealed Liberal sympathies, spent election night outdoors in Quebec City with a crowd of Liberal supporters. They had ventured out from their official summer residence to sit with 'an immense throng' on a nearby grassy knoll where election result updates were posted. 'Announcement of victories for the supporters of Mr Laurier were greeted with tremendous cheers,' the Governor General recorded. With the results clear, he expected a telegram from Tupper to arrange an imminent resignation:

> But instead of this came a message to the effect that although appearances and press reports gave the impression that the Liberal Party had achieved a great victory, yet he hoped to prove to His Excellency that this was not really the case and that in a few weeks time when there had been an opportunity for recounts and inquiries to be made into various elections in which there had been only a small majority, a very different state of affairs would be shown.[11]

Tupper asked Aberdeen to return to Ottawa immediately to discuss the situation but the vice-regal couple administered a subtle snub by lingering for several days in Quebec City before returning to Government House in Ottawa. There, they held picnics on the grounds 'during some days of great heat both physical and political.' In his memoirs, Aberdeen reported 'days of great tension' with the Prime Minister as Tupper insisted the election result not be recognized immediately, the House of Commons not be recalled, and he be allowed to make appointments and to fill vacant Senate seats.

When Aberdeen rejected the idea of an orgy of appointments by an outgoing lame-duck Prime Minister, 'Sir Charles did not hesitate to express his opinion that I was departing from precedents and infringing on the principles of self-government.' For the official record, Aberdeen wrote an account of his unpleasant dealings with Tupper. He noted that behind his refusal to allow the defeated Conservative leader to appoint Senators was the reality that among 78 Senators, there were only five Liberals. If Tupper filled the four available vacancies with more Conservatives, Laurier would not be able to appoint a new senator and cabinet minister of his choice to act as Government Leader in the Senate. Besides, he argued, Tupper's government never had been endorsed by Parliament.

In the face of an unwavering Governor General who kept a written record of the dispute details and refused Tupper's demand that the correspondence between them be destroyed, a bitter Tupper finally resigned on July 2, his 75th birthday, effective July 8. He insisted the resignation was triggered by the Governor General's 'attitude of no-confidence' rather than his election loss.[12] With just 69 days in office, Tupper became Canada's shortest-serving prime minister.

Almost nine decades later during the 1984 election campaign, Tupper's brief occupancy of the prime minister's chair and his brevity record became a footnote in media coverage. Newly selected Liberal leader and Prime Minister John Turner (replacing Pierre Trudeau) chose a downtown Vancouver riding as a personal base for a political comeback while fighting a national election campaign he was clearly losing badly. Party officials decided to hold Turner's Vancouver Quadra nomination meeting at the Sir Charles Tupper Secondary School and a newspaper columnist noted the unfortunate symbolism of holding the event in a school named in honour of the shortest serving Prime minister. Weeks later, Turner led the Liberals to an historic defeat and at 80 days in office, became the second briefest serving prime minister in Canadian history, outdone only by Tupper.

Once the new Parliament opened for business in August 1896 led by the first Liberal government in 18 years, Tupper took his place as Leader of the Opposition. He quickly showed his lingering bitterness by moving several motions demanding that Aberdeen be reprimanded for exceeding his authority. To settle the matter, Prime Minister Laurier referred the file to the Colonial Office in London and the Governor General's written records of the affair were sent overseas for examination. Two years later, Laurier rose in the House of Commons to announce that the Colonial Office had vindicated Aberdeen, concluding that he acted properly by refusing to allow Tupper to fill the vacant Senate seats.[13]

After a summer largely free of politics, Bowell returned to Ottawa to resume his Senate duties during a steamy August filled with political excitement and expectation. He had mused to friends about the welcome prospect of sitting in Parliament without the burden of official responsibilities for the first time in 18 years. However, it was not to be. He soon was handed a new, responsible and time-consuming political job. On August 25, the 54 Conservative senators held a caucus and asked him to become the Senate Conservative leader. Bowell accepted, after voicing some reluctance, and Tupper confirmed him as Opposition Senate Leader. It was a job with parliamentary clout since the Senate had the constitutional obligation to review, debate and vote on all legislation approved by the House of Commons. After almost a quarter century of Conservative parliamentary dominance that included the power to appoint Senators, the party controlled the Upper Chamber and would for the foreseeable future, since Senate appointments were for life.

The governing Liberals were outnumbered more than four to one in the Upper Chamber and although the unelected Senate ultimately was expected to defer to the will of the elected Commons, the Senate Conservative majority under Bowell's leadership had the power to amend, criticize, delay and obstruct the agenda of the government. As a veteran parliamentarian with experience in both Houses, the new Senate Conservative leader knew the rules and how to use them.

Bowell settled in to watch the new Prime Minister, no doubt keenly awaiting Laurier's performance on the crucial Manitoba Schools file. In the dying months of the last Parliament, Laurier's Liberals had blocked the Bowell government from imposing a settlement to protect Manitoba Francophone Catholic minority rights. During the election campaign, the Liberal leader had promised to do what the Conservatives failed to do; reach a deal with Manitoba that would bring an amicable resolution to the issue that had festered for six years as a dangerous infection in the Canadian body politic. Now, the pressure was on the rookie Quebec-based Francophone Catholic Prime Minister to make good on his promise.

Behind Bowell's anticipation of Laurier's performance on the issue lay a history of testy relations between the two men. Laurier had often questioned Bowell's commitment to minority Catholic rights because of his background as an Orange leader, criticized his selection as Prime Minister because of the Orange taint and mocked his strength as a leader. For his part, Bowell referenced the rookie MP's fiery defence of Louis Riel during debates in the mid-1870s and mocked his later poor judgment (in Bowell's view) in supporting free trade with the United States. It turned out that Bowell had a blind spot when it came to sizing up his Liberal opponent. He had consistently underestimated Laurier over the years, disparaging his prospects and questioning his instincts. In 1889, for example, he pronounced himself delighted that new Liberal leader would be speaking on Bowell's home turf. 'I was glad to hear that Laurier was to speak in Belleville because I was quite satisfied what the result would be,' he wrote to a Conservative friend. 'He is a courteous gentlemanly speaker but is a light weight.'[14]

A year later after a Laurier speech in Saint John, New Brunswick, Bowell was equally dismissive. 'Laurier is not a man to "enthuse" any audience,' he wrote of a politician now regularly judged to have been one of Canada's greatest orators.[15] 'He is what might fairly be termed a good, pleasant, agreeable essayist but to take hold of a mixed crowd and work them up to anything like fever heat would require a half dozen old muskets and the death of two or three Riels and then the audience would have to be French.'[16]

On the Manitoba Schools file, Bowell once again misjudged Laurier, this time over-estimating the Liberal leader. He intimated to friends that at least on the Manitoba education file, he expected his political rival would do the right thing to protect the minority rights of his fellow Francophone Catholics. Along with members of the affected Manitoba minority, Bowell would be disappointed. On August 19 when the new Parliament assembled, Laurier's first Throne Speech promised action: 'Immediate steps will be taken to effect a settlement of the Manitoba School Question and I have every confidence that when Parliament next assembles, this important controversy will have been adjusted satisfactorily,' Aberdeen read on behalf of the new Liberal government.[17]

On August 26, Government Senate leader Lawrence Power reported that federal and Manitoba cabinet ministers had already met and 'there is reason to hope that some general basis of a settlement has been arrived at and if this course [negotiation] had been adopted several years ago, I believe this question would never have become what it did become—the basis of partisan warfare.' Hearing those words, Bowell rose to defend the Conservative record against his Halifax critic, disputing the allegation that the Conservatives had erred by refusing to negotiate and simply insisting the province had to submit. The Conservative government always approached the Manitoba government in a friendly way with offers of negotiation but federal overtures were rejected, the former Prime Minister argued. Then he offered a concise description of his view on the need to protect minority rights and the constitution in the face of politicians who would deny them:

> It is not coercion to say to a man who has taken rights from you as an individual and as a community that he must restore them. There is to my mind but one safe course to pursue by any man who attempts to govern or assists in governing this country and that is to take the constitution as it stands and adhere to it as rigidly as possible, maintaining the rights of all classes of the people and more particularly, all minorities.[18]

Then Bowell took his seat to watch Laurier and the Liberals deliver. As Opposition leader, Laurier had trodden a careful, ambiguous path on how he would deal with the Manitoba Liberal government on the Schools issue. In Quebec, he deemed it sufficient to criticize, blaming Conservative inaction on the influence of the Orange Lodge. He once declared: 'Thankfully there are no Orangemen in the Liberal Party.' In an 1895 speech in Montreal, Laurier had mocked the government and its leader Bowell on the issue, drawing laughter from the partisan crowd by asserting: 'If you want to please the Conservatives nowadays, you must not speak of their principles and above all, do not speak of their leader.'[19]

Outside Quebec, Laurier told audiences he had a plan but shared no precise details. At an October, 1895 rally in Morrisburg, south of Ottawa, he promised a vague 'sunny ways' strategy for dealing with the issue, and expression that has entered the language of Canadian politics to the present day both as a summation of Laurier's style and a way to judge Prime Ministers. Before an enthusiastic crowd estimated at 4,000, Laurier said he would not use the Conservative tactic of bluster on the issue. He used as his metaphor the Aesop Fable about a contest between the sun and the wind to see which could succeed in forcing a traveler to remove his coat. The sun and its heat won. 'Well, the government are very windy,' he said. 'The more they have threatened and raged and blown, the more that man Greenway has stuck to his coat. If it were in my power, I would try the sunny way.'[20]

A cliché for judging a Prime Minister's style was born.

The first intimation of progress came on March 25, 1897 when the second Liberal Throne Speech was read to open a new parliamentary session. It announced that a deal had been struck in principle but no details were yet available. The Governor General read from text written by the government:

> A settlement was reached between the two governments which was the best arrangement obtainable under the existing conditions of this disturbing question. I confidently hope that this settlement will put an end to the agitation which has marred the harmony and impeded the development of our country and will prove the beginning of a new era to be characterized by generous treatment of one another, mutual concessions and reciprocal good will.[21]

Hearing the words 'the best arrangement obtainable under the existing conditions,' Bowell's suspicions were aroused. 'I wish I could believe for a moment that the terms of the agreement... meet the approval of the country as a whole and particularly of those who are directly affected by that settlement,' he said in the Senate March 30. However, he could not jump to that conclusion because he had come to believe the Greenway government refused to deal with the Conservatives because of an assumption the Liberals would win the federal election and settle for less.[22]

It took nine more months before Laurier announced final details of the deal in the House of Commons on November 10, although details already had been revealed in the Manitoba Legislature. In essence, it was the same deal Greenway had offered the Bowell/Tupper government the previous year and which had been rejected as falling far short of the constitutional guarantees promised in the Manitoba Act. Bowell's suspicions had been vindicated. It turned out Laurier's 'sunny ways' was another way of saying 'capitulation.' The core of the deal was that constitutional guarantees of government support for French Catholic school instruction were abandoned. French Catholic students would be treated as just another non-Anglo minority in the school system without any special status or rights. 'The right to Catholic teaching and to teaching in the French language was precariously established,' according to sympathetic Laurier biographer Joseph Schull. If enough students were present in the school system and requesting it, 'religious instruction could be given by a priest during the last half hour of each school day and from this period, children of other faiths would be excused. There could be no further separation of children by religious denominations nor could there be special privileges of language for the second of the partner races that had made Confederation.' French-speaking students would have the same status 'as the Germans who were already sprinkled through Manitoba,' Schull concluded. 'They would be on the same basis as the coming hordes [of other immigrants].'[23]

Minority Francophone Manitobans would have to pay school taxes to support the public school system. If they wanted Catholic schools or French Catholic-influenced lessons for their children, they could pay for it themselves. In the Senate, Bowell raged against the 'compromise' as a farce while Laurier and a Liberal delegation traveled to Rome in late November to try to head off feared condemnation from the Vatican. In any event, the visit to the highest levels of Roman Catholic governance failed to persuade senior church officials. In Roman Catholic churches throughout Quebec, priests read a December 8 Papal Encyclical issued by Pope Leo XIII condemning the settlement. The Vatican statement noted that the Canadian Confederation bargain 'had assured the Catholic children the right of being educated in public schools according to the prescription of their conscience. Now, that right the Parliament of Manitoba abolished... Such a law is injurious for our children... The law which has been enacted for the purpose of reparation is defective, imperfect, insufficient.'[24]

Still, despite objections and rallies by the affected Manitoban community, denunciations from the Vatican and Roman Catholic pulpits and occasional parliamentary outbursts by Conservatives over the years, Laurier did not pay a political price for his betrayal of the constitution and the Manitoba minority. Protestant voters warmed up to him, taking his retreat as a sign that Roman Catholic Church did not rule the Catholic prime minister. They also took note of the fact that Protestant rights campaigner and former Conservative star Dalton McCarthy endorsed the deal. Meanwhile, Quebec voters continued to elect Liberals to Parliament, accepting Laurier's claim that it was the best deal he could make in the circumstances.

Almost a decade later, Bowell used his role as Opposition Senate Leader to raise the issue and its legacy again when the Manitoba formula became the template for minority education rules in 1905 legislation creating the provinces of Saskatchewan and Alberta. On July 12, 1905 (ironically the principal Orange celebration day of the year), Liberal Senate House Leader Richard Scott conceded that education rights afforded to Catholic minority students in the new provinces did not amount to much. 'The proposal in the present bill is vastly different from the concessions made by this Parliament in 1875,' he told Bowell. 'Those are a mere skeleton of what Parliament then conferred upon the community but for the sake of peace, the minority are willing to accept them. They will make the best of the situation.' He said Catholic education could be offered only for half an hour at the end of the day 'if the trustees so desire.'[25] While he was a supporter of minority rights, Scott said he accepted the compromise because 'I thought it was much better to yield, far better to accept what had been conceded than to seek to obtain more with the acrimony and bitterness and prejudice that would naturally follow.' Bowell shot back: 'All I can tell him, and I think he knows it, [is] that compromise certainly is not in accord with the sentiments of the vast majority of those who are affected by it.'

While modern day portrayals of Laurier's settling of the Manitoba Schools question usually describe it as an example of his deft handling of difficult and divisive national issues, there still are a few who question Laurier's 'accomplishment'. In a 2002 Senate speech as the governing Liberals were struggling through an internal leadership civil war between forces loyal to Prime Minister Jean Chrétien and rival Finance Minister Paul Martin, Conservative Senator Lowell Murray goaded the Liberals by referencing the Bowell-bolters feud as a cautionary historical precedent for the party. He argued the episode had destroyed the Conservative government and its hold on power while hurting the country's reputation for protection of minorities. Laurier sold them out. The deal 'cost the Manitoba minority their constitutional rights for more than 80 years into the future.'[26]

In a 2016 *Maclean's Magazine* survey of academics about Canadian prime ministers, Laurier was ranked as the second-best prime minister in history for his promotion of tolerance and compromise, among other strengths. University of Fraser Valley professor Barbara Messamore demurred, arguing that Laurier's compromises also could be seen as 'a moral evasion.' She cited the Manitoba deal on minority Francophone education rights as an example because it 'fundamentally represented an abandonment of those rights.'[27]

Some Quebec commentators expressed that same view in Bowell's day as well. In early 1901 after the Quebec City Liberal newspaper *Le Soleil* attacked him for a career marked by Orange Lodge support and anti-Catholic sentiments, a rival French language newspaper jumped to Bowell's defence. 'Sir Mackenzie, Orangeman and Protestant though he is, has so far done more to render justice to the Roman Catholic minority in Manitoba than Sir Wilfrid Laurier, the French Roman Catholic leader,' a January 14 *L'Evenment* editorial thundered in response. 'The ex-premier championed the cause of the minority and if Sir Wilfrid had only acted as a statesman rather than a seeker after place and [popularity], his co-religionists would today be in possession of their constitutional rights.'[28]

Of course, the controversial resolution of the Manitoba education issue was just one of an array of issues facing the new Parliament and a Conservative caucus learning the ropes of being in opposition for the first time in a political generation. As Opposition Senate Leader with the Upper Chamber majority in his caucus, Mackenzie Bowell had to perform a delicate balancing act. The job of Conservative Senators was to hold the Laurier government to account and to criticize and scrutinize legislation and policy proposals sent to the Senate from the Liberal-dominated House of Commons. However, the unelected Senators did not want to be seen as unduly obstructing the will of the popularly elected government.

Bowell orchestrated opposition to a number of controversial Laurier government decisions, in some cases withholding approval and returning them to the Commons for further consideration. A proposal to take $300,000.00 from funds allocated to Manitoba school spending in order to reduce the provincial deficit was defeated. A Laurier attempt to redraw electoral constituency boundaries in a way that Conservatives thought would benefit future Liberal election prospects was rejected, as was a government plan to spend money on a Yukon railway proposed by Liberal business interests.

As is to be expected in the partisan press of the day, Bowell's new role as Senate Opposition leader received mixed reviews. A month after he assumed the role, a glowing Montreal *Star* profile argued that while Liberal Senator Sir Oliver Mowat was the 'titular leader of the Senate' as chief representative of the Laurier government, 'the leading Senator is Sir Mackenzie Bowell. Sir Oliver reigns. Sir Mackenzie governs and governs discreetly and well.' The Conservative newspaper asserted that Bowell would not abuse his power, recognizing that Laurier won the election. 'He is too old a parliamentarian to dream of using the very substantial power he wields to oppose the clearly ascertained wishes of the electorate of the day, nor on the other hand will he always accept the hysterical shriekings of the government organs as inspired expressions of public opinion.' While not obstructing, he and the Conservative Senate caucus 'will provide a wholesome check upon hasty and ill-considered legislation.' The *Star* suggested Bowell had landed on his feet in the election aftermath since Conservative MPs in the House were in a minority for the first time in 18 years while he was 'undisputed leader of a compact and overwhelming majority in the Upper House... We believe in his heart of hearts, Sir

Mackenzie has a feeling that the catastrophe of June 23 [election defeat] was not without its humourous features.'[29]

Government ministers and Liberal-supporting newspapers were not as kind and flattering about Bowell's performance. In an early 1898 Montreal speech, Public Works Minister Joseph-Israel Tarte accused the Conservative Senate majority of being obstructionist and 'not worth the rope to hang them.' The newspaper *La Patrie* had followed up by arguing that if the Senate majority opposed the will of the popularly elected Liberal government, it should be 'annihilated.'[30] Laurier in fact threatened Senate reform but as in most cases of Senate reform initiatives throughout Canadian history, the threat came to naught.

The Toronto *Globe* found a more effective and hurtful way to criticize and goad its old Tory nemesis. When critiquing Bowell's Senate leadership in opposing government proposals, the newspaper touched an exposed nerve by noting that Bowell took his cues about Senate opposition strategy from the Conservative House of Commons Opposition led by Tupper, Foster and Haggart. 'The country will undoubtedly be astonished to find Sir Mackenzie Bowell acting as a chore boy for the nest of traitors,' the *Globe* editors slyly noted in commenting on one 1897 incident. 'The point need not be dwelt upon. Sir Mackenzie knows best what consorts with his own self-respect.'[31] The Liberal newspaper had in fact picked at a wound that Bowell would not let heal. A key under-the-surface reality and irritant of his years as Senate Conservative leader was his lingering anger and resentment over the fact that the party now was run by the men ('traitors' he called them) who had undermined him, criticized him as not qualified to lead and in the end, brought down his administration. Publicly, Bowell played the role of good and loyal Conservative Party soldier, doing what was asked of him for the cause. Even during the leadership crisis, he did not generally assail or denounce his critics publicly. In the interests of the party and a public show of unity, he swallowed his ego and agreed to lead the government for the final three months of the parliamentary session even while Sir Charles Tupper Sr was recognized as the *de facto* party leader and many who had undermined him weeks earlier sat in his cabinet.

Privately, however, Bowell's sense of grievance simmered just beneath the surface against those who now sent him instructions in the Senate. In his last private meeting with Governor General Aberdeen as Prime Minister, his anger boiled about those who betrayed him, even if he would not repeat the sentiments in public. Lady Aberdeen recorded the exchange in her diary. 'He said that he could never forgive those who had acted treacherously to him,' she reported.[32] There are indications that one result of his resentment was a boycott of the Conservative caucus after the party lost power. Typically, in the Canadian parliamentary system, Senators are members of the national caucus and the Senate party leader is a key caucus member, taking part in internal debates so he can understand and defend the position he takes on behalf of the party in the Senate. However, Bowell's personal files housed in the National Archives include an undated and unsigned hand-written note in what appears to be his handwriting recounting a conversation he had with a Liberal Senator (possibly government Senate leader Mowat) while Senate Conservative leader. According to the document saved by Bowell, the Liberal Senator said he had heard a rumor that Bowell was boycotting Conservative caucus. 'It is quite true and unless I change my mind, I shall do so while some of those who pretend to be leaders assume to themselves that mantle,' he recorded as his reply. Later in the conversation, the note suggests Bowell was asked about his relationship with Commons party leaders. 'Certainly I have no leader among those who assume at the present moment to lead the Party in the Commons,' was the recorded response.[33]

Over the years that followed, Bowell also had several opportunities to publicly gain a small measure of revenge against the principal players in the cabinet revolt. A particular target was former finance minister George Foster against whom Bowell seemed to carry the deepest grudge. A close second was former railways and canals minister John Haggart. One of the center-piece moments of payback was a long, rambling, remarkable and bitter 1905 speech Bowell gave in the Senate after both Foster and Haggart had given their own spin on the events of January 1896 that put their disloyalty in a better light. Bowell later justified the speech by arguing that he could not allow his reputation and accomplishments over a 37-year political career be 'besmeared by men of the reputation, politically and otherwise, of the Hon. John Haggart and his associates without a protest and exposure of the chicanery and treachery.'[34]

The pretext for the Bowell speech was a cabinet defection and minor crisis for Prime Minister Laurier that had echoes of the Manitoba Schools issue. Leading Manitoba Liberal Clifford Sifton had resigned from cabinet in a dispute over education and language rules for Francophone Catholic minorities contained in legislation creating the provinces of Saskatchewan and Alberta. They were based on Laurier's 1897 compromise with Greenway. Comparisons with the 1896 bolter crisis had been raised.

Once Bowell started, though, it quickly became evident that the real motive for the speech that lasted several hours was payback for what he saw as self-serving revisionism by his two former ministers. He recalled a request received the previous year from a prominent Conservative asking that he write a letter of support for Foster who was trying to win a North Toronto riding for the Conservatives in the 1904 election. Bowell recounted his reply to the delight of Senate Liberals, 'I humiliated myself quite enough by taking them back.' the Conservative Senate Leader read from a letter of reply he had sent. 'It was done in what was considered the interest of the party then and I have regretted it ever since.' He said he would not write the requested letter of endorsement for his former finance minister. 'I may be all that he and his chums say I am but I have not yet lost self respect,' Bowell read. And he would not 'demean' himself 'by asking my friends to put confidence in him which I do not entertain myself.'[35]

Fred Cook, a veteran parliamentary Press Gallery reporter in the early 1900s, added to the record of Bowell's disdain for Foster. Cook called Bowell 'a good hater,' recounting in a memoir that on a train trip from Montreal to Ottawa, Bowell refused a request from fellow passenger Foster to shake hands and 'let bygones be bygones.' Cook recorded that Bowell had responded in an angry voice 'Go away, I don't want to have anything to do with you' and they never spoke again.[36]

Revenge against Haggart first came in 1900 when Bowell campaigned for an independent Conservative running against the former railways minister in that year's election campaign in his Perth, Ontario riding. Then during his 1905 Senate speech, Bowell said he would regret 'for the rest of my life' accepting Haggart and 'those with whom he was associated in the plot' back into cabinet. He called it a 'fatal political error' on his part and then mused that if he had not called them a nest of traitors at the time 'I ought to have done so.'[37]

Even so, the wounded and resentful 81-year-old political warrior never did turn his fury against Sir Charles Tupper even if the evidence was clear that he had been party to and abetted the cabinet conspirators without ever warning his 'friend' Bowell of the brewing plot. By this time, Tupper also had publicly absolved himself of any responsibility for the Manitoba Schools debacle by blaming Bowell for some bad decision-making. Yet at the end of his speech eviscerating other key players in the plot, Bowell called Tupper 'as upright and honourable a public man as ever sat in Parliament.'

Having finally and publicly aired his pent-up rage against those he felt had betrayed him almost a decade before, Mackenzie Bowell now began to seriously consider his future involvement in the political machine. For several years, he had been musing privately about whether to step back from the pressure and workload he still carried as Conservative Senate leader. He had been in the thick of Canadian and Conservative politics for almost four decades. He was an octogenarian and worn down. Perhaps it was time for party leader Robert Borden (a Nova Scotian who had replaced Tupper in 1901) to bring his own, younger team players into senior party positions as he built the party to challenge the three-term Laurier government.

Mackenzie Bowell had a decision to make.

On July 19, 1905 as the Senate was preparing to adjourn for the summer, Bowell rose from his front row seat to announce his decision. He would retire from the role as Conservative leader in the Senate and he intended 'if I live to attend another session, to take a seat in the rear as soon as one is vacant and let some younger man occupy my present position as leader of the opposition.'[38] He assured the Senate that his decision, four years in the making, was not a reflection on the leader of the party. In fact, he and Borden got along well and at a May 7, 1902 banquet to honour Bowell's work as Conservative Senate leader, Borden had praised him as a key member of Sir John A. Macdonald's governments that worked 'to build Canada.'

Bowell also promised to continue working on the nation's business in his new role as an Opposition backbencher:

> I hope I may be able in future to devote as much time and attention to the business of the Senate as I have in the past but I desire to be relieved of the responsibility and constant attention which must be given to public matters by a Member leading the Opposition in this House.[39]

Bowell said he had asked to be replaced several times during the past several years but had been pressured to stay. The pressure still was there 'but I have become stubborn, determined to follow the inclinations and bent of my own mind at the present moment.' In response to the announcement, Liberal Senate Leader Sir Richard Scott noted Bowell's experience in the sweep of Canadian history. 'There are very few—I might say very very few—gentlemen in the Chamber who are as familiar as the Hon. gentleman with the past history of Canada and the policy which has been pursued by governments that have been in power in Canada for the past 40 years,' he said in tribute.

The Conservative Toronto *Mail and Empire* opined that Bowell had a record 'that does honour to his name and adds luster to his country. There is not in our history a better illustration of the truth that work—constant work —united with rectitude brings its reward than we have in the life of Sir Mackenzie.'[40]

As it turned out, Bowell did not immediately accomplish his goal to slip into a less prominent role. Borden persuaded him to stay on the job until he found the right replacement and it turned out to take a year and one more parliamentary session before Bowell finally could take that seat at the back (actually, he kept his front row seat) when he was replaced by Calgary Senator James Lougheed.

In the years that followed, the Senator from North Hastings often found it difficult to stay out of debates after 40 years of talking in Parliament. 'It was not my intention to speak on this motion,' he said in a typical intervention in December 1907, 'but as the Right Hon. gentleman has indulged in the usual attack on the late government for which I consider myself somewhat responsible, I may be excused if I claim the indulgence of the House for a short time.' Then after a long speech defending the Conservative record, he apologized for taking so much time. Liberal Senate

Leader Scott told him not to apologize. 'We are glad to observe that the Hon. gentleman is in a condition to address this House and hope he may for many years to come be able to do so.'[41] In fact, Bowell had another decade of Senate speeches to make. Many were to 'set the record straight' or to defend his own performance on issues that ranged from Manitoba Schools and the failed 1895 Newfoundland negotiations to customs department affairs, protectionism and defending minority education rights.

As befitting a former Minister of Militia and Defence and a militia officer honoured in the Belleville Armoury for defending the border against Fenian incursions in the 1860s, Bowell used his Senate platform to support the Borden wartime government and its execution of Canada's role in the First World War. He also had a personal stake in the fighting. Bowell had two grandsons at the front in France and Ian Mackenzie Bowell would be wounded and spend the last months of the war in a French hospital.

The 1913 parliamentary debate over a Borden government plan to build a fleet of dreadnought ships for use by Great Britain should war break out gave Bowell a chance to articulate his complicated views as both a British imperialist and a Canadian patriot who supported increased self-governing powers for Canada. The debate divided the Liberal opposition that promoted an independent Canadian navy from the pro-Empire Conservatives. 'Everyone wants a Canadian navy but the people want it to be a British Canadian navy and not an independent Canadian navy,' he insisted in a May 29, 1913 speech. 'While I am an imperialist in my ideas, I do not yield one iota of that autonomy we possess.'[42]

In 1914 at age 90, he intervened in a debate over whether English should be the language of the Canadian wartime shipping industry, arguing that his public life had been dedicated to promoting reconciliation between French and English Canadians. 'Whenever you propound the proposition of imposing either the English language upon the French or the French language upon the English people, you create a feeling of animosity and discontent in the country that should not exist,' he lectured. 'This country is composed of two different races and the less we interfere with either one or the other, the better for the peace and harmony of the country.'[43]

Several days later, he was on his feet again to criticize Opposition Liberal calls for lower tariffs. 'Everyone who knows me knows that I have been a strong protectionist,' said the political high priest of the Conservative high-tariff theology. 'I believe the prosperity of the country today is the result of the policy of 1878 and 1879.'

In recognition of his 90th birthday—which was on December 27, 1913 when Parliament was not sitting—1914 was the year marked by honours and celebrations for Bowell. He was treated as a political celebrity and feted at a Senate banquet that featured 'Green Turtle, brook trout, Egyptian Quail, Punch de Royal and Fromage de Roquefort.'[44] A number of magazine and newspaper profiles (one of which portrayed him as 'Canada's Grand Old Man') marveled at his physical fitness and stamina for work and travel. One anecdote recounted a time when he fell down the stairs at Toronto's exclusive Albany Club that left him unconscious. As worried bystanders speculated that he might be dead, Bowell regained consciousness. 'Sir Mackenzie, who evidently overheard part of what was being said, suddenly opened his eyes, caught sight of portraits of Sir John Macdonald, Sir Charles Tupper, R. L. Borden and other eminent Conservatives that graced the walls. "If I'm dead," he exclaimed, "I'm in very good company indeed".'[45]

In 1916 at age 92, he travelled in early June from Belleville to Vancouver by train to visit son John with a plan to travel to the Yukon to swim in the Yukon River. His family dissuaded him because he had developed a cold so he caught a train east to attend a July Orange Lodge convention in Toronto where he was honoured for 71-years of service to the Order. 'He still stood erect in a jacket and vest with a cane,' remarked at Toronto newspaper covering the convention.[46]

After he turned 93 on the cusp of 1917 with news from the war's Western Front increasingly grim and Bowell worried about his soldier grandsons, he continued to be a regular occupant of his Senate seat when Parliament resumed sittings, although he rarely intervened in debate. But, as the session drew to a close, the old veteran divulged a secret to Senators: he was the ultimate parliamentary packrat with a home library in Belleville that included Hansard debate transcripts and departmental reports dating back to Confederation and in some cases earlier. He offered to let Hamilton Senator George Lynch-Staunton have access after he had complained about not being able to find a report in the parliamentary Library. 'I have about 450 feet of shelving filled with reports of each department for each year and the debates from the time of the Charlottetown meeting at which Confederation was first considered,' he said. Fellow politicians would be welcome to come and browse 'but I will not let any of them take books away because I would probably never see them again.'[47]

On September 20, 1917 as the Senate prepared to adjourn for the year, Bowell took the opportunity to complain that newspapers and the public largely considered the Upper Chamber irrelevant. That day, a final item of business was approval of a proposal to renew a 1913 decision that a reporter and translator of debates be retained by the Senate to prepare reports sent to newspapers in an effort to improve public appreciation and newspaper coverage of Senate work. Bowell opposed the motion even though he had been the originator of the first proposal to improve the profile of the Senate through hiring a reporter. After four years, he had concluded it was a 'useless expenditure' that should be eliminated. Despite receiving stories about the Senate, newspapers ignored them, he complained. 'They have treated the Senate with the same contempt,' said the 25-year veteran of the Upper

Chamber. 'Whether it is because the press consider that this House is useless or that the utterings of the Members are of no consequence to the community is a question they have to consider.'[48] It is a lament that would be familiar to many Canadian Senators a century later.

These were the last words Sir Mackenzie Bowell would speak in the Parliament that had been his second home for half a century. When the Upper House rose that afternoon and Bowell prepared to depart the city for home in Belleville, the cold that had nagged him for the past year had appeared again. He needed some rest.

NOTES

[1] Duffy, John, *Fight of Our Lives: Elections, Leadership and the Making of Canada* (Toronto: HarperCollins Publishers Ltd., 2002), 26.
[2] LAC Bowell Papers, Vol. 94 (June 1, 1893, letter to Barrie, Ontario Senator Sir James Gowan).
[3] ibid, Vol. 106 (undated *Economist Magazine* report on census and economic statistics).
[4] op cit, *Fight of Our Lives*, 32.
[5] ibid, 78.
[6] Hutchison, Bruce, *Mr. Prime Minister 1867–1964* (Toronto: Longman's Canada Ltd., 1964), 112–113.
[7] House of Commons Debates (March 3, 1896.
[8] Saunders, E. M., *The Life and Letters of the Rt. Hon. Sir Charles Tupper,* (Toronto: Castle & Co. Ltd., 1916), 207.
[9] op cit, *Fight of Our Lives*, 83.
[10] Tupper, Sir Charles, *Recollections of Sixty Years in Canada* (Toronto: Castle & Co. Ltd., 1914), 308-309.
[11] WE TWA, *Reminiscences of Lord and Lady Aberdeen*, Vol. II (London: W. Collins Sons & Co., 1925), 34-35.
[12] ibid, 37.
[13] Debates of the House of Commons, 3rd Session, 8th Parliament (June 10, 1898), 7690.
[14] op cit, *The Life and Letters of Rt. Hon. Sir Charles Tupper*, 212.
[15] LAC Bowell Papers, Vol. 90. (Oct. 12, 1889 letter to G.D. Dickson of Belleville).
[16] Greunding, Dennis, *Speeches that Changed Canada* (Toronto: Fitzhenry & Whiteside, 2018), 40.
[17] LAC Bowell Papers, Vol. 91 (December 23, 1890, letter to Saint John Senator John Boyd.), 165-167.
[18] Senate Debates, 1st Session, 8th Parliament, Vol.1 (August 19, 1896), 4.
[19] ibid, (August 26, 1896), 20–29.
[20] LAC Bowell Papers, Vol. 111 (Montreal *Gazette*, February 19, 1895).
[21] op cit, *Fight of Our Lives*, 65.
[22] Debates of the Senate, 2nd Session, 8th Parliament (March 25, 1897), 6.

[23] ibid, 14–15.

[24] Schull, Joseph, *Laurier: The First Canadian* (Toronto: MacMillan of Canada, 1965), 331-332.

[25] Montreal *Star* (January 10, 1898).

[26] Debates of the Senate, 1st Session, 10th Parliament Vol. 1 (July 12, 1905), 565.

[27] Debates of the Senate, 2nd Session, 37th Parliament (October 9, 2002), 90.

[28] *Maclean's Magazine*, October 7, 2016.

[29] LAC Bowell Papers, Vol. 104, File 1, *L'Evenment* article reprinted in the Quebec *Mercury* January 14, 1901.

[30] LAC Bowell Papers, Vol. 129 (Montreal *Star*, September 19, 1896).

[31] Senate Debates, 3rd Session, 8th Parliament (February 8, 1898), 11.

[32] LAC Bowell Papers, Vol. 104, File 1 (*Globe* edition June 24, 1897).

[33] *The Canadian Journal of Lady Aberdeen*, 340–41.

[34] LAC Bowell Papers, Vol. 112, File 1.

[35] Senate Debates, 1st Session, 10th Parliament (March 1, 1905), 84.

[36] ibid, 73–74.

[37] Bosc, Marc (ed.), *Canadian Parliamentary Anecdote* (Peterborough, Ontario: Broadview Press, 1988), 53.

[38] Senate Debates (March 1, 1905), 79.

[39] Senate Debates (July 19, 1905), 934.

[40] Toronto *Mail and Empire* (July 21, 1905).

[41] Senate Debates, 4th Session, 10th Parliament, Vol. 1 (December 3, 1907), 25–36.

[42] Senate Debates, 2nd Session, 12th Parliament (May 29, 1913), 907.

[43] Senate Debates, 3rd Session, 12th Parliament (May 28, 1914).

[44] LAC Bowell Papers, Vol. 134. Bowell preserved the menu from his lavish celebratory dinner in the senate dining room that also included Waldorf salad and 'Tipsy Trifle.'

[45] Craik, W.A., *Canada Magazine*, January 3, 1914.

[46] 'Wonderful Old Man,' article in the Toronto *Daily News* (July 28, 1916).

[47] Senate Debates, 7th Session, 12th Parliament (September 18, 1917), 1179.

[48] ibid (September 20, 1917), 1229.

Chapter 16
BOWELL'S FINAL CHAPTER

One by one they are passing away. As time rolls on, we shall all follow. In the meantime, it is our duty to accept the decrees of Providence in the spirit of resignation.

Mackenzie Bowell after the death of a
Conservative Party elder, May 22, 1883

On Friday, December 14, 1917, 31-year-old Captain G. Harold Holton of the 15th Argyll Light Infantry, Second Canadian Division, was at the Canadian Army frontline base at La Targette near Arras, France, near the Belgian border, when he received the regular mail packet from his wife Minnie at home in Belleville. It contained sad news. Four days earlier, his grandfather Sir Mackenzie Bowell had died. In the life-long diary he recorded daily—including during his three years on the First World War Western Front from 1916 to 1918—Holton flipped back four days to December 10 to update his original entry: 'At La Targett. Grandfather Bowell died at 7:45 pm,' he wrote.[1] In the December 14 entry, he recorded grandfather's life span: '93 years 348 days.'

Holton had learned of grandpa's illness a week earlier when the December 8 mail packet arrived with news from home. It had been a short illness, beginning with a cold that led to pneumonia and several weeks in bed at his daughter' home before succumbing. Bowell died 17 days before his 94th birthday. Until his final illness, he had maintained an active schedule that included daily appearances at the Belleville *Intelligencer* newsroom to tell tales, catch up on the news and write a column. At home, he occupied his time tending a large and lush garden.

With Bowell's death, Holton lost not just an illustrious grandfather but also a military predecessor and a business partner. Their connection ran deep. They shared a military attachment. Capt. Holton's Great War military unit had its roots in a Belleville-based militia unit organized and led by his grandfather in the 1860s during the Fenian raids. Bowell proudly used the title Lieut Col through his life and the grandson's first military experience was a 16-year affiliation with his grandfather's hometown volunteer militia.

According to Holton family records preserved at the Community Archives of Belleville and Hastings County, the two also were executives at the Holton Lumber Company Ltd. in Belleville (lumber manufacturers and dealers, according to a business card in the file), G. H. Holton as secretary treasurer and manager, Sir Mackenzie Bowell as company president. Although Holton was described in a 1936 Belleville *Intelligencer* profile as a 'life-long Liberal' who eventually and unsuccessfully contested a 1946

Toronto by-election as the Liberal candidate, dyed-in-the-wool Conservative Bowell and his Liberal grandson had an easy relationship as evidenced by letters between the two included in the Mackenzie Bowell Papers at Library and Archives Canada. When politics came up, it often was a jocular exchange.

Behind his lifelong public persona as a government fixture, prominent politician, staunch Conservative, Orange leader and newspaperman, Bowell at his core always had been rooted in family.

News of Bowell's death traveled quickly and Liberal leader Sir Wilfrid Laurier was one of the first outside the family to hear it. Laurier was in Winnipeg for an election speech the night of December 10, and just before he left his room at the Fort Garry Hotel to attend the rally, a telegram was delivered informing him of Bowell's death earlier that evening. Laurier biographer Joseph Schull imagined the old leader's reaction to the death of another longtime political colleague and opponent who had crossed parliamentary swords with him for 44 years. 'One more gone of the few who still lingered,' Schull wrote. 'The chief came down to the lobby and passed through to the street. The wind that cut at his throat and knifed through his bones (it was minus 20 degrees F) seemed a little icier.'[2]

For Laurier, it was another piece of melancholy news in the midst of a sad time for the aging political icon. The writing already was on the wall forecasting his personal, imminent political demise after an illustrious career. It was just seven days until the December 17 vote that would almost destroy his party, already deeply split when many of his former senior political allies had deserted him to support the Conservatives and conscription. The election was almost certain to give Robert Borden's Union government a mandate to pursue his war effort and for the first time, impose military conscription in Canada as a way to secure new recruits to populate front lines in the European killing fields.

The French/English divide in Laurier's beloved Canada had never been greater, deeper or more visceral in his lifetime and he sensed it was about to become worse.

In death, Bowell was praised with enthusiasm and admiration that he rarely received during his life, particularly from Liberal-inclined newspapers. The December 11 newspapers across the country spread the news that Laurier had received privately the previous evening. In large boldface letters, the Bowell family-owned Belleville *Intelligencer* filled its front page with the story: 'SIR MACKENZIE BOWELL. BORN DECEMBER 27, 1823. DIED DECEMBER 10, 1917' the headline screamed. Its lead paragraph was effusive in remembrance and praise:

> Sir Mackenzie Bowell has passed but his memory will ever live in the hearts of the thousands who knew him but to love him. All over Canada and in many parts of the world, the news that this great

Canadian has passed to the beyond will bring a feeling of sadness in the loss of a true friend and one whose busy life was full of good works and national service in the upbuilding of Canada as one of the brightest gems in the diadem of the Empire.[3]

The Liberal Toronto *Globe* described it as the end of an era in Canada's half century of history: 'Sir Mackenzie Bowell was one of the very last of a long line of distinguished Canadians whose activities preceded Confederation and who rank among the great builders of the Dominion.' One of his enduring passions, the *Globe* noted, was a life-long membership in the newspaper fraternity. While a politician, senior government player and prime minister during the first half-century of Canada, Bowell 'never ceased to be an editor and to love the smell of printer's ink.'[4]

The Montreal *Gazette* eulogized Bowell as an architect of Canada, the last survivor of Sir John A. Macdonald's nation-building team and a good man. 'He was at all times and to all men kind, considerate and courteous and he will be remembered as typifying Canadian citizenship at its best.'[5]

Bowell's December 13 funeral was one of Belleville's greatest spectacles. Thousands lined the streets from his William Street home to the Bridge Street Methodist Church, which was draped in black for the occasion. Stores and schools were closed for the afternoon in recognition of his accomplishments, and support of Belleville and its school system. 'As the long procession of carriages and many mourners on foot passed the School for the Deaf, the pupils lined the road to honour a man who always worked for public education,' said one description of the day's proceedings.[6]

The Belleville Orange Lodge No.123 organized the funeral march with Orangeman attending from across North America and an honour guard standing at attention. The Ottawa-based Mackenzie Bowell Lodge, which survives in skeletal form into the 21st century, was represented.

Funeral ceremonies began with a short service in his home before the procession to Bridge Street Methodist Church where Rev Dr Charles Scott delivered the homily, praising Bowell for his integrity and ethical life while not passing up a final chance to get a dig in at his former parishioner for not always toeing the church line. Scott told the mourners:

In the few intimate conversations I had with him which it was my privilege to enjoy as his pastor, he made it plain to me that only the richest motives were accentuating him, even when he did not fully meet my wishes as to his church relationship. What a noble life. Nothing could shake his conviction of what was right. Let us be true to our conscientious convictions as he was and we will reach that fellowship above.[7]

After a Masonic funeral service, Bowell was interred in the Belleville Cemetery that he had helped establish and supported over many years as a donor and member of the cemetery board of directors. '[The funeral procession] came to rest near the shore where he first arrived a lifetime ago,' according to an account of the day. 'The little immigrant boy had finished a long and distinguished journey.'[8]

Of course, it couldn't be a Mackenzie Bowell-focused event without some controversy. No senior representatives of the federal government were present despite Bowell's long federal government and parliamentary career, years of senior leadership positions and in his latter years, fervent support for Prime Minister Robert Borden's war strategy. Borden sent a wreath (and later a message to the family), as did the Senate, but no representatives. The Governor General and Manitoba's Lieutenant Governor sent messages of sympathy that were read but there were no significant political players on hand to pay homage, nor did Bowell receive the honour of a State Funeral.

Was it a snub? Some of his later denigrators referenced it as sign of Bowell's insignificance, irrelevance and the low regard in which his contemporaries held him. In a history of the Bridge Street Methodist Church, author J. William Lamb raised the question and then offered some possible explanations beyond Bowell's standing. 'Just why it was not an official state funeral is not clear,' he wrote. 'Government protocol was not clearly spelled out about such matters at that date. Normally the current prime minister would offer a state funeral if the next of kin so wished.' Then, Lamb noted the extraordinary circumstances of the time and competing pressures that dominated public and political priorities. 'At the time of Bowell's death, Parliament was not in session, Borden was traveling across the country seeking a mandate for his newly formed Unionist government, the funeral was only four days before the election and Canada was in the midst of a war… His funeral was notable for who didn't come.'

The traumatic realities of the times provide some context for the muted national acknowledgement of Bowell's death. The country was still reeling in the aftermath of the Halifax Explosion the previous week that killed almost 2,000, injured 9,000 and left 25,000 homeless. Even Parliament Hill was in disarray with MP and Senator offices and debating theatre housed in temporary quarters after fire had destroyed the main parliamentary Centre Block the previous year.[9]

Sir Mackenzie Bowell's death and aftermath could not hope to compete for the attention of the nation and its leaders who were coping with the string of setbacks, disasters and catastrophes that Canadians and their country were enduring in December 1917.

Not for the first time, Mackenzie Bowell's timing was not good.

When the new Parliament began sittings in March, meeting at the Victoria Museum almost a mile south of Parliament Hill, one of the first items of business for Senators was remembering their departed colleague. There was nothing but praise and fond memories. Montreal Liberal H. J. Cloran recalled Bowell's defence of the rights of Manitoba Francophone Roman Catholics to have publicly funded schools. 'He did his utmost—and God will reward him for it—to have equal justice and equal rights given to a small minority in this country and for this he was driven from power,' said the Opposition Senator. 'This will be remembered to him in the annals of our history… If we only had at the head of our affairs more men of his stamp, this country of ours would bear a fairer name abroad and be a happier home for our people.'

Cloran, a former newspaper editor and lawyer appointed to the Senate by Laurier, called Bowell a 'model' example of Canadian leadership and tolerance. 'Notwithstanding that he was the head of an organization which is supposed to be diametrically opposed to Catholic interests… he kept that body within bounds for he was a man who believed in equal rights, equal justice to all classes, all creeds and all races in this Dominion of ours.'[10]

Quebec Liberal Senator and former journalist Laurent-Olivier David remembered Bowell over the 40 years he knew him as a man with 'a deep sense of duty and justice mingled with feelings of benevolence that tempered his combative disposition. His temperament was controlled by a sound judgment and an upright mind and as he was courteous, affable and kind and as his public and private life had been honest and respectable, he enjoyed the confidence and esteem of the Canadian people.'

New Brunswick Conservative Senator Pascal Poirier, a former postmaster for the House of Commons who first met Bowell in 1872 as a House employee and was impressed by how this Anglophone, Orange Ontario MP treated a French-speaking Acadian staff member, ended with a proposed epitaph for his departed friend. 'This I would say of him and have the words engraved on his tombstone: "An honest man has departed this world".'[11]

The tributes that flowed for Bowell in the immediate aftermath of his death were to be expected. Despite their disagreements over policies, priorities and politics, politicians are members of a tight-knit club whose members typically circle the wagons when tragedy, calamity or death visits one of their own. Through the latter years of his life, the celebrations and praise for his record of service and accomplishments seemed genuine. It made Cloran's prediction that Bowell's principled and courageous defence of minority language and education rights would be recorded and remembered 'in the annals of our history' seem like a reasonable bet.

Yet history's judgment has not turned out that way. In the half-century following his death, Bowell's life, legacy and accomplishments all bur faded from the historical record. He was largely invisible and unremarked, at best an asterisk in the story of the political chaos that characterized the nation's business between the death of Macdonald and the rise of Laurier. In the following half century beginning in the 1960s, triggered by the publication of negative portrayals of Bowell in the memoirs of Joseph Pope and diaries of Lady Aberdeen, he was transformed into the butt of historian jokes and a caricature of an embarrassing, failed prime minister and player in Canadian history.

Even on Parliament Hill, where he spent decades at the centre of Canadian political and governmental affairs, there was no public recognition of his role and prominence for more than 85 years after his death. That changed on Monday, June 3, 2002, when a small ceremony was held in a room off the lobby of Parliament Hill's Centre Block for the official unveiling of two new prime ministerial portraits. Sir Mackenzie Bowell and Sir John Abbott would join the 14 already displayed in the prime ministers' portrait gallery that stretches along the corridor in front of the House of Commons.

As has been usual for most interactions between Bowell and Canadian history, creating his portrait-hanging moment was accompanied by some drama and intrigue. First, there was the awkward question of why it had taken Parliament more than eight decades to honour a former prime minister. Paul Szabo, Liberal MP and at the time, parliamentary secretary to the Minister of Public Works and Government Services, was the designated government representative with the job of explaining the long delay. Szabo's explanation was straightforward: during the first 90 years of Confederation, portraits of deceased prime ministers were arranged and paid for by friends or admirers and then donated to the House of Commons. 'For whatever reason, this was not done in the case of prime ministers Abbott and Bowell,' Szabo said. 'It was only years later that a more formal commissioning process was put in place.'[12]

Since the 1950s, the House of Commons has commissioned new portraits to honour former prime ministers and the public works department has footed the bill. Artists are selected by a committee representing Parliament, the Public Works department, the National Gallery of Canada and in Bowell's case, former Dominion Sculptress Eleanor Milne. Toronto artist and University of Toronto art lecturer Joanne Tod was chosen by the committee to produce the Bowell portrait. She was informed of the prestigious commission the morning of September 11, 2001, just minutes before news of the deadly attacks on the World Trade Centre towers in New York City and the Pentagon in Washington began to spread. 'I was thrilled and excited when I got the call but then with the twin towers news, the rest of that day is pretty much a blur,' Tod recalled.[13] 'It didn't turn out to be a day of celebration over getting the job.'

Then the pressure and hard work began, knowing that she had been hired to create a Canadian political image that would take its place in public space within the Parliament Buildings, symbolically and practically at the centre of Canadian politics and political history. She knew almost nothing about Bowell before applying for the commission. She had only seen him in black and white 19th century photographs while the portrait had to be in colour.

As well, Tod had just a few months to create the basis of a portrait that would be scrutinized and judged by parliamentary overseers before a final version was approved, painted and unveiled for viewing by the subject's descendants, members of Canada's political elite and the tens of thousands of tourists who throng to Parliament Hill every year.

She quickly found that the job came with 'a lot of pressure.'

A major handicap was that Bowell was long dead. One of the challenges for a portraitist is to try to capture the personality and the essence of the subject. Bowell's essence clearly was complex, controversial and ancient. However, unlike portraitists of contemporary prime ministers, Tod had no way to become informed through direct connection. No contemporaries with first-hand recollections were around to tell her what he was like, how he talked, what his mannerisms and tics were.

'A good portrait should represent a conversation between the subject and the artist so typically they do want to get to know each other,' observed House of Commons 2017 portrait and art curator Johanna Mizgala. 'It is in part about trying to capture some aspects of that person's personality so that you can factor it into your work.'[14] How could a contemporary painter get inside the personality of a long-dead and controversial public man, particularly one about whom little personal had been preserved in print?

For his image and pose, Tod relied on the collection of Bowell photographs snapped in the 1880s by leading Ottawa photographer William Topley. She chose as the template an 1889 formal pose including scarf and overcoat with fur collar over a morning suit. Then she had to use imagination and 'artistic license' to decide the colour of the coat (dark blue striped) and the likely material as well as the kind of fur and animal skin used in the original garb. Consultation with Toronto furriers led to a conclusion that the lining was beaver and the outside fur was muskrat. So, with the attire decided, how did the artist try to get a sense of what he was *like* as a person? Modern prime ministerial portrait painters usually spend time with their subject before putting brush to canvas. 'I had a séance,' Tod laughed as she described her process. In fact, she read what she could about the man and his times and studied the Topley photograph:

> Sometimes looking at somebody's face reveals quite a lot about them and he seems proud if not arrogant and his stance and the very fancy clothes he wore for the sitting, I just thought "this will be great". The fur and the beard had me right away,' she added. 'I would have liked to have met him. He looked like a fascinating guy who would have been very confident and the fact that he worked as a laborer and was able to do a lot of different things showed in the way he presented.

Joanne Tod's painting of Sir Mackenzie Bowell, displayed in the House of Commons. (Copyright of House of Commons Collection, Ottawa/ Collection de la Chambre des communes, Ottawa.)

Tod also had a few small feuds with the then-parliamentary art curator who was checking in on the project. Bowell was 65 years old at the time of the template photo and his hands and knuckles were enlarged; signs of osteoarthritis. 'I painted what I saw and the curator was none too pleased and wanted me to reduce the size of the inflamed joints which I did not. It was a funny disagreement to have.'

There was one other content dispute the artist did not win... sort of. In the photograph at the top of Bowell's scarf was a discernable small triangular white spot. Tod decided to use artistic license to paint a small patch of Manitoba tartan in that spot as a nod to the fact that a standoff with the Manitoba government over minority French Catholic education rights was at the centre of the political uproar that ended his prime ministerial career. The curator zeroed in on the spot, noticed the colour, asked what it was, received the explanation and insisted it be removed as inauthentic. The Manitoba tartan was not designed and adopted until 1962 and Bowell definitely did not incorporate it into his outfit the day of the photo shoot! Tod relented... and didn't. 'I thought it was subtle enough that it probably wouldn't even be noticed but the curator insisted so I just painted it out. But I can reveal it is still there, just covered.' Like the Prime Minister she was painting, the artist was strong willed and tough. 'Just looking at him, I think he showed a lot of inner toughness. He had to.'

Another modern artist trying to recreate Bowell's likeness came to the same conclusion. Two decades earlier, Moose Jaw, Saskatchewan sculptor Dorothy Yakiwchuk had sized him up and arrived at a similar opinion about his mettle and strength of will as she was preparing to sculpt. The Bowell piece was part of a commission she was given to create sculptures of the 16 prime ministers who had governed Canada to that point.[15] She started the project knowing nothing about Bowell and began by reading what history she could find about his life, including his refusal to back down during the Manitoba Schools dispute with the provincial government.

Yakiwchuk also looked at posed contemporary photos of Bowell, including the Topley collection, but in the end decided not to fashion her image of him based on a formal pose. 'I used the information and let my hands do the interpretation,' she reflected years later. 'I would guess that is my creative process.' In the end, the Mackenzie Bowell she imagined was an informal man relaxing after the leadership crisis was over and he was no longer prime minister. He was sitting in a chair with crossed legs, chin resting on his right hand and face relaxed. 'I saw him as a serious man, comfortable

with himself,' she said. 'He had done what he had to do, what he could and he displayed a mixture of success and pride in that he had accomplished a lot but he was tired. And he was still strong because he believed in himself.'

Yakiwchuk dressed him in a suit for the sculpture but not formally as in many of his 19th century photos. 'I really wanted to portray Prime Minister Bowell as a man who was truly human. He should be allowed to be casual.' It was a representation of an ordinary, relaxed man enjoying the quiet after a life lived through extraordinary, tense, high-volume times.

256

On June 3, 2002, Ottawa presented a sunny, temperate Monday afternoon face for the official unveiling of Tod's Bowell portrait marking Sir Mackenzie's return to Parliament Hill. He would be positioned on the wall directly in front of the House of Commons he first had entered as a rookie MP more than 130 years before and a short hallway walk west from the Senate, 85 years after he last showed up for work.

With descendants of former prime ministers Bowell and Abbott, joined by a smattering of present-day parliamentarians and other invited guests, speeches were made, the shrouds were removed from the portraits and applause followed. Bowell descendants present included great-great grand-children Kathy Holton Masson and Blake Holton. 'It was a really proud moment for us,' Kathy recalled. 'The room was filled and there was a former prime minister, Joe Clark, as well as the Speaker.'

Blake later reflected on Sir Mackenzie Bowell's achievement in traveling from immigrant kid to Prime Minister. 'My dad Mac [Douglas Mackenzie Holton] told me the odds of becoming an NHL player are way better than becoming a PM and I had never thought of it like that,' he said. 'Think of the number of people who have lived in this country and how many are chosen to be prime minister—just 23 so far—and you will understand what an honour it is to lead the country, or to be descended from one who did. That's the way I look at it.'[16]

In retrospect, perhaps the best Parliament Hill epitaph for the fifth Prime Minister of the Dominion of Canada would be to remember again the previously-cited 1925 assessment of legendary senior federal bureaucrat and Laurier biographer O. D. Skelton as he reflected on the cabinet revolt that ultimately pushed Sir Mackenzie Bowell out of the prime minister's office and cemented his reputation as one of Canadian history's losers. Skelton wrote almost three decades after the fact:

> Whatever hidden provocation may have existed, the public were shocked by the indecent publicity of the attacks on the prime minister and the party shaken by the display of jealousy and bad judgment on the part of its leaders. Out of it all, only Mackenzie Bowell himself—perhaps no heaven-born leader but an honourable and straightforward gentleman—emerged with any credit.

NOTES

[1] The 1917 personal daily diary of George Harold Holton containing the December 10 entry was given to the author by Holton's granddaughter MaryJane HoltonSimon of Toronto. She donated the remainder of the lifetime diary

collection to the Archives of Belleville and Hastings County where it now is housed.

[2] Schull, Joseph, *Laurier: The First Canadian* (Toronto: MacMillan of Canada, 1987), 599.

[3] Belleville *Intelligencer* (December 11, 1917), page 1.

[4] Toronto *Globe* (December 11, 1917), page 1.

[5] Montreal *Gazette* (December 12, 1917).

[6] Boyce, Betsy D., *The Accidental Prime Minister* (Ameliasburgh, Ontario: Seventh Town Historical Society, 2001), 319.

[7] Belleville *Intelligencer* (December 14, 1917).

[8] op cit, *The Accidental Prime Minister*, 319.

[9] Lamb, J. William, *Bridging the Years: A History of Bridge Street United/Methodist Church, Belleville 1815–1990* (Winfield, British Columbia: Wood Lake Books, 1990), 242.

[10] Debates of the Senate, 1st Session, 13th Parliament, Vol. 1 (March 21, 1918), 41–42.

[11] ibid, 42.

[12] Speaking notes for Paul Szabo, June 3, 2002.

[13] June 17, 2017 author interview with Joanne Tod.

[14] June 8, 2017 author interview with Johanna Mazgala, Curator, Curatorial Services, House Proceedings, Parliament of Canada.

[15] Information about the sculpting project came from a July 10, 2018 author interview with Dorothy Yakiwchuk from Moose Jaw, Saskatchewan.

[16] February 24, 2017 author interview with Kathy Holton Masson and Blake Holton in Port Hope, Ontario.

BIBLIOGRAPHY

Archival Sources

Library and Archives Canada (LAC)
> Sir Mackenzie Bowell Papers
> Sir John A. Macdonald Papers

Community Archives of Belleville and Hastings County

Provincial Archives of Manitoba
> Premier Thomas Greenway Papers

Newspapers and Periodicals

> *Belleville Intelligencer* (Community Archives of Belleville & Hastings County)
>
> *Toronto Globe* (NAC microfilm)
>
> *Montreal Gazette* (NAC microfilm)
>
> Various clippings in Bowell Papers (NAC)
>
> *The New Yorker*
>
> *The Canadian Courier*
>
> *Maclean's Magazine*
>
> *Canada Magazine*

Library of Parliament

> Debates of the House of Commons 1867–1892. Ottawa: Brown Chamberlain Printer to the Queen's Most Excellent Majesty.
>
> Debates of the Senate 1893–1918. Ottawa: S.E. Dawson to the Queen's/King's Most Excellent Majesty.

Secondary Sources

> Abbott, Elizabeth, *Notes on the Life of Sir John Abbott, Canada's Third Prime Minister: The Reluctant PM* (Montreal, 1997).
>
> Aberdeen, Lord, *WE TWA–Reminiscences of Lord and Lady Aberdeen, Vol. II* (London: W. Collins Sons & Co. 1925).

Adams, Christopher, *Politics in Manitoba* (Winnipeg: University of Manitoba Press, 2008).

Akenson, Donald, *The Irish in Ontario: A Study in Rural History* (Montreal: McGill-Queen's University Press, 1985).

Bosc, Marc, *Canadian Parliamentary Anecdotes* (Peterborough, Ontario: Broadview Press, 1988).

Boyce, Betsy D., *The Accidental Prime Minister* (Ameliasburgh, Ontario: Seventh Town Historical Society, 2001).

Boyce, Gerry, *Belleville, A Popular History* (Toronto: Dundurn Press, 2008).

Canadian Press Association, *A History of Canadian Journalism in Several Portions of the Dominion with a Sketch of the Canadian Press Association 1859–1908* (Toronto: 1908).

Charlesworth, Hector, *Candid Chronicles: Leaves from the Notebook of a Canadian Journalist* (Toronto: The MacMillan Co. of Canada, 1925).

Cook, Tim, *The Madman & the Butcher* (Toronto: Allen Lane Canada, the Penguin Group, 2010).

Craik, W. A., *Canada Magazine*, January 3, 1914.

Creighton, Donald, *John A. Macdonald, the Old Chieftain* (Toronto: The MacMillan Co. of Canada, 1955).

Customs Administration Documents, Library and Archives Canada Microfilm Collection, *Speech of the Hon. Mackenzie Bowell, Minister of Customs* (Ottawa: Queen's Printer, 1889).

Department of Militia and Defence of the Dominion of Canada, *Report for the Half-Year Ended June 30th, 1892*, Library and Archives Canada file COP.CA/D.1

Dominion Methodist Church annual reports, 1890–1896, Dominion-Chalmers United Church, Ottawa.

Duffy, John, *The Fights of Our Lives: Elections, Leadership and the Making of Canada* (Toronto: HarperCollins Publishers, 2002).

Durant, Vincent, *War Horse of Cumberland: the Life and Times of Sir Charles Tupper* (Hantsport, Nova Scotia: Lancelot Press, 1985).

Forsey, Eugene, *A Life on the Fringe* (Toronto: Oxford University Press, 1991).

Friedland, Martin L., *The Case of Valentine Shortis: A True Story of Crime and Politics in Canada* (Toronto: University of Toronto Press, 1986).

Godfrey, Sheldon and Judy, *Burn This Gossip: The True Story of George Benjamin of Belleville, Canada's First Jewish Member of Parliament* (Toronto: The Duke & George Press, 1991).

Granatstein, J. L and Hillmer, Norman, *Prime Ministers: Ranking Canada's Leaders* (Toronto: HarperCollins, 1999).

Gray, Charlotte, *Sisters in the Wilderness: the Lives of Susanna Moodie and Catharine Parr Traill* (Toronto: Penguin Books Canada Ltd, 1999).

Gray, Charlotte, *The Promise of Canada (150 Years—People and Ideas that have Shaped Our Country* (Toronto: Simon and Schuster Canada, 2016).

Green, Lorne, *Chief Engineer, Life of a National Builder–Sandford Fleming* (Toronto: Dundurn Press, 1993).

Greunding, Dennis, *Speeches that Changed Canada* (Toronto: Fitzhenry & Whiteside, 2018).

Gwyn, Richard, *Nation Maker. Sir John A. Macdonald, His Life, Our Times Vol. 2.* (Toronto: Random House Canada, 2011).

Gwyn, Sandra, *The Private Capital* (Toronto: McClelland & Stewart, 1984).

Hadaya, Hagit, *At Home with the Prime Minister: Ottawa Residences of the Prime Ministers Prior to 1952* (Ottawa, 2017).

Hébert, Raymond M. S., *Cautionary Tale* (Montreal: McGill-Queen's University Press, 2004).

Heintzman, Ralph, *The National Policy, 187–1979* (Toronto: University of Toronto Press, 1979).

Hill, O. Mary, *Canada's Salesman to the World: the Department of Trade and Commerce 1892–1939* (Montreal: McGill-Queen's University Press, 1977).

Hiller, James K., 'The 1895 Newfoundland-Canada Confederation Negotiations: A Reconsideration,' *Acadiensis: Journal of the History of the Atlantic Region*, XL No. 2, Fredericton: University of New Brunswick Press, 2011.

Hutchinson, Braden, *The Greater Half of the Continent: Continentalism and the Canadian State in Ontario 1878–1896* (Ottawa: Carleton University Department of History MA Thesis 2008).

Hutchison, Bruce, *Mr. Prime Minister 1867–1964* (Toronto: Longman's Canada Ltd., 1964).

Hutchison, Bruce, *The Incredible Canadian. A Candid Portrait of Mackenzie King* (Don Mills, Ontario: Longmans Canada Ltd., 1952).

Kealey, Gregory S., *Toronto Workers Respond to Industrial Capitalism 1867–1892* (Toronto: University of Toronto Press, 1980).

Kealey, Gregory S., *Introduction to Royal Commission on the Relations of Labor and Capital, 1889* (Toronto: University of Toronto Press, 1973).

Keneally, Thomas, *Australians: From Eureka to the Diggers* (Sydney: Allen & Unwin, 2011).

Lamb, J. William, *Bridging the Years: A History of Bridge Street United/Methodist Church, Belleville 1815–1990* (Winfield, British Columbia: Wood Lake Books, 1990).

Lovell, Crosby Clark, *A History of the Conservative Administrations, 1891 to 1896* (Toronto: University of Toronto PhD dissertation, 1968).

Marjoribanks, Ishbel Maria, *The Canadian Journal of Lady Aberdeen,* see Saywell, John (ed.).

MacGregor, James G., *Father Lacombe* (Edmonton: Hurtig Publishers, 1975).

Martin, Ged, 'John A. Macdonald and the Bottle,' *Journal of Canadian Studies*, Peterborough: Trent University Press, 2006.

McLean, Don, *Fifty Historical Vignettes: Views of the Commons People* (Saskatoon: Gabriel Dumont Institute, 1987)

Miller, J. R., *Equal Rights: The Jesuits' Estates Act Controversy* (Montreal: McGill–Queen's University Press, 1979).

Moore, Christopher, *1867: How the Fathers Made a Deal* (Toronto: McClelland & Stewart, 1977).

Nowlan, Alden, *Smoked Glass* (Toronto: Clark, Irwin & Company, 1977).

O'Flaherty, Patrick, *Lost Country: The Rise and Fall of Newfoundland 1843–1933* (St. John's, Newfoundland: Long Beach Press, 2005).

Sanders, E. L., *Memoir,* Trent University Archives, Mrs. E. Kayser fonds, undated.

Saunders, E. M., *The Life and Letters of the Rt. Hon. Sir Charles Tupper,* (Toronto: Castle & Co. Ltd., 1916), 207.

Rt. Hon. the Earl of Jersey, *Report on the Colonial Conference at Ottawa.* (London: Queen's Printer, 1894).

Rutherford, Paul, *A Victorian Authority: The Daily Press in Late Nineteenth Century Canada* (Toronto: University of Toronto Press, 1982).

Saywell, John (ed.), *The Canadian Journal of Lady Aberdeen, 1893–1898* (Toronto: The Champlain Society, 1960).

Saywell, John T., 'The Crown and the Politicians: The Canadian Succession Question 1891–1896,' *The Canadian Historical Review*, Vol. XXXVII No. 4, 1956.

Sanders, E. M. (ed.), *The Life and Letters of the Rt. Hon. Sir Charles Tupper Vol. 2* (Toronto: Cassell and Co. Ltd., 1916).

Schull, Joseph, *Laurier: The First Canadian* (Toronto: MacMillan of Canada, 1965).

Scott, S. Morley, 'Foster on the Thompson-Bowell Succession,' *Canadian Historical Review*, Vol. XLVIII No. 3.

Senior, Hereward, *Orangeism: The Canadian Phase* (Toronto: McGraw–Hill Ryerson, 1972).

Senior, Hereward, 'Orangeism in Ontario Politics 1872–1896,' *Oliver Mowat's Ontario*, Donald Swainson (ed. (Toronto: Macmillan of Canada, 1972).

Siggons, Maggie, *Riel: A Life of Revolution* (Toronto: HarperCollins Publishers, 1994).

Skelton, Oscar Douglas, *Life and Letters of Sir Wilfrid Laurier* (Toronto: Oxford University Press, 1921).

Steiner, George P., *The Russell House: Social Annex of the House of Commons*, Master's Thesis, McGill University School of Architecture, 1967 (Montreal: McGill University Rare Books Collection).

Taylor, George, *A History of the Rise, Progress, Cruelties and Suppression of the Rebellion in the County of Wexford in the Year 1798, 3rd Edition.* Belleville: M. Bowell, Intelligencer Office, 1864. (Carleton University Archives and Library, Barry Wilson Collection).

Telfer, Thomas G. W., *Ruin and Redemption: The Struggle for a Canadian Bankruptcy Law, 1867–1919* (Toronto: University of Toronto Press; The Osgoode Society for Canadian Legal History, 2014).

The Canadian Press Association, *A History of Canadian Journalism in Several Portions of the Dominion with a Sketch of the Canadian Press Association 1859–1908* (Toronto: 1908).

Thomson, Andrew, *The Sentinel and Orange and Protestant Advocate, 1877–1896: An Orange View of Canada* (Waterloo, Ontario: Master of Arts Thesis for the Department of History, Wilfrid Laurier University, 1983.

Tupper, Sir Charles, *Recollections of 60 Years in Canada* (Toronto: Castle & Co. Ltd., 1914).

Turner, Larry with Stewart, John, *Perth: Tradition and Style in Eastern Ontario* (Perth, Ontario: 1998.

Waite, Peter B., *Canada 1874–1896: Arduous Destiny* (Toronto: McClelland & Stewart, 1971).

Waite, P. B., 'Sir Joseph Pope,' *Dictionary of Canadian Biography*, Vol. 15. University of Toronto/Unversité Laval, 2003.
http://www.biographi.ca/en/bio/pope_joseph_15E.html

Waite, P. B., 'Bowell, Sir Mackenzie,' *Dictionary of Canadian Biography*, Vol. XIV, 1911-1920 (Toronto: University of Toronto Press, 1998).

Waite, P. B., *The Man from Halifax: Sir John Thompson, Prime Minister* (Toronto: University of Toronto Press, 1985).

Wallace, W. Stewart, *The Memoirs of the Rt. Hon. Sir George Foster* (Toronto: The MacMillan Co. of Canada Ltd., 1933).

Printed in the USA
CPSIA information can be obtained
at www.ICGtesting.com
LVHW031557301123
764874LV00006B/163

9 781988 657257